Take the Next Step in Your IT Career

Save 10% on Exam Vouchers*

(up to a $35 value)

*Some restrictions apply. See web page for details.

CompTIA.

Use coupon code WILEY10 during checkout. Redeeming the coupon code is easy:

1. Go to www.comptiastore.com.
2. Browse Certification Vouchers and select the exam voucher you want.
3. Add the voucher to the cart (note that for A+ you will need a separate voucher for each exam).
4. Enter the code WILEY10 on the purchase screen, click Apply and then click Proceed to Checkout to continue and complete the payment process.

CompTIA® Data+® Study Guide

Exam DA0-002

Second Edition

Mike Chapple

Sharif Nijim

SYBEX®
A Wiley Brand

Copyright © 2025 by John Wiley & Sons, Inc. All rights reserved, including rights for text and data mining and training of artificial intelligence technologies or similar technologies

Published by John Wiley & Sons, Inc., Hoboken, New Jersey.
Published simultaneously in Canada.

No part of this publication may be reproduced, stored in a retrieval system, or transmitted in any form or by any means, electronic, mechanical, photocopying, recording, scanning, or otherwise, except as permitted under Section 107 or 108 of the 1976 United States Copyright Act, without either the prior written permission of the Publisher, or authorization through payment of the appropriate per-copy fee to the Copyright Clearance Center, Inc., 222 Rosewood Drive, Danvers, MA 01923, (978) 750-8400, fax (978) 750-4470, or on the web at www.copyright.com. Requests to the Publisher for permission should be addressed to the Permissions Department, John Wiley & Sons, Inc., 111 River Street, Hoboken, NJ 07030, (201) 748-6011, fax (201) 748-6008, or online at http://www.wiley.com/go/permission.

The manufacturer's authorized representative according to the EU General Product Safety Regulation is Wiley-VCH GmbH, Boschstr. 12, 69469 Weinheim, Germany, e-mail: Product_Safety@wiley.com.

Trademarks: Wiley and the Wiley logo are trademarks or registered trademarks of John Wiley & Sons, Inc. and/or its affiliates in the United States and other countries and may not be used without written permission. All other trademarks are the property of their respective owners. John Wiley & Sons, Inc. is not associated with any product or vendor mentioned in this book.

Limit of Liability/Disclaimer of Warranty: While the publisher and author have used their best efforts in preparing this book, they make no representations or warranties with respect to the accuracy or completeness of the contents of this book and specifically disclaim any implied warranties of merchantability or fitness for a particular purpose. No warranty may be created or extended by sales representatives or written sales materials. The advice and strategies contained herein may not be suitable for your situation. You should consult with a professional where appropriate. Further, readers should be aware that websites listed in this work may have changed or disappeared between when this work was written and when it is read. Neither the publisher nor authors shall be liable for any loss of profit or any other commercial damages, including but not limited to special, incidental, consequential, or other damages.

For general information on our other products and services, please contact our Customer Care Department within the United States at (800) 762-2974, outside the United States at (317) 572-3993. For product technical support, you can find answers to frequently asked questions or reach us via live chat at https://sybexsupport.wiley.com.

If you believe you've found a mistake in this book, please bring it to our attention by emailing our reader support team at wileysupport@wiley.com with the subject line "Possible Book Errata Submission."

Wiley also publishes its books in a variety of electronic formats. Some content that appears in print may not be available in electronic formats. For more information about Wiley products, visit our web site at www.wiley.com.

Library of Congress Cataloging-in-Publication Data:

Names: Chapple, Mike author | Nijim, Sharif author
Title: Comptia data+ study guide : exam da0-002 / Mike Chapple, Sharif Nijim.
Description: Second edition. | Hoboken, NJ : John Wiley & Sons Inc, 2025. |
   Series: Sybex study guide | Includes bibliographical references and index.
Identifiers: LCCN 2025027015 | ISBN 9781394320912 paperback |
   ISBN 9781394320936 adobe pdf | ISBN 9781394320929 epub
Subjects: LCSH: Computer industry
Classification: LCC HD9696.2.A2 C48 2025
LC record available at https://lccn.loc.gov/2025027015

Cover Design: Wiley
Cover Image: © Jeremy Woodhouse/Getty Images

To my aspiring computer scientist, Chris. Your mother and I are so proud of you and can't wait to see all of the incredible things that you accomplish! Boiler Up!
—Mike
To Allison, Luca, Olivia, Madeline, and Enzo, thank you for your patience, love, and support – I love you all!
—Sharif

Acknowledgments

Books like this involve work from many people, and as authors, we truly appreciate the hard work and dedication that the team at Wiley shows. We would especially like to thank senior acquisitions editor Kenyon Brown and senior managing editor Pete Gaughan. We have worked with Ken and Pete on multiple projects and consistently enjoy our work with them.

We also greatly appreciated the editing and production teams for the book. First and foremost, we'd like to thank our friend and colleague, Dr. Jen Waddell. Jen provided us with invaluable insight as we worked our way through the many challenges inherent in putting out a book. Jen's a whiz at statistics and analytics, and we couldn't have completed this book without her support. Kezia Endsley continued to serve as a superstar copy editor on this book.

Shahla Pirnia, from the CertMike.com team, played an instrumental role in performing initial reviews and preparing the book for publication. We also benefited greatly from the work of two of our students at Notre Dame. Ricky Chapple did a final read-through of this book to ensure that it was ready to go, and Matthew Howard helped create the instructor materials that accompany this book.

We'd also like to thank the many people who helped us make this project successful, including Janet Wehner, our project editor, who brought years of experience and great talent to the project, and Dhilipkumar Rajendran, our production specialist, who guided us through layouts, formatting, and final cleanup to produce a great book. We would also like to thank the many behind-the-scenes contributors, including the graphics, production, and technical teams who make the book and companion materials into a finished product.

Our agent, Carole Jelen of Waterside Productions, continues to provide us with wonderful opportunities, advice, and assistance throughout our writing careers.

Finally, we would like to thank our families, who support us through the late evenings, busy weekends, and long hours that a book like this requires to write, edit, and get to press.

About the Authors

Mike Chapple, Ph.D., Data+ is author of the best-selling *CISSP ISC2 Certified Information Systems Security Professional Official Study Guide* (Sybex, 2024) and the *CISSP ISC2 Official Practice Tests* (Sybex, 2024). He is an information technology professional with two decades of experience in higher education, the private sector, and government.

Mike currently serves as a teaching professor in the IT, Analytics, and Operations department at the University of Notre Dame's Mendoza College of Business, where he teaches undergraduate and graduate courses on cybersecurity, data management, and business analytics.

Before returning to Notre Dame, Mike served as executive vice president and chief information officer of the Brand Institute, a Miami-based marketing consultancy. Mike also spent four years in the information security research group at the National Security Agency and served as an active-duty intelligence officer in the U.S. Air Force.

Mike has written more than 50 books. He earned both his B.S. and Ph.D. degrees from Notre Dame in computer science and engineering. Mike also holds an M.S. in computer science from the University of Idaho and an MBA from Auburn University.

Learn more about Mike and his other certification materials at CertMike.com.

Sharif Nijim is an associate teaching professor in the IT, Analytics, and Operations department at the Mendoza College of Business at the University of Notre Dame, where he teaches undergraduate and graduate courses in business analytics and information technology.

Prior to Notre Dame, Sharif co-founded and served on the board of a customer data integration company serving the airline industry. Sharif also spent more than a decade building and optimizing enterprise-class transactional and decision support systems for clients in the energy, healthcare, hospitality, insurance, logistics, manufacturing, real estate, telecommunications, and travel and transportation sectors.

Sharif earned both his B.B.A. and M.S. from the University of Notre Dame.

About the Technical Editor

Jennifer Waddell is a teaching professor, assistant department chair, and the director of undergraduate studies in the IT, Analytics, and Operations department at the University of Notre Dame, specializing in the areas of statistical methodology and analytics. Over the last 20 years, she has educated students at the undergraduate, graduate, and executive levels in these disciplines, focusing on their theoretical understanding as well as technical skill implementation. In addition to her time in the classroom, she has worked as a statistical consultant on research projects in healthcare systems and educational services.

Contents at a Glance

Introduction *xxi*

Assessment Test *xxviii*

Chapter 1	Today's Data Analyst	1
Chapter 2	Data Analytics Tools	17
Chapter 3	Understanding Data	43
Chapter 4	Databases and Data Acquisition	83
Chapter 5	Data Quality	145
Chapter 6	Data Analysis and Statistics	197
Chapter 7	Data Visualization with Reports and Dashboards	245
Chapter 8	Data Governance	299

Appendix *349*

Index *365*

Contents

Introduction xxi

Assessment Test xxviii

Chapter 1 **Today's Data Analyst** **1**

Welcome to the World of Analytics 2
Data 2
Storage 3
Computing Power 5
Careers in Analytics 5
The Analytics Process 6
Data Acquisition 7
Cleaning and Manipulation 7
Analysis 7
Visualization 8
Reporting and Communication 9
Analytics Techniques 10
Descriptive Analytics 10
Inferential Analytics 10
Predictive Analytics 10
Prescriptive Analytics 11
Machine Learning, Artificial Intelligence, and Deep Learning 11
Generative AI 12
Robotic Process Automation 13
Data Governance 13
Analytics Tools 14
Summary 16

Chapter 2 **Data Analytics Tools** **17**

Spreadsheets 18
Microsoft Excel 19
Programming Languages 21
R 21
Python 23
Scala 24
SAS 24
Databases and SQL 26
Business Intelligence Software 29
Power BI 29
Tableau 29
Looker 31

	Cloud Infrastructure	32
	Drivers for Cloud Computing	32
	Cloud Service Concepts	33
	Cloud Deployment Models	35
	Public Cloud Providers	36
	Summary	37
	Exam Essentials	37
	Review Questions	39
Chapter 3	**Understanding Data**	**43**
	Exploring Data Types	44
	Structured Data Types	46
	Unstructured Data Types	58
	Categories of Data	63
	Common Data Structures	66
	Structured Data	66
	Unstructured Data	68
	Semi-structured Data	69
	Common File Formats	70
	Text Files	70
	JavaScript Object Notation	72
	Extensible Markup Language (XML)	74
	Hypertext Markup Language (HTML)	75
	Summary	76
	Exam Essentials	77
	Review Questions	78
Chapter 4	**Databases and Data Acquisition**	**83**
	Exploring Databases	84
	The Relational Model	85
	Relational Databases	88
	Nonrelational Databases	94
	Database Use Cases	97
	Online Transactional Processing	97
	Online Analytical Processing	100
	Schema Concepts	101
	Data Acquisition Concepts	107
	Integration	107
	Data Sources and Collection Methods	109
	Working with Data	120
	Data Manipulation	121
	Query Optimization	136
	Summary	139
	Exam Essentials	140
	Review Questions	141

Chapter 5	**Data Quality**	**145**
	Data Inconsistencies	146
	Data Duplication	146
	Data Redundancy	147
	Missing Values	151
	Invalid Data	152
	Nonparametric Data	153
	Data Outliers	153
	Specification Mismatch	154
	Data Type Validation	155
	Data Completeness	156
	Data Transformation Techniques	156
	String Manipulation	156
	Conversion	158
	Augmentation	160
	Scaling	160
	Grouping Techniques	162
	Reduction	163
	Aggregation	166
	Transposition	167
	Exploding	168
	Standardization	168
	Imputation	171
	Parsing	172
	Merging	174
	Appending	175
	Recoding Data	176
	Derived Variables	177
	Deletion	178
	Data Blending	178
	Managing Data Quality	180
	Circumstances to Check for Quality	180
	Automated Validation	182
	Data Quality Dimensions	183
	Data Quality Rules and Metrics	185
	Methods to Validate Quality	188
	Summary	190
	Exam Essentials	191
	Review Questions	192
Chapter 6	**Data Analysis and Statistics**	**197**
	Communication Approaches	198
	Audience	198
	Mock-up	201
	Accessibility	201

	Fundamentals of Statistics	203
	Statistical Functions and Measures	204
	Mathematical	205
	Logical	223
	Date	226
	String	227
	Troubleshooting	229
	Issues	229
	Tools and Methods	232
	Analysis Techniques	234
	Determine Type of Analysis	235
	Types of Analysis	235
	Exploratory Data Analysis	236
	Summary	237
	Exam Essentials	239
	Review Questions	240
Chapter 7	**Data Visualization with Reports and Dashboards**	**245**
	Exploring Visualization Elements	246
	Charts	246
	Maps	252
	Pivot Tables	255
	Infographic	258
	Waterfall	259
	Word Cloud	263
	Understanding Business Requirements	263
	Understanding Design Elements	267
	Cover Page	268
	Executive Summary	269
	Branding	269
	Documentation Elements	277
	Understanding Dashboard Development Methods	279
	Consumer Types	279
	Data Source Considerations	280
	Data Type Considerations	281
	Development Process	282
	Operational Considerations	282
	Delivery Considerations	283
	Static and Dynamic Delivery	283
	Frequency	284
	Data Versioning Techniques	286
	Tactical and Research	287
	Report Validation Techniques	288
	Issues	288
	Techniques	289

		Data Filtering	289
		Reviews	289
		Source Validation	290
		Data Structures	290
		Monitoring Alerts	291
	Summary		291
	Exam Essentials		293
	Review Questions		295
Chapter 8	**Data Governance**		**299**
	Data Management Concepts		300
		Integration	301
		Documentation	302
		Source of Truth	309
		Data Versioning	313
		Metadata	313
		Data Governance Roles	313
	Data Compliance Concepts		315
		National Institute of Standards and Technology (NIST)	315
		Retention	316
		Jurisdictional Requirements	316
		Replication	317
		Storage	318
		Data Ethics	318
		Payment Card Industry (PCI)	319
		Personally Identifiable Information (PII)	320
		Protected Health Information (PHI)	320
		Audit	323
		Classification	323
		Incident Reporting	325
	Data Privacy and Protection		325
		Role-based Access Control (RBAC)	326
		Encryption	327
		Masking	332
		Anonymization	332
		Data Usage	333
		Data Sharing	334
	Data Quality Assurance Practices		334
		International Organization for Standardization (ISO)	335
		Source Control	335
		Unit Test	336
		Requirement Testing	337
		Stress Test	337

User Acceptance Testing (UAT)	338
Data Health Check	339
Automated Data Quality Monitoring	339
Data Profiling	341
Summary	342
Exam Essentials	344
Review Questions	345
Appendix	*349*
Index	*365*

Introduction

If you're preparing to take the Data+ exam, you'll undoubtedly want to find as much information as you can about data and analytics. The more information you have at your disposal and the more hands-on experience you gain, the better off you'll be when attempting the exam. This study guide was written with that in mind. The goal was to provide enough information to prepare you for the test, but not so much that you'll be overloaded with information that's outside the scope of the exam.

We've included review questions at the end of each chapter to give you a taste of what it's like to take the exam. If you're already working in the data field, we recommend that you check out these questions first to gauge your level of expertise. You can then use the book mainly to fill in the gaps in your current knowledge. This study guide will help you round out your knowledge base before tackling the exam.

If you can answer 90 percent or more of the review questions correctly for a given chapter, you can feel safe moving on to the next chapter. If you're unable to answer that many correctly, reread the chapter and try the questions again. Your score should improve.

Don't just study the questions and answers! The questions on the actual exam will be different from the practice questions included in this book. The exam is designed to test your knowledge of a concept or objective, so use this book to learn the objectives behind the questions.

The Data+ Exam

The Data+ exam is designed to be a vendor-neutral certification for data professionals and those seeking to enter the field. CompTIA recommends this certification for those currently working, or aspiring to work, as a data analyst, data architect, business analyst, reporting analyst, operations analyst, or marketing analyst.

The exam covers five major domains:

1. Data Concepts and Environments
2. Data Acquisition and Preparation
3. Data Analysis
4. Visualization and Reporting
5. Data Governance

These five areas include a range of topics, from data types to statistical analysis and from data visualization to tools and techniques, while focusing heavily on scenario-based learning. That's why CompTIA recommends that those attempting the exam have 18–24 months of experience, although many individuals pass the exam before moving into their first data analysis role.

The Data+ exam is conducted in a format that CompTIA calls "performance-based assessment." This means that the exam combines standard multiple-choice questions with other, interactive question formats. Your exam may include several types of questions such as multiple-choice, fill-in-the-blank, multiple-response, drag-and-drop, and image-based problems. More details about the Data+ exam and how to take it can be found here:

```
https://www.comptia.org/en-us/certifications/data
```

You have 90 minutes to take the exam and will be asked to answer up to 90 questions during that time period. Your exam is scored on a scale ranging from 100 to 900, with a passing score of 675.

You should also know that CompTIA is notorious for including vague questions on all of its exams. You might see a question for which two of the possible four answers are correct—but you can choose only one. Use your knowledge, logic, and intuition to choose the best answer and then move on. Sometimes, the questions are worded in ways that would make English majors cringe. Don't let this frustrate you; answer the question and move on to the next one.

CompTIA frequently does what is called *item seeding*, which is the practice of including unscored questions on exams. It does so to gather psychometric data, which is then used when developing new versions of the exam. Before you take the exam, you will be told that your exam may include these unscored questions. So, if you come across a question that does not appear to map to any of the exam objectives—or for that matter, does not appear to belong in the exam—it is likely a seeded question. You never really know whether or not a question is seeded, however, so always make your best effort to answer every question.

Taking the Exam

Once you are fully prepared to take the exam, you can visit the CompTIA website to purchase your exam voucher:

```
https://www.comptia.org/en-us/certifications/
```

When you arrive at the test center, you'll go through a check-in process at the front desk where the exam staff check your identification, take your photograph, and electronically capture your signature.

You will need to bring two forms of identification along with you to the exam. Your primary identification must be a government-issued identification card that contains both a photo and a signature. For example, you might use:

- A passport
- A driver's license
- A military identification card (accepted for in-person exams only)
- A national or state/province-issued identification card
- An alien registration card (green card, permanent resident, visa)

Identification cards printed in a language that does not use Roman characters are only accepted if they were issued from the country where the candidate is taking the exam.

You may use any form of identification for your second source that is current and contains your name and either a photo or a signature.

Currently, CompTIA offers two options for taking the exam: an in-person exam at a testing center and an online exam that you take on your own computer from your home or office. You may not take breaks during your CompTIA exam.

This book includes a coupon for an exam voucher from the CompTIA Store that you may use to save 10 percent on your CompTIA exam registration.

In-person Exams

CompTIA partners with Pearson VUE's testing centers.

Simply set up a CompTIA SSO account (if you don't already have one) and schedule an exam at a Pearson VUE center near you.

On the day of the test, take two forms of identification and make sure to show up with plenty of time before the exam starts. Remember that you will not be able to take your notes, electronic devices (including smartphones and watches), or other materials in with you. You will be provided with a locker to store your items.

Online Exams

CompTIA began offering online exam proctoring in 2020 through the OnVUE online testing system. Candidates using this approach will take the exam at their home or office and be proctored over a webcam by a remote proctor.

Due to the rapidly changing nature of the online testing experience, candidates wishing to pursue this option should check the CompTIA website for the latest details.

After the Data+ Exam

After you finish the exam, you are notified of your score immediately, so you'll know if you passed or failed the test right away. You should keep track of your score report with your exam registration records and the email address you used to register for the exam. If you've passed, you'll receive a handsome certificate in the mail.

Maintaining Your Certification

CompTIA certifications must be renewed on a periodic basis. To renew your certification, you can choose to pass the most recent version of the exam, or complete 20 CEUs (Continuing Education Units) through approved activities during your three-year renewal cycle.

Qualifying activities include:

- Attending a live webinar
- Attending a conference
- Completing a college course
- Completing a training course
- Completing an ACE (American Council on Education) course
- Creating instructional materials used in teaching a course
- Earning a non-CompTIA industry certification
- Completing a CompTIA exam development workshop
- Publishing a book
- Publishing a blog
- Publishing an article or white paper
- Teaching or mentoring
- Work experience

When you sign up to renew your certification, you are asked to agree to the CE program's Code of Ethics, to pay a renewal fee, and to submit the materials required for your chosen renewal method(s).

What Does This Book Cover?

This book covers everything you need to know to pass the Data+ exam.

Chapter 1: Today's Data Analyst
Chapter 2: Data Analytics Tools
Chapter 3: Understanding Data
Chapter 4: Databases and Data Acquisition
Chapter 5: Data Quality
Chapter 6: Data Analysis and Statistics
Chapter 7: Data Visualization with Reports and Dashboards
Chapter 8: Data Governance
Appendix: Answers to the Review Questions

Study Guide Elements

This study guide uses a number of common elements to help you prepare. These include the following:

Summaries   The summary section of each chapter briefly explains the chapter, allowing you to easily understand what it covers.

Exam Essentials   The exam essentials section focuses on major exam topics and critical knowledge that you should take into the test. The exam essentials focus on the exam objectives provided by CompTIA.

Chapter Review Questions   A set of questions at the end of each chapter will help you assess your knowledge and whether you are ready to take the exam based on your knowledge of that chapter's topics.

Interactive Online Learning Environment and Test Bank

This book comes with a number of additional study tools to help you prepare for the exam. They include the following.

Go to https://www.wiley.com/go/sybextestprep to register and gain access to the interactive online learning environment and test bank with study tools.

Wiley/Sybex Online Test Preparation

Wiley's test preparation software lets you prepare with electronic test versions of the introductory assessment test and review questions from each chapter.

Electronic Flashcards

Our electronic flashcards are designed to help you prepare for the exam. Over 100 flashcards will ensure that you know critical terms and concepts.

Glossary of Terms

Wiley provides a full glossary of terms in PDF format, allowing quick searches and easy reference to materials in this book.

Bonus Practice Exams

In addition to the review questions for each chapter, the online environment includes two full 90-question practice exams. We recommend that you use them both to test your preparedness for the certification exam.

Like all exams, the Data+ certification from CompTIA is updated periodically and may eventually be retired or replaced. At some point after CompTIA is no longer offering this exam, the old editions of our books and online tools will be retired. If you have purchased this book after the exam was retired or are attempting to register in the Wiley online learning environment after the exam was retired, please know that we make no guarantees that this exam's online Wiley tools will be available once the exam is no longer available.

Data+ DA0-002 Exam Objectives

CompTIA goes to great lengths to ensure that its certification programs accurately reflect the IT industry's best practices. It does this by establishing committees for each of its exam programs. Each committee consists of a small group of IT professionals, training providers, and publishers who are responsible for establishing the exam's baseline competency level and who determine the appropriate target-audience level.

Once these factors are determined, CompTIA shares this information with a group of hand-selected subject matter experts (SMEs). These folks are the true brainpower behind the certification program. The SMEs review the committee's findings, refine them, and shape them into the objectives that follow this section. CompTIA calls this process a job-task analysis (JTA).

Finally, CompTIA conducts a survey to ensure that the objectives and weightings truly reflect job requirements. Only then can the SMEs go to work writing the hundreds of questions needed for the exam bank. Even so, they have to go back to the drawing board for further refinements in many cases before the exam is ready to go live in its final state. Rest assured that the content you're about to learn will serve you long after you take the exam.

CompTIA also publishes relative weightings for each of the exam's objectives. The following table lists the five Data+ objective domains and the extent to which they are represented on the exam.

Domain	Percent of Exam
1.0 Data Concepts and Environments	20%
2.0 Data Acquisition and Preparation	22%
3.0 Data Analysis	24%
4.0 Visualization and Reporting	20%
5.0 Data Governance	14%

DA0-002 Certification Exam Objective Map

Objective	Chapter
1.0 Data Concepts and Environments	
1.1 Explain data concepts.	Chapters 3, 4
1.2 Identify types of data sources.	Chapter 4
1.3 Identify infrastructure concepts.	Chapter 2

Objective	Chapter
1.4 Identify common data analysis tools.	Chapter 2
1.5 Identify artificial intelligence (AI) concepts.	Chapter 1
2.0 Data Acquisition and Preparation	
2.1 Given a scenario, use data acquisition methods.	Chapter 4
2.2 Given a scenario, perform data exploration to identify possible inconsistencies with a data set.	Chapter 5
2.3 Given a scenario, perform appropriate data transformation and cleansing techniques.	Chapter 5
3.0 Data Analysis	
3.1 Given a set of requirements, determine the appropriate communication approach for data analysis.	Chapter 6
3.2 Given a scenario, select the appropriate statistical method or function.	Chapters 1, 6
3.3 Given a scenario, troubleshoot basic issues using the appropriate tool or method.	Chapter 6
4.0 Visualization and Reporting	
4.1 Given a scenario, use the appropriate visual elements.	Chapter 7
4.2 Given a scenario, use the appropriate delivery or consumption method.	Chapter 7
4.3 Given a scenario, troubleshoot issues using report validation techniques.	Chapter 7
5.0 Data Governance	
5.1 Explain data management concepts.	Chapter 8
5.2 Summarize concepts related to data compliance.	Chapter 8
5.3 Compare and contrast data privacy and protection practices.	Chapter 8
5.4 Compare and contrast data quality assurance practices.	Chapter 8

Exam objectives are subject to change at any time without prior notice and at CompTIA's discretion. Visit CompTIA's website (www.comptia.org) for the most current listing of exam objectives.

Assessment Test

1. A compliance report must be emailed automatically to regulators at 6 a.m. every Monday with the previous week's finalized data. Which delivery approach *best* meets this requirement?
   - **A.** Self-service portal
   - **B.** Push model
   - **C.** Pull model
   - **D.** Real-time interactive dashboard

2. Tonya needs to create a dashboard that will draw information from many other data sources and present it to business leaders. Which one of the following tools is least likely to meet her needs?
   - **A.** Looker
   - **B.** Tableau
   - **C.** Power BI
   - **D.** SAS

3. Ryan is using SQL to work with data stored in a relational database. He would like to add several new rows to a database table. What command should he use?
   - **A.** SELECT
   - **B.** ALTER
   - **C.** INSERT
   - **D.** UPDATE

4. Daniel is working on an ELT process that sources data from six different source systems. Looking at the source data, he finds that data about the sample people exists in two of the six systems. What does he have to make sure he checks for in his ELT process? (Choose the best answer.)
   - **A.** Data duplication
   - **B.** Redundant data
   - **C.** Invalid data
   - **D.** Missing data

5. A marketing director asks for a single page that shows year-to-date revenue, allows quick filtering by region and product line, and lets users drill down to individual sales-rep performance. Which of the following is the best deliverable to meet these requirements?
   - **A.** Monthly static PDF report
   - **B.** Interactive web-based dashboard
   - **C.** Quarterly infographic handout
   - **D.** Ad hoc SQL export in CSV format

6. Alexander wants to use data from his corporate sales, CRM, and shipping systems to try to predict future sales. Which of the following systems is most appropriate? (Choose the best answer.)
   A. Data mart
   B. OLAP
   C. Data warehouse
   D. OLTP

7. Jackie is working in a data warehouse and finds a finance fact table that links to an organization dimension, which in turn links to a currency dimension that is not linked to the fact table. What type of design pattern is the data warehouse using?
   A. Star
   B. Sun
   C. Snowflake
   D. Comet

8. Encryption is a mechanism for protecting data. When should encryption be applied to data? (Choose the best answer.)
   A. When data is at rest
   B. When data is at rest or in transit
   C. When data is in transit
   D. When data is at rest unless you are using local storage

9. What subset of SQL is used to add, remove, modify, or retrieve the information stored within a relational database?
   A. DDL
   B. DSL
   C. DQL
   D. DML

10. Jen wants to study the academic performance of undergraduate sophomores and wants to determine the average GPA (grade point average) at different points during an academic year. What best describes the dataset she needs?
    A. Sample
    B. Observation
    C. Variable
    D. Population

11. Mauro works with a group of R programmers tasked with copying data from an accounting system into a data warehouse. In what phase are the group's R skills most relevent?
    A. Extract
    B. Load
    C. Transform
    D. Purge

12. Omar is conducting a study and wants to capture eye color. What kind of data is eye color? (Choose the best answer).
    A. Discrete
    B. Categorical
    C. Continuous
    D. Alphanumeric

13. Lars is looking at home sales prices in a single ZIP code and notices that one home sold for $938,294 when the average selling price of similar homes is $209,383. What type of data does the $938,294 sales price represent? (Choose the best answer.)
    A. Duplicate data
    B. Data outlier
    C. Redundant data
    D. Invalid data

14. Trianna wants to explore central tendency in her dataset. Which statistic best matches her need?
    A. Interquartile range
    B. Range
    C. Median
    D. Standard deviation

15. Shakira has 15 people on her data analytics team. Her team's charter requires that all team members have read access to the finance, human resources, sales, and customer service areas of the corporate data warehouse. What is the best way to provision access to her team? (Choose the best answer.)
    A. Since there are 15 people on her team, create a role for each person to improve security.
    B. Since there are four discrete data subjects, create one role for each subject area.
    C. Enable multifactor authentication (MFA) to protect the data.
    D. Create a unified role that includes finance, human resources, sales, and customer service data.

16. What is the median of the following numbers?

13, 2, 65, 3, 5, 4, 7, 3, 4, 7, 8, 2, 4, 4, 60, 23, 43, 2

   A. 4
   B. 4.5
   C. 63
   D. 18

17. According to the empirical rule, what percent of the values in a sample fall within three standard deviations of the mean in a normal distribution?

   A. 99.7%
   B. 95%
   C. 90%
   D. 68%

18. Martin is building a database to store prices for items on a restaurant menu. Which one of the following data types is most appropriate for this field?

   A. Decimal
   B. Integer
   C. String
   D. Floating point

19. Harrison is conducting a survey. He intends to distribute the survey via email, and he wants to optionally follow up with respondents based on their answers. What quality dimension is most vital to the success of Harrison's survey? (Choose the best answer.)

   A. Completeness
   B. Accuracy
   C. Consistency
   D. Validity

20. Mary is developing a script that will perform some common analytics tasks. In order to improve the efficiency of her workflow, she is using a package called the tidyverse. What programming language is she using?

   A. Python
   B. R
   C. Ruby
   D. C++

Answers to Assessment Test

1. B. A push model is the best approach because it involves automatically delivering the compliance report to the regulators via email on a scheduled basis, exactly matching the need for weekly delivery at 6 a.m. A self-service portal and a pull model both require the recipients to take action to retrieve the report, which doesn't guarantee timely or consistent access. A real-time interactive dashboard isn't appropriate because it focuses on dynamic data access rather than scheduled delivery of finalized, static reports needed for regulatory compliance.

2. D. SAS is the least likely tool to meet Tonya's needs because, while it is a powerful analytics and statistical software suite, it is not primarily designed for creating interactive dashboards that integrate multiple data sources in a user-friendly way. Looker, Tableau, and Power BI are all widely used business intelligence tools that specialize in data visualization and dashboard creation, allowing users to pull data from various sources and present it in a clear, interactive format for business leaders. SAS is more focused on advanced statistical analysis, data mining, and machine learning rather than real-time dashboarding and visualization.

3. C. The INSERT command is used to add new records to a database table. The SELECT command is used to retrieve information from a database. It's the most commonly used command in SQL, as it is used to pose queries to the database and retrieve the data that you're interested in working with. The UPDATE command is used to modify rows in the database. The CREATE command is used to create a new table within your database or a new database on your server.

4. A. Data duplication is the best answer because the same individuals appear in multiple source systems, meaning there is a risk of repeated records when integrating the data. Daniel must ensure his ELT process properly identifies and resolves duplicate records, either by merging them correctly or eliminating unnecessary repetitions. Redundant data refers to storing the same data multiple times unnecessarily, which is related but not the primary concern in this case. Invalid data pertains to incorrect or improperly formatted values, which is always important but not the main issue arising from multiple sources. Missing data refers to incomplete records, which could be a concern but is not as directly relevant as handling duplicate records in this scenario.

5. B. An interactive web-based dashboard best meets the requirements because it can display year-to-date revenue on a single page, enable quick filtering by region and product line, and support drill-down capabilities to view individual sales rep performance. It offers the flexibility and interactivity needed for real-time data exploration and decision-making. A monthly static PDF report cannot support filtering or drill-downs, limiting its usefulness for dynamic analysis. A quarterly infographic handout is visually appealing but lacks interactivity and timeliness. An ad hoc SQL export in CSV format may provide raw data, but it doesn't offer the user-friendly interface or visual insights needed for effective executive-level review and exploration.

6. C. A data warehouse is the most appropriate system because it integrates data from multiple sources, such as corporate sales, CRM, and shipping systems, to support historical analysis and predictive modeling. Data warehouses are designed for complex queries, reporting, and business intelligence, making them ideal for forecasting future sales. A data mart is a smaller, more specialized subset of a data warehouse, typically focused on a specific department or function, which may not provide the full scope of integrated data Alexander needs. OLAP enables multidimensional analysis but usually operates on data stored in a data warehouse rather than serving as the primary data storage system. OLTP systems are optimized for real-time transactional data rather than historical analysis or predictive modeling.

7. C. The data warehouse is using a snowflake design because the organization dimension links to the currency dimension instead of the fact table linking directly to both. In a snowflake schema, dimensions are normalized into multiple related tables, reducing redundancy but increasing complexity. A star schema would have all dimensions directly connected to the fact table without intermediate links. A sun schema is not a recognized data warehouse design. A comet schema is also not a standard term in data warehousing.

8. B. Encryption should be applied when data is at rest or in transit because both states present security risks. Data at rest, such as stored files or databases, is vulnerable to unauthorized access if not encrypted. Data in transit, such as information being sent over a network, is susceptible to interception and should also be encrypted to prevent eavesdropping. Encrypting only at rest or only in transit leaves potential security gaps. The mention of local storage does not change the need for encryption, as data on local devices can still be accessed or stolen.

9. D. The Data Manipulation Language (DML) is used to work with the data stored in a database. DML includes the SELECT, INSERT, UPDATE, and DELETE commands. The Data Definition Language (DDL) contains the commands used to create and structure a relational database. It includes the CREATE, ALTER, and DROP commands. DDL and DML are the only two sublanguages of SQL.

10. A. The best description is sample because Jen is studying a subset of all undergraduate students—specifically, sophomores—rather than the entire student body. A population would include all undergraduate students or even all students in general, not just sophomores. An observation refers to an individual data point within the dataset, such as one student's GPA at a specific time. A variable represents a characteristic being measured, such as GPA, but does not describe the overall dataset Jen needs.

11. C. The group's R skills are most relevant in the transform phase because R is commonly used for data manipulation, cleaning, and structuring before loading it into a data warehouse. The extract phase involves retrieving raw data from the source system, typically using SQL or ETL tools rather than R. The load phase focuses on inserting data into the data warehouse, which is more about database operations than data transformation. The purge phase involves deleting or archiving old data, which does not typically require R programming.

12. B. Eye color is categorical data because it represents non-numeric labels that describe characteristics such as blue, green, or brown. These values classify individuals into distinct groups without any inherent numerical order or scale. While it's true you can count the number of people with each eye color, that count is a separate summary statistic applied to the categories. That doesn't make the eye color itself discrete data. Discrete data refers specifically to numeric values that result from counting, like the number of children in a household. Continuous data involves measurements that can take on any value within a range, such as height. Alphanumeric data consists of strings containing both letters and numbers, typically used for things like identification codes, not descriptive traits like eye color.

13. B. The $938,294 sales price represents a data outlier because it is significantly higher than the average selling price of similar homes in the same ZIP code. Outliers are values that deviate substantially from the overall pattern of the data. It is not duplicate data, as it does not repeat an existing value. It is not redundant data, which refers to unnecessary duplication of information. It is not invalid data because the price is a possible real-world value, just an unusually high one for that ZIP code.

14. C. Median best matches her need because it is a measure of central tendency, representing the middle value of a sorted dataset. Interquartile range measures data dispersion by capturing the range of the middle 50 percent of values rather than central tendency. Range describes the spread between the highest and lowest values, not the center of the data. Standard deviation measures variability around the mean rather than identifying the central point of the dataset.

15. D. Creating a unified role that includes finance, human resources, sales, and customer service data is the best approach because it simplifies access management by assigning the same permissions to all team members while ensuring they have the necessary read access. Creating a role for each person would be inefficient and difficult to manage. Creating a role for each subject area would require assigning multiple roles to each team member, adding unnecessary complexity. Enabling multifactor authentication (MFA) enhances security but does not address the need for structured and efficient access provisioning.

16. B. To determine the median, the first step is to arrange the numbers in ascending order: 2, 2, 2, 3, 3, 4, 4, 4, 4, 5, 7, 7, 8, 13, 23, 43, 60, and 65. Since there are 18 numbers in the dataset, the median is found by averaging the 9th and 10th values. In this case, the 9th number is 4, and the 10th number is 5, resulting in a median of 4.5. Additionally, the mode is 4, as it appears most frequently, and the range is 63, calculated by subtracting the smallest value, 2, from the largest value, 65. The number of observations is 18.

17. A. According to the empirical rule, 68 percent of values are within one standard deviation, 95 percent are within two standard deviations, and 99.7 percent are within three standard deviations.

18. A. Decimal is the most appropriate data type for storing prices because it allows for precise representation of fractional numbers, which is critical in financial contexts like menu pricing. Decimal types avoid the rounding errors that can occur with floating point representations due to binary approximation. Integer would not work since prices often include cents and require decimals. String is unsuitable because it treats numbers as text, preventing proper numeric operations like sorting or calculations. Floating point allows decimals, but it can introduce precision issues, making it less reliable for storing exact monetary values.

19. A. Completeness is the most vital quality dimension because Harrison needs respondents to provide enough information to enable follow-ups based on their answers. If key responses are missing, he may not be able to effectively analyze the data or reach out to participants. Accuracy ensures the correctness of responses but is secondary to having complete data for follow-ups. Consistency ensures uniformity in responses but does not directly impact whether enough information is provided. Validity ensures the data meets the intended format or criteria but does not guarantee that all necessary responses are present.

20. B. The tidyverse is a collection of packages for the R programming language designed to facilitate the analytics workflow. The tidyverse is not available for Python, Ruby, or C++, all of which are general-purpose programming languages.

Chapter 1

Today's Data Analyst

THE COMPTIA DATA+ EXAM TOPICS COVERED IN THIS CHAPTER INCLUDE:

✔ **Domain 1.0: Data Concepts and Environments**

- 1.5. Identify artificial intelligence (AI) concepts

✔ **Domain 3.0: Data Analysis**

- 3.2. Given a scenario, select the appropriate statistical method or function

Analytics is at the heart of modern business. Virtually every organization collects large quantities of data about its customers, products, employees, and service offerings. Managers naturally seek to analyze that data and harness the information it contains to improve the efficiency, effectiveness, and profitability of their work.

Data analysts are the professionals who possess the skills and knowledge required to perform this vital work. They understand how the organization can acquire, clean, and transform data to meet the organization's needs. They are able to take that collected information and analyze it using the techniques of statistics and machine learning. They may then create powerful visualizations that display this data to business leaders, managers, and other stakeholders.

Welcome to the World of Analytics

We are fortunate to live in the Golden Age of Analytics. Businesses around the world recognize the vital nature of data to their work and are investing heavily in analytics programs designed to give them a competitive advantage. Organizations have been collecting this data for years, and many of the statistical tools and techniques used in analytics work date back decades. But if that's the case, why are we just now in the early years of this Golden Age? Figure 1.1 shows the three major pillars that have come together at this moment to allow analytics programs to thrive: data, storage, and computing power.

Data

The amount of data the modern world generates on a daily basis is staggering. From the organized tables of spreadsheets to the storage of photos, video, and audio recordings, modern businesses create an almost overwhelming avalanche of data that is ripe for use in analytics programs.

Let's try to quantify the amount of data that exists in the world. We'll begin with an estimate made by Google's then-CEO Eric Schmidt in 2010. At a technology conference, Schmidt estimated that the sum total of all of the stored knowledge created by the world

FIGURE 1.1 Analytics is made possible by modern data, storage, and computing capabilities.

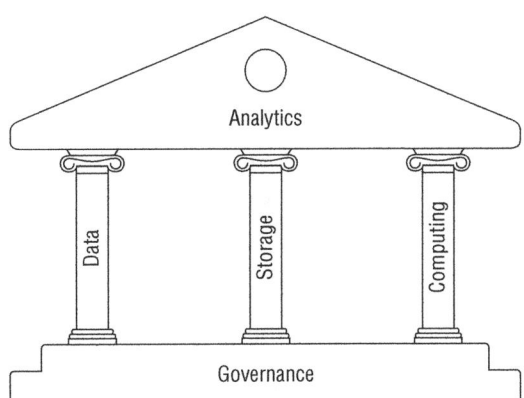

at that point in time was approximately 5 exabytes. To give that a little perspective, the file containing the text of this chapter is around 100 kilobytes. So, Schmidt's estimate is that the world in 2010 had total knowledge that is about the size of 50,000,000,000,000 (that's 50 trillion!) copies of this book chapter. That's a staggering number, but it's only the beginning of our journey.

Now fast-forward just two years to 2012. In that year, researchers estimated that the total amount of stored data in the world had grown to 1,000 exabytes (or one zettabyte). Remember, Schmidt's estimate of 5 exabytes was made only two years earlier. In just two years, the total amount of stored data in the world grew by a factor of 200! But we're still not finished!

In the year 2020, IDC estimates that the world created 59 zettabytes (or 59,000 exabytes) of new information. Compare that to Schmidt's estimate of the world having a total of 5 exabytes of stored information in 2010. If you do the math, you'll discover that this means that on any given day in the modern era, the world generates an amount of brand-new data that is approximately 32 times the sum total of all information created from the dawn of civilization until 2010! Now, *that* is a staggering amount of data!

From an analytics perspective, this trove of data is a gold mine of untapped potential.

Storage

The second key trend driving the growth of analytics programs is the increased availability of storage at rapidly decreasing costs. Table 1.1 shows the cost of storing a gigabyte of data in different years using magnetic hard drives.

Figure 1.2 shows the same data plotted as a line graph on a logarithmic scale. This visualization clearly demonstrates the fact that storage costs have plummeted to the point

TABLE 1.1 Gigabyte Storage Costs over Time

Year	Cost per GB
1985	$169,900
1990	$53,940
1995	$799
2000	$17.50
2005	$0.62
2010	$0.19
2015	$0.03
2020	$0.01
2025	$0.01

FIGURE 1.2 Storage costs have decreased over time.

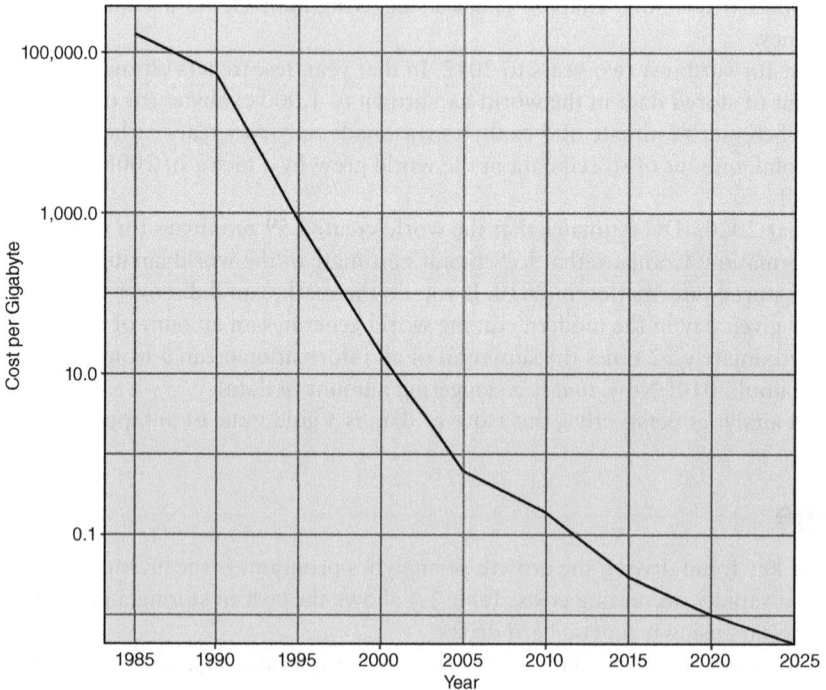

where storage is almost free and businesses can afford to retain data for analysis in ways that they never have before.

Computing Power

In 1975, Gordon Moore, one of the co-founders of Intel Corporation, made a prediction that computing technology would continue to advance so quickly that manufacturers would be able to double the number of components placed on an integrated circuit every two years. Remarkably, that prediction has stood the test of time and remains accurate today.

Commonly referred to as *Moore's Law*, this prediction is often loosely interpreted to mean that we will double the amount of computing power on a single device every two years. That trend has benefited many different technology-enabled fields, among them the world of analytics.

In the early days of analytics, computing power was costly and difficult to come by. Organizations with advanced analytics needs purchased massive supercomputers to analyze their data, but those supercomputers were scarce resources. Analysts fortunate enough to work in an organization that possessed a supercomputer had to justify their requests for small slices of time when they could use the powerful machines.

Today, the effects of Moore's Law have democratized computing. Most employees in an organization now have enough computing power sitting on their desks to perform a wide variety of analytic tasks. If they require more powerful computing resources, cloud services allow them to rent massive banks of computers at very low cost. Even better, those resources are charged at hourly rates, and analysts pay only for the computing time that they actually use.

These three trends—the massive volume of data generated by our businesses on a daily basis, the availability of inexpensive storage to retain that data, and the cloud's promise of virtually infinite computing power—come together to create fertile ground for data analytics.

Careers in Analytics

As businesses try to keep up with these trends, hiring managers find themselves struggling to identify, recruit, and retain talented analytics professionals. This presents a supply-and-demand situation that is problematic for businesses but excellent news for job candidates seeking to break into the field.

In a 2024 survey of executive leaders, Gartner found that 58 percent of CEOs and 62 percent of CFOs believe that artificial intelligence will be the trend with the most significant impact on their industries over the next three years. This will inevitably lead to increased demand for hiring analytics professionals, a fact that was confirmed by the World

TABLE 1.2 Highest-growth Occupations

Rank	Occupation
1	AI and machine learning (ML) specialists
2	Sustainability specialists
3	Business intelligence analysts
4	Information security analysts
5	FinTech engineers
6	Data analysts and scientists
7	Robotics engineers
8	Big Data specialists
9	Agricultural equipment operators
10	Digital transformation specialists

Economic Forum in their 2023 Future of Jobs Report. That study listed occupations with the highest rate of new job creation. The results, shown in Table 1.2, found that AI and machine learning specialists are the most in-demand of any career field, with three other analytics-related fields in the top ten.

The future is bright. There's no reason to anticipate a reduction in this demand any time soon. It's the right time to enter the exciting field of data analytics!

The Analytics Process

Analysts working with data move through a series of different steps as they seek to gain business value from their organization's data. Figure 1.3 illustrates the process they move through as they acquire new data, clean and manipulate that data,

FIGURE 1.3 The analytics process.

analyze it, create visualizations, and then report and communicate their results to business leaders.

Data Acquisition

Analysts work with a wide variety of data, using data sources generated by the business itself or obtained from external sources. For example, data analysts might look at their own organization's sales data (an internal source) and augment it with census data (an external source) as they try to identify new potential markets for their firm's products and services.

In Chapter 3, "Understanding Data," you'll learn about the different data types, data structures, and file formats that analysts might encounter as they carry out data acquisition tasks. In Chapter 4, "Databases and Data Acquisition," you'll learn about the techniques used to collect this data and integrate it with existing systems as well as the use of relational databases to store, maintain, and query those datasets.

Cleaning and Manipulation

In an ideal world, we'd acquire data from internal and external sources and then simply pull it directly into our analysis. Unfortunately, the world of data is far from ideal, and you'll quickly discover (if you haven't already!) that datasets often contain errors, are missing crucial values, or come in a format that simply makes analysis difficult. Analysts spend a large portion of their time cleaning and manipulating data to get it ready for transformation. In fact, many analytics professionals estimate that cleaning and manipulation work consumes 80 percent of the time spent on most analytics projects!

In Chapter 5, "Data Quality," you'll learn more about the cleaning and manipulation work performed by data analysts. You'll discover the common reasons for cleansing and profiling datasets and different data manipulation methods. You'll also learn about the importance of data quality control and techniques you can use to improve the quality of your data.

Analysis

Once you have clean datasets in hand, you're ready to begin analyzing your data. This work typically begins with a process known as *exploratory data analysis* (EDA), which uses simple statistical techniques to summarize a dataset and draw high-level conclusions. EDA creates hypotheses that analysts may further explore using the techniques of machine learning and artificial intelligence.

In Chapter 6, "Data Analysis and Statistics," you'll learn about the tools and techniques of data analysis. You'll learn how to use descriptive statistics to perform EDA. You'll also learn about the processes used to continue analyses, including clarifying business questions, identifying data sources, and applying analytic techniques.

Visualization

The old adage "a picture is worth a thousand words" is as true in the world of analytics as it is in other aspects of life. The human mind excels at processing visual information and isn't so good at handling large quantities of numeric data.

You've already seen this at play once in this chapter. Table 1.1 presented a set of data points on the cost of storage. Looking at that table, you could tell that the cost of storage decreased over time, but you probably had to do a little thinking to reach that conclusion. A quick look at the same data visualized in Figure 1.2 likely led you to the same conclusion without all the mental gymnastics.

The storage dataset was fairly simple, however. Figure 1.4 shows you an excerpt from a 51-row dataset containing the average college tuition in each state. Can you quickly get a sense of the trend from state to state by looking at that data? It's probably not so easy for you.

Figure 1.5 presents the same data in a map-based visualization. Darker shades represent higher tuition costs. We'll bet that you can draw conclusions from this visualization much more quickly than you can from the raw data!

In Chapter 7, "Data Visualization with Reports and Dashboards," you'll learn about different types of data visualizations, including line charts, histograms, infographics, and more. You'll discover how to select a visualization method appropriate for your needs and use it to tell the story of your data.

FIGURE 1.4   Table of college tuition data.

	state	avg_tuition	region
1	AK	19610.00	alaska
2	AL	13736.33	alabama
3	AR	13637.44	arkansas
4	AZ	14760.17	arizona
5	CA	27036.34	california
6	CO	12900.64	colorado
7	CT	22108.86	connecticut
8	DC	36009.50	district of columbia
9	DE	14592.67	delaware
10	FL	16639.59	florida
11	GA	15381.37	georgia
12	HI	10884.00	hawaii
13	IA	26735.68	iowa
14	ID	12851.29	idaho
15	IL	24911.74	illinois
16	IN	22677.10	indiana
17	KS	19973.68	kansas

FIGURE 1.5 Visualization of college tuition data.

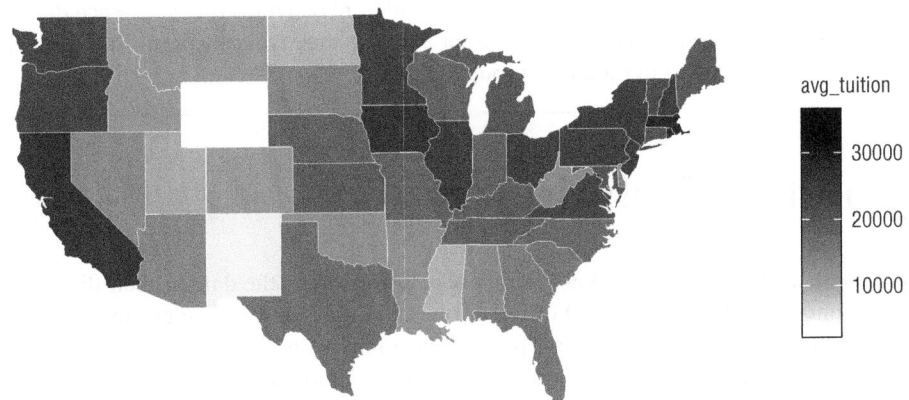

Reporting and Communication

Although visualizations are very useful, they often can't stand alone. In most cases, you'll need to provide business leaders with multiple visualizations as well as supporting text to help communicate the story of your data. That's where *reports* and *dashboards* enter the picture. Reports provide the reader with textual analysis and supporting data in tabular and/or visualization form. They're an extremely common work product in the field of data analytics.

Reports, however, only present a point-in-time analysis. Business leaders often want to monitor business activities in real time using visualizations. Dashboards provide this real-time look at an organization's data using continuously updated visualizations.

Chapter 7 covers reporting and communication in more detail. You'll see examples of different types of reports and dashboards. You'll discover how to translate business requirements into appropriate reporting tools and how to design effective reports and dashboards.

The Analytics Process Is Iterative

While we describe the steps of the analytics process as a series of sequential actions, it's more accurate to think of them as a set of interrelated actions that may be revisited frequently while working with a dataset.

For example, an analyst reviewing a visualization may notice unusual data points that don't seem to belong in the dataset, causing them to return to the data cleaning stage and rerun

> their analysis with the newly cleaned dataset. Similarly, an analyst running an analysis might discover that their analysis would be enriched by adding another source of data, causing them to return to the data acquisition stage.
>
> This process is meant to help you understand the different activities that take place during a data analysis effort and the approximate order in which they typically occur. You shouldn't view it as a rigid process, but rather as a rough guide.

Analytics Techniques

Analysts use a variety of techniques to draw conclusions from the data at their disposal. To help you understand the purpose of different types of analysis, we often group these techniques into categories based on the purpose of the analysis and/or the nature of the tool. Let's take a look at the major categories of analytics techniques.

Descriptive Analytics

Descriptive analytics uses statistics to describe your data. For example, if you perform descriptive analytics on your customer records, you might ask questions like, what proportion of your customers are female? And how many of them are repeat customers?

You can perform descriptive analytics using very basic analysis tools, including simple descriptive statistics and analytic tools. You'll learn more about the use of statistics in descriptive analytics in Chapter 6.

Inferential Analytics

Inferential analytics allows analysts to make generalizations about a population based on a sample of data. For instance, if you survey a subset of your customers to learn about their satisfaction, you can use inferential analytics to draw conclusions about the entire customer base. This type of analysis often involves hypothesis testing, confidence intervals, and regression models to determine relationships, test predictions, and assess whether observed patterns are statistically significant. By doing so, inferential analytics helps analysts make informed decisions about broader populations without needing to examine every single individual.

Predictive Analytics

Predictive analytics seek to use your existing data to predict future events. For example, if you have a dataset on how your customers respond to direct mail, you might use that dataset to build a model that predicts how individual customers will respond to a specific future mailing. That might help you tweak that mailing to improve the response rate by changing the day you send it, altering the content of the message, or even making seemingly minor changes like altering the font size or paper color.

Predictive analytics programs rely on the use of advanced statistical tools and specialized artificial intelligence, machine learning, and deep learning techniques.

Prescriptive Analytics

Prescriptive analytics seek to optimize behavior by simulating many scenarios. For example, if you want to determine the best way to allocate your marketing dollars, you might run different simulations of consumer response and then use algorithms to prescribe your behavior in that context. Similarly, you might use prescriptive analytics to optimize the performance of an automated manufacturing process.

Machine Learning, Artificial Intelligence, and Deep Learning

The work of analytics is intellectually and computationally demanding. Fortunately, you don't always have to do this work yourself; you can rely on automated techniques to help you unlock the hidden value in your data.

Machine learning uses algorithms to discover knowledge in your datasets that you can then apply to help you make informed decisions about the future. That's true regardless of the specific subject matter expertise where you're working, as machine learning has applications across a wide variety of fields. For example, here are some cases where machine learning commonly adds value:

- Segmenting customers and determining the marketing messages that will appeal to different customer groups
- Discovering anomalies in system and application logs that may be indicative of a cybersecurity incident
- Forecasting product sales based on market and environmental conditions
- Recommending the next movie that a customer might wish to watch based on their past activity and the preferences of similar customers
- Setting prices for hotel rooms far in advance based on forecasted demand

Of course, those are just a few examples. Machine learning can bring value to almost every field where discovering previously unknown knowledge is useful—and we challenge you to think of a field where knowledge doesn't offer an advantage!

As we move through the world, we hear the terms *artificial intelligence, machine learning,* and *deep learning* being used almost interchangeably to describe any sort of technique where computers are working with data. Now that you're entering the world of data, it's important to have a more precise understanding of these terms.

FIGURE 1.6 The relationship between artificial intelligence, machine learning, and deep learning.

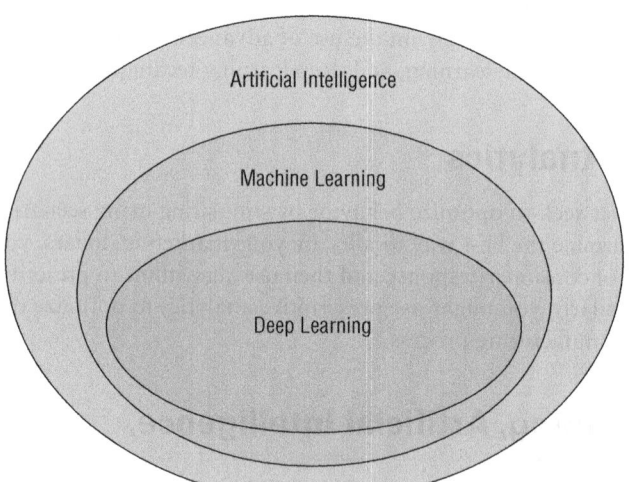

Artificial intelligence (AI) includes any type of technique where you are attempting to get a computer system to imitate human behavior. As the name implies, you are trying to ask computer systems to artificially behave as if they were intelligent. Now, of course, it's not possible for a modern computer to function at the level of complex reasoning found in the human mind, but you can try to mimic some small portions of human behavior and judgment.

Machine learning (ML) is a subset of AI techniques. ML techniques attempt to apply statistics to data problems in an effort to discover new knowledge. Or, in other terms, ML techniques are AI techniques designed to learn.

Deep learning is a further subdivision of machine learning that uses quite complex techniques, known as neural networks, to discover knowledge in a particular way. It is a highly specialized subfield of machine learning that is most commonly used for image, video, and sound analysis.

Figure 1.6 shows the relationships between these fields.

Generative AI

Generative AI is a rapidly growing branch of artificial intelligence that focuses on creating new content, such as text, images, music, and even videos, rather than simply analyzing or interpreting existing data. If you've used tools like ChatGPT, Claude, or Midjourney, you've used generative AI.

At the heart of generative AI are *foundational models*, which are large, pre-trained deep learning models capable of tackling a wide range of tasks. These models are trained on massive datasets to learn general patterns and structures, allowing them to be fine-tuned for specific applications with minimal additional training.

A key category of foundational models is *large language models (LLMs)*, which specialize in processing and generating human language. LLMs are trained on extensive corpora of text to understand the nuances of language, such as grammar, context, and semantics. For example, models like GPT-4 (Generative Pre-trained Transformer 4) can perform tasks ranging from drafting emails and summarizing reports to generating creative writing or answering complex questions. LLMs use advanced deep learning techniques to produce text that often feels human-like, making them indispensable in fields such as customer support, content creation, and coding.

Generative AI builds upon the principles of *natural language processing (NLP)*, a field dedicated to enabling computers to understand and interact with human language. NLP techniques allow generative AI models to parse, interpret, and generate meaningful text. While traditional NLP tasks focused on narrower objectives—such as translating text or identifying sentiment—modern generative AI expands the scope to include creating entirely new and original content.

Robotic Process Automation

Robotic process automation (RPA) is a technology that uses software robots—or "bots"—to automate repetitive, rule-based tasks traditionally performed by humans. These bots are programmed to follow a predefined set of instructions, interacting with digital systems just like a person would, but with greater speed and accuracy. RPA excels at tasks such as data entry, form processing, and system integration, making it an indispensable tool for improving efficiency and reducing human error in business operations.

RPA can assist data analysts by automating time-consuming processes, enabling us to focus on more strategic and value-added work. For instance, RPA can streamline data collection from multiple sources, consolidate the information into a central database, and prepare it for analysis. This is particularly useful in organizations that rely on many legacy systems or deal with large volumes of data spread across different platforms. RPA can automate these tedious tasks and accelerate the analytics workflow.

One of the most impactful applications of RPA in analytics is automated reporting. Generating reports often requires pulling data from various systems, organizing it into the desired format, and applying specific business rules. RPA bots can easily perform these monotonous tasks, ensuring reports are delivered consistently and on time. For example, an RPA bot can automatically extract sales data from a customer relationship management (CRM) system, update a spreadsheet, apply calculations, and generate a report summarizing key performance metrics—all without any manual intervention. This not only saves time but also ensures that stakeholders have access to accurate, up-to-date information for decision-making.

Data Governance

In the beginning of this chapter, we discussed the three major forces that have come together to create the Golden Age of Analytics: data, storage, and computing. In Figure 1.1, we illustrated how those three forces support modern analytics programs. However, there is one element of that figure that we haven't yet discussed. Notice that there is a slab of stone that supports the three pillars of analytics. This slab represents the important role of *data governance* in analytics programs. Without strong governance, analytics programs can't function effectively.

Data governance programs ensure that the organization has high-quality data and is able to effectively control that data. In Chapter 8, "Data Governance," you'll learn the major concepts of data governance and how organizations use *master data management (MDM)* programs to maintain and improve the quality of their data.

Analytics Tools

Software helps analysts work through each one of the phases of the analytics process. These tools automate much of the heavy lifting of data analysis, improving the analyst's ability to acquire, clean, manipulate, visualize, and analyze data. They also provide invaluable assistance in reporting and communicating results.

Some of these tools are well known to most computer users. For example, people are generally familiar with spreadsheet tools such as Microsoft Excel or Google Sheets. Figure 1.7 shows an example of the college dataset used to create Figures 1.4 and 1.5 loaded in Excel.

FIGURE 1.7 Data analysis in Microsoft Excel.

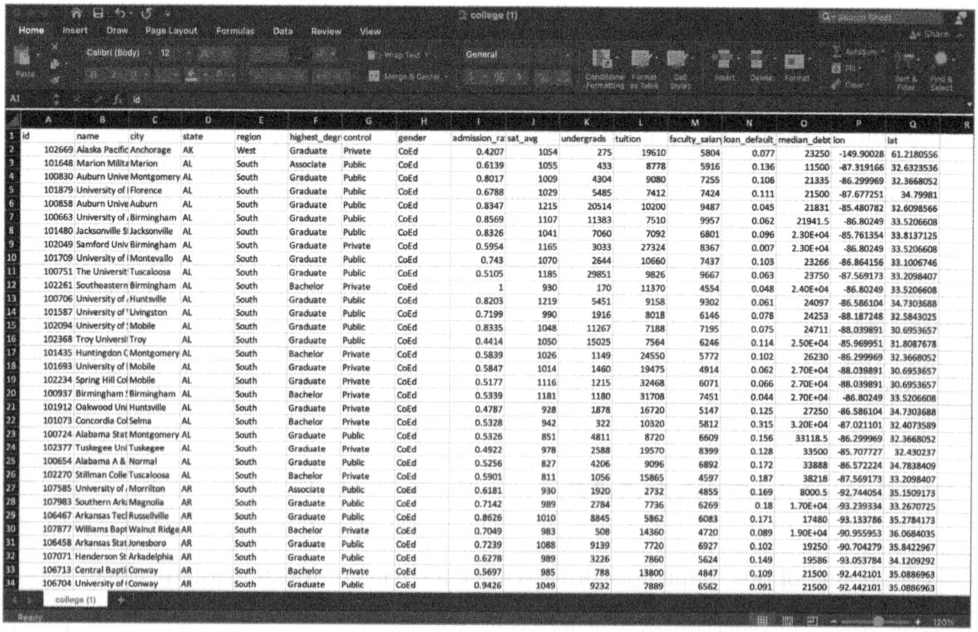

	A	B	C	D	E	F	G	H	I	J	K	L	M	N	O	P	Q
1	id	name	city	state	region	highest_degr	control	gender	admission_ra	sat_avg	undergrads	tuition	faculty_salary	loan_default_	median_debt	lon	lat
2	102669	Alaska Pacific	Anchorage	AK	West	Graduate	Private	CoEd	0.4207	1054	275	19610	5804	0.077	23250	-149.90028	61.2180556
3	101648	Marion Milita	Marion	AL	South	Associate	Public	CoEd	0.6139	1055	433	8778	5916	0.136	11500	-87.319166	32.6323536
4	100830	Auburn Unive	Montgomery	AL	South	Graduate	Public	CoEd	0.8017	1009	4304	9080	7255	0.106	21335	-86.299969	32.3668052
5	101879	University of I	Florence	AL	South	Graduate	Public	CoEd	0.6788	1029	5485	7412	7424	0.111	21500	-87.677251	34.79981
6	100858	Auburn Unive	Auburn	AL	South	Graduate	Public	CoEd	0.8347	1215	20514	10200	9487	0.045	21831	-85.480782	32.6098566
7	100663	University of ,	Birmingham	AL	South	Graduate	Public	CoEd	0.8569	1107	11383	7510	9957	0.062	21941.5	-86.80249	33.5206608
8	101480	Jacksonville S	Jacksonville	AL	South	Graduate	Public	CoEd	0.8326	1041	7060	7092	6801	0.096	2.30E+04	-85.761354	33.8137125
9	102049	Samford Univ	Birmingham	AL	South	Graduate	Private	CoEd	0.5954	1165	3033	27324	8367	0.007	2.30E+04	-86.80249	33.5206608
10	101709	University of I	Montevallo	AL	South	Graduate	Public	CoEd	0.743	1070	2644	10660	7437	0.103	23266	-86.864156	33.1006746
11	100751	The Universit	Tuscaloosa	AL	South	Graduate	Public	CoEd	0.5105	1185	29851	9826	9667	0.063	23750	-87.569173	33.2098407
12	102261	Southeastern	Birmingham	AL	South	Bachelor	Private	CoEd	1	930	170	11370	4554	0.048	2.40E+04	-86.80249	33.5206608
13	100706	University of ,	Huntsville	AL	South	Graduate	Public	CoEd	0.8203	1219	5451	9158	9302	0.061	24097	-86.586104	34.7303688
14	101587	University of '	Livingston	AL	South	Graduate	Public	CoEd	0.7199	990	1916	8018	6146	0.078	24253	-88.187248	32.5843025
15	102094	University of !	Mobile	AL	South	Graduate	Public	CoEd	0.8335	1048	11267	7188	7195	0.075	24711	-88.039891	30.6953657
16	102368	Troy Universi	Troy	AL	South	Graduate	Public	CoEd	0.4414	1050	15025	7564	6246	0.114	2.50E+04	-85.969951	31.8087678
17	101435	Huntingdon C	Montgomery	AL	South	Bachelor	Private	CoEd	0.5839	1026	1149	24550	5772	0.102	26230	-86.299969	32.3668052
18	101693	University of I	Mobile	AL	South	Graduate	Private	CoEd	0.5847	1014	1460	19475	4914	0.062	2.70E+04	-88.039891	30.6953657
19	102234	Spring Hill Col	Mobile	AL	South	Graduate	Private	CoEd	0.5177	1116	1215	32468	6071	0.066	2.70E+04	-88.039891	30.6953657
20	100937	Birmingham !	Birmingham	AL	South	Bachelor	Private	CoEd	0.5339	1181	1180	31708	7451	0.044	2.70E+04	-86.80249	33.5206608
21	101912	Oakwood Uni	Huntsville	AL	South	Graduate	Private	CoEd	0.4787	928	1878	16720	5147	0.125	27250	-86.586104	34.7303688
22	101073	Concordia Col	Selma	AL	South	Bachelor	Private	CoEd	0.5328	942	322	10320	5812	0.315	3.20E+04	-87.021101	32.4073589
23	100724	Alabama Stat	Montgomery	AL	South	Graduate	Public	CoEd	0.5326	851	4811	8720	6609	0.156	33118.5	-86.299969	32.3668052
24	102377	Tuskegee Uni	Tuskegee	AL	South	Graduate	Private	CoEd	0.4922	978	2588	19570	8399	0.128	33500	-85.707727	32.430237
25	100654	Alabama A &	Normal	AL	South	Graduate	Public	CoEd	0.5256	827	4206	9096	6892	0.172	33888	-86.572224	34.7838409
26	102270	Stillman Colle	Tuscaloosa	AL	South	Bachelor	Private	CoEd	0.5901	811	1056	15865	4597	0.187	38218	-87.569173	33.2098407
27	107585	University of ,	Morrilton	AR	South	Associate	Public	CoEd	0.6181	930	1920	2732	4855	0.169	8000.5	-92.744054	35.1509173
28	107983	Southern Ark	Magnolia	AR	South	Graduate	Public	CoEd	0.7142	989	2784	7736	6269	0.18	1.70E+04	-93.239334	33.2670725
29	106467	Arkansas Tec	Russellville	AR	South	Graduate	Public	CoEd	0.8626	1010	8845	5862	6083	0.171	17480	-93.133786	35.2784173
30	107877	Williams Bapt	Walnut Ridge	AR	South	Bachelor	Private	CoEd	0.7049	983	508	14360	4720	0.089	1.90E+04	-90.955953	36.0684035
31	106458	Arkansas Stat	Jonesboro	AR	South	Graduate	Public	CoEd	0.7239	1088	9139	7720	6927	0.102	19250	-90.704279	35.8422967
32	107071	Henderson St	Arkadelphia	AR	South	Graduate	Public	CoEd	0.6278	989	3226	7860	5624	0.149	19586	-93.053784	34.1209292
33	106713	Central Bapti	Conway	AR	South	Bachelor	Private	CoEd	0.5697	985	788	13800	4847	0.109	21500	-92.442101	35.0886963
34	106704	University of (	Conway	AR	South	Graduate	Public	CoEd	0.9426	1049	9232	7889	6562	0.091	21500	-92.442101	35.0886963

FIGURE 1.8   Data analysis in RStudio.

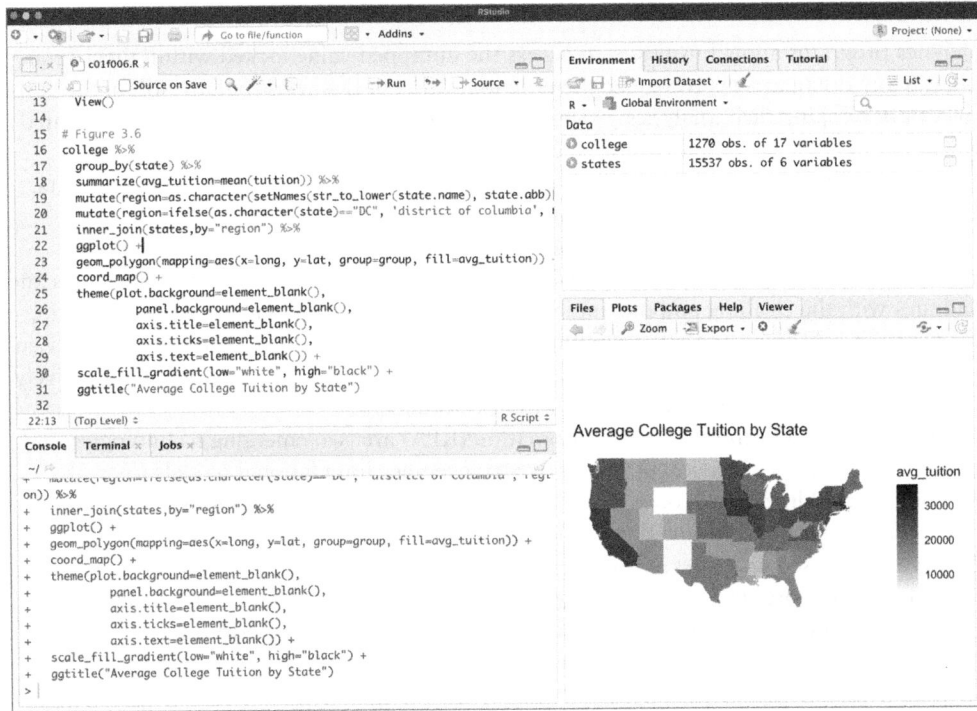

Other analytics tools require more advanced skills. For example, the R programming language is designed to provide analysts with direct access to their data, but it requires learning some basic coding skills. Figure 1.8 shows the RStudio integrated development environment with the code used to create Figure 1.5.

You'll likely work with several different tools in your work as a data analyst. Your choice of tools will depend on the work at hand, the standards used by your organization, and the software licenses available to you. We'll discuss many common analytics tools in Chapter 2, "Data Analytics Tools."

> **Exam Tip**
>
> The bad news is that the Data+ exam covers more than 20 different analytics tools that you'll need to understand to answer test questions. The good news is that you won't need deep knowledge of each of these tools. We'll explore everything that you need to know in Chapter 2.

Summary

Analytics programs allow businesses to access the untapped value locked within their data. Today, many organizations recognize the potential value of this work but are still in the early stages of developing their analytics programs. These programs, driven by the unprecedented availability of data, the rapidly decreasing cost of storage, and the maturation of cloud computing, promise to create significant opportunities for businesses and, in turn, for data professionals skilled in the tools and techniques of analytics.

As analysts develop analytic work products, they generally move through a series of stages. Their work begins with the acquisition of data from internal and external sources and continues with the cleaning and manipulation of that data. Once data is in a suitable form, data professionals apply analytic techniques to draw conclusions from their data, create visualizations to depict the story of their data, and develop reports and dashboards to effectively communicate the results of their work to business leaders.

Generative AI and robotic process automation (RPA) are two emerging technologies reshaping the analytics landscape. Generative AI leverages foundational models to create new content, enabling data professionals to draft reports, summarize insights, and enhance creative tasks with unprecedented efficiency. RPA complements these efforts by automating repetitive, rule-based processes, such as data collection and report generation, freeing analysts to focus on more strategic work. Together, these technologies empower businesses to accelerate analytics workflows, improve accuracy, and unlock new opportunities for innovation in data-driven decision-making.

Chapter 2

Data Analytics Tools

THE COMPTIA DATA+ EXAM TOPICS COVERED IN THIS CHAPTER INCLUDE:

✓ **Domain 1.0: Data Concepts and Environments**
- 1.3. Identify infrastructure concepts
- 1.4. Identify common data analysis tools

Analytics professionals use a wide variety of tools in their work. From simple spreadsheets to complex business intelligence suites, there are many different tools available to help you meet both generalized and specialized analytics needs.

When you're selecting a tool, there are a few important considerations. First, you need the right tool for the job. Just as a carpenter wouldn't use a screwdriver to drive a nail, an analytics professional wouldn't use a spreadsheet to create a machine learning model. Second, you need to choose from the tools available to you. Many analytics tools come with hefty price tags and organizations only license a small subset of them to control costs. Standardizing on a subset of tools also helps improve the ability of teams to work together. If every team in an organization uses different analytics tools, it makes it very difficult for them to collaborate!

> **Exam Tip**
>
> As you prepare for the Data+ exam, you'll need to be familiar with each of the analytics tools discussed in this section. However, you should keep in mind the exact text of this exam objective: "Identify common data analysis tools." While you're expected to know why an analyst would use each of these tools, you're not expected to be able to use all of them yourself.

Spreadsheets

The *spreadsheet* is the most widely used tool in the world of analytics. It's hard to imagine anyone who doesn't use spreadsheets as part of their work because they provide an intuitive way to organize data into rows and columns. Spreadsheet software is installed on pretty much every computer in the modern work environment, and web-based spreadsheets are freely available to anyone.

Spreadsheets are productivity software packages that allow users to create documents that organize any type of data into rows and columns. Users may place any data they like in the spreadsheet and then quickly and easily perform mathematical calculations, such as finding the sum of the values in a row or searching out the minimum, maximum, mean, and median values in a dataset.

Spreadsheets lack any of the constraints of a relational database. While you can certainly organize data in a spreadsheet, there's no requirement that you do so. If you'd like, you can mix numbers, text, dates, and other data elements all in the same column. That does, of course, reduce the usefulness of the spreadsheet, but the user of spreadsheet software has total flexibility in how they organize their data.

The power of spreadsheets comes from the fact that virtually anybody can use one. The barrier to entry is low because they're readily accessible and easy to use. If you need to perform a quick ad hoc data analysis on a fairly small set of data, spreadsheets offer an easy way to do that and then share your work with others.

More formal business needs often stress the capabilities of a spreadsheet. Once the number of people needing to access data grows and you have the desire to keep a centralized and managed data store, these requirements often drive a move of that application from a spreadsheet to a relational database.

Microsoft Excel

Microsoft Excel is the most commonly used desktop spreadsheet application. It's available as a component of the widely deployed Microsoft 365 productivity suite and most modern knowledge workers have access to it.

As with any spreadsheet, you can store data of any kind in an Excel spreadsheet. Figure 2.1 shows an example of an Excel spreadsheet containing data on restaurant

FIGURE 2.1 Table of data in Microsoft Excel.

	A	B	C	D	E	F	G	H	I	J
1	Inspection ID	DBA Name	AKA Name	License #	Facility Type	Risk	Address	City	State	Zip
2	1995829	SUBWAY	SUBWAY	1679112	Restaurant	Risk 1 (High)	8711 S ASHL/	CHICAGO	IL	60620
3	1995817	VENEZUELAN	VENEZUELAN	2424110	Restaurant	Risk 1 (High)	2436 N LINC	CHICAGO	IL	60614
4	1995822	SEVEN TEN	SEVEN TEN	1172093	Restaurant	Risk 1 (High)	1055 E 55TH	CHICAGO	IL	60615
5	1995814	CHISME EXPF	CHISME EXPF	1334960	Restaurant	Risk 1 (High)	5955 S PULA!	CHICAGO	IL	60629
6	1995811	THE NILE RES	THE NILE RES	2334190	Restaurant	Risk 1 (High)	1162 E 55TH	CHICAGO	IL	60615
7	1995752	WINGSTOP	WINGSTOP	2517730	Restaurant	Risk 1 (High)	850 W 63RD	CHICAGO	IL	60621
8	1995226	JOY AND JAN	JOY AND JAN	2073555	Restaurant	Risk 1 (High)	4701 W LAW	CHICAGO	IL	60630
9	1995808	SUSHI MON	SUSHI MON	2517725	Restaurant	Risk 1 (High)	2441 N CLAR	CHICAGO	IL	60614
10	1995807	JEANE KENNI	JEANE KENNI	2215708	Daycare Com	Risk 1 (High)	7600 S PARN	CHICAGO	IL	60620
11	1995802	PEPE'S MEXI(	PEPE'S MEXI(	48820	Restaurant	Risk 1 (High)	1310 E 53RD	CHICAGO	IL	60615
12	1995801	CHILI'S GRILL	CHILI'S GRILL	1937623	Restaurant	Risk 1 (High)	1750 W 119T	CHICAGO	IL	60643
13	1995795	LA FIESTA BA	LA FIESTA BA	1488177	Restaurant	Risk 1 (High)	6424 S PULA!	CHICAGO	IL	60629
14	1995790	DENOVA FRE	MARTHA'S F(	2517805	Grocery Store	Risk 3 (Low)	4459 W DIVE	CHICAGO	IL	60639
15	1995725	UNCLE JOE'S	UNCLE JOE'S	1145333	Restaurant	Risk 1 (High)	10210 S VINC	CHICAGO	IL	60643
16	1973223	TABO SUSHI	PLUM MARKI	2252682	Restaurant	Risk 1 (High)	1233 N WELL	CHICAGO	IL	60610
17	1995781	RED SNAPPEI	RED SNAPPEI	2350305	Restaurant	Risk 1 (High)	1418 E 53RD	CHICAGO	IL	60615
18	1995779	SAMMY'S BR	SAMMY'S BR	2247014	Restaurant	Risk 1 (High)	250 E 103RD	CHICAGO	IL	60628
19	1995776	MONICA'S PI	MONICA'S PI	2522031	Restaurant	Risk 1 (High)	6446-6448 S PULASKI RD	IL	
20	1995773	A WHIZZ KID!	A WHIZZ KID!	2215488	Daycare Abo	Risk 1 (High)	2600 E 83RD	CHICAGO	IL	60617
21	1995769	MONICA'S PI	MONICA'S PI	2326731	Restaurant	Risk 1 (High)	6448 S PULA!	CHICAGO	IL	60629
22	1995766	KENTUCKY FI	KFC	2442911	Restaurant	Risk 1 (High)	5852 S WEST	CHICAGO	IL	60636
23	1995777	CREME DE L/	CREME DE L/	2216029	Daycare Com	Risk 1 (High)	2230 N DOM	CHICAGO	IL	60614
24	1995768	BRIDGEPORT	COFFEE HYD	2277827	Restaurant	Risk 1 (High)	5020 S CORN	CHICAGO	IL	60615
25	1995765	FERNANDEZ	FERNANDEZ	1222819		Risk 3 (Low)	6446 S PULA!	CHICAGO	IL	60629
26	1995751	AKIBA-SCHE(	JEWISH DAY	2275647	School	Risk 1 (High)	5235 S CORN	CHICAGO	IL	60615
27	1995750	LITTLE NEST	LITTLE NEST	2492597	Children's Sei	Risk 1 (High)	5426 W DEV(	CHICAGO	IL	60646

inspections conducted by the city of Chicago. This spreadsheet is organized in the same way you might organize a database table—each column represents a particular data element recorded about each inspection and each row represents a single inspection event.

Excel then allows users to perform calculations and visualizations on their data. You might want to count the total number of restaurant inspections, determine the average length of time that an inspection takes, or compute the number of inspections conducted each day. You can perform almost any simple analysis you might need right in the Excel spreadsheet. Figure 2.2 shows an example of a quick visualization showing the results of inspections conducted by the city.

FIGURE 2.2 Data visualization in Microsoft Excel.

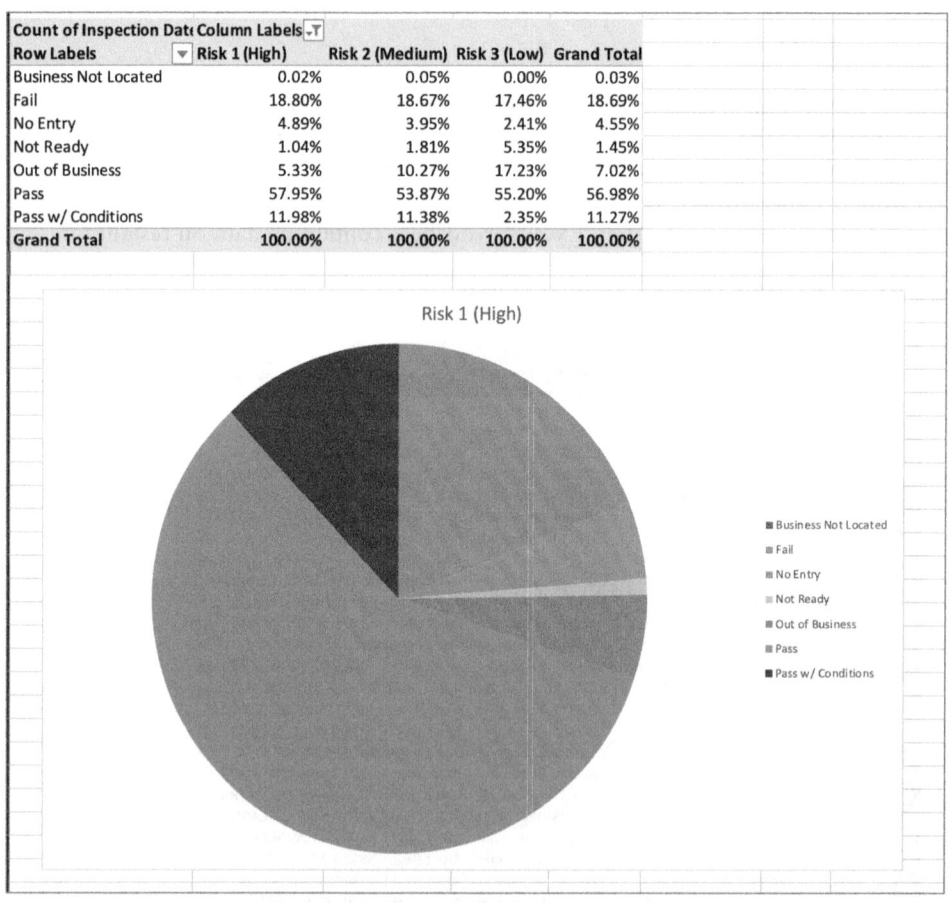

 Microsoft Excel has long held a dominant market share in the spreadsheet market, but competitors do exist. For example, Apple's Numbers spreadsheet software is available to Mac users. Cloud-based spreadsheets such as Google Sheets are also quite popular because they make it easy for multiple people to collaborate on the same spreadsheet. While these other spreadsheets are interesting, you won't need to know about them on the Data+ exam because they're not mentioned in the exam objectives.

Programming Languages

In many cases, business analysts and data scientists need a way to be able to load, manipulate, and analyze data outside of the constraints of software written by another organization. In those cases, they might develop their own software to meet a specific need. In fact, many skilled analysts find it easier to write their own code to perform many analytics tasks than to work within another analytics package.

Programming languages allow skilled software developers to write their own instructions to the computer, allowing them to directly specify the actions that should take place during the analytics process.

> **Exam Tip**
>
> You do not need to know *how* to program on the Data+ exam, and you shouldn't expect any questions that ask you to write or interpret code. You should instead focus on the *purpose* of programming languages and where they might fit into an analytics environment.

R

The *R* programming language is extremely popular among data analysts because it is focused on creating analytics applications. R originally appeared in the 1990s as a statistical programming language that was popular among a niche audience. Three decades later, the language has evolved into one of the most popular languages used by statisticians, data scientists, and business analysts around the world.

R gained rapid traction as a popular language for several reasons. First, it is available to everyone as a free, open source language developed by a community of committed developers. This approach broke the mold of past approaches to analytic tools that relied on proprietary, commercial software that was often out of the financial reach of many individuals and organizations.

R also continues to grow in popularity because of its adoption by the creators of machine learning methods. Almost any new machine learning technique created today quickly becomes available to R users in a redistributable *package*, offered as open source code on the Comprehensive R Archive Network (CRAN), a worldwide repository of popular R code.

One of the most important advances in the R language was the creation of a set of R packages known as the *tidyverse* by Hadley Wickham and other developers. The tidyverse approach to data analysis simplifies the use of the language and makes it accessible to anyone willing to invest a few hours in learning some basic syntax.

Most modern R developers choose to write, test, and deploy their code using an *integrated development environment (IDE)* called RStudio. This graphical interface, shown in Figure 2.3, provides a well-designed environment to manage your code, monitor its progress, and troubleshoot issues that might arise in your R scripts.

FIGURE 2.3   Data analysis using R and RStudio.

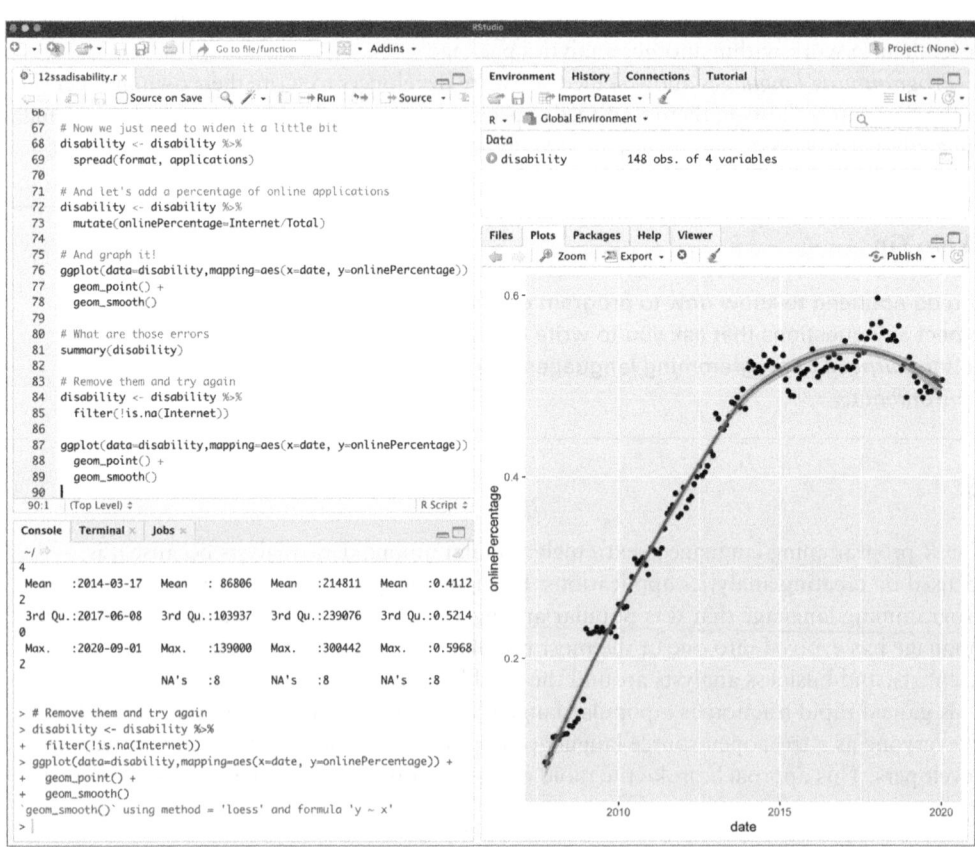

Python

The *Python* programming language is arguably the most popular programming language in use today. Python is about the same age as R, but the major difference between Python and R is that Python is a general-purpose programming language. This means that it is capable of creating software to meet just about any need you might imagine. You can do everything from code a video game to perform a complex data analysis in Python.

With that flexibility, however, comes some complexity. While R is quite popular because of its ease of use, writing software in Python requires some more expertise. Python developers usually have a more formal background in computer science and are familiar with many coding concepts, such as looping and branching, that aren't necessary in most R code.

Python also has specialized libraries that focus on the needs of analysts and data scientists. In particular, the Python Data Analysis Library (pandas) provides a set of tools for structuring and analyzing data. Figure 2.4 shows an example of Python code performing data analysis.

FIGURE 2.4 Data analysis using Python and pandas.

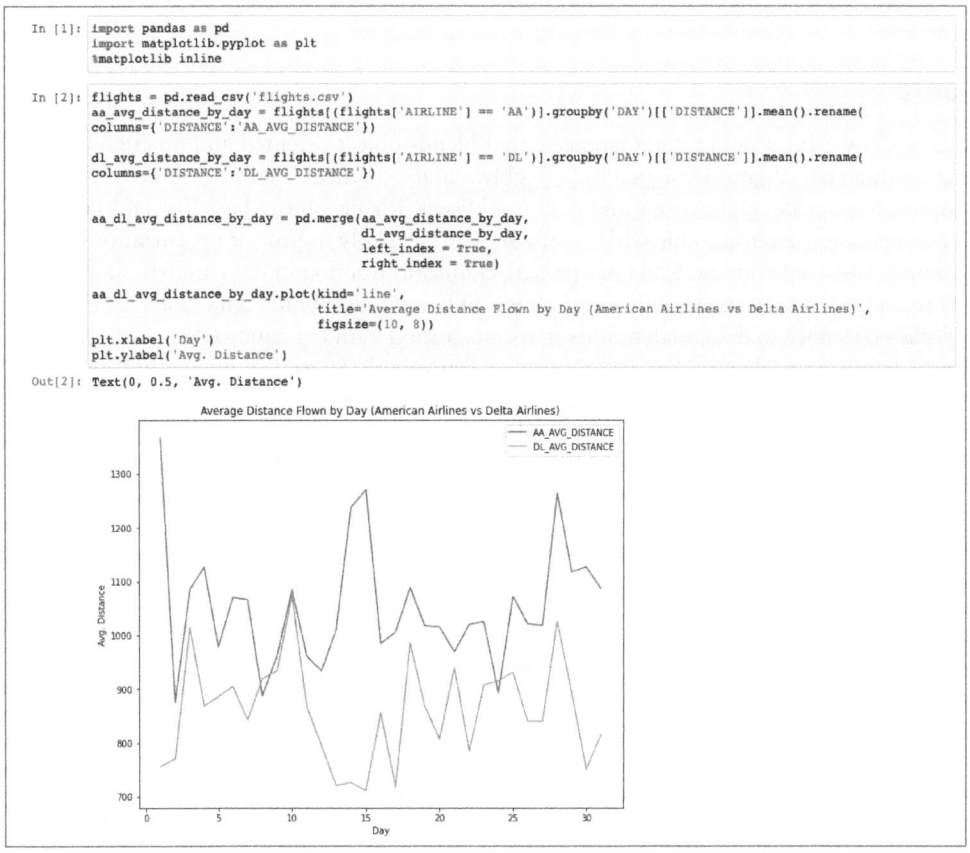

> **Anaconda**
>
> *Anaconda* is an open source distribution of Python and R that simplifies the process of managing packages, dependencies, and environments. It is specifically designed to help analysts and data scientists get up and running quickly without the headaches of configuring complex environments.
>
> One of Anaconda's standout features is its package management system. It includes thousands of pre-built packages for data science and machine learning. Anaconda makes it easy to install and maintain the tools you need for analytics projects. It also includes a built-in environment manager, allowing you to isolate projects and avoid conflicts between package versions.
>
> The Anaconda Navigator is a graphical user interface that allows users to launch applications, manage packages, and create environments without needing to use the command line. It includes tools like Jupyter Notebook for interactive coding, Spyder for traditional development, and even Visual Studio Code for more advanced users.

Scala

Scala is a powerful programming language that blends object-oriented and functional programming paradigms. Designed to be highly scalable (hence its name), Scala excels at complex, large-scale applications and data workflows. It runs on the Java Virtual Machine (JVM), making it interoperable with Java, which is especially useful for organizations with existing Java-based systems. Scala has gained significant traction in data analytics and big data processing due to its flexibility and ability to handle distributed data systems efficiently.

Scala's relevance to data analytics lies in its integration with big data tools, particularly *Apache Spark*, a widely used big data processing framework. Spark is built in Scala, and many data professionals use Scala to write Spark applications for processing massive datasets. This makes Scala an ideal choice for analysts working in environments where speed and scalability are critical, such as streaming analytics or machine learning on distributed datasets.

SAS

SAS is a statistical package that is a long-standing pillar of the statistical software community. It was first released in 1976 and also continues to be widely used today. Figure 2.5 shows an example of a simple data analysis being performed in SAS.

Why is it listed here in a section about programming languages? Well, SAS is both a statistical package and a programming language! While its graphical user interface makes it accessible for users who prefer point-and-click functionality, SAS also includes a powerful scripting language that allows users to write custom programs for data manipulation, analysis, and reporting. This dual nature sets SAS apart, as it caters to both novice users and advanced analysts who need greater flexibility and control over their workflows.

FIGURE 2.5 Analyzing data in SAS.

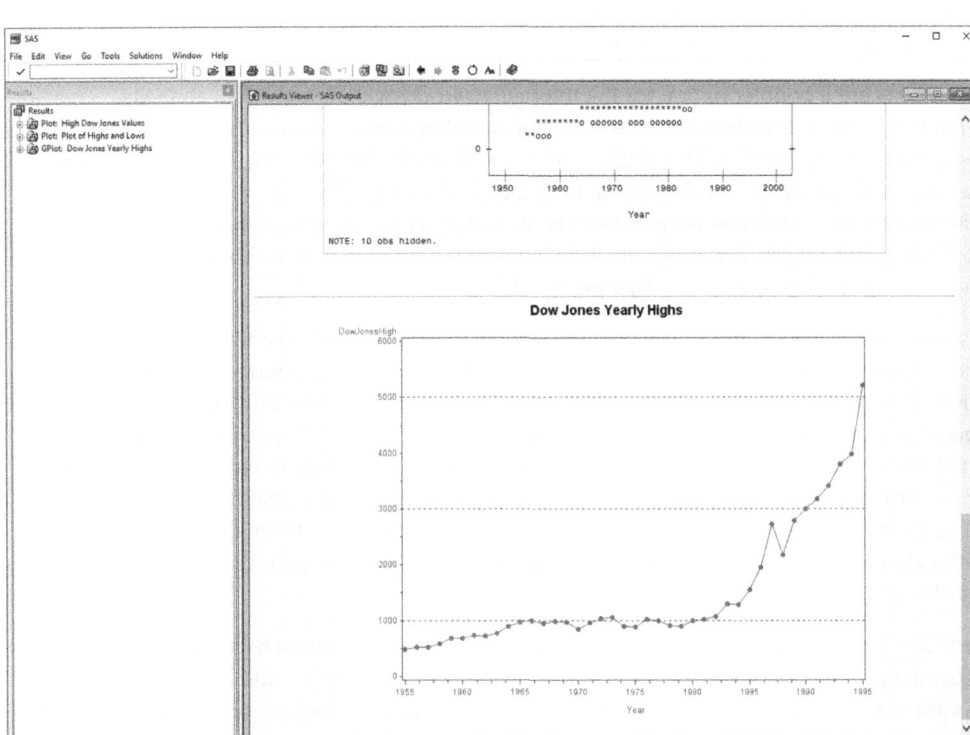

By using SAS as a programming language, analysts can automate repetitive tasks, perform complex data transformations, and create reusable scripts for advanced statistical modeling. This makes SAS an essential tool for professionals working with large datasets or requiring custom analyses that go beyond the capabilities of its graphical interface. Its scripting capabilities also allow for integration with other tools and systems, further enhancing its versatility in data analytics.

Coding Environments

Developers have a few options at their disposal when they write code, and the choice often depends on what they're trying to accomplish and how they like to work.

For the simplest tasks, a *text editor* might be all you need. Text editors are basic programs that let you write and edit code, much like a word processor for text. Popular examples like

Notepad++ or Sublime Text provide features like syntax highlighting to make your code easier to read, but they don't include many advanced tools for running or debugging your code. They're lightweight and great for quick tasks.

Notebooks are a popular option for the interactive work style of many data analysts. A notebook lets you write and execute code in small sections, called *cells*, and immediately see the results right below. This setup is particularly useful for exploring datasets, creating visualizations, or trying out different approaches to a problem. You can also mix code with explanatory text, which is great for documenting your thought process or sharing your work with others. *Jupyter* is the most common notebook platform in analytics, and it supports three languages: Julia, Python, and R.

If you're working on a larger project or need tools to help you debug and manage your code, you might use an IDE, which combines many tools into one interface, including a text editor, a debugger, and sometimes even a way to manage your files and versions of your code. For example, RStudio, which was discussed earlier, is an IDE specifically designed for R programming. It helps you organize your work and makes it easy to create visualizations or perform statistical analysis. Another widely used IDE is Visual Studio (VS) Code, which supports many programming languages, including R and Python. It can be customized with extensions to add functionality like working with Jupyter notebooks directly inside the interface.

Each of these environments has its strengths, and many analysts switch between them depending on the task. If you're new to coding, you might start with a notebook like Jupyter for its ease of use and immediate feedback, then explore IDEs as you tackle more complex projects.

Databases and SQL

The *Structured Query Language (SQL)* is the language of databases. Any time a developer, administrator, or end user interacts with a database, that interaction happens through the use of a SQL command. SQL is divided into two major sublanguages:

- The *Data Definition Language (DDL)* is used mainly by developers and administrators. It's used to define the structure of the database itself. It doesn't work with the data inside a database, but it sets the ground rules for the database to function.
- The *Data Manipulation Language (DML)* is the subset of SQL commands that are used to work with the data inside of a database. They don't change the database structure, but they add, remove, and change the data inside a database.

As you prepare for the exam, you'll need to be familiar with the major commands used in SQL. It's important to understand that you're not responsible for writing or reading SQL commands. You just need to know what the major commands are and when you would use them.

There are three DDL commands that you should know:

- The CREATE command is used to create a new table within your database or a new database on your server.
- The ALTER command is used to change the structure of a table that you've already created. If you want to modify your database or table, the ALTER command lets you make those modifications.
- The DROP command deletes an entire table or database from your server. It's definitely a command that you'll want to use with caution!

There are also four DML commands that you should know:

- The SELECT command is used to retrieve information from a database. It's the most commonly used command in SQL, as it is used to pose queries to the database and retrieve the data that you're interested in working with.
- The INSERT command is used to add new records to a database table. If you're adding a new employee, customer order, or marketing activity, the INSERT command allows you to add one or more rows to your database.
- The UPDATE command is used to modify rows in the database. If you need to change something that is already stored in your database, the UPDATE command will do that.
- The DELETE command is used to delete rows from a database table. Don't confuse this command with the DROP command. The DROP command deletes an entire database table, whereas the DELETE command just deletes certain rows from the table.

Users, administrators, and developers access databases in different ways. First, a developer, administrator, or power user who knows SQL might directly access the database server and send it a SQL command for execution. This often happens through a graphical user interface, such as the Azure Data Studio interface shown in Figure 2.6. This tool allows you to write database queries in SQL, send them to the database, and then view the results.

Utilities like Azure Data Studio can do more than just retrieve data. They also offer a graphical way for database administrators to reconfigure a database. You can click through a series of menus to choose the changes you'd like to make to the database and the utility writes SQL commands that carry out your requests and sends them to the database. As you prepare for the exam, you should also be familiar with some other similar tools available for different databases:

- *MySQL Workbench* is a visual database design tool specifically for MySQL databases. It enables users to create and manage database schemas, write and execute SQL queries, and perform server configuration tasks. Its user-friendly interface makes it popular among developers and database administrators.
- *Compass* is a graphical user interface for MongoDB, designed to help users explore and manipulate their NoSQL databases. It allows for visualizing document structures, creating queries, and managing collections without requiring deep command-line knowledge.

FIGURE 2.6 SQL query using Azure Data Studio.

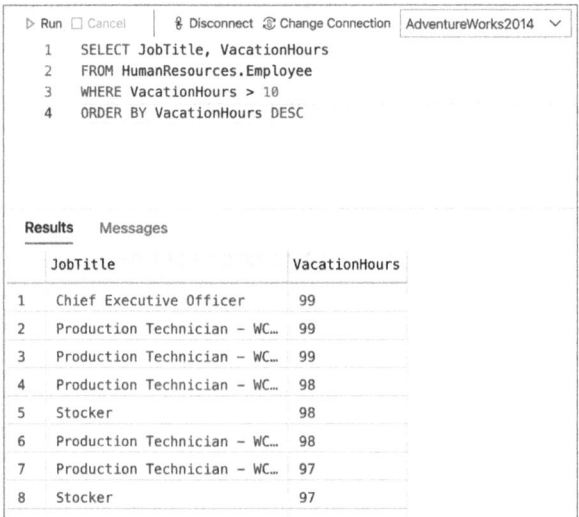

- *DBeaver* is a universal database management tool that supports a wide range of databases, including MySQL, PostgreSQL, Oracle, and SQLite. It provides features such as a visual query builder, data export/import, and ER diagrams, making it a versatile choice for developers and analysts working with multiple database systems.
- *Toad* (Tools for Oracle Application Developers) is a database management tool primarily designed for Oracle databases, although it also supports other platforms. It offers advanced features like code optimization, debugging, and data modeling, helping developers and administrators streamline their workflows.
- Microsoft's *SQL Server Management Studio* is a powerful integrated environment for managing SQL Server databases. It allows users to design, query, and administer databases, providing tools for monitoring performance, creating backups, and automating administrative tasks.

Similarly, many query and report builder tools are available that simplify database access for end users, allowing them to click through a series of menus and drag objects around on the screen to retrieve data from a database. The tool then translates those actions into a SELECT statement that retrieves the desired information from the database.

Finally, computer software can interact with databases programmatically. This just means that software can send SQL commands to the database as part of its activity. For example, when you fill out a form on a company's website, chances are that software is processing that form and then storing a record of your activity in a database.

Business Intelligence Software

Up until this point, the chapter has covered analytics tools that fit into two basic models: programming languages that allow skilled developers to complete whatever analytic task faces them and specialized tools, such as spreadsheets, statistics packages, and machine learning tools that focus on one particular component of the analytics process.

Today, most organizations choose to adopt a *business intelligence* platform that provides powerful capabilities that cross all phases of an analytics process. These tools allow analysts to ingest and clean data, perform exploratory statistical analysis, visualize their data, produce models, make predictions, and communicate and report their results. These packages are normally more expensive than the other tools discussed, but they also provide an end-to-end environment where all of an organization's analysts and developers may work together on analytics projects.

Power BI

Power BI is Microsoft's analytics suite. Power BI is popular among organizations that make widespread use of other Microsoft software because of its easy integration with those packages and cost-effective bundling within an organization's Microsoft enterprise license agreement.

The major components of Power BI include the following:

- *Power BI Desktop* is a Windows application for data analysts, allowing them to interact with data and publish reports for others.
- The *Power BI* service is Microsoft's software-as-a-service (SaaS) offering that hosts Power BI capabilities in the cloud for customers to access.
- *Power BI Mobile* provide users of iOS, Android, and Windows devices with access to Power BI capabilities.
- *Power BI Report Builder* allows developers to create paginated reports that are designed for printing, email, and other distribution methods.
- *Power BI Report Server* offers organizations the ability to host their own Power BI environment on internal servers for stakeholders to access.

Figure 2.7 shows an example of a complex visual dashboard built within the Microsoft Power BI environment to display important information about groundwater quality.

Tableau

Tableau is arguably the most popular data visualization tool available in the market today. The focus of this tool is on the easy ingestion of data from a wide variety of sources and powerful visualization capabilities that allow analysts and business leaders to quickly identify trends in their data and drill down into specific details.

Figure 2.8 shows an example of obesity data for the United States visualized by county using Tableau.

FIGURE 2.7 Communicating a story with data in Microsoft Power BI.

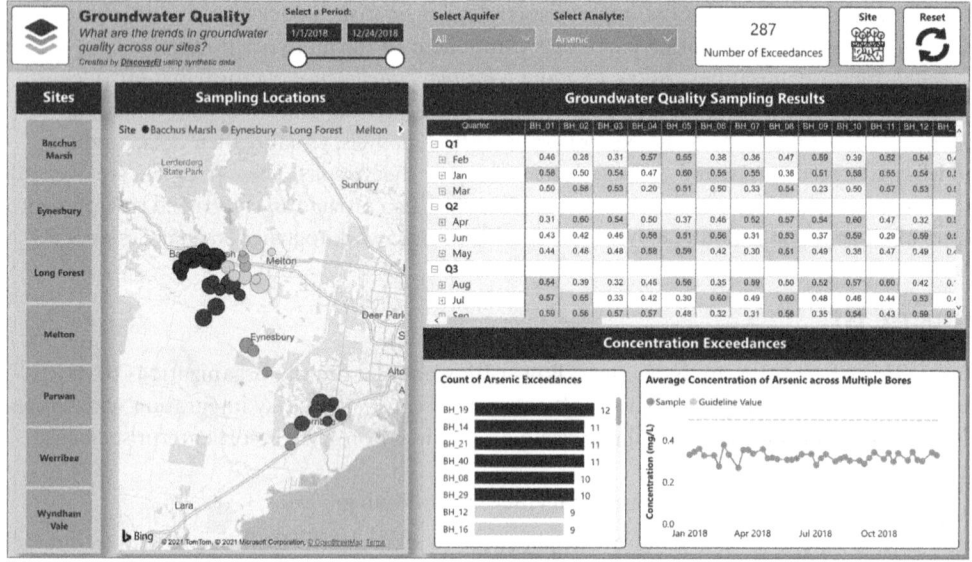

FIGURE 2.8 Visualizing data in Tableau.

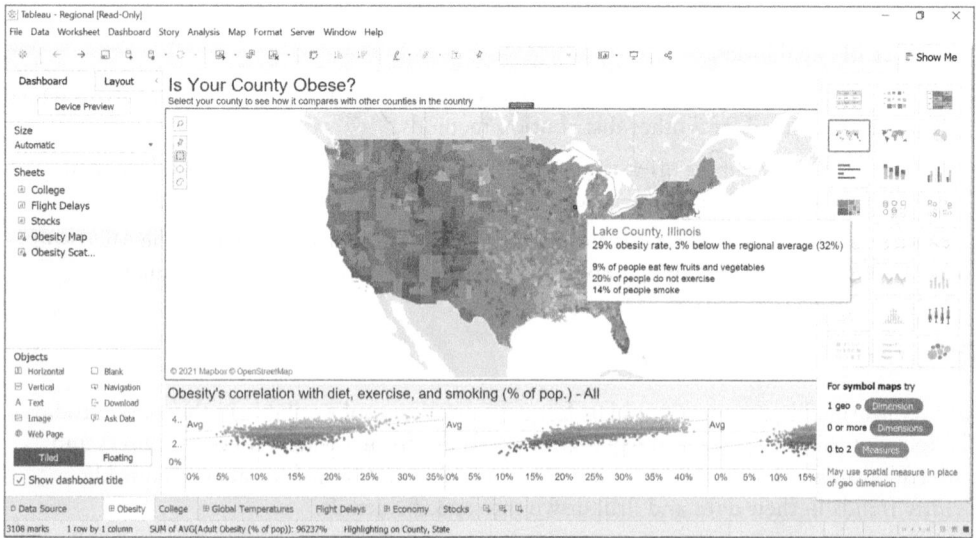

Looker

Looker is another popular SaaS analytics platform, offering access to cloud-based analytics capabilities provided by Google. Unlike traditional BI tools that rely heavily on static reports, Looker provides a highly interactive and flexible approach to data exploration. It connects directly to a variety of databases and data warehouses, leveraging the power of the underlying database to perform queries, rather than requiring data to be extracted and transformed into separate silos. This enables businesses to work with up-to-date data while reducing latency and simplifying workflows.

Figure 2.9 shows an analysis of Google Search data in Looker.

FIGURE 2.9 Visualizing data in Looker.

Cloud Infrastructure

Cloud computing is the delivery of computing services to users over a network. Or, more formally, the National Institute of Standards and Technology (NIST) defines cloud computing as follows:

> A model for enabling ubiquitous, convenient, on-demand network access to a shared pool of configurable computing resources (e.g., networks, servers, storage, applications, and services) that can be rapidly provisioned and released with minimal management effort or service provider interaction.

Drivers for Cloud Computing

Organizations choose the cloud for some or all of their IT workloads for a variety of different reasons.

First, the cloud offers *on-demand* self-service computing. This means that technologists can access cloud resources almost immediately when they need them to do their job. That's an incredible increase in agility for individual contributors and, by extension, the organization. Before the era of on-demand computing, a technologist who wanted to try out a new idea might have to spec out the servers required to implement the idea, gain funding approval, order the hardware, wait for it to arrive, physically install it, and configure an operating system before getting down to work. That might have taken weeks, whereas today the same tasks can be accomplished in the cloud in a matter of seconds. On-demand self-service computing is a true game changer.

Cloud solutions also provide *scalability*. This means that, as the demand on a service increases, customers can easily increase the capacity available to them. This can occur in two ways:

- *Horizontal scaling* refers to adding more servers to your pool. If you run a website that supports 2,000 concurrent users with two servers, you might add a new server every time your typical usage increases by another 1,000 users. Cloud computing makes this quite easy, as you can just replicate your existing server with a few clicks.

- *Vertical scaling* refers to increasing the capacity of your existing servers. For example, you might change the number of CPU cores or the amount of memory assigned to a server. In the physical world, this means opening up a server and adding physical hardware. In the cloud, you can just click a few buttons and add memory or compute capacity.

The cloud also offers rapid *elasticity*. Elasticity is a concept that is closely related to scalability. It refers to both increasing and decreasing capacity as short-term needs fluctuate. If your website starts to experience a burst in activity, elasticity enables you to automatically add servers until that capacity is met and then remove those servers when the capacity is no longer needed.

The cloud offers broad network access. If you have the ability to access the Internet, you can connect to public cloud solutions from wherever you are—in the office, at a coffee shop, or on the road.

Finally, the cloud offers *measured service* as one of its defining characteristics. This means that almost everything you do in the cloud is metered. Cloud providers measure the number of seconds you use a virtual server, the amount of disk space you consume, the number of function calls you make, and many other measures. This allows them to charge you for precisely the services you use—no more and no less. The measured service model is a little intimidating when you first encounter it, but it provides cloud customers with the ability to manage their utilization effectively and achieve the economic benefits of the cloud.

Cloud Service Concepts

Cloud services come in a variety of different concepts. This section discusses the three major service concepts of cloud computing: software as a service, infrastructure as a service, and platform as a service.

Software as a Service

In a *software as a service (SaaS)* model, the public cloud provider delivers an entire application to its customers. Customers don't need to worry about processing, storage, networking, or any of the infrastructure details of the cloud service. The vendor writes the application, configures the servers, and basically gets everything running for customers, who then simply use the service. Very often these services are accessed through a standard web browser, so very little, if any, configuration is required on the customer's end.

Common examples of SaaS applications include email delivered by Google Workspace or Microsoft 365, and storage services that facilitate collaboration and synchronization across devices, such as Box and Dropbox. SaaS applications can also be very specialized, such as credit card processing services and travel and expense reporting management.

Infrastructure as a Service

Customers of *infrastructure as a service (IaaS)* vendors purchase basic computing resources from vendors and piece them together to create customized IT solutions. For example, IaaS vendors might provide compute capacity, data storage, and other basic infrastructure building blocks. The three major vendors in the IaaS space are Amazon Web Services (AWS), Microsoft Azure, and Google Cloud Platform.

IaaS Computing Resources

IaaS computing resources form the backbone of cloud infrastructure, providing organizations with the tools they need to deploy scalable and flexible IT solutions. Two foundational technologies in IaaS are virtual machines (VMs) and containerization, which cater to different use cases and workloads.

Virtual machines are software-based emulations of physical computers, enabling organizations to run applications in isolated environments. Cloud providers like AWS, Azure, and Google Cloud Platform offer highly customizable VMs, allowing customers to configure the number of virtual CPUs, memory, and storage as needed. VMs are particularly suited for legacy applications or workloads that require dedicated resources. They also provide scalability, allowing businesses to add or reduce capacity quickly to adapt to changing demands.

Containerization, on the other hand, packages applications and their dependencies into lightweight, portable units that share the host system's operating system kernel. Containers are often more efficient than VMs, making them ideal for modern, cloud-native applications built on microservices architectures. With services like AWS Elastic Kubernetes Service (EKS), Azure Kubernetes Service (AKS), and Google Kubernetes Engine (GKE), organizations can deploy and manage containers at scale, benefiting from faster startup times and improved resource utilization.

While VMs are ideal for traditional, monolithic applications, containers shine in environments that prioritize agility and portability. Many organizations use both technologies together to balance efficiency, scalability, and compatibility in their cloud infrastructure.

IaaS Storage Resources

IaaS providers offer a variety of storage solutions to meet the diverse needs of their customers. These solutions differ in how they store, access, and manage data.

- *Object storage* is designed for scalability and is ideal for storing unstructured data like images, videos, and backups. In object storage, data is stored as discrete objects, each with a unique identifier, metadata, and content. Popular cloud object storage solutions include Amazon S3, Azure Blob Storage, and Google Cloud Storage.

- *Block storage* breaks data into fixed-size chunks (blocks) and stores them separately, allowing applications to access storage at a lower level. Block storage is highly versatile and ideal for databases, virtual machine disks, and other performance-sensitive workloads. Cloud providers offer block storage solutions like Amazon Elastic Block Store (EBS), Azure Managed Disks, and Google Persistent Disk, which provide low-latency, high-throughput storage options.

- *File storage* provides a familiar hierarchical structure for organizing data into files and directories. It is commonly used for applications that require shared access to files, such as content management systems or home directories. Cloud services like Amazon EFS (Elastic File System) and Azure Files offer scalable file storage with high availability, allowing multiple users or systems to access the same files simultaneously.

- *Local storage* refers to disk storage attached directly to a virtual machine, providing high-performance, low-latency access for applications running on that VM. While local storage offers excellent speed, it is ephemeral—data stored locally does not persist if the VM is stopped or terminated. It's often used for temporary workloads or applications that require fast access to scratch data.

- *Shared storage* enables multiple VMs or containers to access the same storage resource concurrently, often used in clustered applications or workloads requiring high availability. Shared storage solutions leverage network-attached storage (NAS) or other distributed systems to ensure consistent access across environments.

Platform as a Service

In the third tier of public cloud computing, *platform as a service (PaaS)*, vendors provide customers with a platform where they can run their own application code without worrying about server configuration. This is a middle ground between IaaS and SaaS. Users don't need to worry about managing servers, but they are still running their own code.

Cloud Deployment Models

When deploying cloud services, organizations have three primary choices: on-premises private cloud computing, public cloud computing, and hybrid cloud computing.

On-premises/Private Cloud

In the *private cloud* approach, the organization builds and runs its own cloud infrastructure or pays another organization to do so on its behalf. Organizations using the private cloud model want to gain the flexibility, scalability, agility, and cost effectiveness of the cloud but do not want to share computing resources with other organizations. These private clouds may be operated in the organization's own on-premises data center or in a facility owned and/or operated by a partner.

Public Cloud

The *public cloud* uses a different approach: the *multitenancy* model. In this approach, cloud providers build massive infrastructures in their data centers and then make those resources available to all customers. The same physical hardware may be running workloads for many different customers at the same time.

Multitenancy simply means that many different customers share use of the same computing resources. The physical servers that support your workloads might be the same as the physical servers supporting your neighbor's workloads.

In an ideal world, an individual customer should never see the impact of multitenancy. Servers should appear completely independent of each other and enforce the principle of *isolation*. From a security perspective, one customer should never be able to see data belonging to another customer. From a performance perspective, the actions that one customer takes should never impact the actions of another customer. Preserving isolation is the core crucial security task of a cloud service provider.

Of course, sometimes this concept breaks down. If customers do suddenly have simultaneous demands for resources that exceed the total capacity of the environment, performance degrades. This causes slowdowns and outages. Preventing this situation is one of the key operational tasks of a cloud service provider, and they work hard to manage workload allocation to prevent this from happening.

Hybrid Cloud

Organizations adopting a *hybrid cloud* approach use a combination of public and private cloud computing. In this model, they can use the public cloud for some computing workloads, but they also operate their own private cloud for some workloads, often because of data sensitivity concerns.

Public Cloud Providers

The public cloud computing market is dominated by three major providers: Amazon Web Services, Microsoft Azure, and Google Cloud Platform (GCP). Each of these providers offers a wide range of services across the SaaS, IaaS, and PaaS models, providing customers with the flexibility to choose solutions that meet their specific needs.

Amazon Web Services

AWS was the pioneer in the cloud computing space and remains the market leader today. It offers an extensive portfolio of cloud services, including compute, storage, networking, databases, machine learning, and analytics. AWS is known for its global infrastructure, with data centers strategically placed around the world to ensure high availability and low latency. Popular services include Amazon EC2 for scalable virtual servers, Amazon S3 for object storage, and AWS Lambda for serverless computing. AWS's breadth of offerings makes it a go-to choice for organizations ranging from startups to large enterprises.

Microsoft Azure

Azure is Microsoft's cloud platform, and it has rapidly grown into a strong competitor in the cloud space. Azure seamlessly integrates with Microsoft's popular enterprise products, such as Windows Server, SQL Server, and Microsoft 365, making it an appealing choice for organizations already invested in Microsoft's ecosystem. Azure's offerings include virtual machines, Azure SQL Database, and Azure Kubernetes Service for containerized workloads. Azure is also a leader in hybrid cloud solutions, enabling customers to extend their on-premises data centers into the cloud with tools like Azure Arc and Azure Stack.

Google Cloud Platform

GCP, Google's cloud offering, is known for its expertise in data and analytics. Leveraging Google's innovations in artificial intelligence and machine learning, GCP provides services like BigQuery for data warehousing, TensorFlow Enterprise for AI/ML workloads, and

Vertex AI Platform for building and deploying machine learning models. GCP also offers a range of foundational services, such as Compute Engine for virtual machines and Cloud Storage for object storage. Its reputation for strong networking infrastructure and developer-friendly tools makes it a popular choice for technology-driven organizations.

Summary

Data professionals have many different categories of tools at their disposal as they seek to achieve their organization's analytics goals. Spreadsheets are the simplest of these tools, offering a personal productivity solution that is quite flexible and easy to learn. For this reason, spreadsheets remain an indispensable tool in every organization. At the other end of the spectrum, programming languages, such as R and Python, provide software developers with the ability to create their own customized analytics tools.

The reality is that most organizations and analysts want tools that reside somewhere between these extremes. They want tools that are more powerful than spreadsheets, but they don't want to develop those tools themselves. That's where specialized packages that perform statistical analysis and machine learning as well as full-fledged analytics suites enter the picture. The modern analytics organization typically has one or more of these tools at their disposal as they standardize on a set of tools.

Cloud computing plays a pivotal role in modern data analytics by offering scalable, on-demand resources that streamline workflows and enhance flexibility. Infrastructure as a service (IaaS) provides organizations with essential computing resources, such as virtual machines and containerization, to manage data-intensive tasks efficiently. These technologies support the processing, storage, and analysis of vast datasets, accommodating the needs of both traditional and cloud-native applications.

The major cloud providers—AWS, Microsoft Azure, and Google Cloud Platform—offer specialized tools that integrate seamlessly into analytics environments. Object storage solutions, scalable compute instances, and container orchestration platforms empower organizations to analyze data at scale while optimizing resource usage. By leveraging these capabilities, businesses can focus on deriving actionable insights without the overhead of managing physical infrastructure or worrying about performance constraints.

Exam Essentials

Describe the role of the spreadsheet in the modern organization.   Spreadsheets are productivity software packages that allow users to create documents that organize any type of data into rows and columns. They are extremely flexible analytics tools that are available on most modern office computer systems and are very easy to use. The most commonly used spreadsheet software package is Microsoft Excel.

Understand how analytics teams use programming languages. Data professionals with coding skills often turn to programming languages to create their own software analysis tools. This approach frees them of the constraints of other packages and allows them to create software that directly meets their needs. The R programming language is designed specifically for analytics use and is quite easy to learn. Python is a general-purpose programming language that is more difficult to learn but can create virtually any software package.

Know how analysts and developers interact with databases. Relational databases are the primary data stores used in the modern organization. Analysts and developers may interact directly with databases using the Structured Query Language (SQL). SQL has two subcomponents. The Data Definition Language (DDL) defines the structure of the database and contains commands to create, alter, and destroy databases and tables. The Data Manipulation Language (DML) interacts with the data stored in a database and contains commands to add, retrieve, modify, and delete data.

Describe the role of business intelligence suites. Data analytics suites provide powerful capabilities that cross all phases of an analytics process. These tools allow analysts to ingest and clean data, perform exploratory statistical analysis, visualize their data, produce models, make predictions, and communicate and report their results. The business intelligence suites covered on the Data+ exam include Microsoft Power BI, Tableau, and Looker.

Understand the role of cloud providers in modern analytics. Cloud providers such as Amazon Web Services (AWS), Microsoft Azure, and Google Cloud Platform (GCP) play a vital role in delivering scalable, on-demand infrastructure for data analytics. These platforms offer a wide range of services, including computing power, storage solutions, and data analytics tools, enabling organizations to process and analyze vast amounts of data efficiently while reducing the overhead of managing physical infrastructure.

Describe the different cloud and on-premises infrastructure models. Organizations have three primary cloud deployment models to choose from: private, public, and hybrid. Private clouds provide dedicated resources for a single organization, often to meet data security or regulatory requirements. Public clouds rely on shared, multitenant infrastructure to deliver cost-effective, scalable services. Hybrid clouds combine elements of both, allowing businesses to maintain sensitive workloads in private environments while leveraging public clouds for scalability and agility.

Understand the types of cloud storage and their use cases. Cloud storage comes in different forms each designed for specific needs. Object storage is ideal for unstructured data like backups and multimedia files, while file storage provides a hierarchical system for shared access in collaborative environments. Local storage offers high-speed, low-latency access for applications running on virtual machines but lacks persistence. Shared storage supports multiple systems accessing the same data simultaneously, and block storage delivers high-performance, low-latency solutions suitable for databases and virtual machine disks.

Review Questions

The following questions are designed to test your understanding of this chapter's material. You can find the answers in Appendix A.

1. Ricky is a data analyst looking to begin developing his own applications to simplify some reporting and modeling tasks. He does not have experience programming and would like to use a language that will meet his analytics needs but be easy to learn. What language would best meet his needs?
   A. Python
   B. Ruby
   C. C++
   D. R

2. Ann is using the Structured Query Language to retrieve information stored in a relational database table. What DML command should she use to specify the records she would like to retrieve?
   A. INSERT
   B. UPDATE
   C. SELECT
   D. CREATE

3. Which one of the following statements about spreadsheets is incorrect?
   A. Spreadsheet software is available on most modern business computers.
   B. Spreadsheet software is easy to use.
   C. Spreadsheet software provides powerful machine learning capabilities.
   D. Microsoft Excel is the most common example of a spreadsheet.

4. Kevin is helping prepare a computer for a professional statistician who will be performing some quality control analyses for their organization. Which one of the following tools is most likely to meet the statistician's needs?
   A. Tableau
   B. SAS
   C. Looker
   D. Excel

5. Your organization is shifting a series of workloads from an on-premises data center to the cloud. You are working with a vendor that allows you to start up virtual server instances as needed, and then you configure those servers to meet your business requirements. Which cloud service category does this describe?
   A. PaaS
   B. SaaS
   C. DaaS
   D. IaaS

6. Carla works for an organization that is considering using the Anaconda distribution for their analytics development work. Which of the following languages is NOT natively supported by Anaconda?
   A. Python
   B. Scala
   C. R
   D. Anaconda provides native support for Python, Scala, and R

7. Simone works for an organization that is considering using the Jupyter notebook platform. Which one of the following languages is not natively supported by Jupyter?
   A. Scala
   B. R
   C. Julia
   D. Python

8. Lisa is an IT technician with a large organization that uses the Power BI analytics suite. A new data analyst is joining the organization and would like to have a tool installed on their laptop to create paginated reports. What tool would best meet this need?
   A. Power BI Desktop
   B. Power BI Report Server
   C. Power BI Report Builder
   D. Power BI service

9. Xavier is a new data analyst who would like to learn a data visualization package. He would like to use software that specializes in data visualization, integrates with a large number of data sources, and is widely used across organizations. What tool would best meet his needs?
   A. Tableau
   B. Excel
   C. Anaconda
   D. Tidyverse

10. Bob is exploring analytics tools available to his organization and he would like to add a tool that provides a graphical interface for MongoDB. What tool would best meet his needs?
    A. MySQL Workbench
    B. Compass
    C. DBeaver
    D. Toad

11. Which one of the following is a commonly used cloud-based containerization service?
    A. Amazon EKS
    B. Azure SQL
    C. Google BigQuery
    D. Google Vertex AI

12. Piper accidentally created a database table and would like to remove the entire table from the database. What Structured Query Language command would best meet her needs?
    A. DELETE
    B. ALTER
    C. UPDATE
    D. DROP

13. Ty works for a sales organization that stores data from its customer relationship management platform in an AWS S3 data lake. What term best describes this type of storage?
    A. Block storage
    B. Local storage
    C. Shared storage
    D. Object storage

14. What Python library provides data analysts with access to tools that allow them to better structure data?
    A. NumPy
    B. TensorFlow
    C. pandas
    D. Keras

15. Which one of the following is not a standard way for a relational database to receive commands?
    A. SQL query created within a graphical interface
    B. SQL query written directly by an end user
    C. Natural language query written by a customer
    D. SQL query created by software written in Python

16. Wanda is selecting a tool to present analytics reports to business leaders. Which one of the following tools is most likely to meet her needs?

   A. Minitab
   B. SAS
   C. Power BI
   D. Stata

17. Which cloud deployment model is most commonly associated with a consistently multitenant architecture?

   A. Private cloud
   B. Public cloud
   C. Hybrid cloud
   D. IaaS cloud

18. Gwen would like to modify the structure of an existing database table. What SQL command would best meet her needs?

   A. UPDATE
   B. MODIFY
   C. DROP
   D. ALTER

19. Kelly is looking for a programming language for use by her organization's analysts who work with Apache Spark. Which one of the following languages would be most suitable for this purpose?

   A. R
   B. Python
   C. Java
   D. Scala

20. Which one of the following commands is not considered part of the data manipulation language (DML)?

   A. INSERT
   B. SELECT
   C. UPDATE
   D. CREATE

Chapter 3

Understanding Data

THE COMPTIA DATA+ EXAM TOPICS COVERED IN THIS CHAPTER INCLUDE:

✓ **Domain 1.0: Data Concepts and Environments**

  - 1.1. Explain data concepts

We work with data every day in our business and personal lives. But how often do we stop and think about how our data is structured? Effective data analysts understand data in all its forms and how that data fits into their working environment. Knowledge of data includes understanding the various types of data that exist and the different options for storing that data in an enterprise environment. With a basic grounding in how to think about data, you will be well positioned to meaningfully contribute to the collection, organization, and analysis of data.

We kick off this chapter by examining data types that categorize individual pieces of data and exploring considerations for dealing with the range of possible values for different data types. You learn how these building blocks are combined to describe a unique object or event in the sections that follow. You also explore different ways of organizing data and various file formats for facilitating data exchange, system interoperability, and ease of human consumption.

Exploring Data Types

To understand data types, it is best first to understand data elements. A *data element* is an attribute about a person, place, or thing containing data within a range of values. Data elements also describe characteristics of activities, including orders, transactions, and events. Consider the data in Table 3.1, which illustrates some simple information about domesticated animals. You can see that the data elements include the name, type, breed, date of birth, height, and weight for each animal in the table. The column headings name the data element, while each row is an example value for that element.

Now that you understand what data elements are, let's explore how they relate to data types. A *data type* limits the values a data element can have. Consider the information in Table 3.1. Pet Name, Animal Type, and Breed Name are all words. Meanwhile, the Date of Birth column contains numbers and slashes that identify a specific date. Height and Weight are both numbers. Each of these groupings represents a particular data type.

Individual data types support structured, unstructured, and semi-structured data. Let's explore the differences between these categories.

TABLE 3.1 Pet Data

Pet Name	Animal Type	Breed Name	Date of Birth	Height (Inches)	Weight (Pounds)
Jack	Dog	Corgi	3/2/2018	10	26.3
Viking	Dog	Husky	5/8/2017	24	58
Hazel	Dog	Labradoodle	7/3/2016	23	61
Schooner	Dog	Labrador Retriever	8/14/2019	24.3	73.4
Skippy	Dog	Weimaraner	10/3/2018	26.3	63.5
Alexander	Cat	American Shorthair	10/4/2017	9.3	10.4

Tabular Data

Tabular data is data organized into a table, made up of columns and rows. A table represents information about a single topic. Each *column* represents a uniquely named field within a table, also called a variable, about a single characteristic. The contents of each column contain values for the data element as defined by the column header. Consider the pet data in Table 3.1. The Pet Name column contains the names of a given animal.

Each *row* represents a record of a single instance of the table's topic. Looking at the row for Jack in Table 3.1, you see that he is a dog of breed Corgi, his birth date, and his height and weight information. All the information in that row is about Jack.

It is helpful to think of tabular data as rectangular data. It is easy to draw a rectangle around the data. The top of the rectangle is defined by columns, while rows define the left side of the rectangle.

The intersection of a row and column contains a specific value. Looking at the intersection of Jack and Breed Name in Table 3.1 tells you that Jack is a Corgi. If you want to identify Hazel's breed, you look at where her row intersects with the Breed Name column and see that she is a Labradoodle.

Spreadsheets, including Microsoft Excel, Google Sheets, and Apple Numbers, are practical tools for representing tabular data. A *relational database management system* (*RDMS*), commonly called a database, extends the tabular model. Instead of having all data in a single table, a relational database organizes related data across multiple tables. The connection between tables is known as a *relationship*. Oracle, Microsoft SQL Server, MySQL, and

PostgreSQL are examples of database software. Tabular data is the concept that underpins both spreadsheets and relational databases.

You learn more about relational databases and their nonrelational counterparts in Chapter 4, "Databases and Data Acquisition."

Structured Data Types

Structured data is tabular in nature, organized into rows and columns. Structured data is what typically comes to mind when looking at a spreadsheet. With clearly defined column headings, spreadsheets are easy to work with and understand. In a spreadsheet, cells are where columns and rows intersect.

Consider the dataset in Figure 3.1. It contains basic information about a group of people. When you read the column headings, you get a good sense of the kind of data that you're going to find in that column. For example, when you see the Weight (Pounds) column, you expect to see numeric values. In the Address field, you expect to see text. Looking more closely, you can see that the data values are consistent for each column. For example, all the height and weight information uses numbers instead of words. Taken as a whole, Figure 3.1 is an example of highly structured data, with defined columns, an expectation for what the rows will contain, and consistent columnar values in each row.

Let's explore some of the most common data types that give structured data its structure.

Character Strings

The character data type limits data entry to only valid characters. Characters can include the alphabet that you might see on your keyboard, as well as numbers. Depending on your needs, multiple data types are available that can enforce character limits.

String is the most widely used data type for storing character-based data. Strings are appropriate when a data element consists of both numbers and letters. Consider the Address field in Figure 3.1. To accurately represent a given street address, both the house number and the street name are required.

The string data type is ideal for storing product stock-keeping units (SKUs). It is common in the retail clothing space to have a unique SKU for each item available for sale. If you sell jeans, you may stock products from Armani Jeans, Diesel, Lee Jeans, Levi's, and Wrangler.

FIGURE 3.1 Person data.

First Name	Last Name	Date of Birth	Height (inches)	Weight (pounds)	Hair Color	Eye Color	Address	City	State	Zip Code
Chris	Stuzman	4/3/1976	78	183	brown	black	193 Main St	Stevens Point	Wisconsin	54481
Amy	Robinson	5/8/1985	72	134	black	hazel	388 Walnut St	Mobile	Alabama	36602
Tom	Henkel	8/23/1947	68	155	blond	green	3942 N. Beech S	Amarillo	Texas	79111
Cindy	Sturm	10/17/1991	66	159	brown	blue	881 Fir Rd	San Diego	California	92104
Dave	O'Leary	2/14/1983	70	196	red	blue	941 Hickory Ln	Fort Collins	Colorado	80526
Robin	Richardson	12/8/1986	64	167	grey	green	4024 W Division	Chicago	Illinois	60651

FIGURE 3.2 SKU example.

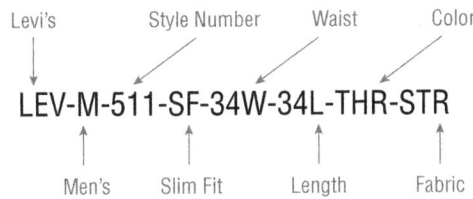

FIGURE 3.3 U.S. QWERTY keyboard layout.

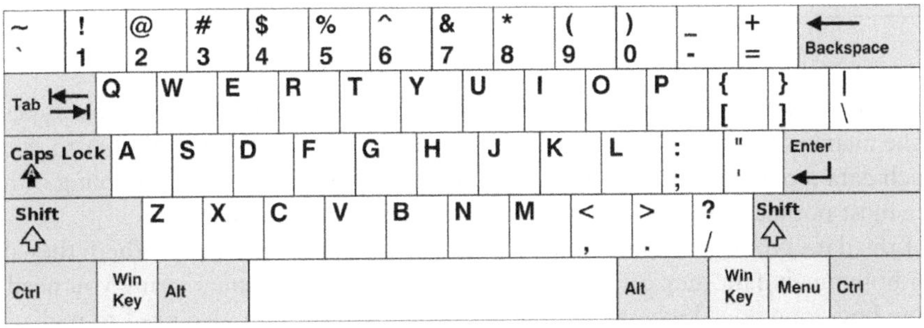

To keep track of all the manufacturer, size, color, and fit combinations in your inventory, you might use an SKU similar to the one depicted in Figure 3.2. Tracking inventory at the SKU level allows you to manage availability in your online and in-store systems, all courtesy of the string data type.

There are times when it is necessary to impose even stricter limits on character-related data to exclude numbers. For example, consider the State data element in Figure 3.1. If the system contains state names from the United States, it would be appropriate to restrict the string to contain only alphabetic characters.

Consider a data entry example. Suppose you operate an online retail system. To deliver orders, you need address information for the intended recipients. This information comes from the customers themselves, since they can specify where orders should be shipped. Any time a person interacts with a computer, there is the potential for a data entry error. Suppose someone wanted to enter Montana for the state component of their address.

Take a look at the positioning of the O and 0 keys in Figure 3.3, depicting the U.S. QWERTY keyboard layout. These two keys are very close together. Many people press these keys with the fourth finger of their right hand, making a data entry error that much more likely. A person could supply the value "M0ntana" instead of the intended "Montana." If you restrict the field to contain only alphabetic characters, trying to input the erroneous value would result in an error.

TABLE 3.2 Selected Character Data Types and Maximum Size

Data Type Name	Oracle	Microsoft SQL Server	MySQL
char	2,000 bytes	8,000 bytes	255 bytes
varchar2	4,000 bytes	-	-
varchar	-	8,000 bytes	64 KB
CLOB	128 TB	2 GB	64 KB
varchar(max)	-	2 GB	-
LONGTEXT	-	-	4 GB

Each database software has its unique method of implementing character data types to handle the nuances related to character data. The most significant difference has to do with how much data a particular data element can contain. Table 3.2 shows a sampling of how the three most popular databases provide data types for character data.

All of the data types shown in Table 3.2 support alphanumeric data. Where they differ is on how much data they can handle. Before defining a column a string you need to determine how long your longest-possible text value will be. You also need to realize that while data types may have the same names, they are implemented differently by software vendors. There are also individual data types, like CLOB and LONGTEXT, that are vendor-specific. Finally, you need to be aware of the absolute limits imposed by the database you are using.

With spreadsheets, configuring a given cell or range of cells as a text-only data type takes more effort than when using a database. It is not possible to accomplish this with one of the native data types provided by the software. Instead, limiting to just text requires a formula. Figure 3.4 shows an example of how to use a formula to perform this level of validation in Microsoft Excel. Suppose a person tries to input a value containing numbers or symbols into a cell where the formula is active. Figure 3.5 illustrates the resulting error message.

Character Sets

When selecting string data types, you need to think about the character set you are using to input and store data when using a database. Databases use character sets to map, or encode, data and store it digitally. The ASCII encoding standard is based on the U.S. English alphabet. ASCII accommodates both the upper and lowercase English alphabet and numbers, mathematical operators, and symbols, as shown earlier in Figure 3.3.

Many languages include accent marks, extending the Latin alphabet. For example, Akrapovič is a Slovenian manufacturer. To store the č in Akrapovič, you need to encode that value appropriately. In addition, there are many languages, including Arabic, Chinese, Japanese, and Korean, which use symbols as opposed to extending the Latin alphabet. For example, قط is the Arabic word for "cat." Several encoding standards exist that accommodate non-Latin characters. One of the most common is Unicode Transformation Format-8 (UTF-8), which allows non-Latin characters to be input by a user and stored in a file or database.

Many languages use the letter n to indicate that a Unicode standard is in use. For example, a character string of type `nvarchar` would use Unicode encoding.

It is necessary to realize that individual characters may consume multiple bytes, impacting the length of a character string you can store in a character data type.

FIGURE 3.4 Excel text-only formula.

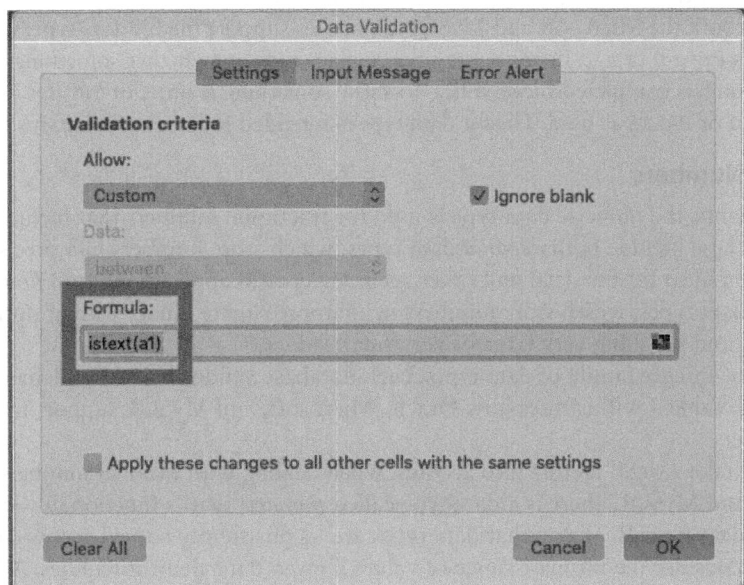

Numeric

When numbers exclusively make up values for a data attribute, *numeric* becomes the data type of choice. This data type appears to be simple and obvious based on its name. As seen with the character data type, implementation nuances about numeric

FIGURE 3.5 Text-only data validation restriction.

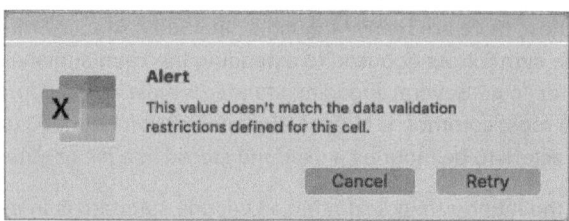

are essential to understand. Databases accommodate two types of numeric data types: *integer* and *numeric*.

Whole Numbers

The *integer*, and all its subtypes, are for storing whole numbers. As seen with the string family of data types, implementation differences exist across databases. Table 3.3 illustrates how Oracle, Microsoft, and MySQL support whole numbers.

Note that both the Microsoft and MySQL databases support the bit data type, which can be empty or store a 0 or a 1. In computer science, flags indicate whether something is on or off, or if a function has completed successfully. To show something is on, 1 or TRUE is used. For a value of off, 0 or FALSE is used. The bit data type is intended for storing the status of a flag.

Fractional Numbers

In all its variants, the numeric data type is used for fractional numbers that include a decimal point. These include both *decimal* data types, which store numbers in a precise base-10 representation ideal for financial and other accuracy-critical applications, and *floating point* (or "float") data types, which store numbers in an approximate binary format optimized for performance and handling very large or very small values.

As with the integer family of data types, each database vendor has its implementation nuances. Table 3.4 illustrates how Oracle, Microsoft, and MySQL support fractional numbers.

You must take several factors into account when dealing with rational numbers. In both SQL Server and MySQL, there is a data type called *numeric* that is functionally equivalent to the decimal data type. Realizing that data types are inconsistently named across databases, you need to consider the ultimate range of values a given data element handles. All the data types in Table 3.4 store numbers to a configurable number of significant digits. There are scientific use cases that require an even greater number of significant digits; additional numeric data type variants exist to accommodate that need.

Boolean Values

Boolean values are the simplest data type possible. They consist of a single bit, which can have one of only two possible values: 0 or 1. In a Boolean value, 0 represents false, while 1

TABLE 3.3 Selected Integer Data Types and Value Range

Data Type Name	Oracle	Microsoft SQL Server	MySQL
bit	-	0 and 1	0 and 1
tinyint	-	0 to 255	0 to 255
smallint	-32,768 to 32,767	-32,768 to 32,767	-32,768 to 32,767
int	-2,147,483,648 to 2,147,483,647	-2,147,483,648 to 2,147,483,647	-2,147,483,648 to 2,147,483,647
bigint	-9,223,372,036,854,775,808 to 9,223,372,036,854,775,807	-9,223,372,036,854,775,808 to 9,223,372,036,854,775,807	-9,223,372,036,854,775,808 to 9,223,372,036,854,775,807

TABLE 3.4 Selected Integer Data Types and Value Range

Data Type Name	Oracle	Microsoft SQL Server	MySQL
number	-10^{125} to 10^{125}, up to 38 significant digits	-	-
decimal	-	-10^{38} to 10^{38}, up to 38 significant digits	Up to 65 digits in total, so the range depends on the number of digits assigned to the whole and fractional components
binary_float	1.17549E-38F to 3.40282E+38F	-	-
Binary_Double	2.22507485850720E-308 to 1.79769313486231E+308	-	-

represents `true`. Boolean values are a fundamental data type in most programming languages and database systems, serving as the basis for logical operations and decision-making processes.

At their core, Boolean values are used to express conditions or outcomes that can have only two possibilities. For example, a Boolean value might represent whether a user is logged in (`true`) or not (`false`), or whether a transaction was successful (`true`) or failed (`false`). Booleans are commonly used in comparisons, control structures, and filtering operations.

In databases, Boolean fields are particularly useful for flags or binary states. For instance, a column named `IsActive` might indicate whether an account is active or inactive, while a `HasPaid` column might track whether an invoice is paid or unpaid.

Boolean values are also critical for conditional logic. In programming, expressions that evaluate to `true` or `false`, such as comparisons (5 > 3 or `username == "admin"`), are used in constructs like `if` statements, loops, and filters. These expressions determine whether certain sections of code should execute or whether specific rows of data should be included in a query result.

Date and Time

Gathered together under the broad category of *date*, day of year and time of day are data elements that appear with great frequency. As illustrated in Table 3.5, databases have various data types for handling date- and time-related information. As seen with character and numeric data types, nuances exist across different databases. Selecting the appropriate date-related data type depends on the data you need to store.

For example, suppose you operate a veterinary clinic and need to store birth date information for pets. In that case, you need to store the year, month, and day. With those three components of date, you can effectively administer medication and determine when to schedule annual veterinary appointments.

TABLE 3.5 Selected Date and Time Data Types

Data Type Name	Oracle	Microsoft SQL Server	MySQL
`date`	YYYY-MM-DD hh:mm:ss	YYYY-MM-DD	YYYY-MM-DD
`datetime2`	-	YYYY-MM-DD hh:mm:ss.sss[.fractional seconds]	-
`time`	-	hh:mm:ss.sss[.fractional seconds]	hh:mm:ss.ss[.fractional seconds]
`timestamp`	YYYY-MM-DD hh:mm:ss.sss[.fractional seconds]	-	hh:mm:ss.ss[.fractional seconds]
`year`	-	-	YYYY

There are many occasions when it is more appropriate to include time, in addition to the day, month, and year. For instance, consider package tracking information for companies like FedEx, United Parcel Service, or DHL. Consumers want to know where a specific package is up to the minute. The company itself may need second-level details to optimize labor, infrastructure investments, and route planning.

Spatial Values

Spatial values are a specialized data type used to represent geographic and geometric data in databases and programming environments. These values capture spatial features such as points, lines, polygons, and more complex shapes, allowing for the storage and analysis of location-based data.

Spatial data is typically divided into two broad categories:

- *Geometric data* is used to describe shapes and objects in a flat, two-dimensional space (e.g., xy or xyz coordinates). Common examples include the layout of a building or the boundaries of a parcel of land.
- *Geographic data* represents locations and shapes on Earth's surface, typically associated with latitude and longitude coordinates. This category is used for applications like mapping, navigation, and geospatial analysis.

Spatial values are essential in fields like urban planning, logistics, environmental science, and location-based services. They power applications such as mapping services, navigation systems, geographic information systems (GIS), and augmented reality.

Unique Identifiers

Unique identifiers are an important part of modern databases and other software systems. They are used to ensure that every record, object, or resource can be distinctly recognized. They help eliminate ambiguity, prevent duplication, and ensure reliable operations.

There are two major implementations of unique identifiers: *globally unique identifiers (GUIDs)* and *universally unique identifiers (UUIDs)*. They are essentially identical, other than the fact that UUIDs are based upon an open standard, while GUIDs are a specific Microsoft implementation of that standard. Both GUIDs and UUIDs are 128-bit values that are normally represented in hexadecimal form. Here are a few example GUID values:

- 8bb53e8e-a738-4e03-9a56-2f901348d3e5
- 3f329350-5368-4a63-9d3d-4373f76899ab
- f713d0be-1b33-4a14-b8cd-74ac021e0809
- 2900f6d0-dbad-41a4-8f2c-b948126f9934
- 5e19fb77-f9b6-4d0f-8ac0-47f9fb3eb0b7
- 6ab34a08-4e39-40df-9508-8ead92010ccf

Unique identifiers are commonly used as primary keys in databases. Unlike sequential numeric IDs, UUIDs allow records to be uniquely identified even when data is created across multiple systems or merged from different sources. For example, in a distributed application where multiple databases operate independently, UUIDs ensure that each record remains unique without requiring a centralized system for generating IDs. This makes UUIDs particularly valuable for large-scale, distributed systems or environments where data synchronization is critical.

There are some drawbacks to using unique identifiers in place of sequential values, however. Unique identifiers are much larger than basic numeric identifiers, requiring more storage space and sometimes affecting database indexing performance. They may also be less efficient for certain types of queries, such as those that rely on sequential order. Additionally, their length and complexity make them difficult to read and work with manually, which can be a challenge during debugging or troubleshooting.

Currency

Many people use spreadsheets to manage their finances. Organizations typically use enterprise-scale software for the same purpose, with the data residing in a database. While financial data is numeric, people prefer seeing the numbers displayed as a specific currency. For example, consider the Number, Dollar, and Euro columns in Figure 3.6. The column headings indicate what each column contains. The currency symbols in each cell tell the reader what the data represents, even if the column headings have scrolled off the screen.

Especially in this context, it is essential to differentiate between data formatting and data storage. Data storage contains the actual value for a given data element. Data formatting takes a given data value and then formats it for display purposes. Data formatting is common when dealing with currency and date data types.

The numeric data in all the columns of Figure 3.6 are numerically equivalent. Figure 3.7 illustrates a sampling of currencies available for formatting in a Google spreadsheet.

Of the databases mentioned in this chapter, only Microsoft SQL Server has data types specifically for storing currency. Table 3.6 illustrates these two data types. Both of these data types offer four digits of precision after the decimal point.

FIGURE 3.6 Numeric data formatted as different currencies.

Number	Dollar	Euro
1.2	$1.20	€1.20
1.14	$1.14	€1.14
1.12	$1.12	€1.12
1.18	$1.18	€1.18
1.13	$1.13	€1.13
1.11	$1.11	€1.11
1.11	$1.11	€1.11
1.33	$1.33	€1.33
1.33	$1.33	€1.33
1.29	$1.29	€1.29
1.39	$1.39	€1.39
1.33	$1.33	€1.33
1.39	$1.39	€1.39
1.47	$1.47	€1.47
1.37	$1.37	€1.37
1.26	$1.26	€1.26
1.24	$1.24	€1.24
1.24	$1.24	€1.24
1.13	$1.13	€1.13
0.95	$0.95	€0.95
0.9	$0.90	€0.90
0.92	$0.92	€0.92

FIGURE 3.7 Currency formats in Google Sheets.

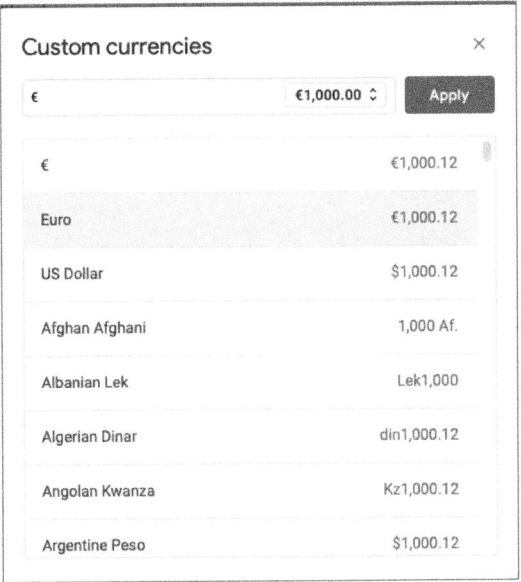

56 Chapter 3 ▪ Understanding Data

While the currency data types exist, it is more common to use a numeric data type for storing currency data. Limiting a calculation to only four digits of precision after the decimal point can lead to incorrect rounding errors. Consider Figure 3.8, which illustrates retrieving values from a database. The money_table_example table contains columns defined as money for both sales price and price. The percentage column in the query result is calculated by taking the sales price divided by the price and then multiplying the result by 100. Figure 3.9 illustrates the same calculation in a spreadsheet, and Figure 3.10 shows the result of 18 divided by 22 in a calculator.

Recall that the money data type uses only four digits after the decimal. For this reason, the database incorrectly calculates the percentage as 81.81 instead of the spreadsheet's correct evaluation of 81.82.

TABLE 3.6 Currency Data Types in Microsoft SQL Server

Data type name	Range of Values
smallmoney	–214,748.3648 to 214,748.3647
money	–922,337,203,685,477.5808 to 922,337,203,685,477.5807

FIGURE 3.8 Incorrect percentage due to money data type.

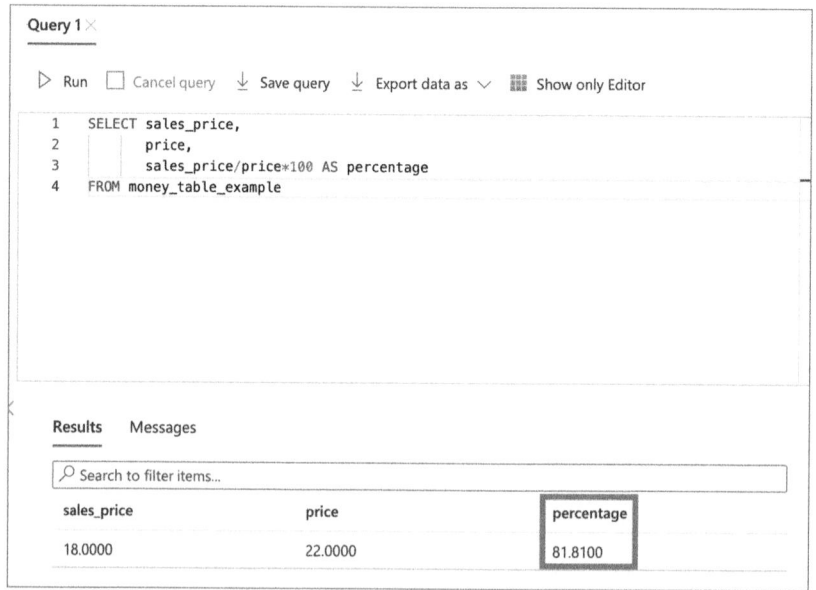

FIGURE 3.9 Correct percentage as calculated by a spreadsheet.

FIGURE 3.10   Unrounded calculation in a calculator.

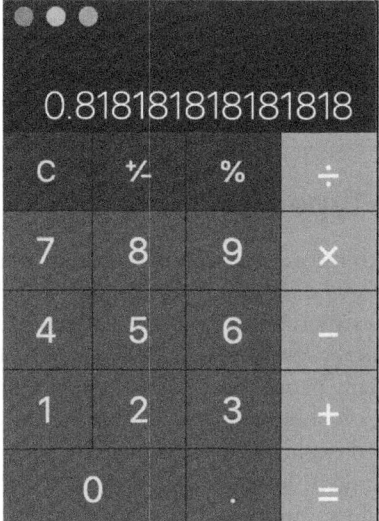

FIGURE 3.11   Correct percentage when using a numeric data type.

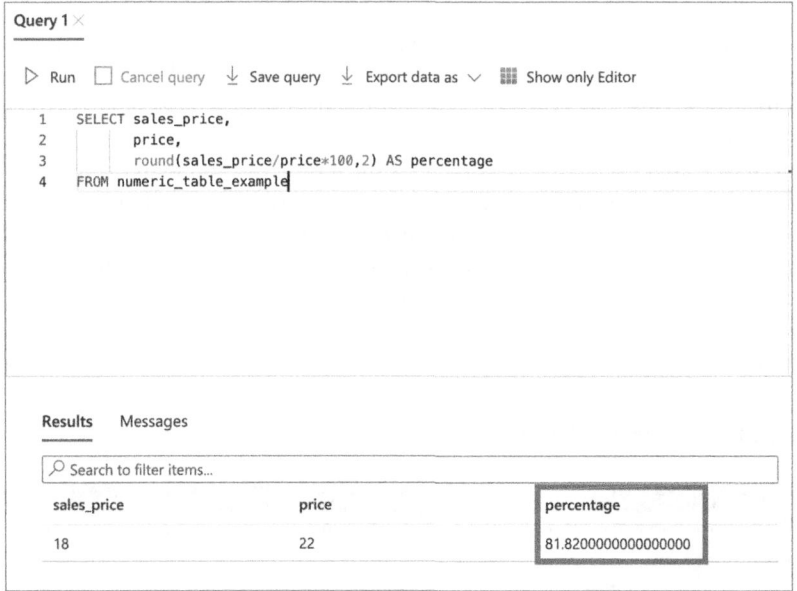

While SQL Server does support two currency-specific data type variants, most databases do not. As the rounding error in Figure 3.8 shows, it is best to use a numeric data type to store currency-related data. Figure 3.11 illustrates that the rounded results are mathematically accurate using the numeric data type for both `sales_price` and `price`.

> **Exam Tip**
>
> As you prepare for the Data+ exam, you should recognize the difference between storing a data type and formatting it to facilitate human interpretation. Take care not to automatically infer a data type based on formatting.

Unstructured Data Types

While much of the data used to record transactions is highly structured, most of the world's data is *unstructured*. Unstructured data is any type of data that does not fit neatly into the tabular model. Examples of unstructured data include digital images, audio recordings, video recordings, and open-ended survey responses. Analyzing unstructured data creates a wealth of information and insight. Many people have camera-enabled smartphones, and using video for conversations and meetings is commonplace. To capture and analyze unstructured data, you can use data types designed explicitly for that purpose.

Consider the pet data depicted in Table 3.1. Suppose the veterinary office wants to augment their records to include digital images of the animals. To accommodate that requirement, you need to use an unstructured data type.

Binary

Binary data types are one of the most common data types for storing unstructured data. They support any type of digital file you may have, from Microsoft Excel spreadsheets to digital photographs. These file types are generically called *binary large objects (BLOBs)*.

When considering which binary data type to use, file size tends to be the limiting factor. You need to select a data type that is as large as the largest file you plan on storing.

The most common types of unstructured data are audio, image, and video data. Spreadsheets are consumer applications designed to manage highly structured data, but they're often not very good at storing binary data. Figure 3.12 illustrates the result of trying to integrate images into the pet information spreadsheet in Excel. While it is possible to place images within the spreadsheet, it is impossible to store the images within a cell. However, Google Sheets does allow the storing of binary data within a cell, as shown in Figure 3.13.

FIGURE 3.12 Images in Excel.

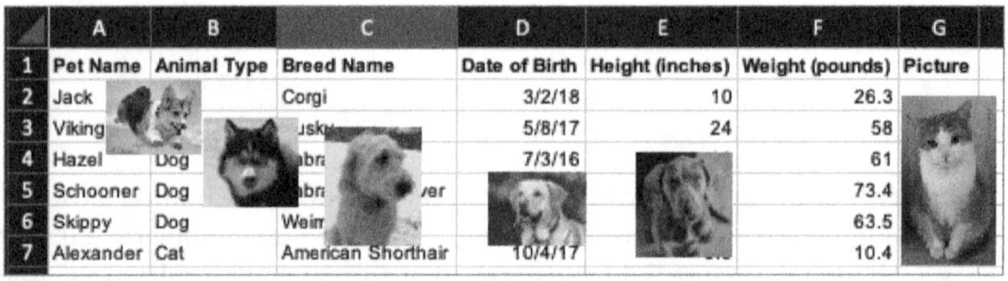

FIGURE 3.13 Binary data in a Google spreadsheet.

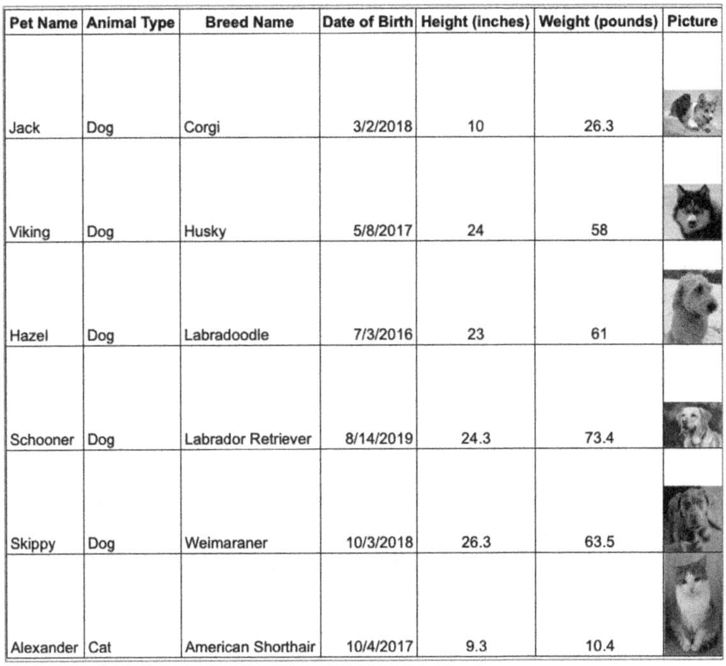

Pet Name	Animal Type	Breed Name	Date of Birth	Height (inches)	Weight (pounds)	Picture
Jack	Dog	Corgi	3/2/2018	10	26.3	
Viking	Dog	Husky	5/8/2017	24	58	
Hazel	Dog	Labradoodle	7/3/2016	23	61	
Schooner	Dog	Labrador Retriever	8/14/2019	24.3	73.4	
Skippy	Dog	Weimaraner	10/3/2018	26.3	63.5	
Alexander	Cat	American Shorthair	10/4/2017	9.3	10.4	

TABLE 3.7 Selected Binary Data Types and Maximum Sizes

Data Type Name	Oracle	Microsoft SQL Server	MySQL
tinyblob	-	-	255 bytes
mediumblob	-	-	16 MB
binary	2,000 bytes	8,000 bytes	255 bytes
varbinary	2,000 bytes	8,000 bytes	64 KB
varbinary(max)	-	2 GB	-
longblob	-	-	4 GB
BLOB	128 TB	-	64 KB

Databases offer a much more sophisticated collection of data types for storing binary data, as Table 3.7 illustrates. Note that the maximum size is per row, not per table. Once again, note the inconsistency in naming, as well as the supported size.

Audio

Audio data can come from a variety of sources. Whenever you interact with a customer service agent and hear "this call may be recorded for quality assurance purposes," your conversation is probably being recorded and stored for later analysis. The impact of capturing, storing, and analyzing audio data has led to the development of *avalanche detection systems*. These systems listen for and detect the acoustic characteristics of an avalanche. With real-time notification capabilities, these systems reduce the time it takes for emergency services to respond and alert hikers to treacherous conditions.

In order to ingest audio data into a system and make it available for processing, data is first captured via a microphone. The data is then digitized and stored. Audio can be stored in its raw form, which consumes the most storage space. Alternatively, it can be encoded with a compression algorithm to reduce the amount of space required. Regardless of if it is in raw or compressed form, storing audio requires a data type designed to handle raw binary data.

Images

Image data can come from a variety of sources. People take more than 1 trillion photographs every calendar year, fueled by the ubiquity of camera-enabled smartphones and relatively low storage costs. Each digital picture is a piece of unstructured data. Examining Figure 3.14, it is easy for a human to identify the contents of the photograph. However, it is

FIGURE 3.14   Photograph of racing motorcycles.

FIGURE 3.15 Motorcycle search results.

a binary file to a computer, ultimately stored as a series of ones and zeros. Applying artificial intelligence algorithms for image processing over a set of digital photos allows people to look for the objects they contain. Figure 3.15 illustrates the search results for the word "motorcycle" in a digital image library.

Image data has applicability across several industries. For example, dentists use digital X-rays to augment a person's dental record. Magnetic resonance imaging scans, used for soft tissue investigations, are added to a person's health record. Insurance companies provide mobile applications to upload photographs of accident scenes. As the use of image data grows, understanding how it is stored is vital for the modern data analyst.

Resolution is the most significant factor that governs how much space is required to store an image. The greater the resolution, the more detail an image contains, and the more storage space it needs. Similar to compressing audio data, there are a variety of ways to encode and store images, including the JPEG, GIF, TIFF, and PNG formats. Storing images in a database requires a data type designed to handle raw binary data, such as `varbinary` or `BLOB`.

Video

Video data is growing at a similar pace to image data. In the consumer space, people upload videos to YouTube, Instagram, and TikTok every day. Police officers wear body cameras to create a video record of enforcement situations. Image processing algorithms examine videos to detect everything from traffic congestion to intruders in the home.

As is the case with audio data, the resolution has a significant impact on the storage a video consumes. Video duration is also another factor that impacts storage size. Consider Table 3.8, which approximates the space required for storing a still image, one minute of audio data, and one minute of video data as recorded on a modern smartphone. Every minute of video is equivalent to over 50 individual images, or more than 200 minutes of audio.

TABLE 3.8 Approximate Storage Needs

	Still Image	Audio (1 Minute)	Video (1 Minute)
Space consumed (KB)	2,048	503	102,400

Large Text

There are times when it is appropriate to store a significant amount of text data. It is the combination of words into sentences that result in classifying large text as unstructured data. You may need to explore text data to detect nuance, humor, sarcasm, and inferential meaning. For example, you may need to keep the complete transcript of a legal proceeding, public address, or verbose open-ended survey responses. What differentiates large text from the text and string data types is size. When considering Table 3.9, keep in mind that 2 GB of character data is approximately 500,000 pages of text.

Once again, note that data type names differ across vendor products. For example, Table 3.2 shows that Oracle has the `varchar2` text data type. Oracle currently implements `varchar` as a synonym for `varchar2`. However, Microsoft's implementation of varchar is vastly different. In Oracle, since the `varchar` data type is a synonym of `varchar2`, it is limited to 4,000 bytes. Meanwhile, Microsoft's implementation of `varchar` supports up to 2 GB. To handle larger amounts of text, Oracle created the proprietary *character large object (CLOB)* data type.

> **Exam Tip**
>
> As you prepare for the Data+ exam, you should be familiar with the different types of structured and unstructured data that you might encounter. Be prepared to evaluate a situation and select the most appropriate data type to store a piece of data.

TABLE 3.9 Selected Binary Data Types and Maximum Sizes

Data Type Name	Oracle	Microsoft SQL Server	MySQL
`varchar(max)`	-	2 GB	-
`longtext`	-	-	4 GB
`CLOB`	128 TB	2 GB	64 KB

> **File Extensions**
>
> When you store files on a disk or other storage media, they are saved with a filename (provided by the user) and a file extension. The extension is normally a three- or four-character abbreviation that describes the file format and it is appended to the filename, separated by a period. For example, the file `analytics.txt` has the name `analytics` and the extension `txt`, indicating that it is a text file.
>
> When you prepare for the Data+ exam, you'll need to know the following common file extensions:
>
> | Extension | Description |
> | --- | --- |
> | .csv | Comma-separated values (CSV) file |
> | .xlsx | Excel file |
> | .json | JavaScript Object Notation (JSON) file |
> | .txt | Text file |
> | .jpg or .jpeg | JPEG image file |
> | .dat | Data file (generic extension) |

Categories of Data

We try to fit data into structured and unstructured categories. The reality is that the world is not black and white, and not all data fits neatly into structured and unstructured categories. Semi-structured data represents the space between structured spreadsheets and unstructured videos.

As illustrated in Table 3.1, a veterinary practice may be interested in collecting structured data about the animals under its care. When mapping data attributes to data types, there are additional considerations regarding the actual values to be stored.

Quantitative vs. Qualitative Data

Regardless of structure, data is either *quantitative* or *qualitative*. Quantitative data consists of numeric values. Data elements whose values come from counting or measuring are quantitative. In Table 3.1, the Height and Weight columns are quantitative. Quantitative data answers questions like "How many?" and "How much?"

Qualitative data frequently consists of text values. Data elements whose values describe characteristics, traits, and attitudes are all qualitative. In Table 3.1, Pet Name, Animal Type, and Breed Name are all qualitative. Qualitative data answers questions like "Why?" and "What?"

Discrete vs. Continuous Data

Numeric data comes in two different forms: *discrete* and *continuous*. A helpful way to think about discrete data is that it represents measurements that can't be subdivided. You may intuitively think of discrete data as using whole numbers, but that doesn't have to be the case. For example, if a fundraising organization sells chickens in half-chicken increments, you can buy 1.5 chickens. However, you can't buy .25 chickens.

Another way to think about it is that discrete data is useful when you have countable, or listable, outcomes. For example, a veterinary clinic may be interested in the number of dogs and cats under its care. Figure 3.16 shows the aggregation of the pet from Table 3.1. The Total data element is an example of discrete data, as it contains the value 5 for Dog and 1 for Cat. A veterinary practice would not care for 5.5 dogs or 2.25 cats.

Instead of counting, when you measure things like height and weight, you are collecting continuous data. While whole numbers represent discrete data, continuous data typically need a decimal point and can be continuously divided using additional decimal places by using more sophisticated measurement tools. Two dogs in Table 3.1 have their height recorded to the tenth of an inch. Similarly, weight is recorded to the tenth of an inch for three dogs and one cat. Figure 3.17 shows the continuous measure of average height and weight information by animal.

Both the Average Height and Average Weight calculations for dogs result in numbers to the hundredths. These averages will change as the animals' weight changes and as the veterinarian's practice grows and adds animals. In addition, the degree of precision in terms of weight measurement could change. For example, the vet could start recording weight information to the hundredths instead of the tenths. The Height and Weight attributes from Table 3.1, as well as the Average Height and Average Weight from Figure 3.17, are examples of continuous data elements.

Qualitative data is discrete, but quantitative data can be either discrete or continuous data. For example, age is a continuous variable, but you may treat a person's age in years as discrete. A good rule of thumb is that discrete applies when counting while continuous applies when measuring.

> **Exam Tip**
>
> As you prepare for the Data+ exam, make sure you can distinguish between qualitative and quantitative data, as well as discrete and continuous data.

FIGURE 3.16 Discrete data example.

Animal Type	Total
Dog	5
Cat	1

FIGURE 3.17 Continuous data example.

Animal Type	Total	Average Height	Average Weight
Dog	5	21.52	56.44
Cat	1	9.3	10.4

Categorical Data

In addition to quantitative, numeric data, there is categorical data. Text data with a known, finite number of categories is categorical. When considering an individual data element, it is possible to determine whether or not it is categorical. Let's continue to identify each data element of the pet dataset in Table 3.1. Animal Type is a good example of categorical data. As represented, this column separates the data into two categories: dog and cat. As additional dogs or cats enter into care, they fall within the existing categories.

That said, the range of accepted values for a given category can change over time. For instance, suppose the veterinarian branches out beyond small animal care and starts caring for horses. It is possible to expand the range of acceptable values in a category to accommodate this change.

You can also use categories to enforce data validation when someone is first entering data. Category enforcement has the effect of improving data quality. For example, suppose the veterinarian decides to care only for cats and dogs. To streamline operations, the veterinarian has a website built so that clients can schedule appointments online. Suppose the intent is to limit online appointments for only dogs and cats. In that case, the website can implement a drop-down menu where the only options for the animal type are "dog" and "cat." If someone had a mouse, hamster, or gerbil, the validation check prevents the scheduling of an appointment.

Dimensional Data

Dimensional modeling is an approach to arranging data to facilitate analysis. Dimensional modeling organizes data into fact tables and dimension tables. Fact tables store measurement data that is of interest to a business. A veterinary practice may want to answer some questions about appointments. A table holding appointment data would be called a *fact table*.

Dimensions are tables that contain data about the fact. For appointment data, the veterinarian's office manager may want to understand who was at an appointment and if any procedures were performed. In Figure 3.18, the Appointments table is the fact table. The Veterinarians, Owners, Procedures, and Pets tables are all dimensions that can answer questions about appointments.

Dimensional data contains groupings of individual attributes about a given subject. For example, taken as a whole, the pets dataset from Table 3.1 can be called the "pets" dimension. You can imagine that the "owners" dimension in Figure 3.18 contains biographic information about a pet's owner, identifying who was present at an appointment. When combined with data from additional dimensions, data elements from each dimension add detail about the facts in the fact table.

FIGURE 3.18 Dimension illustration.

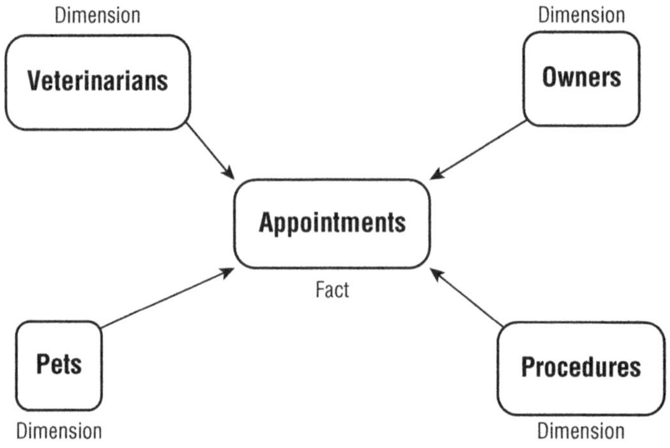

```
     Dimension                              Dimension
   ┌─────────────┐                       ┌─────────────┐
   │ Veterinarians│                      │   Owners    │
   └──────┬──────┘                       └──────┬──────┘
          │                                     │
          ↓                                     ↓
              ┌─────────────┐
              │ Appointments│
              └──────┬──────┘
                    Fact
          ↑                                     ↑
          │                                     │
   ┌──────┴──────┐                       ┌──────┴──────┐
   │    Pets     │                       │  Procedures │
   └─────────────┘                       └─────────────┘
     Dimension                              Dimension
```

When relationships between dimensions become more complex, such as when a single fact relates to multiple dimension entries, you use a *bridge table* to resolve these many-to-many relationships. For instance, if a single appointment involves multiple veterinarians or procedures, storing this relationship in the fact table or in a single dimension becomes challenging. In such cases, a bridge table is an intermediary to capture these many-to-many relationships.

You will explore dimensional modeling in greater detail in Chapter 4.

Common Data Structures

To facilitate analysis, data needs to be stored in a consistent, organized manner. When considering structured data, several concepts and standards inform how to organize data. On the other hand, unstructured data has a wider variety of storage approaches.

Analysts need to be able to perform their roles as efficiently as possible. It is common to use multiple tools to analyze data. Improved integration and interoperability between tools makes it easier for analysts to be productive. As a result, several concepts have become standardized. Let's explore the similarities and differences in how structured and unstructured data is defined and organized.

Structured Data

Tabular data is structured data, with values stored in a consistent, defined manner, organized into columns and rows. Data is *consistent* when all entries in a column contain the same type of value. This method of organization facilitates aggregation. For example, you can add each

FIGURE 3.19   Data entry errors.

	A	B	C	D	E	F
1	Pet Name	Animal Type	Breed Name	Date of Birth	Height (inches)	Weight (pounds)
2	Jack	Dog	Corgi	3/2/2018	10	26.3
3	Viking	Dog	Husky	5/8/2017	24	58
4	Hazel	Dog	Labradoodle	7/3/2016	23	61
5	Schooner	Dog	Labrador Retriever	8/14/2019	24.3	73.4
6	Skippy	Dog	Weimaraner	10/3/2018	26.3	63.5
7	Alexander	Cat	American Shorthair	10/4/2017	9.3	10.4
8	Dog	Thor	German Shepherd	10/3/2020	28	95

FIGURE 3.20   Data entry error identified in a summary.

Animal Type	Total
Dog	5
Cat	1
Thor	1

value in the Weight column in Table 3.1 to get the total weight for all animals. Structured data also makes summarization easy, since you can compute the average height for each animal in Table 3.1. It is common to perform summarization across groups. Figure 3.17 illustrates summarization at the categorical level.

However, structured data does not translate directly to data quality. For example, suppose a new dog named Thor became a patient. When Thor's data was input into the system, a person transposed the Pet Name and Animal Type values, as highlighted in Figure 3.19. Since both Pet Name and Animal Type are character data types, nothing from a structural standpoint prevents this mistake. However, if you were to perform the same summarization as in Figure 3.16, the result would be what is represented by Figure 3.20. A person looking at the summary in Figure 3.20 would immediately know that something is amiss from a data quality standpoint, as "Thor" is not a type of animal.

Just as there is an expectation that the values in a given column are consistent, it is a convention that each row contains data about a single record. In Figure 3.19, each row contains data about a single animal. Once again, nothing structural prevents a person from incorrectly putting data about Thor into Alexander's row. However, the intent is that each row's data pertains to a single animal.

It is a best practice to specify a *key* that uniquely identifies all values for a given row. In Figure 3.19, no column enforces uniqueness across rows. Consider this possible, though unlikely, scenario: a Labradoodle named Hazel, born on 7/3/2016, measuring 23 inches tall and weighing 61 pounds, becomes a new patient. Since all of her information is identical to an existing animal, nothing in the structure exists to differentiate the two. Figure 3.21

FIGURE 3.21 Pet ID as a key.

Pet ID	Pet Name	Animal Type	Breed Name	Date of Birth	Height (inches)	Weight (pounds)
1	Jack	Dog	Corgi	3/2/2018	10	26.3
2	Viking	Dog	Husky	5/8/2017	24	58
3	Hazel	Dog	Labradoodle	7/3/2016	23	61
4	Schooner	Dog	Labrador Retriever	8/14/2019	24.3	73.4
5	Skippy	Dog	Weimaraner	10/3/2018	26.3	63.5
6	Alexander	Cat	American Shorthair	10/4/2017	9.3	10.4
7	Thor	Dog	German Shepherd	10/3/2020	28	95
8	Hazel	Dog	Labradoodle	7/3/2016	23	61

illustrates how to address this storage issue. The Pet ID column has a data type of integer and contains a unique number for each row. With Pet ID as the key, you can differentiate between the Hazel in rows 3 and 8.

Unstructured Data

Unstructured data is qualitative, describing characteristics about an event or an object. Images, phrases, audio or video recordings, and descriptive text are all examples of unstructured data. There is very little that is common about different kinds of unstructured data. Since the data is highly variable, its organizational and storage needs are different from structured data. Unstructured data also represents a significant opportunity. A *Forbes* study shows that more than 90 percent of businesses need to manage and derive value from unstructured data.

Machine data is a common source of unstructured data. Machine data has various sources, including Internet of Things (IoT) devices, smartphones, tablets, personal computers, and servers. As machines operate, they create digital footprints of their activity. This data is unstructured and can identify machine-to-machine interaction. Although some may think of machine data as digital exhaust, it is a treasure trove just waiting to be exploited by organizations.

A wide variety of technologies has emerged to facilitate the storage of unstructured data. Operationally, these technologies are similar to how a key in a tabular dataset identifies its associated values. With unstructured data, the key is a unique identifier, whereas the value is the unstructured data itself.

Consider the log entry shown in Figure 3.22. As an example of machine data, it represents a single entry within a log file generated when accessing a specific image on the Internet. The log entry contains a mix of seemingly random strings, timestamps, IP addresses, URLs, and browser metadata.

Object storage facilitates the storage of unstructured data. The key-value concept underpins the design of object storage. The key is a unique identifier, and the value is the unstructured data itself. In Figure 3.23, the key is the filename, and the value is the contents of the file itself. Note that in this figure, each file is of a different type. The `word document.docx`

FIGURE 3.22 Unstructured data: log entry.

```
a67c0359188d9f84be33da6007b9f3697a5ad6b733826d1fc1457fd0cf6f376e global_sbn [02/
Feb/2021:18:46:56 +0000] 129.74.45.248 - FCDBECB76E3AE654 REST.GET.OBJECT lp_ima
ge-1.jpeg "GET /lp_image-1.jpeg HTTP/1.1" 304 - - 172032 10 - "https://s3.consol
e.aws.amazon.com/s3/object/global_sbn?region=us-east-1&prefix=lp_image-1.jpeg" "
Mozilla/5.0 (Macintosh; Intel Mac OS X 10_15_7) AppleWebKit/537.36 (KHTML, like
Gecko) Chrome/88.0.4324.96 Safari/537.36" - u+g8xLT4ji5dgMlB9VdXVXr5X2I2vFOnWb22
g9LUgyp+lTIzC4pGoOn8kUJTOcAYM1e1VUPYL6s= - ECDHE-RSA-AES128-GCM-SHA256 - global_
sbn.s3.amazonaws.com TLSv1.2
```

FIGURE 3.23 Files in object storage.

Name	Type	Last modified	Size	Storage class
word document.docx	docx	April 23, 2021, 14:24:32 (UTC-04:00)	72.3 KB	Standard
textfile.txt	txt	April 23, 2021, 14:22:58 (UTC-04:00)	2.1 KB	Standard
spreadsheet.xlsx	xlsx	April 23, 2021, 14:22:33 (UTC-04:00)	52.0 KB	Standard
png image.png	png	April 23, 2021, 14:24:45 (UTC-04:00)	7.1 KB	Standard
pdf document.pdf	pdf	April 23, 2021, 14:24:15 (UTC-04:00)	104.5 KB	Standard
lp_image-8.jpeg	jpeg	February 2, 2021, 13:39:36 (UTC-05:00)	172.3 KB	Standard

FIGURE 3.24 Keys and values in object storage.

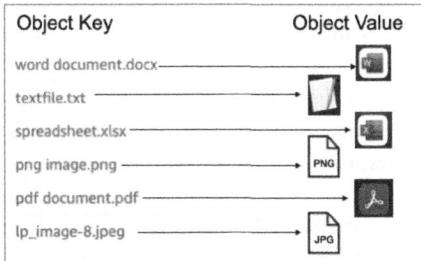

is a Microsoft Word file, `textfile.txt` contains plain-text data, and the `png image.png` and `lp_image-8.jpeg` objects are digital images.

To access the contents of a file, you need to know its key. Figure 3.24 illustrates how an individual key serves as a reference to its unstructured data.

Semi-structured Data

Semi-structured data is data that has structure and that is not tabular. Email is a well-known example of semi-structured data. Every email message has structural components, including recipient, sender, subject, date, and time. However, the body of an email is unstructured text, while attachments could be any type of file.

The need to make semi-structured data easier to work with has led to the emergence of semi-structured formatting options. These formatting options use separators or tags to provide some context around a data element. Let's explore common file formats for transporting semi-structured data.

Common File Formats

Common file formats facilitate data exchange and tool interoperability. Several file formats have emerged as standards and are widely adopted. As a modern data analyst, you will need to recognize all of these formats and be familiar with common use cases for each type.

Text Files

Text files are one of the most commonly used data file formats. As the name implies, they consist of plain text and are limited in scope to alphanumeric data. One of the reasons text files are so widely adopted is their ability to be opened regardless of platform or operating system without needing a proprietary piece of software. Whether you are using a Microsoft Windows desktop, an Apple MacBook, or a Linux server, you can easily open a text file. Text files are also commonly referred to as flat files.

When machines generate data, the output is commonly stored in a text file. For example, the unstructured log entry, as illustrated in Figure 3.22, is an excerpt taken from a plain-text file.

A unique character known as a *delimiter* facilitates transmitting structured data via a text file. The delimiter is the character that separates individual fields. A delimiter can be any character. Over the years, the comma and tab grew into widely accepted standards. Various software packages support reading and writing delimited files using the comma and the tab. In addition, many coding languages have libraries that make it easy to write comma- or tab-delimited files. When a file is comma-delimited, it is known as a *comma-separated values* (CSV) file. Similarly, when a file is tab-delimited, it is called a *tab-separated values* (TSV) file.

Suppose you have the pet data from Table 3.1 in a Google spreadsheet. Figure 3.25 illustrates how it is possible to download the data as either a comma- or tab-delimited file. Microsoft Excel also supports CSV and TSV as options.

Note that the columns in Figure 3.26 do not line up with each other. The width of each column is variable, only as long as it needs to be to store the data in each row.

You may think that all CSV files represent structured data. Consider Figure 3.27, containing an excerpt from playback-related events from a Netflix viewer. Every column header except for Playtraces is structured. However, note the contents of the Playtraces field within the rectangle. It contains quite a bit of text that appears to have a structure of its own.

FIGURE 3.25 Exporting data as CSV or TSV.

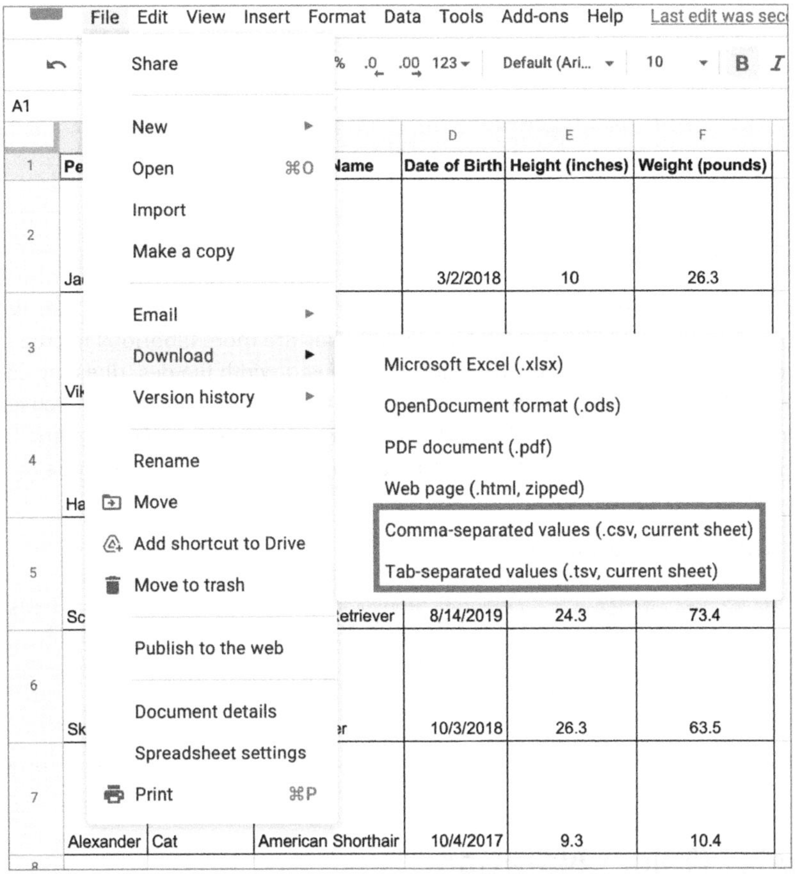

FIGURE 3.26 Contents of a CSV file.

```
Pet Name,Animal Type,Breed Name,Date of Birth,Height (inches),Weight (pounds)
Jack,Dog,Corgi,3/2/2018,10,26.3
Viking,Dog,Husky,5/8/2017,24,58
Hazel,Dog,Labradoodle,7/3/2016,23,61
Schooner,Dog,Labrador Retriever,8/14/2019,24.3,73.4
Skippy,Dog,Weimaraner,10/3/2018,26.3,63.5
Alexander,Cat,American Shorthair,10/4/2017,9.3,10.4
```

FIGURE 3.27 Semi-structured CSV.

```
Profile Name,Title Description,Device,Country,Playback Start Utc Ts,Playtraces
Jackson,"The Office (U.S.): Season 8: ""Jury Duty""",Sony Sony Android TV 2019 M1 Smart TV,US,2020-11-05 04:22:29
,"[{""eventType"":""start"",""sessionOffsetMs"":0,""mediaOffsetMs"":1000},{""eventType"":""playing"",""sessionOff
setMs"":2217,""mediaOffsetMs"":1000},{""eventType"":""paused"",""sessionOffsetMs"":76295,""mediaOffsetMs"":73833}
,{""eventType"":""repos"",""sessionOffsetMs"":76296,""mediaOffsetMs"":87500},{""eventType"":""playing"",""session
OffsetMs"":76857,""mediaOffsetMs"":87500},{""eventType"":""stopped"",""sessionOffsetMs"":1184351,""mediaOffsetMs""
:1194036}]"
```

Fixed-Width Files

Before it was common to use delimited files with variable-length columns, flat files were fixed-width, as illustrated in Figure 3.28. Fixed-width files are more laborious to create, since they require a few extra steps. The first row in a fixed-width file describes the column names. For the data rows, you first need to determine the maximum length of each column. Then, you must pad values that are shorter than that maximum length. For numeric fields, you accomplish padding by prepending a leading zero. For text fields, this is done by prepending or appending spaces.

FIGURE 3.28 Fixed-width file.

```
Pet_ID Pet_Name  Animal_Type Breed_Name         Date_of_Birth Height_(inches) Weight_(pounds) Picture
0001       Jack  Dog                  Corgi       03/02/2018  10.0            26.3
0002      Viking Dog                  Husky       05/08/2017  24.0            58.0
0003       Hazel Dog           Labradoodle        07/03/2016  23.0            61.0
0004    Schooner Dog     Labrador Retriever       08/14/2019  24.3            73.4
0005      Skippy Dog             Weimaraner       10/03/2018  26.3            63.5
0006   Alexander Cat     American Shorthair       10/04/2017  09.3            10.4
```

JavaScript Object Notation

JavaScript Object Notation (JSON) is an open standard file format, designed to add structure to a text file without incurring significant overhead. One of its design principles is that JSON is easily readable by people and easily parsed by modern programming languages. Languages such as Python, R, and Go have libraries containing functions that facilitate reading and writing JSON files.

Consider Figure 3.29, which illustrates data about the first two pets from Table 3.1, formatted as JSON. As a person, it is easy to see that the information corresponding to an individual pet is within curly braces, with name-value pairs corresponding to the data elements and values.

To illustrate how a machine processes this same information, Figure 3.30 shows how the entire pet data, formatted as JSON, is read using the Python programming language. Figure 3.31 illustrates reading the same file using the R programming language. Note that R, which facilitates statistical analysis of data, has a summary command, the results of which

FIGURE 3.29 Pet data JSON example.

```
[
  {
    "Pet ID": 1,
    "Pet Name": "Jack",
    "Animal Type": "Dog",
    "Breed Name": "Corgi",
    "Date of Birth": "3/2/2018",
    "Height (inches)": 10,
    "Weight (pounds)": 26.3
  },
  {
    "Pet ID": 2,
    "Pet Name": "Viking",
    "Animal Type": "Dog",
    "Breed Name": "Husky",
    "Date of Birth": "5/8/2017",
    "Height (inches)": 24,
    "Weight (pounds)": 58
  },
```

FIGURE 3.30 Reading JSON in Python.

```
# Import the json package in order to read files formatted as JSON
import json

# Read in each line in the JSON file.
with open('./c2pets.json') as f:
    pets = json.load(f)

# Print out the entire data structure
print(pets)

[{'Pet ID': 1, 'Pet Name': 'Jack', 'Animal Type': 'Dog', 'Breed Name': 'Corgi', 'Date of Birth': '3/2/2018', 'H
eight (inches)': 10, 'Weight (pounds)': 26.3}, {'Pet ID': 2, 'Pet Name': 'Viking', 'Animal Type': 'Dog', 'Breed
Name': 'Husky', 'Date of Birth': '5/8/2017', 'Height (inches)': 24, 'Weight (pounds)': 58}, {'Pet ID': 3, 'Pet
Name': 'Hazel', 'Animal Type': 'Dog', 'Breed Name': 'Labradoodle', 'Date of Birth': '7/3/2016', 'Height (inches
)': 23, 'Weight (pounds)': 61}, {'Pet ID': 4, 'Pet Name': 'Schooner', 'Animal Type': 'Dog', 'Breed Name': 'Labr
ador Retriever', 'Date of Birth': '8/14/2019', 'Height (inches)': 26.3, 'Weight (pounds)': 73.4}, {'Pet ID': 5,
'Pet Name': 'Skippy', 'Animal Type': 'Dog', 'Breed Name': 'Weimaraner', 'Date of Birth': '10/3/2018', 'Height (
inches)': 26.3, 'Weight (pounds)': 63.5}, {'Pet ID': 6, 'Pet Name': 'Alexander', 'Animal Type': 'Cat', 'Breed N
ame': 'American Shorthair', 'Date of Birth': '10/4/2017', 'Height (inches)': 9.3, 'Weight (pounds)': 10.4}, {'P
et ID': 7, 'Pet Name': 'Thor', 'Animal Type': 'Dog', 'Breed Name': 'German Shepherd', 'Date of Birth': '10/3/20
20', 'Height (inches)': 28, 'Weight (pounds)': 95}]

# Print the information for the first pet only
pets[0]

{'Pet ID': 1,
 'Pet Name': 'Jack',
 'Animal Type': 'Dog',
 'Breed Name': 'Corgi',
 'Date of Birth': '3/2/2018',
 'Height (inches)': 10,
 'Weight (pounds)': 26.3}
```

illustrate some summary statistics about the pet data. The summary statistics are convenient, as it shows six dogs and only one cat in this dataset. It also shows the quartile breakdowns for height and weight.

JSON formats can become extremely complex. It's possible to have *nested structures* in your JSON files, where one JSON object contains another object, called a nested object. Those nested objects can also contain their own nested objects, through many levels of recursion!

FIGURE 3.31 Reading JSON in R.

```r
1  library(tidyverse) # Load library to easily chain commands with pipes
2  library(jsonlite)  # Load library for interacting with JSON
3  library(lubridate) # Load library for manipulating dates
4
5  # Read in the JSON data
6  jsonpets <- fromJSON("./c2pets.json")
7  # Convert to appropriate data types, as Animal Type and Breed Name
8  # are categorical variables, and Date of Birth is a date.
9  jsonpets <- jsonpets %>%
10    mutate(`Animal Type` = as.factor(`Animal Type`),
11           `Breed Name` = as.factor(`Breed Name`),
12           `Date of Birth` = mdy(`Date of Birth`))
13 summary(jsonpets)
14 jsonpets
```

```
> summary(jsonpets)
     Pet ID       Pet Name         Animal Type         Breed Name
 Min.   :1.0   Length:7           Cat:1     American Shorthair:1
 1st Qu.:2.5   Class :character   Dog:6     Corgi             :1
 Median :4.0   Mode  :character             German Shepherd   :1
 Mean   :4.0                                Husky             :1
 3rd Qu.:5.5                                Labradoodle       :1
 Max.   :7.0                                Labrador Retriever:1
                                            Weimaraner        :1
  Date of Birth         Height (inches)   Weight (pounds)
 Min.   :2016-07-03    Min.   : 9.30     Min.   :10.40
 1st Qu.:2017-07-21    1st Qu.:16.50     1st Qu.:42.15
 Median :2018-03-02    Median :24.00     Median :61.00
 Mean   :2018-06-01    Mean   :20.99     Mean   :55.37
 3rd Qu.:2019-03-09    3rd Qu.:26.30     3rd Qu.:68.45
 Max.   :2020-10-03    Max.   :28.00     Max.   :95.00
> jsonpets
  Pet ID Pet Name Animal Type         Breed Name Date of Birth
1      1     Jack         Dog              Corgi    2018-03-02
2      2   Viking         Dog              Husky    2017-05-08
3      3    Hazel         Dog        Labradoodle    2016-07-03
4      4 Schooner         Dog Labrador Retriever    2019-08-14
5      5   Skippy         Dog         Weimaraner    2018-10-03
```

Extensible Markup Language (XML)

Extensible Markup Language (XML) is a markup language that facilitates structuring data in a text file. While conceptually similar to JSON, XML incurs more overhead because it makes extensive use of tags. *Tags* describe a data element and enclose each value for each data element. While these tags help readability, they add a significant amount of overhead.

Consider Figure 3.32, which illustrates an XML representation for a single pet. Note that for each data element, there is an open tag that defines the element, followed by its value and a closing tag. Compared with the JSON in Figure 3.29, XML results in a file roughly double in size. Although this is insignificant for small files, the impact is much more profound when dealing with data in the gigabyte and terabyte range.

In 1999, XML was the data format of choice and facilitated *Asynchronous JavaScript and XML (Ajax)* web development techniques. AJAX allowed client applications, written in HTML, to retrieve data from a server asynchronously. Without having to wait for a server response, the speed with which dynamic web pages operated increased. With JSON as a lighter-weight alternative to XML, it is becoming increasingly popular when interacting asynchronously between a web browser and a remote server.

Hypertext Markup Language (HTML)

Hypertext Markup Language (HTML) is a markup language for documents designed to be displayed in a web browser. HTML pages serve as the foundation for how people interact with the web. Similar to XML, HTML is a tag-based language. Figure 3.33 illustrates the creation of a table in HTML containing the data for a single pet. Figure 3.34 illustrates how a browser processes an HTML of fully populated pet data to display it to people.

Most people interact with HTML as interpreted by a web browser. HTML has become increasingly sophisticated over the years, with the ability for developers to create web pages that dynamically display content, adjust to different screen sizes, and play videos. Among the many tags that HTML supports is the image (IMG) tag. It is possible to display a picture for each pet in the table using image tags. Figure 3.35 illustrates the code that makes this happen.

FIGURE 3.32   Representing a single animal in XML.

```
 1  <?xml version="1.0" encoding="UTF-8"?>
 2  <pet>
 3      <PetID>1</PetID>
 4      <PetName>Jack</PetName>
 5      <AnimalType>Dog</AnimalType>
 6      <BreedName>Corgi</BreedName>
 7      <DateOfBirth>03/02/2018</DateOfBirth>
 8      <Height>10</Height>
 9      <Weight>26.3</Weight>
10  </pet>
```

FIGURE 3.33   Representing a single animal in HTML.

```
 1  <!DOCTYPE html>
 2  <html>
 3  <table class="table table-bordered table-hover table-condensed">
 4  <thead><tr><th title="Field #1">Pet ID</th>
 5  <th title="Field #2">Pet Name</th>
 6  <th title="Field #3">Animal Type</th>
 7  <th title="Field #4">Breed Name</th>
 8  <th title="Field #5">Date of Birth</th>
 9  <th title="Field #6">Height (inches)</th>
10  <th title="Field #7">Weight (pounds)</th>
11  </tr></thead>
12  <tbody><tr>
13  <td align="right">1</td>
14  <td>Jack</td>
15  <td>Dog</td>
16  <td>Corgi</td>
17  <td>3/2/2018</td>
18  <td align="right">10</td>
19  <td align="right">26.3</td>
20  </tr>
21  </tbody></table>
22  </html>
```

FIGURE 3.34 HTML table in a browser.

Pet ID	Pet Name	Animal Type	Breed Name	Date of Birth	Height (inches)	Weight (pounds)
1	Jack	Dog	Corgi	3/2/2018	10	26.3
2	Viking	Dog	Husky	5/8/2017	24	58
3	Hazel	Dog	Labradoodle	7/3/2016	23	61
4	Schooner	Dog	Labrador Retriever	8/14/2019	26.3	73.4
5	Skippy	Dog	Weimaraner	10/3/2018	26.3	63.5
6	Alexander	Cat	American Shorthair	10/4/2017	9.3	10.4
7	Thor	Dog	German Shepherd	10/3/2020	28	95

FIGURE 3.35 Displaying an image in an HTML table.

```
1  <!DOCTYPE html>
2  <html>
3  <table class="table table-bordered table-hover table-condensed">
4  <thead><tr><th title="Field #1">Pet ID</th>
5  <th title="Field #2">Pet Name</th>
6  <th title="Field #3">Animal Type</th>
7  <th title="Field #4">Breed Name</th>
8  <th title="Field #5">Date of Birth</th>
9  <th title="Field #6">Height (inches)</th>
10 <th title="Field #7">Weight (pounds)</th>
11 <th title="Field #8">Picture</th>
12 </tr></thead>
13 <tbody><tr>
14 <td align="right">1</td>
15 <td>Jack</td>
16 <td>Dog</td>
17 <td>Corgi</td>
18 <td>3/2/2018</td>
19 <td align="right">10</td>
20 <td align="right">26.3</td>
21 <td><img src="https://global_sbn.s3.amazonaws.com/jack.jpeg"> </td>
22 </tr>
```

Summary

When dealing with data, you need to think through the data values you are working with, because doing so influences your choice of data type. When using structured data, you may be working with dates, numbers, text, or currency data. Whether the data is discrete, continuous, or categorical, choosing the appropriate data type can help boost data quality. There are also data types for storing unstructured data, such as images, audio, and video.

If you are working with structured data, you should start thinking about it in a tabular fashion. Getting structured data into unique rows and consistent columns is the first step on the path to preparing data for analysis. Structured data fits well into CSV files, a popular format for exchanging data via flat files.

When you have to incorporate additional metadata or represent a complex data structure, you need capabilities beyond what a flat file provides. Formatting the data as JSON or XML is a viable alternative.

The modern analyst frequently works with data sources over the Internet. Understanding that HTML is the standard for structuring web pages is crucial to developing the ability to interact with data over the Internet programmatically.

Exam Essentials

Consider the values of what you will store before selecting data types. Data types are used to store different kinds of values. When dealing with numeric information, the best option is a numeric data type that can accommodate decimals. For sequences of whole numbers, an integer data type is a good choice. Be wary of using currency-specific data types—that can lead to calculation errors. For text values, the string data type is the optimal choice. When dealing with dates, you will want to consider whether you need to store the time as well. For binary data, including audio, video, and images, you should use a BLOB data type.

Know that you can format data after storing it. While data types determine how data gets stored, formatting data governs how data will be displayed to a person. You may want to store numeric data to many decimal places but round to the hundredths for display purposes. Similarly, numeric data can be formatted and displayed as a currency. Dates are possibly the most commonly formatted data type, since the same information may need to be displayed differently depending on cultural norms.

Consider the absolute limits of values that you will use before selecting data types. When selecting data types, consider the range of values that a data element can contain. Suppose the values need to fall within a given, defined range. In that case, you must select a data element that can support discrete data. If the data element's range is unknown, a data element that supports continuous data is necessary.

Explain the differences between structured and unstructured data. Individual data elements fall along the structured data continuum. At one end, there is highly structured, rectangular data. Structured data is organized into columns and rows. Each column has a consistent data type, and each row contains data about one data subject. Unstructured data does not fit neatly into a column. Looking for similarities or differences in unstructured data requires more advanced analytical techniques than structured data.

Understand the differences in common file formats. Common file formats make it easy for people to read a file's contents and facilitate interoperability between tools. Delimiters separate variable-length fields in a file. The comma and the resultant CSV file are among the most commonly used formats for exchanging text files. To provide additional metadata about data values and support more complex data structures, XML and JSON were developed. JSON is a preferred format, given its low overhead, especially when compared with XML.

Review Questions

The following questions are designed to test your understanding of this chapter's material. You can find the answers in Appendix A.

1. While UA 769 contains numeric components, selecting a string data type is the best option if you store this information in a single field. Since there is no date information contained in UA 769, the date data type is not appropriate. Using a CLOB would be wasteful, as this is a short text string.

    A. Date
    B. Numeric
    C. CLOB
    D. String

2. Voice transcripts are unstructured digital audio files. As such, the BLOB data type is the only viable choice. The string, numeric, and date data types are all structured data types.

    A. String
    B. Numeric
    C. BLOB
    D. Date

3. In order to facilitate precise mathematical operations on financial data, a numeric data type is the most appropriate choice. Smallmoney does not support values in excess of $1 million. Both smallmoney and money are subject to rounding errors. While string could be used to store financial records, the data would have to be converted to numeric in order to facilitate mathematical operations.

    A. String
    B. Smallmoney
    C. Money
    D. Numeric

4. Hazel needs to store video recordings for subjects participating in a psychological experiment. There are 300 participants in the experiment, and each session is 45 minutes long. Presuming the video is captured using a modern smartphone at a rate of 102,400 KB per minute, which of the following data types does Hazel need to select if she is storing these videos in a database?

    A. `varbinary`
    B. BLOB
    C. CLOB
    D. Numeric

5. Alexander is doing research on literary works and wants to store the title, complete text, and community-sourced rating in a database. The longest book included in his study is *Atlas Shrugged* by Ayn Rand, coming in at 1,168 pages. Presuming that Alexander is working in an Oracle database, which of the following data types should he choose?

   A. BLOB
   B. CLOB
   C. `varchar`
   D. Numeric

6. Barnali is analyzing defects at a manufacturing plant. In order to inform her work, she tracks the number of defective control arms that come down the assembly line on an hourly basis. What kind of data is represented by the number of defects?

   A. Discrete
   B. Continuous
   C. Categorical
   D. String

7. Haroon is choosing a pair of running shoes. In the past, he has found a size 10 to be too small and size 10.5 to be uncomfortable. While he would like to be able to order a size 10.25, it is simply not available as shoes are sold in half-size increments. What kind of data is represented by shoe size?

   A. Discrete
   B. Continuous
   C. Categorical
   D. String

8. Amdee is measuring her feet to help her figure out what shoe size to order. At 9.75 inches, that places her between a U.S. size 8 and a U.S. size 8.5 shoe. What kind of data does Amdee's measured foot size represent?

   A. Discrete
   B. Continuous
   C. Categorical
   D. String

9. Connor is aggregating temperature information from 5,000 Internet of Things temperature sensors at disparate locations around his farm. What type of measure is temperature, and what is an appropriate data type to contain these values?

   A. Discrete; integer
   B. Discrete; numeric
   C. Continuous; integer
   D. Continuous; numeric

10. Zahara is conducting a survey to collect opinions about a recent theatrical release. She is capturing this via an open-ended text response field on a web form. What category of data does this represent?

   A. Quantitative
   B. Qualitative
   C. Categorical
   D. Dimensional

11. Jed wants to track his expenditures in a spreadsheet containing check number, date, recipient, and amount. What kind of data is Jed working with?

   A. Unstructured
   B. Semi-structured
   C. Structured
   D. Machine

12. Amy is interested in exploring the Netflix viewing history, including Profile Name, Title Description, Device, Country, Playback Start Times, and Playtraces, for her household. Navigating to the account export screen, which option should she select in order to facilitate analysis using the Python programming language?

   A. CSV
   B. Text file
   C. HTML
   D. XML

13. Zeke is experimenting with home automation. Reading the application programming interface (API) guide, he sees that commands can be issued in the following syntax:

    ```
    {
        "commands": [
            {
                "component": "main",
                "capability": "switch",
                "command": "off",
                "arguments": []
            }
        ]
    }
    ```

    Which data format does the API require?

    A. JSON
    B. TSV
    C. CSV
    D. XML

14. Maura is a data engineer tasked with a new system integration. She has been given the following sample file to help her understand how to parse files of a similar type:
    ```
    {
        "VIN": "WP0ZZZ99Z5S73824",
        "Manufacturer": "Porsche",
        "Model": "Carrera S",
        "Horsepower": 443,
        "Torque": 390
    }
    ```
    Which data format does the API require?
    A. JSON
    B. TSV
    C. CSV
    D. XML

15. Chris is a financial analyst who wants to use Microsoft Excel to perform what-if analysis on data extracted from his corporate accounting system. To make the data extract easy to import, which of the following file formats should he specify?
    A. CSV
    B. JSON
    C. XML
    D. YAML

16. Claire is a web developer working on an interactive website. While she is programming in JavaScript, which of the following file types is essential to test her work in a web browser?
    A. CSV
    B. JSON
    C. HTML
    D. XML

17. Claire has just received a spreadsheet of streaming media use data, and one of the columns contained the following data:
    `[{"eventType":"start","sessionOffsetMs":0,"mediaOffsetMs":0},{"eventType":"playing","sessionOffsetMs":3153,"mediaOffsetMs":0},{"eventType":"stopped","sessionOffsetMs":4818,"mediaOffsetMs":559}]`

    While the spreadsheet is displaying this data as a single piece of text, Claire feels like there is structure to the data. Is Claire correct, and if so, how are the contents of the column formatted?
    A. No; it is plain text.
    B. No; it is machine data.
    C. Yes; it is JSON.
    D. Yes; it is plain text.

18. Jorge is transferring data from a mainframe to his laptop so that he can upload it into a Google spreadsheet for analysis. Looking at the file from the mainframe, he sees that it uses `^%` as a delimiter. To make it easy to load into the Google spreadsheet, what should Jorge do?

   A. Nothing, the file will load just fine.

   B. Nothing, you cannot transfer data from a mainframe to a laptop.

   C. Use software on the mainframe instead of a Google spreadsheet.

   D. Convert the `^%` into a comma or a tab.

19. Eleanora has been tasked with analyzing web server logs to better understand where website visitors are coming from. Every time a person visits a website, an entry containing multiple items, including IP address, destination page, and current time, is automatically made in the log. What type of data is this?

   A. Machine data

   B. Undefined data

   C. Automatic data

   D. Web data

20. Dave is a graphic designer who wants to build a website to show off his portfolio. For each item in his portfolio, he wants to show the client name, date of commission, and a thumbnail image of the artwork. While he can accomplish this by building out a table in HTML, what category of data best describes what he wants to do?

   A. Unstructured

   B. Semi-structured

   C. Structured

   D. Machine

Chapter 4

Databases and Data Acquisition

THE COMPTIA DATA+ EXAM TOPICS COVERED IN THIS CHAPTER INCLUDE:

✔ **Domain 1.0: Data Concepts and Environments**

- 1.1 Explain data concepts
- 1.2. Identify types of data sources

✔ **Domain 2.0: Data Acquisition and Preparation**

- 2.1. Given a scenario, use data acquisition methods

In Chapter 3, "Understanding Data," you learned how organizations rely on structured and unstructured data to meet their business needs. You also learned about various tools available for analyzing data. Every data analytics tool requires data to facilitate insights. Data exists in multiple locations, shapes, sizes, and formats. Gaining familiarity with where data comes from, how to manipulate it, and how to store it is essential for today's data analytics professionals.

The vast majority of transactional systems generate structured data, and we need technology platforms to store all of that data. Relational databases are a foundational technology platform that allows us to keep our data organized and easy to retrieve when we need it.

We collect data from many sources to derive insights. For example, a financial analyst may seek to understand why some retail outlets are more profitable than others. The analyst could look at the individual records for each store. However, with thousands of items across hundreds of stores, looking at individual records would take too much time. Developing an understanding of profitability requires summarizing the data for each store. Databases make it easier to answer this question using powerful aggregation and summarization features.

In this chapter, you examine the two main database categories: relational and nonrelational. You learn several different database design approaches for storing structured data. Building on this foundation, you learn about common database design practices. You proceed to dive into the details of working with databases and explore techniques and design patterns for moving data between systems. You examine tools and techniques that will help you answer questions using data. This chapter wraps up by exploring methods for collecting data. Equipped with this knowledge, you will clearly understand database structure, how data flows between systems, and how to improve your ability to derive actionable insights from data.

Exploring Databases

There are many different database options to choose from when an organization needs to store data. While many database products exist, they belong to one of two categories: *relational* and *nonrelational*. One of the oldest and most mature databases is the relational database. Relational databases excel at storing and processing structured data. As you discovered in Chapter 3, much of the world's data is unstructured. The need to interact with unstructured data is one of the reasons behind the rise of nonrelational databases.

Although databases fall into two categories, many systems we interact with daily produce tabular data. *Tabular data*, or *rectangular data*, is organized in a table format consisting of rows and columns. Each row represents a single observation or record, while each column represents a variable or attribute of the data. Since tabular data is highly structured, most of this chapter goes deeper into relational databases, their design, and how to use them.

The Relational Model

In 1969, IBM's Edgar F. Codd developed the relational model for database management. The relational model builds on the concept of tabular data. In the relational model, an *entity* contains data for a single subject. When creating an IT system, you need to consider all the entities required to make your system work. You can think of entities as nouns because they usually correspond to people, places, and things.

Consider again the veterinary clinic example from Chapter 3. They have to store data about the animals they treat and the people who own those animals. The clinic needs one entity for data about animals and a separate entity for data about people to accomplish this goal. Figure 4.1 shows the structure of the Animal and Person entities.

An *entity instance* identifies a specific example of an entity. Considering the Animal entity in Figure 4.1, an entity instance is a particular animal. Looking at Table 4.1, all of the information about Jack represents an entity instance.

For both entities in Figure 4.1, the bolded word in the header is the entity's name. For example, suppose you want to know where to look for data about a specific person. The Person entity in Figure 4.1 is a clear choice since it stores data about people.

Understanding that the header corresponds to the name of an entity, look at the rows of the Person entity. Each row represents an individual attribute associated with a person.

FIGURE 4.1 The (a) Animal entity and (b) Person entity in a veterinary database.

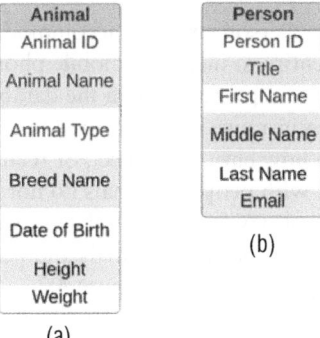

TABLE 4.1   Animal Data

Animal_ID	Animal_Name	Animal_Type	Breed_Name	Date_of_Birth	Height (Inches)	Weight (Pounds)
1	Jack	Dog	Corgi	3/2/2018	10	26.3
2	Viking	Dog	Husky	5/8/2017	24	58
3	Hazel	Dog	Labradoodle	7/3/2016	23	61
4	Schooner	Dog	Labrador Retriever	8/14/2019	24.3	74.4
5	Skippy	Dog	Weimaraner	10/3/2018	26.3	64.5
6	Alexander	Cat	American Shorthair	10/4/2017	9.3	10.4
7	Éowyn	Cat	American Shorthair	5/22/2024	8.4	8.8
8	Euclid	Cat	American Shorthair	4/3/2020	9	10

FIGURE 4.2   Relationship connecting Animal and Person.

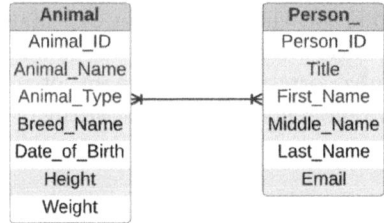

Suppose you want to enhance the Person entity to accommodate a mobile phone number. You would just edit the Person entity to include a mobile phone attribute.

Each of these entities becomes a separate table in the database, with a column for each attribute. Each row represents an instance of the entity. The power of the relational model is that it also allows us to describe how entities connect, or relate, to each other. The veterinary clinic needs to associate animals with people. Animals do not have email addresses, cannot schedule appointments, and cannot pay for services. Their owners, on the other hand, do all of these things. There's a relationship between animals and people, and we can include this relationship in the database design, as shown in Figure 4.2.

The *entity relationship diagram* (ERD) is a visual artifact of the data modeling process. It shows the connection between related entities. The line in Figure 4.2 illustrates that a *relationship* exists between the Animal and Person entities. A relationship is a connection between entities. The symbols adjacent to an entity describe the relationship.

Cardinality refers to the relationship between two entities, showing how many instances of one entity relate to instances in another entity. You specify cardinality in an ERD with various line endings. The first component of the terminator indicates whether the relationship between two entities is optional or required. The second component indicates whether an entity instance in the first table is associated with a single entity instance in the related table or if an association can exist with multiple entity instances. Figure 4.3 illustrates the possible combinations for representing relationships.

With an understanding of ERD line endings, let's apply it to Figure 4.2. Reading the diagram aloud from left to right, you say, "An individual animal belongs to at least one and possibly many people." Reading from right to left sounds like, "A specific person has at least one and possibly many animals."

A *unary relationship* is when an entity has a connection with itself. For example, Figure 4.4 illustrates a unary relationship where a single manager has multiple employees.

A *binary relationship* connects two entities, as shown in Figure 4.2. A *ternary relationship* connects three entities. For example, you might use a ticket entity to connect a venue, a performing artist, and a price.

FIGURE 4.3 ERD line endings.

Relationship Description	Cardinality Symbol
Optional relationship, at most one instance	 ———O+
Required relationship, at most one instance	 ———++
Optional relationship, potentially infinite instances	 ———O<
Required relationship, potentially infinite instance	 ———+<

FIGURE 4.4 Unary relationship.

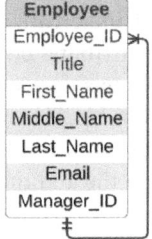

FIGURE 4.5 Entity relationship diagram.

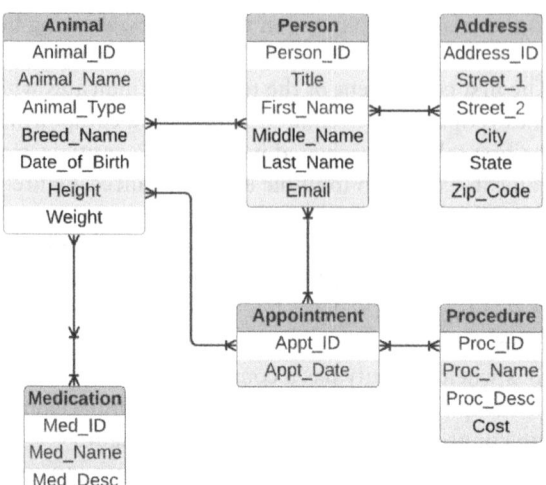

Binary relationships are the most common and easy to explore, whereas unary and ternary are comparatively complex and rare.

As you think about a database that would support an actual veterinary clinic, you're probably realizing that it would need to store more information than we've already discussed. For example, we'd need to store addresses, appointments, medications, and procedures. Database designers would continue to add entities and relationships to the diagram until it meets all of the veterinary clinic's business needs, such as the one shown in Figure 4.5.

Apart from being a helpful picture, the entity relationship diagram also serves as the technical blueprint from which you can build a relational database. The ability to read ERDs helps you understand the structure of a relational database. ERDs are particularly useful when formulating how to retrieve information from multiple tables spread across the database since the ERDs allow you to visualize the connections between entities.

Relational Databases

Relational databases are pieces of software that let you make an operational system out of an ERD. You start with a relational model and create a physical design. Relational entities correspond to database tables, and entity attributes correspond to table columns. When creating a database table, the ordering of columns does not matter because you can specify the column order when retrieving data from a table. When an attribute becomes a column, you assign it a data type. Completing all of this work results in a diagram known as a *schema*. You can think of a schema as an ERD with the additional details needed to create a database. For example, the relational model in Figure 4.2 becomes the schema in Figure 4.6.

FIGURE 4.6 Database schema.

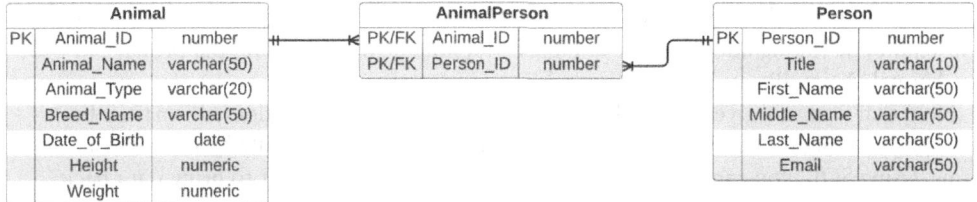

TABLE 4.2 Person Data

Person_ID	Title	First_Name	Middle_Name	Last_Name	Email
10000	Mr	Paul		Tupy	pault@example.com
10001	Ms	Emma	M	Snyder	esnyder@example.com
10002	Ms	Giustina	Marguerite	Rossi	gmrossi@example.com
10003	Mr	Giacomo	Paolo	Mangione	gpman@example.com
10004	Mrs	Eleonora	B	Mangione	eman@example.com
10005	Ms	Leila	Abir	Abboud	leila@example.com
10006	Mr	Chris	Thomas	Bregande	christb@example.com

Note that the two entities in Figure 4.2 become three tables in Figure 4.6. The new AnimalPerson table is necessary because you need to resolve a many-to-many relationship with an *associative table*. An associative table is both a table and a relationship. Recall that an animal can belong to more than one person, and a person can have more than one animal. An associative table lets you identify the relationship between a specific animal and a particular person with a minimum amount of data duplication. Let's examine the tables and their data in more detail to see the Animal, AnimalPerson, and Person tables in action.

With the schema design complete, you can build the tables. Once you have the tables, you can load them with data. Table 4.1 shows what the Animal entity from Figure 4.1 looks like with data.

Similarly, the Person entity from Figure 4.1 corresponds to Table 4.2. The first column in both Table 4.1 and Table 4.2 is an identifier with a numeric data type. In both cases, these identifier columns (Animal_ID and Person_ID) are the *primary keys* for the table. A primary key is one or more attributes that uniquely identify a specific row in a table. It is best to use a *synthetic primary key*, which is simply an attribute whose only purpose is to contain unique values for each row in the table. In Table 4.1, Animal_ID is a synthetic primary key, and the number 3 is arbitrarily assigned to Hazel. The number 3 has no meaning beyond its ability to uniquely identify a row. Nothing about Hazel's data changes if her Animal_ID was 7 instead of 3. Taking another look at Figure 4.6, note how PK denotes the primary key for the Animal, AnimalPerson, and Person tables.

Note that within a given table, the actual sequencing of the rows does not matter. For example, you might want to retrieve data from Table 4.2 alphabetically by first or last name. Using SQL, you can easily specify the order in which you want to bring data back from a table.

You can imagine the data in Tables 4.1 and 4.2 existing as separate tabs in a spreadsheet. Suppose both Hazel and Alexander belong to the Mangione family. There is nothing in the data that connects an animal to a person. To link the two tables, you need a *foreign key*. A foreign key is one or more columns in one table that points to corresponding columns in a related table. Frequently, a foreign key references another table's primary key. Looking at the AnimalPerson table in Figure 4.6, FK denotes a foreign key. The Person_ID in the AnimalPerson table points to the Person_ID in the Person table. You can't put a row in the AnimalPerson table if the Person_ID doesn't exist in the Person table. Similarly, you can't use an Animal_ID in AnimalPerson if it doesn't exist in the Animal table.

Every row in a relational database must be unique. In Table 4.1, each row contains data about a specific animal, whereas each row in Table 4.2 refers to a particular person. Since the Mangione family has multiple animals, you need an associative table to describe the relationship between Animal and Person. Table 4.3 shows data from the AnimalPerson table in Figure 4.6.

Suppose you want to send an email reminder about an upcoming appointment for a pet. Figure 4.7 shows an email template with placeholder values.

To populate the email template, you need the person's title, last name, and email address from Table 4.2 and the corresponding pet's name and animal type from Table 4.1. To pull data from a relational database table, you perform a *query*. You compose queries using a programming language called *Structured Query Language (SQL)*.

TABLE 4.3 AnimalPerson Table

Animal_ID	Person_ID
3	10003
3	10004
6	10003
6	10004

FIGURE 4.7 Email template.

> Dear <Title> <Last_Name>,
>
> This is a reminder to let you know that your <Animal_Type> <Animal_Name> is due for an annual appointment. Please schedule one at your convenience.
>
> Regards,
>
> Your Friendly Family Vet

FIGURE 4.8 Reminder appointment email.

> Dear Mr. Mangione,
>
> This is a reminder to let you know that your Dog Hazel is due for an annual appointment. Please schedule one at your convenience.
>
> Regards,
>
> Your Friendly Family Vet

Your query needs to perform a *database join* to retrieve the data to substitute in the email reminder. A join uses data values from one table to retrieve associated data in another table, typically using a foreign key.

The first row in Table 4.3 represents the relationship between Mr. Mangione and Hazel. To send Mr. Mangione an email, you take 10003, the value for Person_ID in the first row of Table 4.3, and join it to Table 4.2. Using 10003, you retrieve Mr. Mangione's title, last name, and email address. To retrieve Hazel's information, you perform a similar join. You get 3 for Animal_ID from Table 4.3 and look up Hazel's information in Table 4.1. The result is the email that gets sent, shown in Figure 4.8. Note that if you send an email for each row in Table 4.3, both Mr. and Mrs. Mangione get emails about Hazel the Dog and Alexander the Cat.

Foreign keys enforce *referential integrity*, or how consistent the data is in related tables. Consider Figure 4.9, which shows why referential integrity is crucial to enforcing data quality. Suppose you try to add a row to the middle table, specifying 6 for the Animal_ID and 99999 as the Person_ID. The foreign key on Animal_ID checks the table to the left to ensure a row exists with the Animal_ID of 6. The new record passes this check because there is a record with Animal_ID 6 for the cat named Alexander. When a similar check

FIGURE 4.9 Referential integrity illustration.

Animal ID	Animal Name	Animal Type	Breed Name	Date of Birth	Height (inches)	Weight (pounds)
1	Jack	Dog	Corgi	3/2/2018	10	26.3
2	Viking	Dog	Husky	5/8/2017	24	58
3	Hazel	Dog	Labradoodle	7/3/2016	23	61
4	Schooner	Dog	Labrador Retriever	8/14/2019	24.3	73.4
5	Skippy	Dog	Weimaraner	10/3/2018	26.3	63.5
6	Alexander	Cat	American Shorthair	10/4/2017	9.3	10.4

Animal ID	Person ID
3	10003
3	10004
6	10003
6	10004
6	99999

Person ID	Title	First Name	Middle Name	Last Name	Email
10000	Mr	Paul		Tupy	pault@example.com
10001	Ms	Emma	M	Snyder	esnyder@example.com
10002	Ms	Giustina	Marguerite	Rossi	gmrossi@example.com
10003	Mr	Giacomo	Paolo	Mangione	gpman@example.com
10004	Mrs	Eleonora	B	Mangione	eman@example.com
10005	Ms	Leila	Abir	Abboud	leila@example.com
10006	Mr	Chris	Thomas	Bregande	christb@example.com

happens on Person_ID, there is no row corresponding to the Person_ID 99999 in the table on the right. Therefore, adding the new row fails, and the relationship between the tables is maintained.

In Table 4.3, the Animal_ID column is a foreign key that points to the Animal_ID primary key in Table 4.1. Looking at the first data row in Table 4.3, Animal_ID 3 refers to Hazel. Similarly, the Person_ID column points to the Person_ID column in Table 4.2, with 10003 identifying Giacomo Mangione. The combination of both Animal_ID and Person_ID is what makes each row in Table 4.3 unique. Taken together, Animal_ID and Person_ID represent a *composite primary key*. As the name implies, a composite primary key is a primary key with more than one column. While Figure 4.2 describes a relational model, Figure 4.6 shows modifications necessary to create tables for storing data.

Relational databases are complicated to operate at scale. A *database administrator* (DBA) is a highly trained person who understands how database software interacts with computer hardware. A DBA looks after how the database uses the underlying storage, memory, and processor resources assigned to the database. A DBA also looks for processes that are slowing the entire database down.

Address Referential Integrity Example

Let's explore another example of how foreign keys enforce referential integrity. Suppose an organization has an order management system that stores customers' information and addresses, as shown in Figure 4.10.

With an understanding of cardinality, you can read that ERD in Figure 4.10 and see that:

- A specific customer can have many addresses, while a particular address belongs to a single customer.
- A specific address has a single address type, while a particular address type can apply to many different addresses.
- A specific address has a single state, while a particular state can exist in many different addresses.

FIGURE 4.10 Customer ERD.

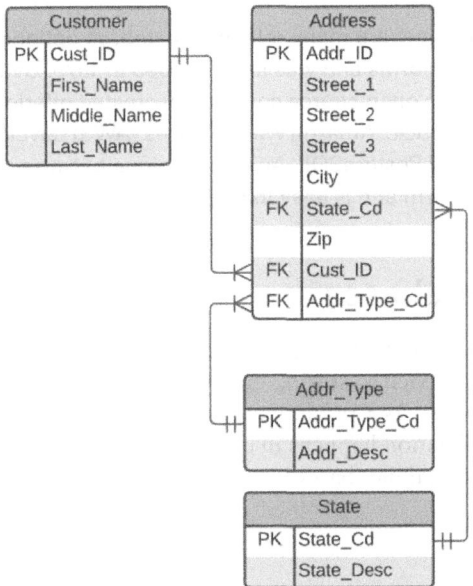

FIGURE 4.11 Foreign key data constraint.

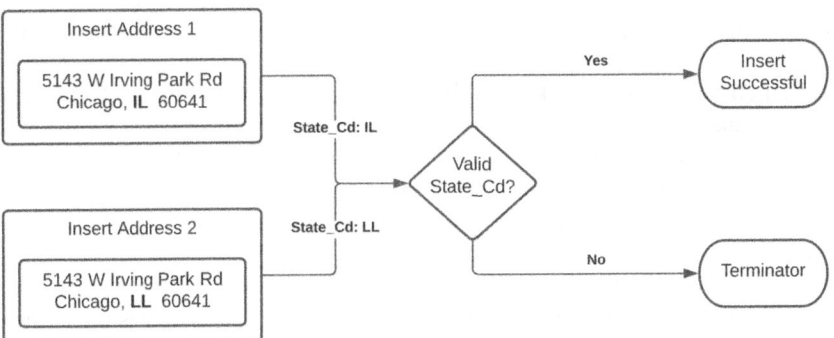

Implementing the relationships from an ERD enforces data constraints. For example, Figure 4.10 shows that an individual address must have a relationship with a state. You use foreign keys to implement data constraints in a database, like the relationship connecting Address with State. The FK designation for the State_Cd attribute on the Address entity in Figure 4.10 indicates that State_Cd is a foreign key. With a foreign key constraint in place, the database will not allow you to insert an address unless it exists in the State table, as shown in Figure 4.11.

> **Relational Database Providers**
>
> From a software standpoint, there are many relational database options. Oracle is one of the most mature database platforms and was first released in 1979. Over time, Microsoft developed SQL Server, and the open-source community created offerings including MySQL, MariaDB, and PostgreSQL. Amazon Web Services (AWS) developed Aurora, which is compatible with MySQL and PostgreSQL. Aurora is unique because it takes advantage of AWS's underlying cloud platform and is easy to scale.

Nonrelational Databases

A nonrelational database does not have a predefined structure based on tabular data. The result is a highly flexible approach to storing data. However, the data types available in relational databases are absent. As a result, you need to know more about the data itself to interact with it. Data validation happens in code, as opposed to being done in the database. Examples of nonrelational databases include *key-value, document, column family*, and *graph*.

Key-value

A key-value database is one of the simplest ways of storing data. Data is stored as a collection of keys and their corresponding values. A key must be globally unique across the entire database. The use of keys differs from a relational database, where a given key identifies an individual row in a specific table. There are no structural limits on the values of a key. A key can be a sequence of numbers, alphanumeric strings, or some other combination of values.

The data that corresponds with a key can be any structured or unstructured data type. Since there are no underlying table structures and few limitations on the data that can be stored, operating a key-value database is much simpler than a relational database. It also can scale to accommodate many simultaneous requests without impacting performance. However, since the values can contain multiple data types, the only way to search is to have the key.

One reason for choosing a key-value database is when you have lots of data and can search by a key's value. Imagine an online music streaming service. The key is the name of a song, and the value is the digital audio file containing the song itself. When a person wants to listen to music, they search for the name of the song. With a known key, the application quickly retrieves the song and starts streaming it to the user.

Document

A document database is similar to a key-value database, with additional restrictions. In a key-value database, the value can contain anything. With a document database, the value is

FIGURE 4.12 JSON person data.

```
{
  "firstName": "George",
  "lastName": "Villeneuve",
  "address": {
    "streetAddress": "123 Sample St",
    "city": "Chicago",
    "state": "IL",
    "postalCode": "60601"
  },
  "phoneNumbers": [
    {
      "type": "mobile",
      "number": "312-555-1234"
    },
    {
      "type": "office",
      "number": "312-555-6789"
    }
  ]
}
```

restricted to a specific structured format. For example, Figure 4.12 is an example of using JSON as the document format.

With a known, structured format, document databases have additional flexibility beyond what is possible with key-value databases. While searching with a known document key yields the fastest results, searching using a field within the document is possible. Suppose you are storing social network profiles. The document key is the profile name. The document itself is a JSON object containing details about the person, as Figure 4.12 shows. With a document database, it is possible to retrieve all profiles that match a specific ZIP code. This searching ability is possible because the database understands the document's structure and can search based on data within the document.

Column Family

Column family databases use an index to identify data in groups of related columns. A relational database stores the data in Table 4.2 in a single table, where each row contains the Person_ID, Title, First_Name, Middle_Name, Last_Name, and Email columns. In a column family database, the Person_ID becomes the index, while the other columns are stored independently. This design facilitates distributing data across multiple machines, which enables handling massive amounts of data. The ability to handle large data volumes is due to the technical implementation details of how these databases organize and store. From a design standpoint, column family databases optimize performance when you need to examine the contents of a column across many rows.

The main reason for choosing a column family database is its ability to scale. Suppose you need to analyze U.S. stock transactions over time. With daily trade volumes of over 6 billion records, processing that amount of data on a single database server is not feasible. It is in situations like this where column family databases shine.

Graph

Graph databases specialize in exploring relationships between pieces of data. Consider Figure 4.6, which shows the tables required to indicate which animals belong to which people. Figure 4.13 illustrates how a graph models data from Tables 4.1 and 4.2. Each animal and person represents a *node* in the graph. Each node can have multiple *properties*. Properties store specific attributes for an individual node. The arrow connecting nodes represents a *relationship*.

Relational models focus on mapping the relationships between entities. Graph models map relationships between actual pieces of data. In Figure 4.6, you need three tables to represent the relationship between animals and their people, with the associative table serving as the index that connects a specific animal to a specific person. Meanwhile, Figure 4.13 represents the same data using the graphical approach of directly-connected nodes. The direct linking of related nodes is known as *index-free adjacency*, which lets you represent relationships between individual pieces of data without needing an associative table.

FIGURE 4.13   Data in a graph.

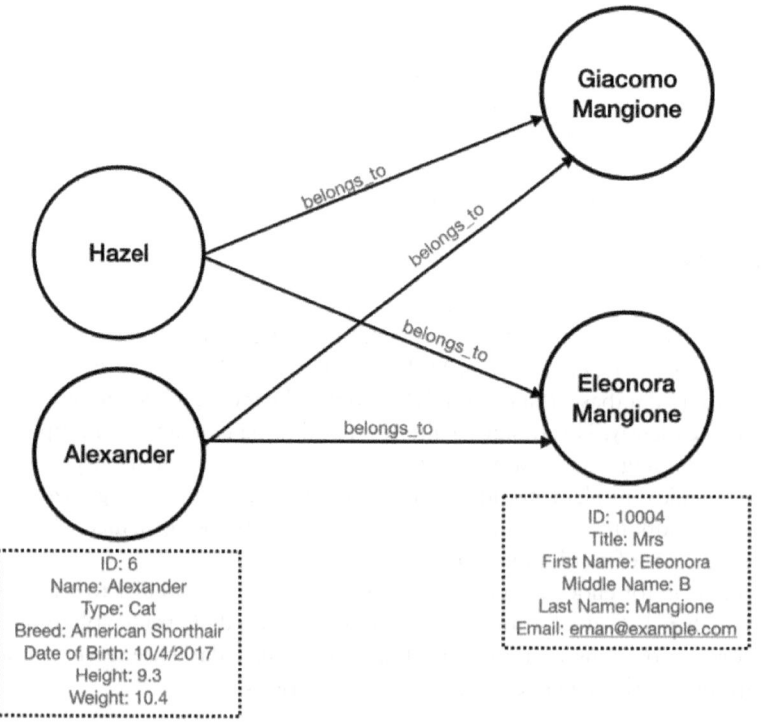

With the benefit of index-free adjacency, graph databases offer performance advantages over their relational counterparts. Graphs are an optimal choice if you need to create a recommendation engine, as graphs excel at exploring relationships between data. For example, when you search for a product on an e-commerce website, the results are frequently accompanied by a collection of related items. Understanding the connection between products is a challenge that graphs solve with ease.

Database Use Cases

Different business needs require different database designs. While all databases store data, the database's structure needs to match its intended purpose. Business requirements impact the design of individual tables and how they are interconnected. Transactional and reporting systems need different implementation approaches to serve the people who use them efficiently. Databases tend to support two major categories of data processing: *Online Transactional Processing* (OLTP) and *Online Analytical Processing* (OLAP).

Online Transactional Processing

OLTP systems handle the transactions we encounter every day. Example transactions include booking a flight reservation, ordering something online, or executing a stock trade. While the number of transactions a system handles on a given day can be very high, individual transactions process small amounts of data. OLTP systems balance the ability to write and read data efficiently.

Based on the data in Table 4.1, Table 4.2, and Table 4.3, suppose Giacomo Mangione wants to book an annual visit appointment for his cat, Alexander. Suppose both Giacomo and Alexander already exist in the database that supports the appointment system, as shown in Figure 4.14.

To book an appointment, Giacomo logs in to the vet clinic's website. When Giacomo logs in, the system retrieves his information from the Person table. Using the Animal_IDs corresponding to his Person_ID in the AnimalPerson table, the system displays a list of Giacomo's animals. Selecting Alexander from the list, Giacomo specifies a date and time of his choosing. Giacomo's input represents all the data necessary to create an appointment record, which Table 4.4 illustrates.

In Table 4.4, the AnmlPers_ID identifies Giacomo and Alexander. The Appt_ID is a system-generated synthetic key while Giacomo supplies the Date and Time. To retrieve the rest of the details about the person and the animal, you need to join the tables together using the foreign key to primary key relationship.

For this appointment, Alexander is due for a complete blood count and blood chemistry panel. The details about each procedure are in the Procedure table in Figure 4.14. The AppointmentProcedure table provides the link between a given appointment and all of the procedures performed during that appointment.

FIGURE 4.14 Vet clinic transactional schema.

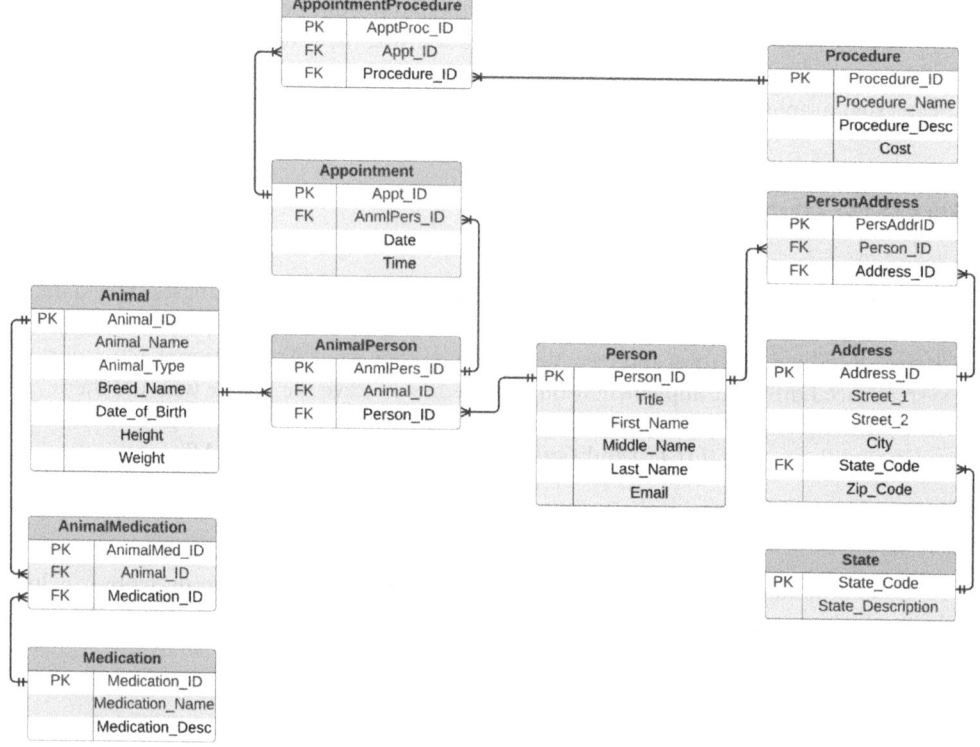

TABLE 4.4 Appointmentnt Booking

Appt_ID	AnmlPers_ID	Date	Time
53	10003	5/5/2022	13:00

Normalization

Normalization is a process for structuring a database in a way that minimizes duplication of data. One of the principles is that a given piece of data is stored once and only once. As a result, a normalized database is ideal for processing transactions.

FIGURE 4.15 Data in first normal form.

Person_ID (PK)	Person_Name	Addr_Code	Addr_Desc	Street	City	State_Code	State_Desc
10003	Giacomo	H	Home	123 State St.	Chicago	IL	Illinois
10003	Giacomo	W	Work	51 Work St.	Chicago	IL	Illinois
10004	Eleonora	H	Home	123 State St.	Chicago	IL	Illinois

First normal form (*1NF*) is when every row in a table is unique and every column contains a unique value. Consider Figure 4.15, where there are separate rows for Giacomo and Eleonora. While Giacomo and Eleonora have the same home address, appending Eleonora's name in the Person_Name column to Giacomo's in the first row would violate 1NF. However, since each row is unique, Figure 4.15 is in 1NF.

Second normal form (*2NF*) starts where 1NF leaves off. In addition to each row being unique, 2NF applies an additional rule stating that all nonprimary key values must depend on the entire primary key. To get to 2NF, the table from Figure 4.15 evolves into the tables in Figure 4.16. Note that the Person_Address table has a composite primary key composed of Person_ID and Addr_ID. The values of both Addr_Code and Addr_Desc are associated with the composite primary key.

Suppose Eleonora starts working from home and updates the Addr_Desc for her row with the value Work. That causes data corruption, as the Addr_Code corresponds to the Addr_Desc. Addr_Desc depends on Addr_Code, and with that change, H would mean both Home and Work.

Third normal form (*3NF*) builds upon 2NF by adding a rule stating all columns must depend on only the primary key. Evolving Figure 4.16 into 3NF results in Figure 4.17. If Eleonora starts working from home, the only value that needs to change is Addr_Code in the Person_Address table. The description for each type of address is in the Addr_Code table. Similarly, the description for each state code is in the State_Code table. The result is that there is little redundancy in the data's storage location and that keys enforce the relationships between tables. Databases in 3NF are said to be highly normalized.

FIGURE 4.16 Data in second normal form.

Person

Person_ID	Person_Name
10003	Giacomo
10004	Eleonora

Person_Address

Person_ID (PK)	Addr_ID (PK/FK)	Addr_Code	Addr_Desc
10003	500	H	Home
10003	501	W	Work
10004	500	H	Home

Address

Addr_ID (PK)	Street	City	State_Code	State_Desc
500	123 State St.	Chicago	IL	Illinois
501	51 Work St.	Chicago	IL	Illinois

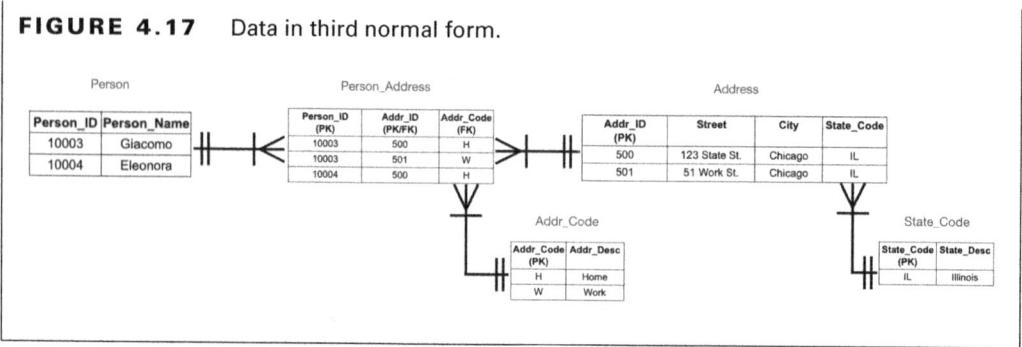

FIGURE 4.17   Data in third normal form.

Online Analytical Processing

OLAP systems focus on the ability of organizations to analyze data. While OLAP and OLTP databases can both use relational database technology, their structures are fundamentally different. OLTP databases need to balance transactional read and write performance, resulting in a highly normalized design. Typically, OLTP databases are in 3NF.

On the other hand, databases that power OLAP systems have a denormalized design. Instead of having data distributed across multiple tables, denormalization results in wider tables than those found in an OLTP database. It is more efficient for analytical queries to read large amounts of data for a single table instead of incurring the cost of joining multiple tables together.

Imagine you want to create a summary of the clinic's interaction history with a family's pets, as shown in Figure 4.18. Using the normalized OLTP database from Figure 4.14, you need to retrieve data from the Procedure, AppointmentProcedure, Appointment, AnimalPerson, and Animal tables. The greater the number of joins, the more complex the query. The more complex the query, the longer it takes to retrieve results.

FIGURE 4.18   Yearly spend by animal.

Animal ID	Name	Breed	Visit Year	Total Spend
3	Hazel	Labradoodle	2022	30
3	Hazel	Labradoodle	2021	30
3	Hazel	Labradoodle	2020	50
3	Hazel	Labradoodle	2019	30
3	Hazel	Labradoodle	2018	175
3	Alexander	Domestic Shorthair	2022	50
3	Alexander	Domestic Shorthair	2021	30
6	Alexander	Domestic Shorthair	2020	100
6	Alexander	Domestic Shorthair	2019	30
6	Alexander	Domestic Shorthair	2018	30

FIGURE 4.19 CostSummary table.

CostSummary	
PK	Animal_ID
PK	Visit_Year
	Name
	Breed
	Total_Spend

Consider the table in Figure 4.19, whose structure easily supports the data in Figure 4.18. It is possible to create the summary in Figure 4.18 using the OLTP database from Figure 4.14. However, the CostSummary table in Figure 4.19 greatly simplifies that operation.

Schema Concepts

The design of a database schema depends on the purpose it serves. Transactional systems require a highly normalized design that eliminates redundant data storage, whereas a denormalized design is more appropriate for analytical systems. A denormalized design prioritizes improving read performance, which may cause the same data to exist multiple times instead of once.

A *data warehouse* is a database that aggregates data from many transactional systems for analytical purposes, while a *data mart* is a subset of a data warehouse. Data warehouses serve the entire organization, whereas data marts focus on the needs of a particular department. For data warehouses and data marts, several design patterns exist for modeling data. It is crucial to realize that the structure of a database schema impacts analytical efficiency, particularly as the volume of data grows. In addition to a schema's design, it is vital to consider the lifecycle. Lifecycle considerations include where data comes from, how frequently it changes, and how long it needs to persist. OLAP systems like data warehouses and data marts typically use a star or snowflake design.

Star

The *star schema* design to facilitate analytical processing gets its name from what the schema looks like when looking at its entity relationship diagram, as Figure 4.20 illustrates. Star schemas are denormalized to improve read performance over large datasets.

At the center of the star is a *fact table*. Fact tables chiefly store numerical facts about a business. In Figure 4.20, the schema design centers on reporting on the cost and profitability of procedures. Qualitative data, including names, addresses, and descriptions, is stored in a series of *dimension tables* that connect to the main fact table.

Consider Figure 4.20, which has the Procedure_Facts table at the center of the star. This table makes it straightforward to calculate overall profitability. If you want to explore profitability for cats, you need to join the Procedure_Facts table to the Animal_Dimension. Similarly, you can join in the Procedure_Dimension table to understand profitability by

FIGURE 4.20 Star schema example.

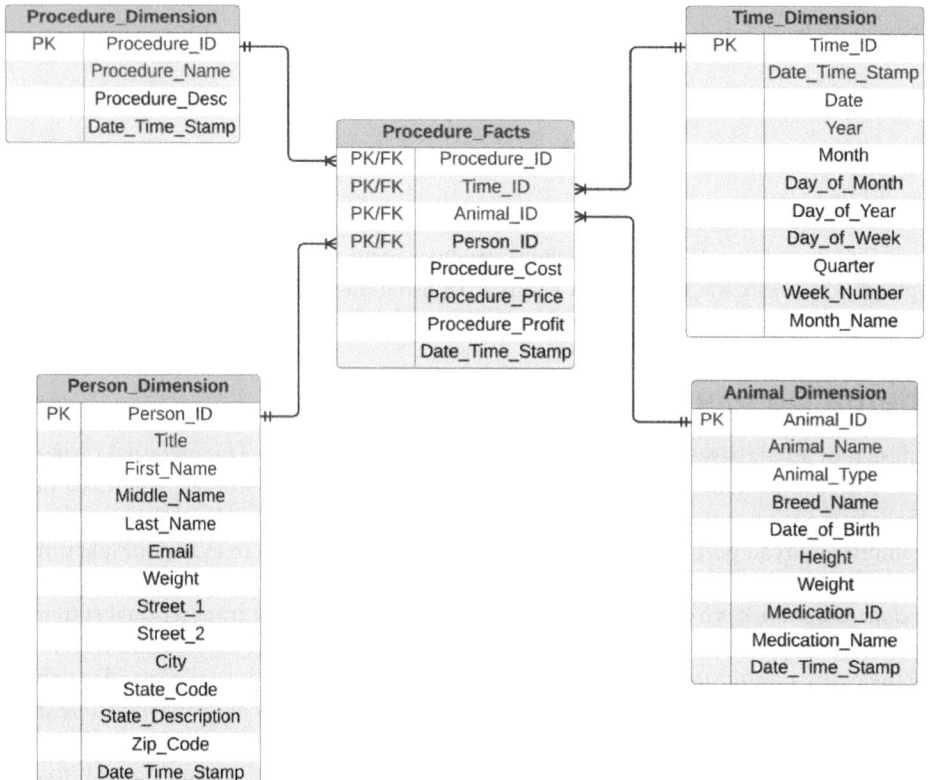

procedure name. The Time_Dimension is unique in that it makes it easy to look at profitability by day of week, quarter, month, or any other time-related attribute.

With a fact table surrounded by dimension tables, the queries to answer questions are simple to write and understand. Suppose you want to understand the aggregate cost of all procedures performed on dogs. In Figure 4.21, the OLTP Query shows how to answer that question using the transactional schema from Figure 4.14. The Star Schema Query provides the same answer, using the schema in Figure 4.20.

Even if you have never seen SQL before, you can appreciate that the four INNER JOIN statements in the OLTP Query indicate that you need five tables to get the result. In contrast, the single INNER JOIN in the Star Schema Query requires two tables. Now imagine that you want to get procedure cost by animal type and ZIP code. Crafting that query using the schema in Figure 4.14 requires you to bring in the Person, PersonAddress, and Address tables. Using the star schema from Figure 4.20, you only need to add the Person_Dimension table.

FIGURE 4.21 OLTP and OLAP query example.

OLTP Query

```
Select SUM(procedure_cost)
FROM procedure
INNER JOIN appointmentprocedure
ON procedure.procedure_id = appointmentprocedure.procedure_id
INNER JOIN appointment
ON appointmentprocedure.appt_id = appointment.appt_id
INNER JOIN animalperson
ON appointment.anmlpers_id = animalperson.anmlpers_id
INNER JOIN animal
ON animalperson.animal_id = animal.animal_id
WHERE animal_type = 'Dog'
```

Star Schema Query

```
Select SUM(procedure_cost)
FROM procedure_facts
INNER JOIN animal_dimension
ON procedure_facts.animal_id = animal_dimension.animal.id
WHERE animal_type = 'Dog'
```

When data moves from an OLTP design into a star schema, there is a significant amount of data duplication. As such, a star schema consumes more space than its associated OLTP design to store the same data. These additional resource needs are one of the factors that makes data warehouses expensive to operate.

Snowflake

Another design pattern for data warehousing is the *snowflake schema*. As its name implies, the schema diagram looks like a snowflake. Snowflake and star schemas are conceptually similar in that they both have a central fact table surrounded by dimensions. Where the approaches differ is in the handling of dimensions. With a star, the dimension tables connect directly to the fact table. With a snowflake, dimensions have subcategories, which gives the snowflake design its shape. A snowflake schema is less denormalized than the star schema.

Recall that in a star schema, dimensions are one join away from the fact table. With a snowflake schema, you may need more than one join to get the data you are looking for. Consider the Day, Quarter, and State lookup tables in Figure 4.22. The data for State_Description is in the State table. In Figure 4.20, State_Description exists in the Person_Dimension.

Recall that as the number of tables in a schema grows, queries become more complicated. For example, suppose you want to get procedure cost on a quarter-by-quarter basis and include Quarter_Name in the output. Using a star schema, you need two tables to answer this question. With the snowflake from Figure 4.22, you need three.

A snowflake schema query is more complex than the equivalent query in a star schema. Part of the trade-off is that a snowflake schema requires less storage space than a star schema. Consider where State_Description exists in Figure 4.20 and Figure 4.22. When

FIGURE 4.22 Snowflake example.

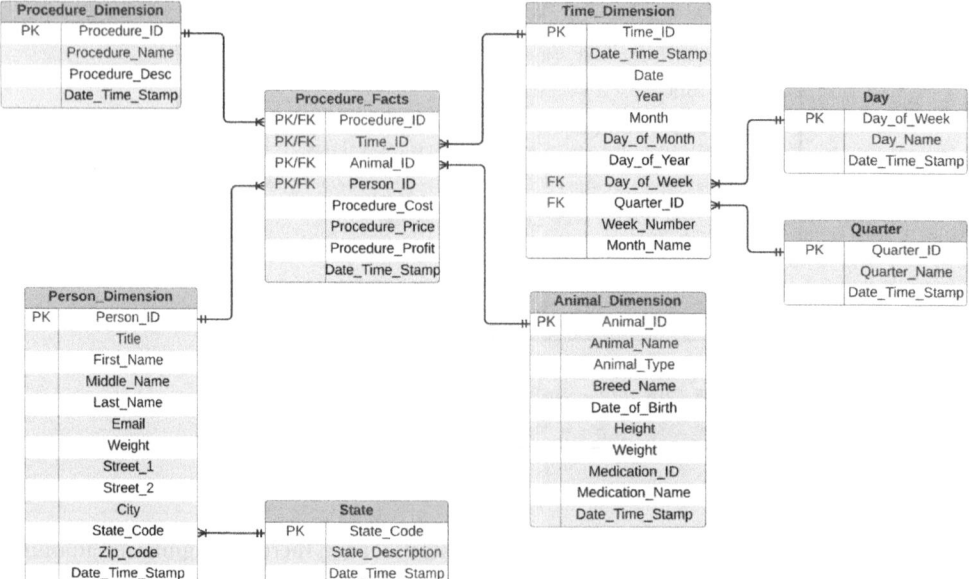

State_Description is in a separate lookup table, it also consumes much less storage space. Imagine that there are 1 billion rows in the Person_Dimension table. In a star schema, the State_Description is stored 1 billion times. With a snowflake schema, you only end up storing State_Description 50 times—once for each of the 50 U.S. states.

Data warehouses often use snowflake schemas, since many different systems supply data to the warehouse. Data marts are comparatively less complicated, because they represent a single data subject area. As such, data marts frequently use a star schema approach.

> **Exam Tip**
>
> As you prepare for the Data+ exam, keep in mind that the amount of storage a database needs decreases as a function of the degree of normalization. OLTP databases are highly normalized. Meanwhile, OLAP databases are denormalized and typically have greater storage requirements.

Dimensionality

Dimensionality refers to the number of attributes a table has. The greater the number of attributes, the higher the dimensionality. A *dimension table* provides additional context around data in fact tables. For example, consider the Person_Dimension table in Figure 4.22, which contains details about people. If you need additional data about people, add columns to Person_Dimension.

It is crucial to understand the types of questions an analyst will need to answer when designing dimension tables. For example, a vice president of sales may want to examine profitability by geographical region and time of year. They may want to zoom in and look at product sales by day to gauge the effectiveness of a marketing campaign. They may also want to better understand trends by product and product family.

One dimension you will frequently encounter is time. It is necessary to answer questions about when something happened or when something was true. For example, to understand historical profitability, you need to keep track of pricing at the product level over time. One way to accomplish this is to add a start and end date to each product's price.

Consider Table 4.5, reflecting the price history for a 17 mm socket in a product dimension table. This table illustrates one approach to handling time. The last price change went into effect on January 1, 2025. The value for this date goes in the End_Date column for the $7.39 price and the Start_Date column for the $6.29 price. With this approach, it is easy to identify a 17 mm socket price on any given day after its original on-sale date.

Imagine a time-specific dimension that allows grouping by various time increments, including the day of the year, day of the week, month, and quarter. Using timestamp data types for both the Start_Date and End_Date columns in Table 4.5 makes it easy to calculate the average price for all sockets regardless of the level of time detail.

One of the criteria to consider is how quickly a dimension changes over time. Consider a geographic dimension table containing the 50 U.S. states. Ever since Hawaii became the 50th state in 1959, the number of states has remained constant. Looking forward, it is unlikely that additional states will enter the union with great frequency. In this context, geography is an example of a *slowly changing dimension*. However, other geographic attributes change more quickly. For example, a person's street address is more likely to change than the number of states in the United States.

TABLE 4.5 Product Dimension

Product_ID	Product_Name	Price	Start_Date	End_Date
53	17 mm socket	5.48	1993-01-01 00:00:00	2003-01-01 00:00:00
53	17 mm socket	5.89	1998-01-01 00:00:00	2013-01-01 00:00:00
53	17 mm socket	5.99	2002-01-01 00:00:00	2020-05-03 00:00:00
53	17 mm socket	6.23	2010-05-03 00:00:00	2020-05-31 00:00:00
53	17 mm socket	8.59	2018-05-31 00:00:00	2020-10-31 00:00:00
53	17 mm socket	7.39	2022-10-31 00:00:00	2021-01-01 00:00:00
53	17 mm socket	6.29	2025-01-01 00:00:00	9999-12-31 23:59:59

Regardless of the speed at which a dimension changes, you need to handle both current and historical data.

Handling Dimensionality

There are multiple ways to design dimensions. Table 4.5 illustrates the start and end date approach. An understanding of this method is required to write a query to retrieve the current price. Another method extends the snowflake approach to modeling dimensions. You have a product dimension for the current price and a product history table for maintaining price history. One advantage of this approach is that it is easy to retrieve the current price while maintaining access to historical information.

Another approach is to use an indicator flag for the current price. This approach requires another column, as shown in Table 4.6. The indicator flag method keeps all pricing data in a single place. It also simplifies the query structure to get the current price. Instead of doing date math, you look for the price where the Current flag equals "Y."

It is also possible to use the effective date approach to handling price changes. Consider Table 4.7, which illustrates this approach. In the table, each row has the date on which the given price goes into effect. The assumption is that the price stays in effect until there is a price change, at which point a new row is added to the table.

There is additional complexity with the effective date approach because queries have to perform date math to determine the price. Looking at the table, the price of 8.59 went into effect on May 31, 2018. The price changes on October 31, 2022. To retrieve the price on

TABLE 4.6 Current Flag

Product_ID	Product_Name	Price	Start_Date	End_Date	Current
53	17 mm socket	8.59	2018-05-31 00:00:00	2020-10-31 00:00:00	N
53	17 mm socket	7.39	2022-10-31 00:00:00	2021-01-01 00:00:00	N
53	17 mm socket	6.29	2025-01-01 00:00:00	9999-12-31 23:59:59	Y

TABLE 4.7 Effective Date

Product_ID	Product_Name	Price	Effective_Date
53	17 mm socket	8.59	2018-05-31 00:00:00
53	17 mm socket	7.39	2022-10-31 00:00:00
53	17 mm socket	6.29	2025-01-01 00:00:00

October 3, 2022, you know that October 3 falls after May 31 and before October 31. As such, the price on May 31 is current on October 3. While it is possible to code this logic in SQL, it complicates the queries.

Data Acquisition Concepts

To perform analytics, you need data. Data can come from internal systems you operate, or you can obtain it from third-party sources. Regardless of where data originates, you need to get data before analyzing it to derive additional value. This section explores methods for integrating data from systems you own. It also explore strategies for collecting data from external systems.

Integration

Data from transactional systems flow into data warehouses and data marts for analysis. Recall that OLTP and OLAP databases have different internal structures. You need to retrieve, reshape, and insert data to move data between operational and analytical environments. You can use a variety of methods to transfer data efficiently and effectively.

One approach is known as *extract, transform, and load* (ETL). As the name implies, this method consists of three phases.

- **Extract:** In the first phase, you extract data from the source system and place it in a staging area. The goal of the extract phase is to move data from a relational database into a plain text file, or flat file, as quickly as possible.
- **Transform:** The second phase transforms the data. The goal is to reformat the data from its transactional structure to the data warehouse's analytical design.
- **Load:** The purpose of the load phase is to ensure data gets into the analytical system as quickly as possible.

Extract, load, and transform (ELT) is a variant of ETL. With ELT, data is extracted from a source database and loaded directly into the data warehouse. Once the extract and load phases are complete, the transformation phase gets under way. One key difference between ETL and ELT is the technical component performing the transformation. With ETL, the data transformation takes place external to a relational database, using a programming language like Python. ELT uses SQL and the power of a relational database to reformat the data.

ELT has an advantage in the speed with which data moves from the operational to the analytical database. Suppose you need to get massive amounts of transactional data into an analytical environment as quickly as possible. In that case, ELT is a good choice, especially when the data warehouse has a lot of hardware capacity. Whether you choose ETL or ELT is a function of organizational need, staff capabilities, and technical strategy.

> **ETL Vendors**
>
> Whether you choose ETL or ELT for loading your data warehouse, you don't have to write transformations by hand. Many products support both ETL and ELT. Before you pick one, carefully evaluate the available free and paid options to determine the one that best fits your needs and system architecture goals.

An *initial load* occurs the first time data is put into a data warehouse. After that initial load, each additional load is a *delta load*, also known as an *incremental load*. A delta load only moves changes between systems. Figure 4.23 illustrates a data warehouse that launches in January and uses a monthly delta load cycle. The initial load happens right before the data warehouse becomes available for use. All of the transactional data from January becomes the delta load that initiates on the first of February. Figure 4.23 illustrates a monthly delta-load approach that continues throughout the year.

The frequency with which delta loads happen depends on business requirements. Depending on how fresh the data needs to be, delta loads can happen at any interval. Hourly, daily, and weekly refreshes are typical.

When moving data between systems, you have to balance the speed and complexity of the overall operation. Suppose you operate nationally within the United States and start processing transactions at 7 in the morning and finish by 7 in the evening. The 12 hours between 7 p.m. and 7 a.m. represent the *batch window*, or time period available, to move data into your data warehouse. The duration of a batch window must be taken into account when designing a delta load strategy.

> **Exam Tip**
>
> You need to understand the time available for performing delta loads into your data warehouse. Regardless of how long your batch window is, think carefully about moving current data into the data warehouse without losing history.

FIGURE 4.23 Delta load example.

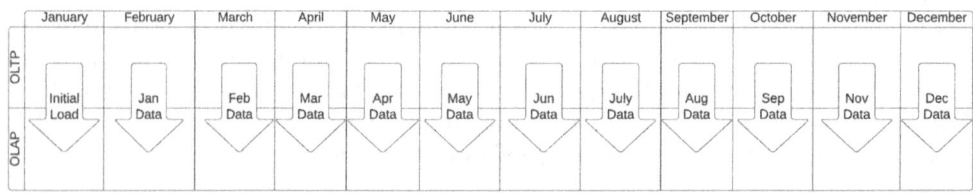

Data Sources and Collection Methods

Data is the lifeblood of every organization, whether an organization realizes it or not. City planners need data about traffic flow to inform road improvement projects. Airlines need data about the status of their aircraft to stage replacement parts at the appropriate repair facilities. Online retailers use search and purchase data to inform inventory levels and product recommendations. Insurance companies incorporate claim and weather data to develop pricing models for insurance premiums.

Organizations use internal and external data sources to improve overall analytical capabilities. For example, suppose you work in the analytics department for MotoWanderer, a national provider of motorcycle rentals. The Chief Operations Officer asks whether there is a need to rebalance the motorcycle fleet across MotoWanderer's existing locations. Meanwhile, the Chief Executive Officer wants to evaluate whether expanding to a new geographic region is profitable, and the head of internal logistics wants to predict the best time, place, and type of motorcycle to add to the fleet.

Internal databases are an excellent place to start when analyzing how to grow MotoWanderer's business. While starting with internal data about your motorcycle fleet, customers, and rental history, augmenting this internal data can improve analytical accuracy. Additional data you may wish to obtain includes weather data, tourism patterns, and competitors in the motorcycle rental business. This extra data can come from various sources, including federal and state open data portals, other public data sources, and private purveyors of data.

Application Programming Interfaces (APIs)

An *application programming interface (API)* is a structured method for computer systems to exchange information. APIs provide a consistent interface to calling applications, regardless of the internal database structure. APIs hide *how* they accomplish their given piece of business logic so calling applications can focus on *what* data the API provides. Since APIs abstract the underlying datastore from the calling application, applications frequently use APIs as a data source. From a data structure and storage perspective, some APIs serve data from transactional databases, while others use analytical data stores. The internal data structure does not matter as long as the API returns the appropriate data to the calling system. APIs can be transactional, returning data as JSON objects. APIs can also facilitate bulk data extraction, returning CSV files.

APIs represent a specific piece of business functionality. Let's return to the motorcycle rental business. Say one of MotoWanderer's repeat customers logs into the company's website. The web application personalizes the customer experience by using an internal database to retrieve the customer's profile information, including their name and most frequently visited locations. The MotoWanderer organization wants the same profile information available to customer service agents in its call center to provide excellent customer service.

In Figure 4.24, both the web application and the call center application directly access the corporate database with SQL. Duplicating the same code across multiple systems makes maintenance a challenge. When the SQL needs updating, it must happen in two places.

FIGURE 4.24 Direct database access.

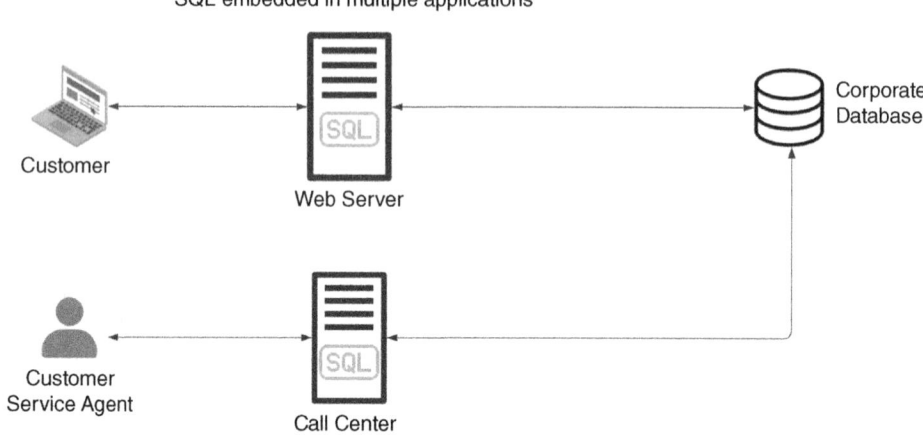

Figure 4.25 illustrates the benefits of using an API. Instead of directly embedding SQL in separate applications, you place it within a single GetProfile API. Centralizing the profile retrieval logic provides consistent customer profile information to any calling application. You can easily connect the API to the customer-facing web server and internal-facing call center application. When MotoWanderer wants to improve the in-store customer experience by getting employees access to customer profile information, all it has to do is connect the in-store application to the GetProfile API.

Web Services

Many smartphone applications need a network connection, either cellular or Wi-Fi, to work correctly. Smartphones need network connections because much of the data these applications need is not on the smartphone itself. Instead, data is found in private and public data sources and is accessible via a *web service*. A web service is an API you can call via *Hypertext Transfer Protocol* (HTTP), the language of the web.

While a web service is an API, an API does not have to be a web service. Consider the call center application from Figure 4.25. Suppose that instead of being accessible via a web browser, you need to install the application on each customer service agent's computer, the same way you install Microsoft Excel or PowerPoint. In this case, it is likely that the application accesses the API directly using a private network connection, not as a web service.

Suppose you want to get weather-related data. The National Centers for Environmental Information (NCEI) is a U.S. federal agency within the National Oceanic and Atmospheric Administration (NOAA) office. The NCEI is an authoritative source for weather data. It makes that data publicly available via a web service–enabled API.

FIGURE 4.25 Database access with an API.

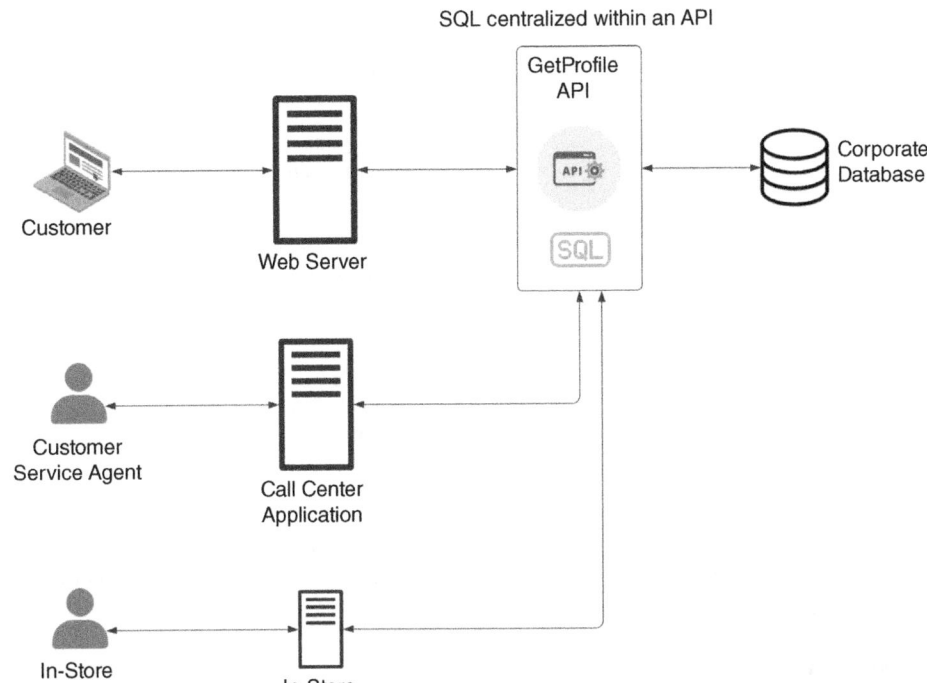

Many APIs, like those from the NCEI, require an *API key*. If you imagine an API as the door behind which data treasures exist, an API key is what unlocks the door. API providers generate a unique API key for each calling application. Centralized creation and distribution of API keys allow the provider to understand who is using the API and to turn off individual keys' access in the event of abuse.

Open data providers like NCEI make API keys available for free. You register for an API using an email address. After registering, you receive your unique API key in an email. Other data purveyors charge for API access. For example, Google has excellent APIs for static and dynamic map information. In addition to having to register for an API, you incur a nominal charge for each API call. The more you use an API, the more you have to pay. Other API providers take a tiered approach, where you get a limited number of API calls for free, after which you have to pay.

If you own a smartphone, most applications on your phone require data from an external system to function. For example, in the United States, weather data may come from the National Oceanic and Atmospheric Administration. In Europe, the European Centre for Medium-Range Weather Forecasts provides weather data, while the India Meteorological Department makes weather data available in India. In your weather application, if you

FIGURE 4.26 Weather API example.

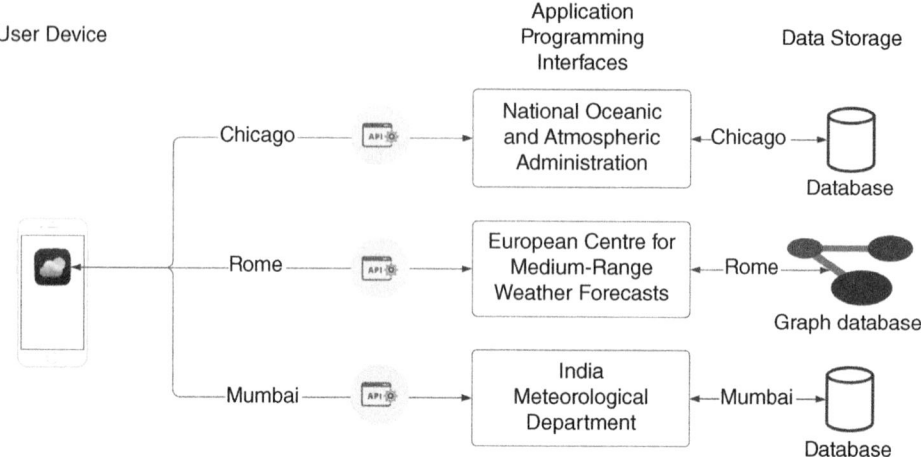

include Chicago, Rome, and Mumbai in your list of favorite cities, you are effectively sourcing weather data from multiple data brokers. Figure 4.26 illustrates how the weather application on a smartphone retrieves data from multiple weather data providers.

Web Scraping

Some of the data you want may not be available internally as an API or publicly via a web service. However, data may exist on a website. As shown in Chapter 2, data can present itself in an HTML table on a web page. If data exists in a structured format, you can retrieve it programmatically. Programmatic retrieval of data from a website is known as *web scraping*.

You can use software bots to scrape data from a website. Many modern programming languages, including Python and R, make it easy to create a web scraper. Instead of using an API or a web service, a web scraper reads a web page similar to a browser, such as Chrome, Safari, or Edge. Web scrapers read and parse the HTML to extract the web page's data.

The search results for some websites span multiple web pages. Your web scraper has to account for pagination to ensure that you are not leaving any data behind. The scraper must understand how many result pages exist and then iterate through them to harvest the data.

 Remember that programmatically scraping a website may violate its terms of service. If you persist in programmatically collecting data in violation of a website's terms, the website provider may block your ability to access the site.

Files

Files are a common way to integrate systems and obtain data. In Chapter 3, "Understanding Data," you explored various types of files. Many systems offer the option to export data as a CSV file due to the simplicity with which a CSV represents rows and columns and how easy it is to load the data from a CSV file into a database table. In the United States, Data.gov (https://data.gov) makes more than 250,000 datasets available for public use, and the Bureau of Labor and Statistics (BLS) makes economic data available (https://www.bls.gov). You can retrieve data from Data.gov or the BLS in various file formats. CSV, XLS, and JSON are among the most common formats.

Files are also a common way to integrate external systems. For example, suppose a company outsources its payroll processing. Instead of having a direct connection between the payroll processing provider and the company's internal payroll system, a much more common design pattern is to generate a file and securely transmit it to the payroll processor.

One thing to remember about files is that they do not contain data types. The receiving system is responsible for determining the appropriate data type. For example, consider the animal data from Table 4.1. A CSV representation of the first two lines looks like this:

```
Animal_ID,Animal_Name,Animal_Type,Breed_Name,Date_of_Birth,
Height,Weight 1,Jake,Dog,Corgi,3/2/2018,10,26.3
```

If you receive this data in CSV form, you need to specify the data type for each field in the file. For example, computing the average weight becomes challenging if you store the Weight column as character data. Since aggregation functions typically operate on numeric data, you must convert the data from character to numeric to compute the average weight.

Logs

Log files are another common source of data. Servers generate internal log files documenting system access and other operational health details. Every time a person visits a website, the web server makes an entry in its local log file, including:

- **Date and time:** Date and time the request was made.
- **Internet protocol address (IP address):** The IP address of the calling client.
- **Request method:** The HTTP method used in the request, with GET, POST and PUT among the most common.
- **URL/PATH:** The URL or path requested by the client, typically the name of a web page or an artifact on the web page, like a CSV file.
- **HTTP status code:** The status code returned by the web server. Some of the most common statuses include success, failure, permission denied, and file not found.
- **Bytes sent:** The response size from the server to the client, in bytes.
- **User-agent:** Details about the client's browser and operating system

Web server logs help answer compelling questions for an organization. For instance, when a retailer wants to understand if an email campaign succeeded in driving traffic to their website, they aggregate the number of log entries within a specific date and time window. To better connect with customers and tailor the design of specific advertisements, advertising agencies use the User-Agent log entry to learn about the types of devices their customers use. From an operational standpoint, system administrators monitor unsuccessful HTTP status codes to check for references to retired pages.

Log files represent a treasure trove of data. As with CSV files, log files don't specify data types. Fortunately, many open-source and commercially available packages help analyze web logs. If you're a Python programmer and want to prepare log files for ongoing analysis, Lars is a Python framework for loading web server logs into relational databases. Nagios is an open-source package that analyzes logs, and SolarWinds offers a paid software package that centralizes log data for ongoing analysis.

Data Repositories

Before analyzing the data within files and log files, you must first preprocess the files to transform the data so it's ready for analysis. After conversion, it is common to combine this log data with other data sources to conduct ongoing analysis. Organizations frequently have multiple internal data repositories that store data in preparation for analysis.

Data Silos

A *data silo* is a repository of data controlled by one department or organization that is isolated from other parts of the organization. This data is typically not easily accessible to others outside that specific group, which creates barriers to sharing and analyzing information across teams. Figure 4.27 illustrates two operational systems for an airline. The first system contains loyalty information about the airline's customers, while the second system handles flight reservations. For this example, presume both databases are data silos, only accessible by their respective teams.

FIGURE 4.27   Database with overlapping content.

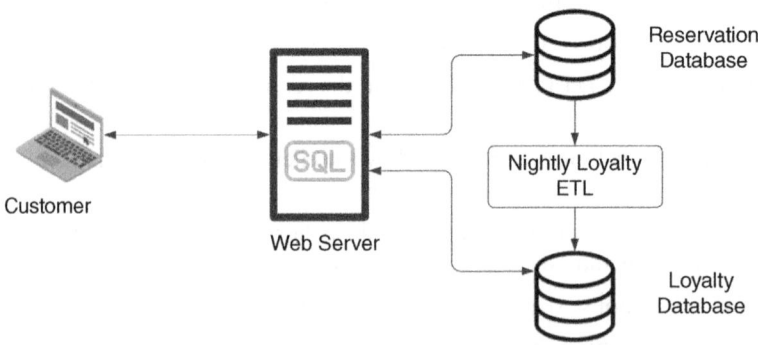

Customer reservation information, including name, address, date of birth, origin, and destination, all exist in the Reservation database. Customer information, including name, address, and date of birth, also exists in the Loyalty database.

The airline determines loyalty status using attributes including the number of flight segments, total distance traveled, and ticket value. As these attributes exist in the Reservation database, a nightly ETL job updates the Loyalty database. While it is crucial to appropriately calculate a customer's loyalty score, having customer information in two separate databases illustrates another data silo challenge: duplicate data.

Suppose a customer updates her home address when making a reservation. Since the Loyalty database still contains the old home address, the airline must update the ETL process to include address data. However, it's also possible for a customer to update address information in the Loyalty database. Having the customer's address information in two data silos complicates the operational situation, as the airline needs to implement business logic to determine the source of truth for customer address information, then propagate that new address information to the other system.

Integrating the Reservation and Loyalty databases reduces the complexity of this situation. You can consolidate common attributes, like name and address, into a single set of tables. Instead of independent data silos, you end up efficiently storing common attributes in a single location.

Data Warehouses

A *data warehouse* is a database containing data from many transactional systems for analytical purposes. Transactional data may come from the independent systems that power a company's human resources, sales, marketing, and product divisions. Since transactional systems have tables optimized for transaction processing, ETL or ELT jobs transform and reshape transactional data for loading into the warehouse.

Figure 4.28 illustrates the flow of data from transactional systems into a data warehouse. Data from the Reservation and Loyalty databases flows through an ELT process for transformation on the way into the warehouse. For illustrative purposes, Aircraft Maintenance, Customer Support, and Customer Relationship Management data also flows through an ETL process.

The frequency of ELT and ETL jobs depends on business requirements. For example, reservation analysts need reservation data that is as close to real-time as possible. Meanwhile, analysts working on a predictive model to determine the location and quantity of spare aircraft parts can work with data that is 24 hours old. Therefore, the Reservation ELT job must run as frequently as possible while the Aircraft Maintenance ETL runs once daily.

A data warehouse facilitates analytics across the entire company. Once in the warehouse, analysts use tools like Tableau and Looker to develop insights from the data.

Data Marts

A *data mart* is a subset of a data warehouse. Data warehouses serve the entire organization, whereas data marts focus on the needs of a particular department. Data marts have a similar internal table structure to data warehouses. For example, suppose an organization wants to

FIGURE 4.28 Data warehouse.

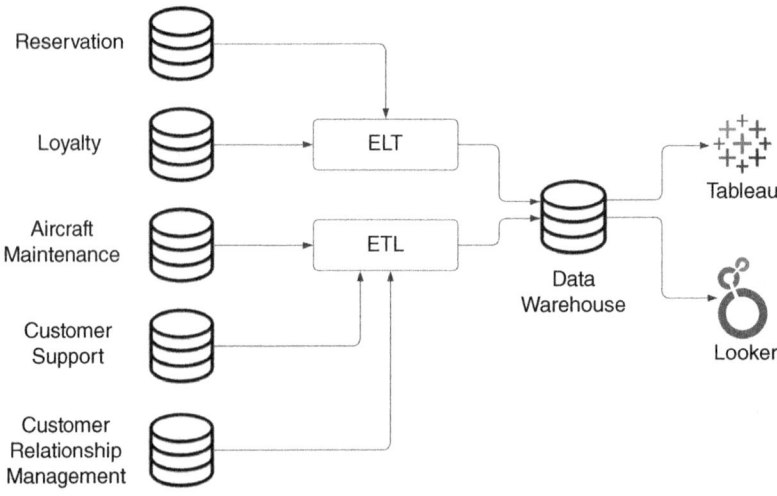

FIGURE 4.29 Data mart.

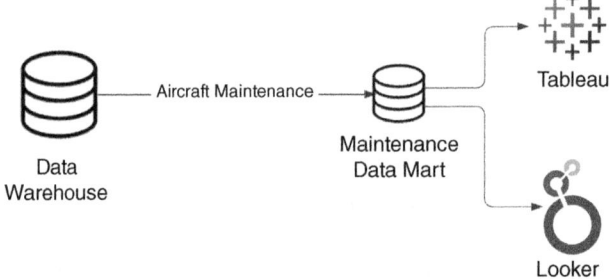

analyze its employees to understand retention and career evolution trends. To satisfy that use case, you can create a data mart focusing on the human resources subject area from the data warehouse.

In the airline example, consider the analysts working on the placement and timing of spare parts. Reservation, Loyalty, Customer Support, and Customer Relationship Management data do not inform this analysis. Figure 4.29 illustrates a Maintenance Data Mart using Aircraft Maintenance data from the data warehouse.

For data warehouses and data marts, several design patterns exist for modeling data. It is crucial to realize that the structure of a database schema impacts how you analyze its contents. An efficient database structure is particularly important as data volumes grow. In addition to a schema's design, it is essential to consider the data lifecycle. Lifecycle considerations include where data comes from, how frequently it changes, and how long it needs to persist.

Data Lakes

A *data lake* stores raw data in its native format instead of transforming it for storage in a database. Data lakes can contain images and other unstructured data. Semi-structured data, like JSON documents, can also be found in a data lake. Data lakes can also include highly structured data.

Data lakes are helpful for machine learning and data science in big data environments. Using a data lake is more complex than a data warehouse or data mart, as it requires additional knowledge about the raw data to make it analytically useful. Applications and relational databases enforce a structure that encapsulates business rules and business logic, both of which are missing in a data lake.

Following the airline example, suppose that in addition to structured data from internal systems, the airline captures audio recordings from its call center, social media interactions, and customer reviews. Instead of processing and transforming all this data into a data warehouse, the airline stores it in a data lake. This raw data is then available for various teams to analyze as needed. For example, the marketing team might analyze social media and reservation data to understand customer preferences, while the IT team may use log data to identify potential security risks.

The data lake allows each department to access relevant information in its raw form, providing a single, flexible repository that supports multiple analytics needs across the organization.

Data Lakehouses

A *data lakehouse* combines the data lake storage with a data warehouse's structured management aspects. A data lakehouse handles structured and unstructured data, allowing for large-scale data processing and analytics while maintaining data conforming to data governance policies.

Data lakehouses overcome the limitations of data lakes and data warehouses by providing a single platform for storing and analyzing data, regardless of its format. Recall that data lakes store raw data and lack the context that the originating applications and databases provide, while a data warehouse doesn't contain unstructured or semi-structured data. A data lakehouse is a best-of-both-worlds approach, combining the ability to analyze raw and structured data while supporting business intelligence tools like Tableau.

Continuing the airline example, the airline uses structured reservation records, semi-structured survey response data, and unstructured call center recordings to develop a comprehensive customer analytics solution. The airline stores all this data in one place using a data lakehouse. The lakehouse facilitates traditional analytics, like generating reports on customer reservation history. The lakehouse also supports machine learning, such as performing sentiment analysis on call center interactions.

Human-in-the-Loop

There are times when the data you seek exists only in people's minds. For example, you can extract the most popular and profitable motorcycling destination from your existing internal data. You can get weather information from an API packaged as a web service. You can glean insight into competitive pricing by scraping your competitors' websites. Even with all

FIGURE 4.30 Single question survey.

of these data sources, you may still want insight into how customers feel about the services you provide.

Surveys

One way to collect data directly from your customers is by conducting a *survey*. The most simplistic surveys consist of one question and indicate customer satisfaction. For example, Figure 4.30 illustrates a survey collection approach in the airline industry. As people board their aircraft, they walk past a small machine with two buttons on it. In response to the question, the people press either the happy face or the unhappy face. Although single-question surveys don't provide any depth as to why people feel positively or negatively, they provide an overall indicator of satisfaction.

Surveys can be much more complicated than a single question. For example, suppose you want a comprehensive understanding of customer satisfaction. In that case, you design a sophisticated survey that presents people with different questions depending on their answers. Complex survey logic lets you gather additional detail as to why a person has a particular opinion.

You can design surveys to achieve your data collection goals and your audience. You can tailor a survey to collect data on how your employees feel about the effectiveness of their manager, or more broadly, about your organization's approach to pay and benefits. You may want feedback on a customer appreciation event or training session. As long as you know the objective of a survey, you can design one to accomplish your goals.

As you can imagine, survey design is an entire discipline, and question design significantly impacts the quality of data the survey obtains. As you design a survey, you want to keep in mind how you will analyze the data you collect. Numeric data is easy to analyze using a variety of statistical methods. Free-response questions result in unstructured text data, which is more challenging to interpret. You need to clearly understand what is essential to your organization and what decisions you will make using the output to develop and administer an impactful survey.

Survey Tools

Instead of designing a custom application to collect survey data, several survey products let you design complex surveys without worrying about building a database. Qualtrics is a powerful tool for developing and administering surveys. Figure 4.31 shows what it is like to build a survey in Qualtrics.

FIGURE 4.31 Qualtrics survey build.

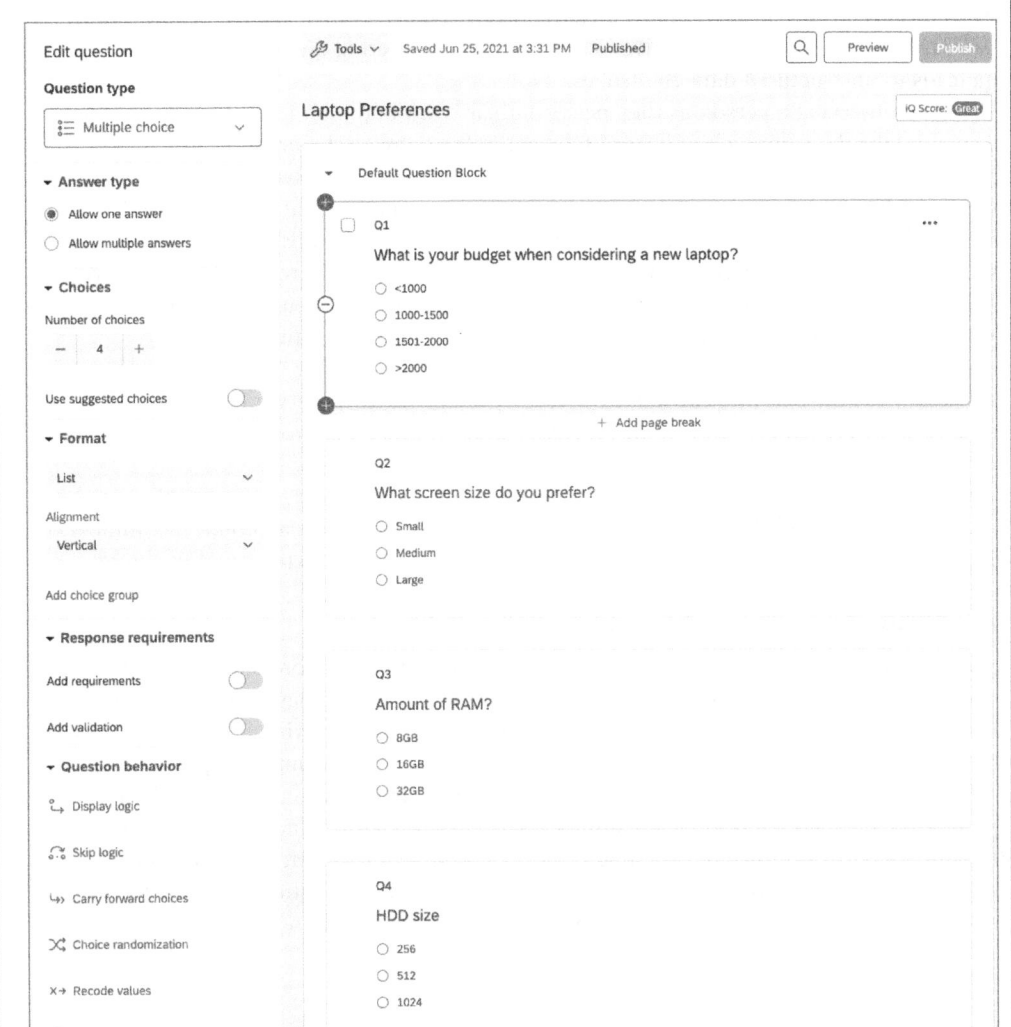

What makes Qualtrics so compelling is its API, which you can use to integrate survey response data into a data warehouse for additional analysis.

Observation

Observation is the act of collecting primary source data, from either people or machines. Observational data can be qualitative or quantitative. Collecting qualitative observational data leads to unstructured data challenges.

Imagine observing a person as they perform their work and interact with their colleagues. When you take this approach, it is hard to account for nonverbal communication. You also may struggle to collect data about what people do subconsciously. Returning to the motorcycle rental business, imagine a mechanic going through a post-rental examination. He may augment the post-ride checklist with his experience and intuition. For example, he may decide to change the brake pads and tighten the clutch lever if he perceives the motorcycle was subject to abuse. That may lead him to intuitively look at particular areas of the vehicle for indications of abuse before signing off on the security deposit return.

Asking someone to write down everything they do or the number of times they do something can introduce bias into the data. Developing methods for observation is one way to record what is happening in an environment accurately. Of course, you need to account for the bias of the observer.

Quantitative observations are much easier to collect and interpret. For example, suppose you are trying to establish the defect rate on a production line. You can count the number of vehicles that come off the line, as well as how many fail post-production quality checks.

Sampling

Regardless of the data acquisition approach, you may end up with more data than is practical to manipulate. Imagine you are doing analytics in an Internet-of-Things environment, in which 800 billion events occur daily. Though it is possible, ingesting and storing 800 billion records is a challenging task. Manipulating 800 billion records takes a lot of computing power.

Suppose you want to analyze one day's worth of data. In that case, the 800 billion records represent the total *population*, or the number of events, available. Since manipulating 800 billion records is unwieldy, you might collect a *sample*, or subset, of the overall population. Once you have collected sample data, you can use statistical methods to make generalizations about the entire population. For more detail on these methods, see Chapter 6, "Data Analysis and Statistics."

Working with Data

Determining an appropriate database structure, identifying data sources, and loading a database takes a considerable amount of effort. To turn a database design into an operational database ready to accept data, you use the *Data Definition Language* (*DDL*) components of SQL. DDL lets you create, modify, and delete tables and other associated database objects.

With all of that work complete, the foundation is in place to derive impactful insights. To generate insights, a productive analyst must be comfortable using the *Data Manipulation*

Language (*DML*) capabilities of SQL to insert, modify, and retrieve information from databases. While DDL manages the structure of a database, DML manages the data in the database.

The DML components of SQL change very slowly. As long as relational databases exist, you will need to understand SQL to work with them. It is worth learning SQL, as the foundational knowledge of DML operations will serve you well.

Data Manipulation

When manipulating data, one of four possible actions occurs:

- Create new data.
- Read existing data.
- Update existing data.
- Delete existing data.

The acronym *CRUD* (*Create, Read, Update, Delete*) is a handy way to remember these four operations.

SQL uses verbs to identify the type of activity a specific statement performs. For each CRUD activity, there is a corresponding DML verb, as Table 4.8 illustrates. These verbs are known as *keywords*, or words that are part of the SQL language itself.

Reading and manipulating data is commonplace on the path to creating insights. To that end, the focus here is on options that affect reading data. Before jumping in, it is helpful to understand the syntax of a query.

Figure 4.32 illustrates the basic structure of a SQL query that reads from a database. SELECT, FROM, and WHERE are all reserved words that have specific meaning in SQL.

TABLE 4.8 Data Manipulation in SQL

Operation	SQL Keyword	Description
Create	INSERT	Creates new data in an existing table
Read	SELECT	Retrieves data from an existing table
Update	UPDATE	Changes existing data in an existing table
Delete	DELETE	Removes existing data from an existing table

FIGURE 4.32 SQL SELECT statement.

```
SELECT  <what>
FROM    <source>
```

The SELECT clause identifies the columns from the table(s) that are retrieved. If you want to list the name and animal type from Table 4.1, the SELECT portion of the query will look like this:

```
SELECT Animal_Name
      ,Breed_Name
```

The FROM clause in a query identifies the source of data, which is frequently a database table. Both the SELECT and FROM clauses are required for a SQL statement to return data, as follows:

```
SELECT Animal_Name
      ,Breed_Name
FROM   Animal
```

As the queries in Figure 4.21 illustrate, it is possible to specify more than one location for data by joining tables together.

SQL Considerations

The keywords in SQL are case-insensitive. However, the case-sensitivity of column names and values depends on the database configuration.

Consider the following query:

```
Select Animal_Name, Breed_Name from Animal
```

The previous query returns the same results as this query:

```
SELECT Animal_Name, Breed_Name FROM Animal
```

SQL can also span multiple lines. For example, rewriting the previous query as follows will return identical results:

```
SELECT Animal_Name
      ,Breed_Name
FROM   Animal
```

How a query appears is a function of organizational conventions. Factors that influence convention include database configuration, query efficiency, and how easy it is for people to read and understand the query.

Two dashes next to each other denote a comment in SQL. A database doesn't evaluate any text after two dashes. Consider the following query:

```
SELECT Animal_Name  -- column for animal name
      ,Breed_Name   -- column for animal breed
FROM   Animal       -- name of the table
```

> The text after the two dashes are comments that improve the readability of SQL code. While not necessary for such a simple query, comments provide valuable context when working with complex queries.

Filtering

Examining a large table in its entirety provides insight into the overall population. To answer questions that an organization's leadership has typically requires a subset of the overall data. Filtering is a way to reduce the data down to only the rows that you need.

One way to filter data is with the DISTINCT clause within a SELECT statement to retrieve unique values from a column. For example, Table 4.1 has eight rows but only two animal types. By adding a DISTINCT to the SELECT clause, the result set would contain one row for cat and another for dog:

```
SELECT DISTINCT Animal_Type
FROM   Animal
```

To filter data, you add a WHERE clause to a query. Note that the column you are filtering on does not have to appear in the SELECT clause. To retrieve the name and breed for only the dogs from Table 4.1, you modify the query as follows:

```
SELECT Animal_Name
      ,Breed_Name
FROM   Animal
WHERE  Animal_Type = 'Dog'
```

Filtering and Logical Operators

A query can have multiple filtering conditions. You need to use a logical operator to account for complex filtering needs. For example, suppose you need to retrieve the name and breed for dogs weighing more than 60 pounds. In that case, you can enhance the query using the AND logical operator, as follows:

```
SELECT Animal_Name
      ,Breed_Name
FROM   Animal
WHERE  Animal_Type = 'Dog'
AND    Weight > 60
```

The AND operator evaluates the Animal_Type and Weight filters together, only returning records that match both criteria. OR is another frequently used logical operator. For example, suppose you want to see the name and breed for all dogs and any animals that weigh more than ten pounds regardless of the animal type. The following query delivers the answer to that question:

```
SELECT Animal_Name
      ,Breed_Name
```

```
FROM     Animal
WHERE    Animal_Type = 'Dog'
OR       Weight > 10
```

Complex queries frequently use multiple logical operators at the same time. It is good to use parentheses around filter conditions to help make queries easy for people to read and understand.

Data warehouses often contain millions, billions, or even trillions of individual data records. Filtering data is essential to making effective use of these massive data stores.

Sorting

When querying a database, you frequently specify the order in which you want your results to return. The ORDER BY clause is the component of a SQL query that makes sorting possible. Similar to how the WHERE clause performs, you do not have to specify the columns you are using to sort the data in the SELECT clause.

For example, suppose you want to retrieve the animal and breed for dogs over 60 pounds, with the oldest dog listed first. The following query delivers the answer:

```
SELECT    Animal_Name
          ,Breed_Name
FROM      Animal
WHERE     Animal_Type = 'Dog'
AND       Weight > 60
ORDER BY  Date_of_Birth ASC
```

If you want to return the youngest dog first, you change the ORDER BY clause as follows:

```
SELECT    Animal_Name
          ,Breed_Name
FROM      Animal
WHERE     Animal_Type = 'Dog'
AND       Weight > 60
ORDER BY  Date_of_Birth DESC
```

The ASC keyword at the end of the ORDER BY clause sorts in ascending order, whereas using DESC with ORDER BY sorts in descending order. If you are sorting on multiple columns, you can use both ascending and descending as appropriate. Both the ASC and DESC keywords work across various data types, including date, alphanumeric, and numeric.

Date Functions

As seen in Table 4.5 and Table 4.6, date columns are frequently found in OLAP environments. Date columns also appear in transactional systems. Storing date information about an event facilitates analysis across time. For example, you may be interested in first-quarter sales performance or outstanding receivables on a rolling 60-day basis. Fortunately, there is an abundance of functions that make working with dates easy.

The most important thing to note is that you have to understand the database platform you are using and how that platform handles dates and times. Since each platform provider uses different data types for handling this information, you need to familiarize yourself with the functions available from your provider of choice.

Logical Functions

Logical functions can make data substitutions when retrieving data. Remember that a SELECT statement only retrieves data. The data in the underlying tables does not change when a SELECT runs. Consider Table 4.9, which enhances Table 4.1 by adding a Sex column. Looking at the values for Sex, you can see that this column contains code values. To understand the description for each code value in a sound relational model, the Sex column from Table 4.9 is a foreign key pointing to the Sex column in Table 4.10.

Suppose you want to retrieve the name and sex description for each animal, as Table 4.11 illustrates. One way to accomplish this is by joining the two tables together, retrieving the Animal_Name from Table 4.9 and Sex_Description from Table 4.10.

TABLE 4.9 Augmented Animal Data

Animal_ID	Animal_Name	Animal_Type	Breed_Name	Sex	Date_of_Birth	Height (Inches)	Weight (Pounds)
1	Jack	Dog	Corgi	M	3/2/2018	10	26.3
2	Viking	Dog	Husky	M	5/8/2017	24	58
3	Hazel	Dog	Labradoodle	F	7/3/2016	23	61
4	Schooner	Dog	Labrador Retriever	M	8/14/2019	24.3	74.4
5	Skippy	Dog	Weimaraner	F	10/3/2018	26.3	64.5
6	Alexander	Cat	American Shorthair	M	10/4/2017	9.3	10.4
7	Éowyn	Cat	American Shorthair	F	5/22/2024	8.4	8.8
8	Euclid	Cat	American Shorthair	M	4/3/2020	9	10

TABLE 4.10 Sex Lookup Table

Sex	Sex_Description
M	Male
F	Female

TABLE 4.11   Desired Query Results

Animal_Name	Sex
Jack	Male
Viking	Male
Hazel	Female
Schooner	Male
Skippy	Female
Alexander	Male
Éowyn	Female
Euclid	Male

When writing SQL, there are frequently many ways to write a query and create the same results. Another way to generate the output in Table 4.10 is by using the `IFF` logical function. The `IFF` function has the following syntax:

`IFF(boolean_expression, true_value, false_value)`

As you can see from the syntax, the `IFF` function expects the following three parameters:

- **Boolean expression:** The expression must return either TRUE or FALSE.
- **True value:** If the Boolean expression returns TRUE, the `IFF` function will return this value.
- **False value:** If the Boolean expression returns FALSE, the `IFF` function will return this value.

The following query, using the `IFF` function, generates the results in Table 4.11:

```
SELECT  Animal_Name
       ,IFF(Sex = 'M', 'Male', 'Female')
FROM    Animal
```

Note that with the `IFF` approach, the values for Male and Female come from the function parameters, not from the source table (see Table 4.9). Suppose the description in the underlying table gets modified. In that case, the results of the `IFF` query will not reflect the modified data.

Table 4.12 shows the results of the following query, which also uses the `IFF` function.

```
SELECT  Animal_Name
       ,IFF(Sex = 'M', 'Boy', 'Girl')
FROM    Animal
```

IFF is just one example of a logical function. When using logical functions, you need to balance their convenience with the knowledge that you are replacing data from the database with the function's coded values. The ability to do this type of substitution is a real asset when dividing data into categories.

Aggregate Functions

Summarized data helps answer questions that executives have, and aggregate functions are an easy way to summarize data. Aggregate functions summarize a query's data and return a single value. While each database platform supports different aggregation functions, Table 4.13 describes functions that are common across platforms. Be sure to familiarize yourself with the functions available in your platform of choice.

TABLE 4.12 Modified IFF Query Results

Animal_Name	Sex
Jack	Boy
Viking	Boy
Hazel	Girl
Schooner	Boy
Skippy	Girl
Alexander	Boy
Éowyn	Girl
Euclid	Boy

TABLE 4.13 Common SQL Aggregate Functions

Function	Purpose
COUNT	Returns the total number of rows of a query.
MIN	Returns the minimum value from the results of a query. Note that this works on both alphanumeric and numeric data types.
MAX	Returns the maximum value from the results of a query. Note that this works on both alphanumeric and numeric data types.
AVG	Returns the mathematic average of the results of a query.
SUM	Returns the sum of the results of a query.
STDDEV	Returns the sample standard deviation of the results of a query.

You can also use aggregate functions to filter data. For example, you may want a query that shows all employees who make less than the average corporate salary. Aggregate functions also operate across subsets of data. For instance, you can calculate total sales by month with a single query.

Concatenation

Concatenation is the merging of separate variables into a single variable. Concatenation is a highly effective technique when dealing with a source system that stores components of a single variable in multiple columns. The need for concatenation frequently occurs when dealing with date and time data. Concatenation is also useful when generating address information. For example, you want to send an email campaign using first and last names from independent columns. You can concatenate the first and last names together for use in the campaign.

Suppose you are working on aggregating temperature sensor data for the National Weather Service. On the left side of Figure 4.33 is a data sample from a North Kingston, Rhode Island, weather station. Note that the sensor stores the day, month, and year as individual numeric variables. You want to merge the day, month, and year into a single date variable to make it easier to use date functions in your analysis tools. Combining this data is straightforward, as programming languages, including SQL, Python, and R, have functions that make concatenation easy.

In SQL, concatenation happens as part of the SELECT clause. Depending on the database engine, the concatenation character is either the double pipe (||) or plus sign (+). For instance, Oracle uses the double pipe for concatenation, while Transact-SQL for Microsoft SQL Server uses the plus sign. In Oracle, the SQL statement that creates the concatenated data in Figure 4.33 looks like this:

```
SELECT  Reporting_Station
       ,Temperature
       ,Day || '/' || Month || '/' || Year
FROM    <Source Data>
```

Note that concatenation operations literally combine fields. Consider the data in Table 4.14, which consists of first and last names.

FIGURE 4.33 Creating a date variable with concatenation.

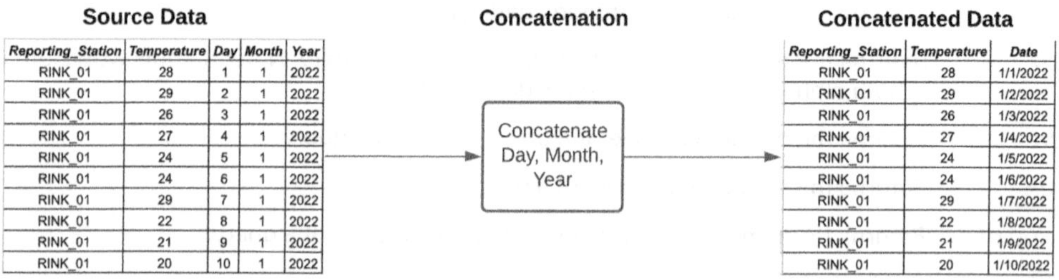

Source Data

Reporting_Station	Temperature	Day	Month	Year
RINK_01	28	1	1	2022
RINK_01	29	2	1	2022
RINK_01	26	3	1	2022
RINK_01	27	4	1	2022
RINK_01	24	5	1	2022
RINK_01	24	6	1	2022
RINK_01	29	7	1	2022
RINK_01	22	8	1	2022
RINK_01	21	9	1	2022
RINK_01	20	10	1	2022

Concatenation: Concatenate Day, Month, Year

Concatenated Data

Reporting_Station	Temperature	Date
RINK_01	28	1/1/2022
RINK_01	29	1/2/2022
RINK_01	26	1/3/2022
RINK_01	27	1/4/2022
RINK_01	24	1/5/2022
RINK_01	24	1/6/2022
RINK_01	29	1/7/2022
RINK_01	22	1/8/2022
RINK_01	21	1/9/2022
RINK_01	20	1/10/2022

TABLE 4.14 Name Table

First_Name	Last_Name
Basheer	Rossi
Enzo	Ivanac

Suppose you need to concatenate the first and last names as part of a mail merge and write the SQL statement as follows:

```
SELECT   First_Name || Last_Name AS FullName
FROM     Name_Table
```

Table 4.15 shows the result for this query:

The good thing about SQL is that it does precisely what you tell it to, which, in this case, is not what you intend. To get a space between the first and last name, you must add a space character as part of the concatenation in the SELECT:

```
SELECT   First_Name || ' ' || Last_Name AS FullName
FROM     Name_Table
```

This modified query would generate the desired result shown in Table 4.16.

TABLE 4.15 Concatenation Output without a Space

FullName
BasheerRossi
EnzoIvanac

TABLE 4.16 Concatenation Output with a Space

FullName
Basheer Rossi
Enzo Ivanac

Grouping

It is common for an organization to want aggregations across subsets, or groups, of data. In SQL, you accomplish this by introducing the GROUP BY clause. To function properly, every column in the SELECT clause must either be in an aggregate function or in the GROUP BY clause. To retrieve the average height and weight of animals by animal type from Table 4.9, you use the GROUP BY clause as follows:

```
SELECT    Animal_Type
         ,AVG(Height) AS AvgHeight
         ,AVG(Weight) AS AvgWeight
FROM      Augmented_Animal_Data
GROUP BY Animal_Type
```

Table 4.17 shows the output of the query. The AVG aggregation function applies to the Height and Weight columns, while the Animal_Type column is in both the SELECT and GROUP BY clauses.

As Table 4.17 illustrates, the GROUP BY clause first retrieves the unique values from the Animal_Type column, then applies the AVG aggregation function on the Height and Weight columns, calculating the averages for each group.

You can apply the GROUP BY clause to multiple columns. To get average height and weight by animal type and breed name, you just add the breed name to the SELECT and GROUP BY clauses:

```
SELECT    Animal_Type
         ,Breed_Name
         ,AVG(Height) AS AvgHeight
         ,AVG(Weight) AS AvgWeight
FROM      Augmented_Animal_Data
GROUP BY Animal_Type, Breed_Name
```

Nested Queries

A *nested query*, or *subquery*, is a SQL query embedded in another query. A helpful design pattern uses aggregation functions within a nested query. To inform cat owners that their pets are overweight, you need to identify every cat weighing more than the

TABLE 4.17 Concatenation Output with a Space

Animal_Type	AvgHeight	AvgWeight
Cat	8.9	9.73
Dog	21.52	56.84

TABLE 4.18 Nested Query Result Set

Animal_Name	Weight
Alexander	10.4
Euclid	10

average cat. Using the augmented animal data in Table 4.9, consider the following nested SQL query:

```
SELECT    Animal_Name -- outer query
          ,Weight
FROM      Augmented_Animal_Data
WHERE     Animal_Type = 'Cat'
AND       Weight > (
                    SELECT AVG(Weight) -- inner query/
                                       -- nested query/subquery
                    FROM <Augmented Animal Data>
                    WHERE Animal_Type = 'Cat'
                   )
```

In this query, the inner query resolves before the outer query, calculating the average weight for cats, which is 9.73 pounds, as Table 4.17 shows. The comparison operator in the outer query compares cat weights from the outer query with the average weight calculated by the inner query. Table 4.18 illustrates the result set of this nested query.

Working with Multiple Tables

When writing queries, it is common to need data from multiple related tables. Writing SQL that uses more than one table is easy because of the JOIN clause. A *join* is a SQL operation that combines rows from two or more tables. Joins allow for data retrieval across multiple tables, helping create a unified view of data spread across different entities.

The main join types include:

- INNER JOIN
- OUTER JOIN
- CROSS JOIN

Inner Join

An *inner join* uses the columns in a join condition whose values exist in two tables to retrieve matching data from those tables. Typically, the join condition involves the first table's foreign key and the second table's primary key. Recall that an IFF function created the query results in Table 4.11. Since the values for Male and Female are hard-coded in the function, that approach would not reflect any changes to the underlying tables.

A better approach to generating the output in Table 4.11 is with an inner join. Using the data from Table 4.9 and 4.10, consider the following query:

```
SELECT     Animal_Name           -- Column from the augmented animal data table
           ,Sex_Description.     -- Column from the Sex Lookup Table
FROM       Augmented_Animal_Data -- name of first table
INNER JOIN Sex_Lookup_Table      -- name of second table
ON         Augmented_Animal_Data.Sex = Sex_Lookup_Table.Sex -- join condition
```

The join condition in this query uses two columns: the Sex column from Table 4.9, which is a foreign key that references the primary key Sex column in Table 4.10. The INNER JOIN clause is the most common type of join. When you see SQL statements that say JOIN instead of INNER JOIN, the SQL performs an inner join.

You can retrieve data from more than two tables by adding additional INNER JOIN clauses. Consider the following query that retrieves the animal name, animal type, owner first name, and owner last name using the data from Table 4.1, Table 4.2, and Table 4.3:

```
SELECT     Animal_Name     -- Column from the animal table
           ,Animal_Type    -- Column from the animal table
           ,First_Name     -- Column from the person table
           ,Last_Name      -- Column from the person table
FROM       Animal_Table    -- name of first table, Table 4.1
INNER JOIN AnimalPerson    -- name of second table, Table 4.3
ON         Animal_Table.Animal_ID = AnimalPerson.Animal_ID -- 1st join condition
INNER JOIN Person_Table    -- name of second table, Table 4.2
ON         Person_Table.Person_ID = AnimalPerson.Person_ID -- 2nd join condition
```

Table 4.19 shows the result of this query. In this case, the query pulls information from the Animal and Person tables, using the inner joins to the AnimalPerson table to match the appropriate records.

Outer Join

An *outer join* returns all rows from one table, regardless of whether a row matches data from the second table. If the join condition matches, an outer join returns data from the

TABLE 4.19   Result Set from a Multi-Join Query

Animal_Name	Animal_Type	First_Name	Last_Name
Hazel	Dog	Giacomo	Mangione
Hazel	Dog	Eleonora	Mangione
Alexander	Cat	Giacomo	Mangione
Alexander	Cat	Eleonora	Mangione

FIGURE 4.34 Outer join types.

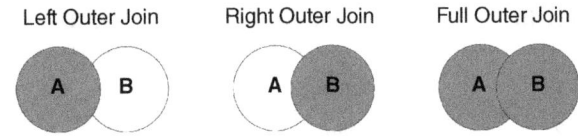

FIGURE 4.35 Animal and vet data.

Animal

Animal_ID	Vet_ID	Animal_Name
A1	V1	Euclid
A2	V2	Éowyn
A3	V3	Hazel

Vet

Vet_ID	Vet_Name
V1	Bowen
V2	Carter
V3	Rashid
V4	Ivanac

second table. If the join condition does not match, the outer join returns null values from the second table. The three main types of outer joins are:

- `LEFT OUTER JOIN`: Returns all rows from the first table
- `RIGHT OUTER JOIN`: Returns all rows from the second table
- `FULL OUTER JOIN`: Returns all rows from both tables

Figure 4.34 uses shading to illustrate the results of a left, right, and full outer join. Let's explore the different types of outer joins using the data in Figure 4.35.

Consider the following SQL statement:

```
SELECT     *                              -- retrieve all columns
FROM       Animal                         -- name of first table
LEFT OUTER JOIN Vet                       -- name of second table
ON         Animal.Vet_ID = Vet.Vet_ID     -- join condition
```

The outer join will retrieve every record from the left (animal) table, and if the join condition matches, the appropriate data from the right (vet) table, resulting in the output in Table 4.20. In this case, every row in the animal table has a corresponding row in the vet table. Note that the Vet_ID column appears twice since the column exists in both the animal and vet tables.

Now consider a right outer join using the same join condition, as follows:

```
SELECT     *                              -- retrieve all columns
FROM       Animal                         -- name of first table
RIGHT OUTER JOIN Vet                      -- name of second table
ON         Animal.Vet_ID = Vet.Vet_ID     -- join condition
```

TABLE 4.20 Left Outer Join Results

Animal_ID	Vet_ID	Animal_Name	Vet_ID	Vet_Name
A1	V1	Euclid	V1	Brown
A2	V2	Éowyn	V2	Carter
A3	V2	Hazel	V2	Carter

TABLE 4.21 Right Outer Join Results

Animal_ID	Vet_ID	Animal_Name	Vet_ID	Vet_Name
A1	V1	Euclid	V1	Brown
A2	V2	Éowyn	V2	Carter
A3	V2	Hazel	V2	Carter
NULL	*NULL*	*NULL*	V3	Rashid
NULL	*NULL*	*NULL*	V4	Ivanac

This query returns all veterinarians and the animals they serve. Since Rashid and Ivanac are new vets and have yet to see any animals, there are no matching rows in the Animal table for their Vet_IDs, leading to the results in Table 4.21.

It is vital to note that the only difference between a left outer join and a right outer join is the order in which you specify the tables when writing the query. For example, you can use a left outer join to generate the same functional results in Table 4.21 by reversing the order of the tables in the query:

```
SELECT    *                              -- retrieve all columns
FROM      Vet                            -- name of first table
LEFT OUTER JOIN Animal                   -- name of second table
ON        Animal.Vet_ID = Vet.Vet_ID     -- join condition
```

However, since this query reverses the order of the tables, Table 4.22 shows that the Vet_ID and Vet_Name columns also appear in reverse order.

Cross Join

A *cross join* creates a Cartesian product of two tables by matching every row from the first table with every row in the second table. There is no join condition for a cross join, as its

TABLE 4.22 Right Outer Join Results

Vet_ID	Vet_Name	Animal_ID	Vet_ID	Animal_Name
V1	Brown	A1	V1	Euclid
V2	Carter	A2	V2	Éowyn
V2	Carter	A3	V2	Hazel
V3	Rashid	NULL	NULL	NULL
V4	Ivanac	NULL	NULL	NULL

purpose is to combine all records from both tables. Here's what a CROSS JOIN clause looks like using the tables from Figure 4.33:

```
SELECT     *        -- retrieve all columns
FROM       Animal   -- name of first table
CROSS JOIN Vet      -- name of second table
```

With three rows in the Animal table and four rows in the Vet table, Table 4.23 illustrates that the cross join generates 3 x 4 = 12 rows of output.

While cross joins are uncommon, you can use one to calculate all possibilities pairings of vets and animals. In a retail setting, a cross join can pair all products with all shipping locations.

Caution with Cross Joins

Be incredibly careful before executing a CROSS JOIN on two tables. It's a good idea to count the rows in both tables before executing the cross join to understand how many rows the query will generate. Performing a CROSS JOIN on relatively small tables generates lots of output. With 10,000 rows in one table and 20,000 rows in another, a CROSS JOIN generates 200,000,000 rows of output!

System Functions

Each database platform offers functions that expose data about the database itself. One of the most frequently used system functions returns the current date. The current date is a component of transactional records and enables time-based analysis in the future. The current date is also necessary for a system that uses an effective date approach.

System functions also return data about the database environment. For example, whenever a person or automated process uses data from a database, they need to establish a *database session*. A database session begins when a person/program connects to a database. The session lasts until the person/program disconnects. For example, a poorly written query

TABLE 4.23 Cross Join Results

Animal_ID	Vet_ID	Animal_Name	Vet_ID	Vet_Name
A1	V1	Euclid	V1	Brown
A1	V1	Euclid	V2	Carter
A1	V1	Euclid	V3	Rashid
A1	V1	Euclid	V4	Ivanac
A2	V1	Éowyn	V1	Brown
A2	V1	Éowyn	V2	Carter
A2	V1	Éowyn	V3	Rashid
A2	V1	Éowyn	V4	Ivanac
A3	V1	Hazel	V1	Brown
A3	V1	Hazel	V2	Carter
A3	V1	Hazel	V3	Rashid
A3	V1	Hazel	V4	Ivanac

can consume most of the resources available to the database. When that happens, a database administrator can identify and terminate the problematic session.

Query Optimization

Writing a SQL query is straightforward. Writing a SQL query that efficiently does what you intend can be more difficult. There are several factors to consider when creating well-performing SQL.

Parametrization

Whenever a SQL query executes, the database has to *parse* the query. Parsing translates the human-readable SQL into code the database understands. Parsing takes time and impacts how long it takes for a query to return data. Effective use of parameterization reduces the number of times the database has to parse individual queries.

Suppose you operate a website and want to personalize it for your customers. Login details serve as parameters to the query to retrieve your information for display. After logging in, a customer sees a welcome message identifying them by name.

Figure 4.36 provides an example of the web server creating a hard-coded query. Examining the WHERE filter in the query, you see that it matches the string 'Gerald'. When Gerald logs in, the database parses the query, executes it, and returns Gerald's information.

FIGURE 4.36 Hard-coded SQL query.

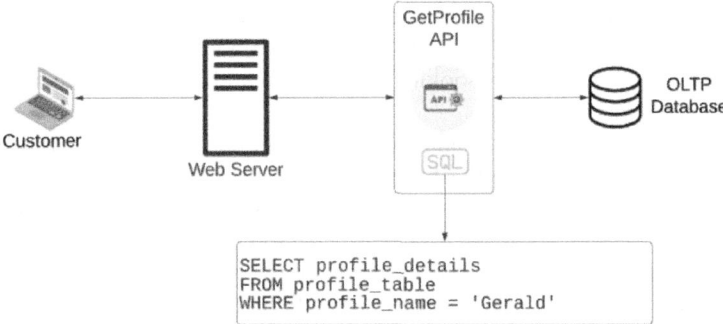

FIGURE 4.37 Parameterized SQL query.

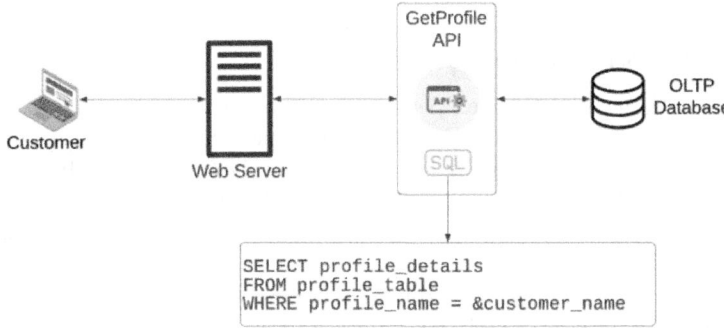

In this situation, when Gina logs in, the WHERE filter looks specifically for "Gina." Since Gerald is different from Gina, the database treats this as a new query and parses it. The time it takes to parse becomes problematic at scale. Imagine 1,000 people all logging in at the same time. The database sees each of these queries as unique and ends up parsing 1,000 times.

Figure 4.37 illustrates how to address this potential performance problem using parameterization. Instead of looking specifically for an exact string match for every customer, the query uses a variable called &customer_name. The code in the web server populates the variable with the appropriate customer name. To the database, this appears as a single query. While the value of &customer_name changes for every customer, the database parses it only once.

Indexing

When retrieving data from a table, the database has to scan each row until it finds the ones that match the filters in the WHERE clause. The process of looking at each row is called a *full table scan*. A full table scan is like flipping through every page in a book to find a specific piece of data. For small tables, full table scans happen quickly. As data volumes increase, scanning the entire table takes a long time and is not efficient. To speed up query performance, you need a *database index*.

A database index works like the index in the back of a book. Instead of looking at each page in a book to find what you are looking for, you can find a specific page number in the index and then go to that page.

A database index can point to a single column or multiple columns. When running queries on large tables, it is ideal if all of the columns you are retrieving exist in the index. If that is not feasible, you at least want the first column in your SELECT statement to be covered by an index.

If a query is running slowly, look at the indexes on the underlying tables. If you think a new index would help improve query performance, discuss it with a database administrator. The administrator will look at other factors that impact performance and will have the permissions to create an index if necessary.

While indexing improves query speed, it slows down create, update, and delete activity. An indexing strategy needs to match the type of system the database supports, be it transactional or reporting.

Data Subsets and Temporary Tables

When dealing with large data volumes, you may want to work with a subset of records. For example, suppose an organization has 1,000,000 customers. Each of those customers places 200 orders per year, and there are 10 years of data in the data warehouse. In this situation, the Order table in the data warehouse would have 2 billion rows. If you want to explore trends for a specific customer's order history, it would not be efficient to query the main Order table.

It is possible to create a temporary table to make the data more manageable. Temporary tables can store the results of a query and are disposable. Depending on the database platform, temporary tables automatically get removed when the active session ends. Using temporary tables is an effective method of creating subsets for ad hoc analysis.

For example, you can establish a database session, create a temporary table with the order history for a single customer, run queries against that temporary table, and disconnect from the database. When the session disconnects, the database automatically purges any temporary tables created during the session.

Execution Plan

An *execution plan* shows the details of how a database runs a specific query. Execution plans are extremely helpful in troubleshooting query performance issues. They provide additional information about how a query is spending its time.

For example, an execution plan can tell you if a slow-running query uses a full table scan instead of an index scan. In this case, it could be that the query is poorly written and not using the existing indexes. It also could be that a column needs a new index.

Looking at execution plans is an integral part of developing efficient queries. It is worth understanding the nuances of how to interpret execution plans for the database platform you use. If you need help understanding an execution plan, get in touch with your local database administrator.

Summary

Databases are technology platforms for processing and storing data. There are two primary types of databases: relational and nonrelational. Relational databases are ideal when you have tabular data, while there are numerous nonrelational offerings when you need more flexibility than the structure a relational database imposes.

Using a relational database as a technology platform, you can build transactional or analytical databases to address business needs. Transactional (OLTP) and analytical (OLAP) databases require different schema design approaches. Since a transactional database needs to balance reading and writing data, it follows a highly normalized schema design.

On the other hand, analytical databases prioritize reading data and follow a denormalized approach. The star and snowflake schema designs are two approaches to structuring data for analysis. Both methods implement dimensional modeling, which organizes quantitative data into facts and qualitative data into dimensions.

There are multiple ways to acquire data for analysis. For example, most data warehouses source data from transactional systems. You can use an ETL or ELT approach to copy data from a transactional system. ETL leverages technology external to a relational database to transform data, while ELT uses the power of a relational database to do the transformation. Depending on the rate of change and data volume, you can take a complete refresh or delta load approach.

You can also acquire data from external sources. APIs are integration components that encapsulate business logic and programmatically expose data. Interacting with APIs to source data for both transactional and analytical purposes is common. You may also need to scrape data from a website or pull data from a public database.

Sometimes, you need primary source data that you can't obtain programmatically. In that case, you may end up conducting a survey or directly observing people and processes.

Once you have data in a relational database, you need to be comfortable manipulating it. Structured Query Language (SQL) is the standard for relational data manipulation. You can filter, sort, compare, and aggregate data with SQL queries. You can also create groups, perform aggregation at the group level, and combine data from multiple tables using inner and outer joins.

There are times when you will be working with large volumes of data that impact performance. There are several approaches you can take to mitigate performance issues. When writing frequently executed queries, parametrization reduces the database's parsing load. Reducing the number of records you're working with is another viable approach, which you can achieve by subsetting the data and using temporary tables. If queries take longer than expected, work with a database administrator to review the query's execution plan and ensure you have the appropriate indexing strategy.

Exam Essentials

Describe the characteristics of OLTP and OLAP systems. The two main categories of relational databases are transactional (OLTP) and analytical (OLAP). Transactional systems use highly normalized schema design, which allows for database reads and writes to perform well. Analytical systems are denormalized and commonly have a star or snowflake schema. Remember that a star design simplifies queries by having a main fact table surrounded by dimensions. A snowflake design is more normalized than a star. While this approach reduces storage requirements, the queries are more complex than in a star schema.

Describe approaches for handling dimensionality. It is crucial to keep track of how data changes over time to perform historical analysis. Although an effective date approach is valid, the SQL queries to retrieve a value at a specific point in time are complex. A table design that adds start date and end date columns allows for more straightforward queries. Enhancing the design with a current flag column makes analytical queries even easier to write.

Understand integration and how to populate a data warehouse. The more data an organization has, the more impactful the analysis it can conduct. The extract, transform, and load (ETL) process copies data from transactional to analytical databases. Suppose an organization wants to use the power of a relational database to reformat the data for analytical purposes. In that case, the order changes to extract, load, and transform. Regardless of the approach, remember that a delta load migrates only changed data.

Differentiate between data collection methods. Data can come from a variety of sources. An organization may scrape websites or use publicly available databases to augment its data. While web scraping may be the only way to retrieve data, it is better if a published application programming interface exists. An API is more reliable since its structure makes for a consistent interface. If you want to capture the voice of the customer, a survey is a sound approach. Collecting data through observation is a great way to validate business processes and collect quantitative data.

Describe how to manipulate data and optimize queries. Analytical databases store massive amounts of data. Manipulating the entire dataset for analysis is frequently infeasible. To efficiently analyze data, understand that SQL has the power to filter, sort, and aggregate data. When focusing on a particular subject, creating a subset is an ideal approach. Although it is possible to create permanent tables to house subsets, using a temporary table as part of a query is viable for ad hoc analysis. When an analytical query performs poorly, use its execution plan to understand the root cause. It is wise to work with a database administrator to understand the execution plan and ensure that indexes exist where they are needed.

Review Questions

The following questions are designed to test your understanding of this chapter's material. You can find the answers in Appendix A.

1. Brandon is trying to understand why the personalization features of his website performs poorly under heavy load. Looking at the query that retrieves customer profile information, he sees that the web application is hard-coding the customer's identifying number into each query, then using the Customer_ID column to retrieve profile data. Looking at the execution plan, Brandon sees that the query is performing optimally. What does he need to do to resolve the performance issue? Choose the best answer.
   A. Check to ensure there is an index to the Customer_ID column.
   B. Review the execution plan for the query with a DBA.
   C. Remove the personalization features due to the performance problems.
   D. Change the application code to use query parameters instead of hard-coding.

2. Julie works for an online retailer and has two tables: one contains customer information, and the other contains order information. The order table has a foreign key referencing the primary key in the customer table. Which join should she use to retrieve customers and their associated orders?
   A. INNER JOIN
   B. LEFT OUTER JOIN
   C. RIGHT OUTER JOIN
   D. CROSS JOIN

3. Claire operates a travel agency and wants to automatically recommend accommodation, rental car, and entertainment packages based on her customers' interests. What type of database should Claire select?
   A. Relational
   B. Graph
   C. Key-value
   D. Column family

4. Evan needs to retrieve information from two separate tables to create a month-end credit card summary. What should he use to join the tables together?
   A. Primary key
   B. Foreign key
   C. Synthetic primary key
   D. Referential integrity

5. Taylor wants to investigate how manufacturing, marketing, and sales expenditures impact overall profitability for her company. Which of the following systems is most appropriate? Choose the best answer.
   A. OLTP
   B. OLAP
   C. Data warehouse
   D. Data mart

6. J. R. needs to move data into his data warehouse. One of his primary concerns is how fast data can get into the warehouse. As he thinks about approaches for transferring data, which of the following is the *best* option?
   A. Initial load
   B. Delta load
   C. ETL
   D. ELT

7. Riley is designing a data warehouse and wants to make writing queries that track customer satisfaction over time as simple as possible. What could she add to her table design to accomplish her goal? Choose the best answer.
   A. Current flag
   B. Start date
   C. Middle date
   D. End date

8. Richard is designing a data warehouse and wants to minimize query complexity. What design pattern should he follow?
   A. Avalanche
   B. Star
   C. Snowflake
   D. Quasar

9. Razia is working on understanding population trends by county across the United States. Considering the rate of change, which of the following *best* describes county name?
   A. Static dimension
   B. Slowly changing dimension
   C. Rapidly changing dimension
   D. Fluid dimension

10. Zaiden is debating between a snowflake and a star schema design for a data warehouse. Which of the following is not a factor in his selection?
    A. Storage space
    B. Query complexity
    C. Number of records in the fact table
    D. Degree of normalization

11. Madeline wants to collect data about how her competitor prices products. She can see this information after logging in to her competitor's website. After some initial struggles, Madeline creates a web scraper to harvest the data she needs. What does she need to do next? Choose the best answer.
    A. Check the terms of service.
    B. Load the data into an OLTP database.
    C. Load the data into an OLAP database.
    D. Figure out how to parse JSON.

12. Maurice manages an organization of software developers with deep expertise in Python. He wants to make use of this expertise to move data between transactional systems and the data warehouse. In what phase are Python skills most relevant?
    A. Extract
    B. Transform
    C. Load
    D. Purge

13. Ellen is collecting data about a proprietary manufacturing process and wants to control for any bias that workers may have. What type of data collection approach is most appropriate?
    A. Survey
    B. Sample
    C. Public database
    D. Observation

14. George wants to integrate data from his city's open data portal. Reading the website, he sees that he can download the data he wants as a CSV file. After manually downloading the file, he writes the code to transform the data and load it into his database. Presuming the data changes once a month, what can George do to ensure he has the most up-to-date data from the city? Choose the best answer.
    A. Manually check the city's website every day.
    B. Contact the city and encourage the development of an API.
    C. Automate the process that downloads, transforms, and uploads the CSV file.
    D. Nothing, George has already successfully loaded the data.

15. Martha is designing a nightly ETL process to copy data from an order processing system into a data warehouse. What should she do to replicate the data she needs efficiently without losing historical data? Choose the best answer.
    A. Complete purge and load
    B. Delta load
    C. ELT
    D. Use an ETL product

16. Bob manages a production line and is worried that defects are not being accurately reported. What is the best way for him to obtain the true number of defects?
    A. Survey the production staff.
    B. Test a sample of finished goods.
    C. Observe the final quality check process.
    D. Use historical data to establish a trend.

17. Barb wants to understand which product costs the least. What aggregate function can she use in her SQL query to get this answer?
    A. COUNT
    B. MAX
    C. MIN
    D. AVG

18. Elena is an analyst at a multinational corporation. She wants to focus her analysis on transactions that took place in Italy. What is the first thing she should do to make efficient use of resources?
    A. Filter out transactions for all countries except Italy.
    B. Filter out transactions for Italy.
    C. Aggregate transactions across the European Union.
    D. Subset the data to a specific Italian province.

19. Jeff is an analyst at a company that operates in the United States. He wants to understand profitability trends by region, state, and county. What should he do next? Choose the best answer.
    A. Aggregate data at the county level.
    B. Aggregate data by region, state, and county.
    C. Use effective date logic to determine current profitability.
    D. Make sure there is an index on the county column.

20. Gretchen is trying to create a list of purchases in chronological order. What clause does she need to add to her SQL query?
    A. ORDER BY
    B. SELECT
    C. FROM
    D. WHERE

Chapter 5

Data Quality

THE COMPTIA DATA+ EXAM TOPICS COVERED IN THIS CHAPTER INCLUDE:

✓ **Domain 2.0: Data Acquisition and Preparation**
  - 2.2. Given a scenario, perform data exploration to identify possible inconsistencies with a dataset
  - 2.3. Given a scenario, perform appropriate data transformation and cleansing techniques

In Chapter 3, "Understanding Data," you learned about sources of data and the design differences between transactional and analytical databases. With this knowledge of data sources and retrieval methods under your belt, you can now consider issues that impact data quality.

Businesses need high-quality data to create the kinds of analysis that organizations rely on for decision making. While the data we use in these analyses isn't perfect, understanding each dataset's limitations will help you identify any data transformation work you must complete before proceeding with analysis.

This chapter explores the reasons why data needs transformation. With a scenario providing context, this chapter explores the data manipulation techniques that best prepare data for analysis. Zooming out, it walks through data quality scenarios and examines methods for resolving data quality issues.

Data Inconsistencies

Analysts are often eager to jump straight to analyzing data. As discussed in Chapter 4, "Databases and Data Acquisition," data warehouses aggregate multiple data sources and provide a platform for conducting analysis. However, each data source has unique quality issues and associated inconsistencies, which need resolution before finding its way into a data warehouse. Whether designing an *extract, transform, and load* (*ETL*) process or digging into a new set of data warehouse tables, an analyst needs to examine each data source and resolve any underlying quality issues. This section explores some common reasons for cleaning and profiling datasets.

Data Duplication

Data duplication occurs when data representing the same transaction is accidentally duplicated within a system. Suppose you want to open a spreadsheet on your local computer. To open the spreadsheet, you locate the file and double-click it. This method of opening documents establishes muscle memory that associates double-clicking with the desired action.

Suppose you are shopping online for flights between Chicago and San Francisco. Once you identify a flight that meets your scheduling needs, you proceed to a web page to complete your purchase. Unintentionally, you double-click the purchase button. Instead of purchasing one ticket for your upcoming travels, you create two. The first is intentional, whereas the second is a duplicate.

Humans are primarily responsible for creating duplicate data. System architects work diligently to prevent duplicate data from being created. The best way to resolve duplicate data is to prevent its creation in the first place. One common approach to stopping duplicate data before it gets into a system is a visual warning to alert users. If you've ever purchased something online, you probably have received a warning, such as "Please wait while your transaction is being processed. Clicking Purchase Now again may result in a duplicate charge on your credit card."

Having multiple data sources for the same data elements is also a source of duplicate data. Consider the scenario in Figure 5.1, where Allison wants to update her billing address. She speaks with Jackson, who inputs her address information into the Sales database. After some time, Allison moved and wanted to update her billing address. This time, she speaks with Rachel. Instead of updating Allison's existing billing information, Rachel adds a new billing address. At this point, Allison has duplicate data in the Sales system.

The company has a duplicate resolution process to resolve duplicate data issues. This process looks for customers with multiple billing addresses, validates the correct address, and updates the Sales database by removing the duplicate record.

Data Redundancy

While duplicate data typically comes from accidental data entry, redundant data happens when the same data elements exist in multiple places within a system. Frequently, data redundancy is a function of integrating multiple systems.

For example, multiple source systems that perform different business functions and use shared data elements create the conditions for data redundancy. When a record changes in one system, there is no guarantee that its new value will change in another system. Since there is no certainty of data synchronization, a data element can have conflicting values

FIGURE 5.1 Duplicate data resolution process.

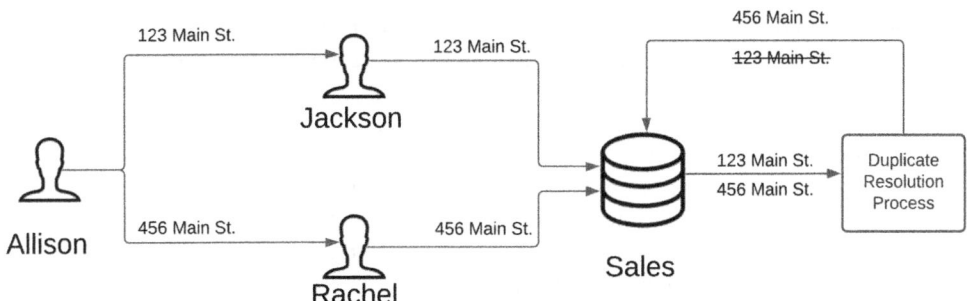

FIGURE 5.2 Illustration of multiple data sources.

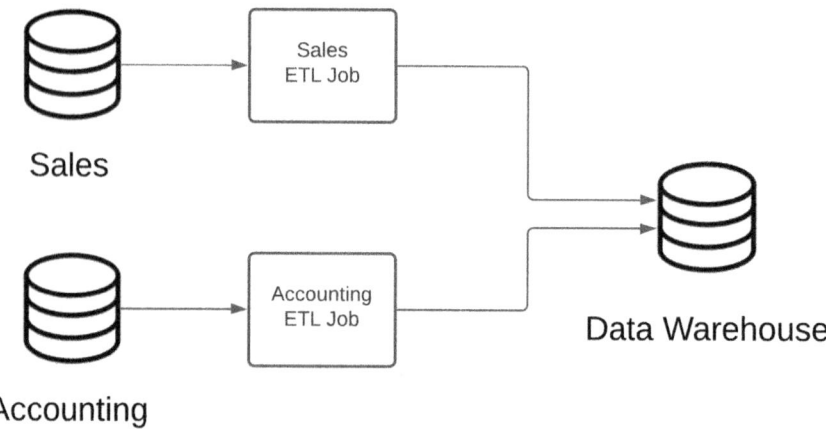

across systems. Dealing with redundant data is a persistent challenge when integrating multiple data sources.

Figure 5.2 illustrates two transactional systems feeding a single data warehouse. In this illustration, the Sales ETL job connects to the sales database and copies data into the warehouse. Independently, the Accounting ETL job copies accounting data into the warehouse. Suppose a salesperson enters a customer's address information into the Sales system. After the customer orders, an accounting clerk enters the same address information into the Accounting system for billing purposes. Now that the same information exists in two places, the potential for a data redundancy problem exists.

Suppose the salesperson processes an address change after talking with a customer. The Sales system would have the new address, leaving the Accounting system out of date. Different systems have different addresses for the same customer.

The customer's address in the data warehouse depends on how the ETL jobs function. Recall from Chapter 4 that ETL jobs can be either a full load, replacing data entirely, or a delta load, moving only changes between systems. If they perform a full reload and the Accounting ETL job processes before Sales, the old address ends up in the warehouse. If the ETL jobs perform delta loads, the new address ends up in the warehouse since its value in the Sales system is more recent than in the Accounting system. Either way, the address data in the transactional systems contain different values.

There are several options for resolving redundant data. One approach synchronizes changes to shared data elements between the Accounting and Sales systems. However, technical or political realities can make synchronizing source systems unfeasible.

Figure 5.3 illustrates how an integrated ETL approach addresses this redundant data problem while maintaining accurate historical data. This integrated ETL process takes a delta load approach. When an address changes, the ETL job sets the effective end date for

Data Inconsistencies   149

FIGURE 5.3   Resolving redundancy with an integrated ETL process.

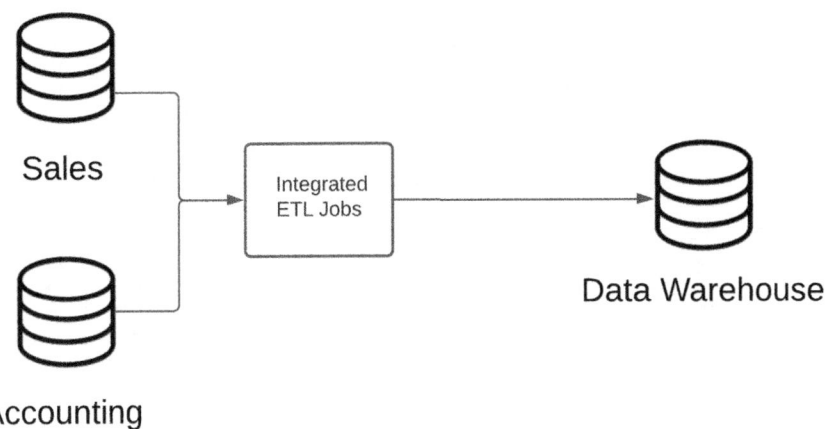

FIGURE 5.4   Redundant data.

	A	B	C	D	E	F	G	H
1	Project Number	Client Name	Employee Number	Employee First Name	Employee Last Name	Job Class	Bill Rate	Billable Hours
2	42523	Bosch	68	Isabel	Diehl	DBA	175	40
3	95003	Tenneco	68	Isabel	Diehl	DBA	175	35
4	95003	Tenneco	68	Isabel	Diehl	DevOps Engineer	215	28
5	42523	Bosch	69	Roland	Clem	Developer	128	150
6	37724	Johnson Controls	80	Igor	Stravinsky	Developer	128	304
7	37724	Johnson Controls	492	Johann	Bach	Senior Developer	200	58
8	95003	Tenneco	69	Roland	Clem	Developer	128	103
9	95003	Tenneco	73	Ferdinand	Kamienski	Project Manager	190	40
10	95003	Tenneco	39	Bruce	Logan	DevOps Engineer	215	67
11	30243	ZF Friedrichshafen	69	Roland	Clem	Developer	128	43
12	30243	ZF Friedrichshafen	80	Igor	Stravinsky	Developer	128	64
13	30243	ZF Friedrichshafen	492	Johann	Bach	Senior Developer	200	86
14	30243	ZF Friedrichshafen	39	Bruce	Logan	DevOps Engineer	215	57
15	30243	ZF Friedrichshafen	73	Ferdinand	Kamienski	Project Manager	190	40

the old address and inserts a new row for the current address. The additional ETL logic ensures that the warehouse contains the correct values. While the data discrepancy between the Sales and Accounting systems still needs resolution, the analyst has the proper customer address in the data warehouse.

Another root cause of data redundancy is an inappropriate database design. For example, consulting companies bill clients by the hour. To that end, consultants need to keep track of client projects, employees, and job roles. Figure 5.4 illustrates a poorly designed transactional table for storing billing information.

Examining Figure 5.4 more closely, note that there are multiple redundant data issues. Rows 2, 3, and 4 illustrate Isabel Diehl's billable hours and job roles on the Bosch and

FIGURE 5.5 Name change issue.

Project Number	Client Name	Employee Number	Employee First Name	Employee Last Name	Job Class	Bill Rate	Billable Hours
42523	Bosch	68	Isabel	Diehl	DBA	175	40
95003	Tenneco	68	Isabel	Diehl	DBA	175	35
95003	Tenneco	68	Isabel	Diehl	DevOps Engineer	215	28
69937	Akrapovič	68	Isabel	Chanteaux	DBA	175	35
42523	Bosch	69	Roland	Clem	Developer	128	150
37724	Johnson Controls	80	Igor	Stravinsky	Developer	128	304
37724	Johnson Controls	492	Johann	Bach	Senior Developer	200	58
95003	Tenneco	69	Roland	Clem	Developer	128	103
95003	Tenneco	73	Ferdinand	Kamienski	Project Manager	190	40
95003	Tenneco	39	Bruce	Logan	DevOps Engineer	215	67
30243	ZF Friedrichshafen	69	Roland	Clem	Developer	128	43
30243	ZF Friedrichshafen	80	Igor	Stravinsky	Developer	128	64
30243	ZF Friedrichshafen	492	Johann	Bach	Senior Developer	200	86
30243	ZF Friedrichshafen	39	Bruce	Logan	DevOps Engineer	215	57
30243	ZF Friedrichshafen	73	Ferdinand	Kamienski	Project Manager	190	40

FIGURE 5.6 Transactional design.

Project Number	Client Name		Project Number	Employee Number	Job Class	Billable Hours		Employee Number	Employee First Name	Employee Last Name
30243	ZF Friedrichshafen		30243	39	DevOps Engineer	57		39	Bruce	Logan
37724	Johnson Controls		95003	39	DevOps Engineer	67		68	Isabel	Chanteaux
42523	Bosch		42523	68	DBA	40		69	Roland	Clem
69937	Akrapovič		95003	68	DBA	35		73	Ferdinand	Kamienski
95003	Tenneco		69937	68	DBA	35		80	Igor	Stravinsky
			95003	68	DevOps Engineer	28		492	Johann	Bach
			30243	69	Developer	43				
			42523	69	Developer	150		Job Class	Bill Rate	
			95003	69	Developer	103		DBA	175	
			30243	73	Project Manager	40		Developer	128	
			95003	73	Project Manager	40		DevOps Engineer	215	
			30243	80	Developer	64		Project Manager	190	
			37724	80	Developer	304		Senior Developer	200	
			30243	492	Senior Developer	86				
			37724	492	Senior Developer	58				

Tenneco projects. The only meaningful difference between these rows is the Project Number, Client Name, Job Class, and Billable Hours. The other data elements are all redundant.

For example, suppose Isabel changes her last name and works on a new project, as shown in Figure 5.5. Since this is a transactional table, Isabel's last name should change in rows 2, 3, and 4. Similarly, if the consulting organization wants to increase the bill rate for a developer, rows 6, 7, 9, 12, and 13 all have to change.

While the table in Figure 5.5 is fine for analytical purposes, it illustrates why transactional databases are often in third normal form, as discussed in Chapter 4. Restructuring the tables is the best way to resolve a data redundancy issue. Figure 5.6 provides an example of solving data redundancy through restructuring.

Figure 5.6 has tables for storing information on projects and employees. The associative table connects employees, their job class, and their role in a project. With this design, no data attribute exists redundantly.

Missing Values

Another issue that impacts data quality is the concept of missing values. *Missing values* occur when you expect an attribute to contain data, but nothing is there. Missing values are also known as null values. A *null value* is the absence of a value. A null is not a space, blank, or other character. There are situations when allowing nulls makes sense. Suppose you are storing data about people and have a column for Middle Initial. Since only some have a middle initial, the Middle Initial column should be optional. When a column optionally contains data, it is *nullable*, meaning the column can contain null values. However, be aware that having nulls in a dataset poses calculation challenges.

Suppose a temperature sensor logs the maximum observed temperature to a table daily, as shown in Figure 5.7. An analyst expects the Temperature column to contain a value for each date. However, there was a failure on January 4, 2025, and while a record for that date exists, no temperature data is present. Since the value for the Temperature attribute for that date is absent, its value is null.

Null values present several challenges depending on the tools you use to analyze data. For example, if you use the AVG function in SQL to find the numeric average of the data from Figure 5.7, you will get a number because the AVG function excludes null values.

However, if you read a CSV file using the Python or R programming language, the null value for January 4 poses a problem. Trying to calculate the average, which was successful in SQL, results in an error in Python and R as the equivalent functions in those languages do not handle null values.

FIGURE 5.7 Missing temperature value.

	Date	Temperature
1	**Date**	**Temperature**
2	1/1/2025	17
3	1/2/2025	15
4	1/3/2025	14
5	1/4/2025	
6	1/5/2025	15
7	1/6/2025	16
8	1/7/2025	17
9	1/8/2025	10
10	1/9/2025	8
11	1/10/2025	2
12	1/11/2025	-2
13	1/12/2025	6
14	1/13/2025	9
15	1/14/2025	16
16	1/15/2025	13

To handle missing values, you first have to check for their existence. SQL offers functions to check for null and functions that can replace a null with a user-specified value. There are similar functions in both Python and R.

Invalid Data

Invalid data indicates values outside the valid range for a given attribute. An invalid value violates a business rule instead of having an incorrect data type. As such, you have to understand a system's context to determine whether a value is invalid.

For example, consider the temperature sensor that generates the data in Figure 5.7. The Date column has a date data type, and the Temperature column is numeric. You can presume the temperature sensor measures external air temperature in Fahrenheit and is somewhere on Earth. With those constraints in mind, consider the data in Figure 5.8.

All of the values in Figure 5.8 belong to their respective data type. Historically, temperatures on Earth are between −140 and 140 degrees Fahrenheit. With this context, it becomes clear that −99,999 is an unrealistic value for temperature. The value is clearly invalid despite being numeric.

Invalid values violate business rules, not technical rules. For example, −99,999 is a valid number, but it is an invalid temperature for a location on Earth. As such, programming languages do not have native functions that definitively tell you whether or not a given value is invalid. As a data professional, it's up to you to work with software developers to create these rules based on your organization's unique needs. When considering data types, numeric and date data is comparatively easy to check for invalid values.

FIGURE 5.8 Invalid temperature value.

	A	B
	Date	Temperature
2	1/1/2020	17
3	1/2/2020	15
4	1/3/2020	14
5	1/4/2020	-99999
6	1/5/2020	15
7	1/6/2020	16
8	1/7/2020	17
9	1/8/2020	10
10	1/9/2020	8
11	1/10/2020	2
12	1/11/2020	-2
13	1/12/2020	6
14	1/13/2020	9
15	1/14/2020	16
16	1/15/2020	13

Text data is more complex. One thing that leads to invalid character data is an absence of referential integrity within a database. If two tables have a relationship but no foreign keys, the conditions for invalid character data exist. Implementing relationships appropriately reduces the likelihood of invalid character data. As you learned in Chapter 4, enforcing referential integrity is an excellent way to improve data quality.

Nonparametric Data

Nonparametric data is data collected from categorical variables, which you read about in Chapter 3. Sometimes, the categories indicate differentiation, and sometimes, they have a rank order associated with them. In this latter case, the rank order of the values holds the significance, not the individual values themselves.

For example, when a person with abdominal pain seeks medical attention, the attending physician asks the person to rate their pain. Since individuals experience pain differently, the doctor uses the scale in Figure 5.9 to assess discomfort. The interval between each face is inconsistent, as people have differing perceptions of pain.

Suppose the person indicates the first face in the "severe" category in response to the "rate your pain" question. While the face itself means nothing, its relative position gives the physician insight into the person's level of distress. With that context, the doctor checks for appendicitis and might order an X-ray or ultrasound to further inform treatment options.

On the other hand, suppose the person says their pain level is in the mild range. Instead of ordering additional tests, the doctor performs a physical examination to rule out appendicitis and may advise a carbonated beverage or antacid to relieve the comparatively mild distress.

Chapter 6, "Data Analysis and Statistics," explores nonparametric data and statistical approaches to testing it in greater detail.

Data Outliers

A *data outlier* is a value that differs significantly from other observations in a dataset. Consider the real estate sale price example in Figure 5.10. All of the properties are on the same street, city, and state. Most of the properties have a sale price between $128,000 and $153,000. However, the property at 130 Main Street has a sale price of $26,496,400. That is a dramatic difference from the rest of the sales prices.

With outliers, you need to understand why they exist and whether they are valid in the context of your analysis. For example, suppose you investigate why the property at 130

FIGURE 5.9 Pain rating scale.

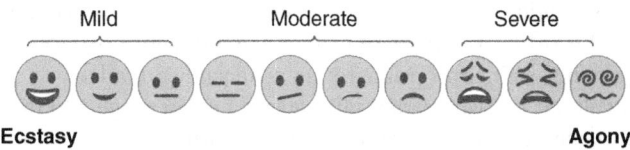

FIGURE 5.10 Real estate sales outlier.

	A	B	C	D
1	**Address**	**City**	**State**	**Sale Price**
2	123 Main St	Sampletown	Iowa	$130,000
3	124 Main St	Sampletown	Iowa	$153,000
4	125 Main St	Sampletown	Iowa	$134,000
5	126 Main St	Sampletown	Iowa	$142,000
6	127 Main St	Sampletown	Iowa	$148,000
7	128 Main St	Sampletown	Iowa	$128,000
8	129 Main St	Sampletown	Iowa	$137,000
9	130 Main St	Sampletown	Iowa	$26,496,400
10	131 Main St	Sampletown	Iowa	$144,000

Main Street is more expensive than the other properties on the same street. During your investigation, you find that 130 Main Street is a commercial property, while all the other properties are residential dwellings. If your analysis is on residential real estate prices, you want to remove 130 Main Street from the dataset.

If 130 Main Street is not a commercial property, it is possible that a data entry error created the outlier. In that case, you need to rectify the mistake by replacing the bad data with the actual value.

Outliers exist regardless of data type. Chapter 6 examines statistical methods for identifying outliers in greater detail.

Specification Mismatch

A specification describes the target value for a component. A *specification mismatch* occurs when an individual component's characteristics are beyond the range of acceptable values. For example, suppose you want to add a room to a house and buy 15 wooden studs. Looking at the blueprint for the addition, you need wooden studs with a rectangular cross-section measuring 2 inches by 4 inches (2×4). When purchasing the studs, you want to ensure all 15 have a consistent cross-section.

Selecting boards at the local home improvement store, you notice that one doesn't match the other 14. Getting out your tape measure, you find that its cross-section is 2 inches by 6 inches (2×6). While 2×6 is a standard size for dimensional lumber, there is a specification mismatch, as that specific board doesn't match your blueprint. To prevent complications while building the addition, you put the 2×6 back on the shelf and find a 2×4.

In manufacturing, a specification mismatch causes a component to fail post-production quality checks. Understanding a specification's tolerance is crucial to maintaining quality. For example, if a 2×4 is off by a 16th of an inch, it is suitable for use. However, that measurement discrepancy isn't appropriate for an artificial heart valve.

When data is invalid, it has values that fall outside a given range. On the other hand, a specification mismatch occurs when data doesn't conform to its destination data type.

For example, you might load data from a file into a database. You'll have a specification mismatch if the destination column is numeric and you have text data. To resolve this mismatch, you must validate that the inbound data consistently maps to its target data type.

Data Type Validation

Data type validation ensures that values in a dataset have a consistent data type. Consider the schema excerpt in Figure 5.11. The primary keys for the Manufacturer and Model expect integer values, while the Manufacturer_Name and Model_Name are characters. Recall from Chapter 4 that the foreign key on Manufacturer_ID enforces referential integrity between the two tables.

Now, imagine that you need to load the data from Figure 5.12 into the schema in Figure 5.11. The first nine rows load successfully, while the tenth row fails because the identifier consists of two asterisks, which is not a valid integer.

FIGURE 5.11 Automotive schema excerpt.

Manufacturer		
PK	Manufacturer_ID	integer
	Manufacturer_Name	character

Model		
PK	Model_ID	integer
	Model_Name	character
FK	Manufacturer_ID	integer

FIGURE 5.12 List of automotive manufacturers.

	A	B
1	**Identifier**	**Manufacturer**
2	1	Lexus
3	2	Lincoln
4	3	Maserati
5	4	Mazda
6	5	Mercedes-Benz
7	6	MINI
8	7	Mitsubishi
9	8	Nissan
10	9	Pontiac
11	**	Porsche
12	11	RAM
13	12	Scion
14	13	Subaru
15	14	Toyota
16	15	Volkswagen
17	16	Volvo

How the load process handles the data type validation failure determines whether the remaining rows load successfully. Depending on the tool, a single failure may cause the load process to stop. Alternatively, the load process might write each failed record to an error file before loading the remaining records.

Programming languages, including SQL, Python, and R, all have data type validation functions. Use these functions to validate the data type for each column in a data file before attempting a database load. It's in your best interest to detect and remediate data type issues as early as possible to ensure the data is ready for analysis.

Data Completeness

Data completeness is the minimum amount of information you need to fulfill a business objective. Imagine putting together a jigsaw puzzle and discovering at the end that you are missing a couple of pieces. In this context, data completeness ensures you have all the pieces you need to complete the puzzle.

To check for completeness, examine your dataset for null values. Checking for null or missing values as part of any ETL process is a good idea. To prevent missing data, work with your user experience team to ensure that when people must enter data into a system, any required fields are mandatory in the user interface. Consider performing automated data audits on a periodic basis to check for missing data in your analytics environment.

Data Transformation Techniques

There are several potential issues to be aware of when working with data. Invariably, you'll need to clean up data inconsistencies. When preparing data for analysis, you should create a data plan that specifies what your data needs to look like and then develop steps to cleanse and transform your data. With these ideas in mind, this section explores some of the data transformation and cleansing techniques you can use to resolve potential data quality issues.

String Manipulation

String manipulation is a technique for programmatically modifying text to improve data consistency. Text data originates from many sources. For example, a person may type their address into a web form. If you're running a survey and asking open-ended questions, people type their answers as free text. One objective of storing data in a database is to ensure the data is clean and consistent. Whenever you process text data, there is a high likelihood that you will have to transform it before loading it into a database.

Suppose you receive address data as a CSV file and need to load it into a database. Figure 5.13 shows sample CSV input and the structure of the corresponding table in the database.

FIGURE 5.13 CSV data and database table.

CSV Input File

```
5401 Norris Canyon Rd,Unit 306,,San Ramon, CA,94583
4710 Johnston Street,,,Lafayette,LA,70503
1302 east 6th St,,,Tulsa,OK,74120
```

Destination Database Table

Address	
PK	Address_ID
	Street_Line_1
	Street_Line_2
	Street_Line_3
	City
	State
	Postal_Cd

Examining the CSV input file data, there are several issues that need resolution to ensure clean data in the destination database table. The issues include:

- Line 1: Remove the leading space before CA
- Line 2: Convert Street to St
- Line 3: Covert east to E

An efficient way to manipulate text is by using *regular expressions* (*RegEx*). Regular expressions let you match patterns in text. Many languages, including Python and R, have string manipulation libraries that use regular expressions to define a text pattern and then replace the pattern with other text. Components of a regular expression include:

- **Anchors:** Anchors refer to the position in a string, with the ^ character matching the start of a line and the $ character matching the end of a line.
- **Boolean:** Boolean logic allows for matching more than one value. For example, neighbor|neighbour matches both "neighbor" and "neighbour."
- **Character classes:** Character classes include the ability to match multiple values for a given character. For example, the [12] pattern matches either 1 or 2. Other examples include \d for matching any digit and \s for matching any whitespace (spaces, tabs, etc.).
- **Literals:** Literals match exactly the literal characters in a text string.
- **Quantifiers:** Quantifiers let you specify the number of times to match a pattern. For example, the * quantifier matches zero or more occurrences of a pattern, while the + quantifier matches one or more.
- **Wildcard:** A wildcard matches any character. For example, the . character matches any single character.

Considering the three lines of text from Figure 5.13, you could write three specific regular expressions to match the pattern for each case. After matching the pattern, you must replace it with the desired value.

To remove the whitespace after a comma, you could write the following regular expression:

`,\s+`

Reading the previous expression, it looks for a comma and one or more white spaces after the comma.

The following regular expression matches the pattern Street in the second line of the CSV input file in Figure 5.13:

`, Street`

Note that this example uses a literal character space instead of \s. Using the \s character class is also appropriate to match this pattern.

To match east in the third line of the input file, you can use the following regular expression:

`\seast\s`

Note that in the previous regular expression, \s denotes whitespace, and east is the string literal "east".

While you don't always have to write regular expressions, understanding what they are and how they work is vital to manipulating strings and cleansing data. You may write RegEx directly when doing ETL. If you are doing ELT and using the database to transform data, many database platforms implement the TRIM() function to remove characters from a string. For more specifics on how the TRIM() function works, consult the documentation for your database.

> **More on Regular Expressions**
>
> While incredibly powerful, regular expressions can be very complex. Some books and websites focus only on regular expressions, so don't get overwhelmed. The RegEx 101 website (`https://regex101.com`) is a great place to start if you want to build and test your regular expressions.

Conversion

It is frequently necessary to convert data as it flows between systems. Before reaching the analytics environment, you need to understand how many conversions happen for each data source. Figure 5.14 illustrates how customer order data flows through three different systems

FIGURE 5.14 Three opportunities to impact data quality.

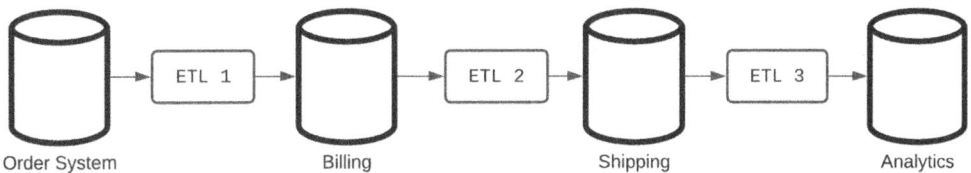

FIGURE 5.15 Data conversion issue.

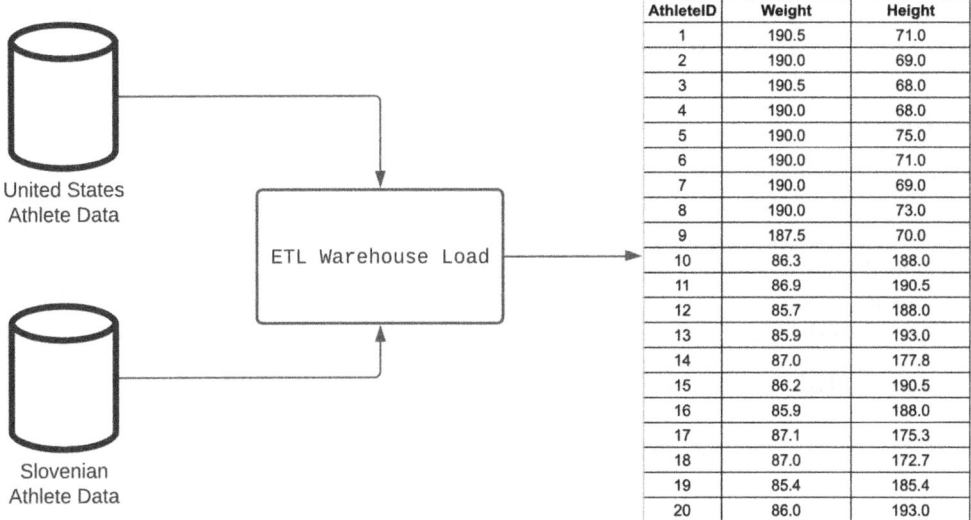

AthleteID	Weight	Height
1	190.5	71.0
2	190.0	69.0
3	190.5	68.0
4	190.0	68.0
5	190.0	75.0
6	190.0	71.0
7	190.0	69.0
8	190.0	73.0
9	187.5	70.0
10	86.3	188.0
11	86.9	190.5
12	85.7	188.0
13	85.9	193.0
14	87.0	177.8
15	86.2	190.5
16	85.9	188.0
17	87.1	175.3
18	87.0	172.7
19	85.4	185.4
20	86.0	193.0

and ETL processes before reaching its destination. Each ETL is an intrahop within the organization and presents an opportunity to transform data incorrectly.

Data conversion is another possible source of data quality issues. Specifically, attribute values need to use consistent units of measure. In Figure 5.15, the values for the Weight and Height columns abruptly change starting with AthleteID 10.

One possible reason for this change is that the ETL process somehow transposed the values for Weight and Height. However, the source of this inconsistency is a conversion issue. AthleteIDs 1 through 10 come from the U.S. Athlete Data source, which has Weight in pounds and Height in inches. Starting with AthleteID 10, the remaining records are from the Slovenian Athlete Data source, which uses the metric system. As such, Weight is in kilograms and Height is in centimeters. To fix this conversion issue, you need to modify the ETL Warehouse Load process to be aware of the source data differences and convert the data appropriately.

Augmentation

You may need to augment the data you have to do the analysis you are attempting. *Augmentation* is the process of adding attributes not found within your original dataset. For example, the athlete data from Figure 5.15 contains Weight and Height. While important, these two variables do not give a complete picture of an athlete. If you were analyzing Olympic athletes, you would augment the original data with the athlete's sport to include attributes relevant to that sport.

For example, to explore performance in the 100-meter dash, you should augment the Weight and Height data to include the athlete's sex and the wind speed. While the values of sex and height are unlikely to experience significant fluctuations over time, weight and wind speed are event-specific. A reduction in weight or a considerable tailwind could result in a faster time, so augmenting the original dataset with these additional attributes leads to better analysis. The data you need to augment datasets is as unique as the analysis challenge you're working on solving.

Scaling

In the context of data transformation, *scaling* is changing the range of a numeric variable to ensure consistent measurement and improve the ability to compare across variables. Scaling is typical when comparing columns whose measurements use different units. After scaling is complete, the dataset is ready for ongoing analysis.

For example, suppose you want to compare the height and weight of a group of athletes. As Figure 5.16 shows, height is in inches, and weight is in pounds. Since inches and pounds

FIGURE 5.16 Raw athlete data.

AthleteID	Weight (pounds)	Height (inches)	MileTime (seconds)
1	190.5	71	315
2	190	69	338
3	190.5	68	377
4	190	68	319
5	190	75	334
6	190	71	343
7	190	69	341
8	190	73	365
9	187.5	70	361
10	189.5	74	377
11	188.5	75	340
12	189	74	356
13	188	76	353
14	190	70	336
15	190	75	330
16	190	74	341
17	190	69	367
18	190	68	321
19	190	73	367
20	190	76	327

FIGURE 5.17 Scaled athlete data.

AthleteID	Scaled Weight	Scaled Height	MileTime (seconds)
1	1.000	0.375	315
2	0.833	0.125	338
3	1.000	0.000	377
4	0.833	0.000	319
5	0.833	0.875	334
6	0.833	0.375	343
7	0.833	0.125	341
8	0.833	0.625	365
9	0.000	0.250	361
10	0.667	0.750	377
11	0.333	0.875	340
12	0.500	0.750	356
13	0.167	1.000	353
14	0.833	0.250	336
15	0.833	0.875	330
16	0.833	0.750	341
17	0.833	0.125	367
18	0.833	0.000	321
19	0.833	0.625	367
20	0.833	1.000	327

describe different attributes, comparing the numerical values of the height and weight columns doesn't make sense. With the data from Figure 5.16, the weight column will take on greater importance than height simply because its values are greater.

To compare height and weight, you need to scale the data. Figure 5.17 shows the data after using the min-max normalization technique that sets 0 and 1 as the lower and upper limits for numeric column values. Normalizing the data in this way lets you compare weight and height.

Min-Max Normalization

If you're curious about how the min-max normalization, consider its mathematical definition:

$$x' = \frac{x - min(x)}{max(x) - min(x)}$$

Let's walk through it using the height data for AthleteID 1 in Figure 5.17. You first need find the minimum value of the Height column, which is 68. Then, find the maximum value of the

Height column, which is 76. For AthleteID 1, the value you want to convert is 71. Once you have these values, you can plug them into the formula as follows:

$$0.375 = \frac{71 - 68}{76 - 68}$$

Min-max normalization is one of the most straightforward approaches to normalizing data.

Grouping Techniques

Frequently, you will need to transform your data into groups. This section explores two approaches you might take: clustering and binning.

Clustering

Clustering is a technique that forms groups of similar data points using shared attributes. One goal of clustering is to use hidden patterns within a dataset to create groups whose members have something in common. Imagine you have a bag with assorted candies and want to organize it using their similarities. You might put chocolate-based candies in one pile, sour-flavored candies in a second pile, and fruit-flavored candies in a third. This grouping process is similar to what clustering accomplishes.

Companies frequently use clustering to create groups of customers. Suppose you are working on bringing a new product to market and want to identify which of your customers you should target. For each of your customers, you have their annual income, age, and spending habits. Applying a clustering algorithm to the customer data would look at customer similarities and create groups using those similarities. You might end up with something like:

- Cluster 1: Young, low-income customers who spend moderately
- Cluster 2: Middle-aged, high-income customers who spend lavishly
- Cluster 3: Older customers, average-income who spend moderately

From there, your marketing team creates catchy names for the clusters to socialize and explain the groupings internally, as people remember names better than they remember cluster numbers:

- Cluster 1: The Hopefuls
- Cluster 2: The Opportunity
- Cluster 3: The Owls

You want to start with as much data as possible to facilitate clustering. In addition to your customers' income, age, and spending habits, you would augment the dataset with as many other attributes as you have. The additional attributes can include sex, marital status, number of children, work status, education, location, and so on.

Binning

Binning is a way of grouping continuous numerical data into categories. These categories are known as *bins*. Binning is useful when you want to aggregate and abstract underlying data. For example, the United States Census Bureau publishes data using the following broad age categories:

- Under 18 years of age
- 18 to 64 years of age
- 65 years of age and over

If you've ever taken a survey, you've likely encountered binning during data collection. Figure 5.18 illustrates an age intake question that makes survey participants feel comfortably anonymous.

When binning, you can create whatever groupings make sense for the task. For instance, the age categories in Figure 5.18 may make sense in a product satisfaction survey. When working with weather data in Fahrenheit, meteorologists commonly use 10 as the bin size, using phrases like "low temperatures in the 40s and highs in the 70s."

Reduction

When dealing with big data, it is frequently unfeasible and inefficient to manipulate the entire dataset during analysis. *Reduction* is the process of shrinking an extensive dataset without negatively impacting its analytical value. There are a variety of reduction techniques from which you can choose. Selecting a method depends on the type of data you have and what you are trying to analyze. Dimensionality reduction and numerosity reduction are two techniques for data reduction.

Dimensionality Reduction

Dimensionality reduction removes attributes from a dataset. Removing attributes reduces the dataset's overall size. For instance, suppose you want to explore a person's weight as a function of time using the Weight Log data in Figure 5.19. Although the Weight Log has 12 attributes, you only need the Date and Weight for your purposes. If you end up needing the day of the week for future analysis, you can derive it from the values in the Date column.

Note that Figure 5.19 illustrates dimensionality reduction using SQL. However, you can remove dimensions from any programming language, including Python or R.

Numerosity Reduction

Another technique is *numerosity reduction*, which reduces the overall volume of data. Suppose you are working with a decade's worth of Weight Log data from Figure 5.19 and want to identify the most frequently occurring weight. A decade of 365 observations per year

FIGURE 5.18 Survey question.

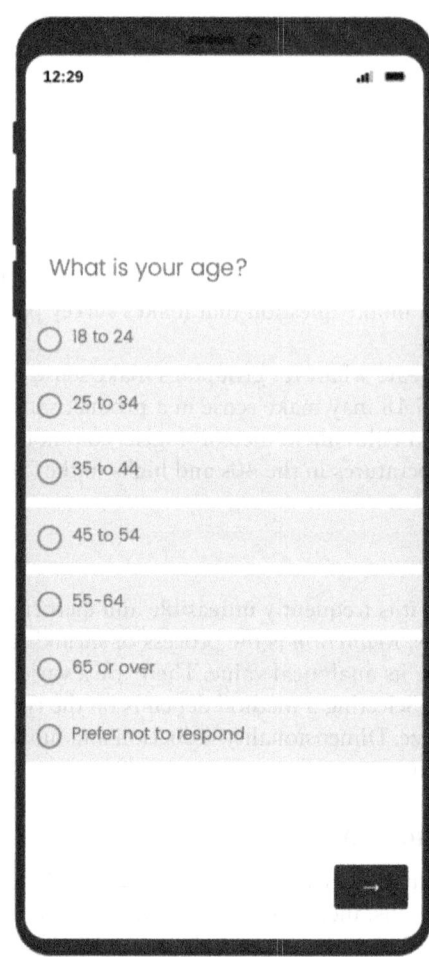

FIGURE 5.19 Dimensionality reduction example.

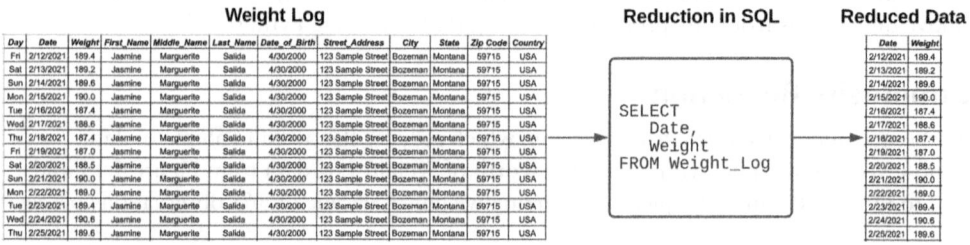

represents 3,650 individual data points per person. If you are studying 10,000 people, the total number of data points jumps to 36.5 million. Your laptop or desktop may lack the computing power to manipulate 36.5 million records. As data volumes grow, numerosity reduction can improve the efficiency of your analysis.

One way to reduce the volume of quantitative data is by creating a *histogram*. You can create a histogram in Python, R, and many visualization-specific tools. A histogram is a diagram made up of rectangles, or bars, that show how frequently a specific value occurs. When creating a histogram, you can configure the width of a rectangle to represent a range of values.

Consider the two histograms in Figure 5.20. Both diagrams represent 10 years of Weight Log data. However, the histogram on the left is for a single person's data, whereas the one on the right uses the data for 10,000 people. Note the difference in the y-axis. When dealing with a single person, the number of observations of 190 pounds is between 600 and 700. With 10,000 people, the number swells to more than 4 million. Regardless of the number of data points, both histograms convey the number of times each weight occurs in the data.

Whether you're dealing with data from one person or from 10,000 people, histograms are great at reducing the number of data points you have to consider. Glancing at a histogram is a much more efficient way of analyzing data, especially when an alternative is combing through millions of rows of data.

Another approach to reducing the data is through *sampling*. Sampling is a technique that selects a subset of individual records from the initial dataset. There are many sampling approaches to take depending on dataset characteristics. The most straightforward technique is a random sample and applies in many cases. Consider the pair of histograms in Figure 5.21. The diagram on the left uses the complete data for 10,000 people, whereas the one on the right uses a random sample from the original dataset. The histograms are roughly the same shape. The big difference is in the time to produce these diagrams. A standard laptop can

FIGURE 5.20 Numerosity reduction with histograms.

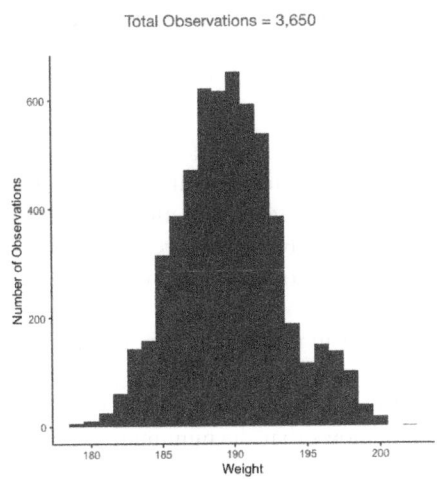
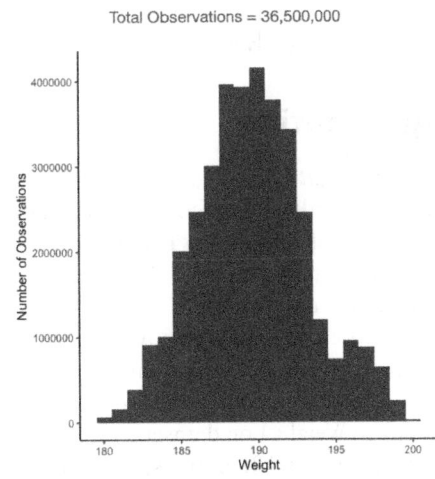

FIGURE 5.21 Sampling and histograms.

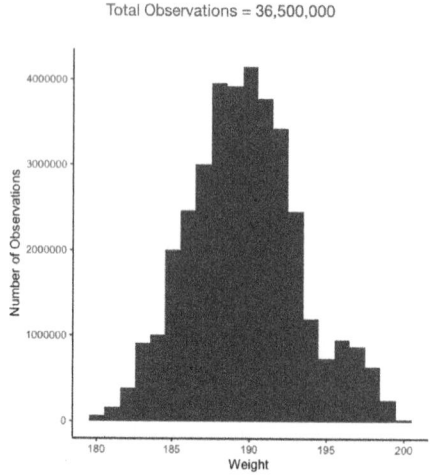
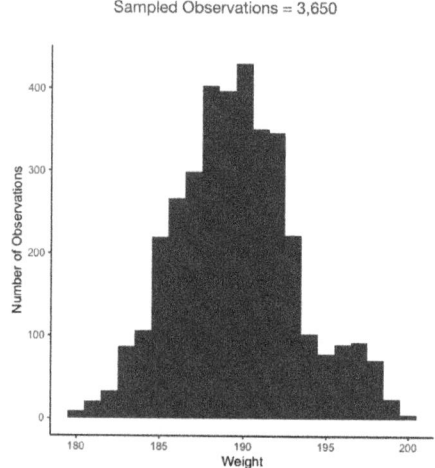

FIGURE 5.22 Summary statistics.

```
         Weight
Min.    :180.0
1st Qu.:187.5
Median :189.6
Mean   :189.8
3rd Qu.:192.0
Max.   :199.8
```

process the entire dataset in about 45 seconds while creating the sample-based histogram, which takes only 0.2 seconds. As data volumes increase, sampling is a common approach for improving an analyst's efficiency.

Aggregation

Data aggregation is the summarization of raw data for analysis. When you are dealing with billions of individual records, a data summary can help you make sense of it all. Recall that a daily log of activity for 10,000 people over 10 years produces 36.5 million records. You might want to know facts about the data that would be difficult to figure out by looking through the data by hand.

Suppose you want to know the lowest and highest weights in the Weight Log data from Figure 5.19. Instead of searching through the data, you can use calculations that operate on the data, giving you what you need. Figure 5.22 shows some summary statistics for the complete Weight Log dataset. For example, this summary shows that the minimum weight in the dataset is 180 pounds, while the maximum is 199.8.

Aggregating data provides answers that help make decisions. Imagine you are on a road trip. While traveling, running out of fuel is the last thing you want to do. Onboard computers summarize your control inputs and give you a meaningful metric: distance to empty. With an understanding of how far you can travel with the fuel remaining, you have the data you need so you can stop, refuel, and avoid being stranded.

Aggregation is also a means of controlling privacy. Suppose you have payroll information for an organization with 100,000 employees and only one chief executive officer (CEO). If you look at salary information by job role, it will expose the CEO's salary. However, if you aggregate the data and examine average compensation, the CEO's privacy is intact.

Transposition

Transposing data is when you want to turn rows into columns or columns into rows to facilitate analysis. Suppose you have sales data with details for each salesperson and their sales territory. Figure 5.23 shows a sample of this sales data. Corporate leadership likely wants to track total sales per salesperson by fiscal year. The first step is to transpose the data.

When transposing, each value from a column becomes a new row. Transposing the data from Figure 5.23, you wind up with Figure 5.24. In this case, the transposed data could be more helpful, especially if you imagine thousands of rows of sales data.

To organize the data to benefit leadership, you can combine the transposition of the FiscalYear column with the aggregation of Sales data to generate the table in Figure 5.25. Combining aggregation with transposition is a powerful data manipulation technique. With this approach to organizing the data, you get a column for each fiscal year and total sales

FIGURE 5.23 Sales data.

SalesPersonID	280	280	280	280	280	280
FirstName	Pamela	Pamela	Pamela	Pamela	Pamela	Pamela
LastName	Ansman-Wolfe	Ansman-Wolfe	Ansman-Wolfe	Ansman-Wolfe	Ansman-Wolfe	Ansman-Wolfe
SalesTerritory	Northwest	Northwest	Northwest	Northwest	Northwest	Northwest
Sales	$24,432.61	$10,993.39	$4,076.39	$32,673.04	$20,628.57	$32,492.60
FiscalYear	2011	2012	2012	2012	2012	2012

FIGURE 5.24 Transposed sales data.

SalesPersonID	FirstName	LastName	SalesTerritory	Sales	FiscalYear
280	Pamela	Ansman-Wolfe	Northwest	$24,432.61	2011
280	Pamela	Ansman-Wolfe	Northwest	$10,993.39	2012
280	Pamela	Ansman-Wolfe	Northwest	$4,076.39	2012
280	Pamela	Ansman-Wolfe	Northwest	$32,673.04	2012
280	Pamela	Ansman-Wolfe	Northwest	$20,628.57	2012
280	Pamela	Ansman-Wolfe	Northwest	$32,492.60	2012

FIGURE 5.25 Combining transposition with aggregation.

SalesPersonID	FirstName	LastName	SalesTerritory	FY2011	FY2012	FY2013	FY2014
286	Lynn	Tsoflias	Australia	$0.00	$0.00	$184,105.70	$1,237,705.23
282	José	Saraiva	Canada	$106,251.73	$2,171,995.26	$1,388,793.28	$2,259,378.09
278	Garrett	Vargas	Canada	$9,109.17	$1,254,087.33	$1,179,530.57	$1,166,720.15
277	Jillian	Carson	Central	$46,695.56	$3,496,243.82	$3,940,665.19	$2,582,198.97
290	Ranjit	Varkey Chudukatil	France	$0.00	$360,245.82	$1,770,366.53	$2,379,276.58
288	Rachel	Valdez	Germany	$0.00	$0.00	$371,973.20	$1,455,093.52
275	Michael	Blythe	Northeast	$63,762.92	$2,399,593.15	$3,765,459.20	$3,065,087.73
280	Pamela	Ansman-Wolfe	Northwest	$24,432.61	$1,533,075.67	$587,779.21	$1,179,815.11
283	David	Campbell	Northwest	$69,473.00	$1,291,904.81	$1,151,080.99	$1,217,486.55
284	Tete	Mensa-Annan	Northwest	$0.00	$0.00	$958,999.53	$1,353,546.16
279	Tsvi	Reiter	Southeast	$104,419.33	$3,037,174.76	$2,159,685.19	$1,869,733.48
281	Shu	Ito	Southwest	$59,708.32	$1,953,000.66	$2,439,216.08	$1,975,080.50
276	Linda	Mitchell	Southwest	$5,475.95	$3,013,884.39	$4,064,078.24	$3,283,568.85
289	Jae	Pak	United Kingdom	$0.00	$963,345.11	$4,188,307.00	$3,351,686.53

for each salesperson by territory. This data representation makes it easy to view performance across fiscal years at a glance. This format also makes it easier to visualize data, which is explored in detail in Chapter 7, "Data Visualization with Reports and Dashboards."

Exploding

Exploding data is a technique that takes complex data from a single row and transforms it into multiple rows. While exploding and transposition transform the shape of data, exploding operates on nested data structures, while transposition converts between rows and columns. Figure 5.26 contains details about two variants of the Porsche 911. Examining the JSON, multiple values exist for colors, interior materials, and wheel designs.

To explode data from Figure 5.26, each member of the nested data elements becomes a row. For example, exploding the color category results in a row for each vehicle variant and color combination. Table 5.1 shows the results of exploding the color category.

Since interior materials and wheel designs exist as nested structures, as shown in Figure 5.26, you could explode each attribute into a separate table. Depending on your objective, you could create one large, exploded table containing a row for each combination. Fortunately, there are software libraries that facilitate exploding data. Pandas, a popular data manipulation Python library, has a method specifically for exploding data.

Standardization

In a complex analytics environment with multiple source systems, it is essential to standardize data into a consistent format. *Standardization* is converting data into a consistent format to ensure uniformity and comparability across datasets.

FIGURE 5.26 Vehicle JSON.

```
{
  "car": {
    "make": "Porsche",
    "model": "911",
    "year": 2024,
    "variants": [
      {
        "name": "Carrera",
        "engine": {
          "type": "3.0L Twin-Turbo Flat-6",
          "horsepower": 379,
          "torque": 331,
          "transmission": {
            "type": "8-Speed PDK Automatic",
            "manual_option": true
          }
        },
        "options": {
          "colors": ["Schwarz Black", "Carrara White Metallic", "Jet Black Metallic"],
          "interior_materials": ["Leather", "Alcantara"],
          "wheel_designs": ["Standard", "Turbo", "Exclusive Design"]
        }
      },
      {
        "name": "Turbo S",
        "engine": {
          "type": "3.8L Twin-Turbo Flat-6",
          "horsepower": 640,
          "torque": 590,
          "transmission": {
            "type": "8-Speed PDK Automatic",
            "manual_option": false
          }
        },
        "options": {
          "colors": ["Guards Red", "Gentian Blue Metallic", "GT Silver Metallic"],
          "interior_materials": ["Leather", "Full Leather", "Carbon Fiber"],
          "wheel_designs": ["Turbo S", "RS Spyder", "Exclusive Design"]
        }
      }
    ]
  }
}
```

For example, you may have corporate naming conventions that enforce standard column names across databases. If upstream systems don't conform to these standard names, the ETL process needs to reconcile the data on the way into the analytics environment.

You may also need to standardize date formats, categorical values ("IA" versus "Iowa"), phone numbers, and units of measure. While ETL engineers are responsible for actually implementing standardization, there are external sources of data that can help. For example, the U.S. Postal Service partners with the mailing industry to create a standardized format for address information. This standard address format aids the efficient processing and delivery of mail. Online retailers need a valid shipping address when processing customer orders. Validating the shipping address as early as possible is the best way to ensure high-quality address data.

TABLE 5.1 Exploded Vehicle Data

Name	Color
Carrera	Schwarz Black
Carrera	Carrara White Metallic
Carrera	Jet Black Metallic
Turbo S	Guards Red
Turbo S	Gentian Blue Metallic
Turbo S	GT Silver Metallic

FIGURE 5.27 Address standardization.

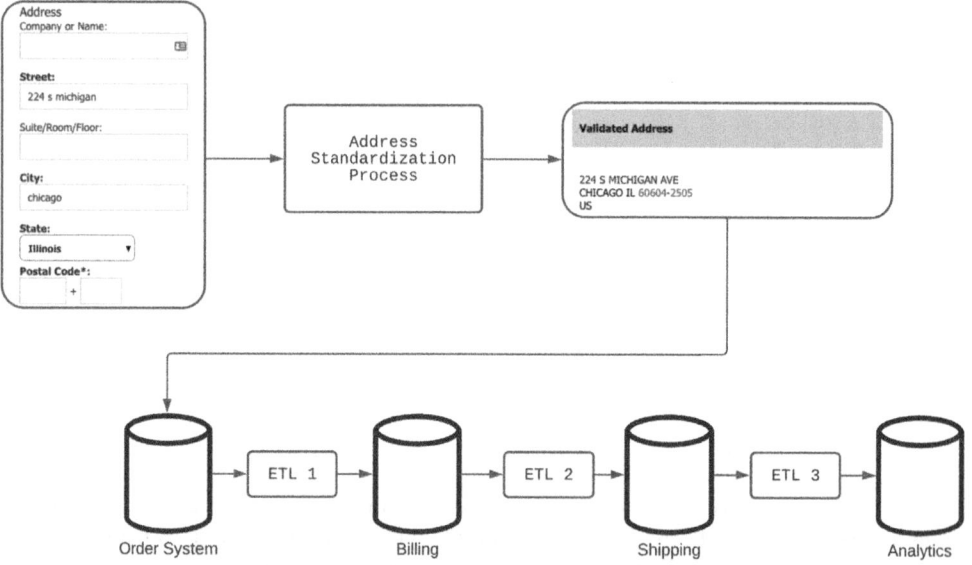

Suppose a customer submits their address information into the ordering system. Figure 5.27 shows the difference between a customer submission and the postal standard. Specifically, the customer submission is missing the designation for Avenue, and the ZIP code is absent. The address standardization process compares customer input with postal standards and generates a validated address. After the customer confirms the validated address, it makes its way into the order system. From then on, the ETL processes serve as a pass-through, sending the data without examining data values.

Imputation

Imputation is a technique for dealing with missing values by replacing them with substitutes. When merging multiple data sources, you may have a dataset with many nulls in a given column. If you are collecting sensor data, it is possible to have missing values due to collection or transmission issues.

For example, Figure 5.28 is a log of someone who tracks their weight daily. Looking at the data, we see four days where there is no recorded weight.

There are many potential reasons why the data is missing. Perhaps the person is using a smart scale, and the scale has lost its network connection. It could be that the person used a manual scale and forgot to record the value. Another possibility is that the person didn't get on the scale on those four days. Regardless of the reason, the analyst must decide how to handle the missing data. Here are a few approaches an analyst can use for imputing values:

- **Remove missing data:** With this approach, you can remove rows with missing values without impacting the quality of your overall analysis.

- **Replace with zero:** With this approach, you replace missing values with a zero. Whether or not it is appropriate to replace missing data with a zero is contextual. Zero isn't a proper value in this scenario, as a person's weight should be a positive number. In addition, replacing missing data with a zero, in this case, will have an extraordinary impact on the overall average weight.

- **Replace with overall average:** Instead of using a zero, you can compute the average weight value for all rows with data and then replace the missing weight values with that calculated average.

FIGURE 5.28 Weight log with missing values.

	A	B	C
1	Day	Date	Weight
2	Fri	2/12/2021	189.4
3	Sat	2/13/2021	
4	Sun	2/14/2021	
5	Mon	2/15/2021	190.0
6	Tue	2/16/2021	187.4
7	Wed	2/17/2021	188.6
8	Thu	2/18/2021	187.4
9	Fri	2/19/2021	
10	Sat	2/20/2021	
11	Sun	2/21/2021	190.0
12	Mon	2/22/2021	189.0
13	Tue	2/23/2021	189.4
14	Wed	2/24/2021	190.6
15	Thu	2/25/2021	189.6

- **Replace with most frequent (mode):** Alternatively, you can take the most frequently occurring value, called the *mode*, and use that as the constant.
- **Closest value average:** With this approach, you use the values from the rows before and after the missing values. For example, to replace the missing measurements for 2/13/2021 and 2/14/2021, take the values from 2/12/2021 and 2/15/2021 to compute the average.

Figure 5.29 illustrates the impact of four of these approaches to imputation on the overall average for this dataset.

Parsing

Raw data can contain columns with composite or distributed structural issues. A composite issue is when a raw data source combines multiple distinct values within a single character column. When this happens, each value in a composite column has data representing more than one attribute. Composite columns need to be split into their component parts to aid analysis.

Consider the string parsing process in Figure 5.30. In the source data, one column contains values representing both sex and age range. You can use string manipulation functions in your programming language of choice to convert the original column into two new columns.

Similarly, it is possible to have a distributed structural issue when data in a single column spreads across multiple columns. When that happens, you need to combine the individual columns. Whenever you have composite or distributed structural data issues, you must manipulate the strings before starting your analysis.

FIGURE 5.29 Various imputation techniques.

Day	Date	Weight	Zero	Overall_Average	Most_Often (Mode)	Closest_Value_Average
Fri	2/12/2021	189.4	189.4	189.4	189.4	189.4
Sat	2/13/2021		0.0	189.1	187.4	189.7
Sun	2/14/2021		0.0	189.1	187.4	189.7
Mon	2/15/2021	190.0	190.0	190.0	190.0	190.0
Tue	2/16/2021	187.4	187.4	187.4	187.4	187.4
Wed	2/17/2021	188.6	188.6	188.6	188.6	188.6
Thu	2/18/2021	187.4	187.4	187.4	187.4	187.4
Fri	2/19/2021		0.0	189.1	187.4	188.7
Sat	2/20/2021		0.0	189.1	188.7	188.7
Sun	2/21/2021	190.0	190.0	190.0	190.0	190.0
Mon	2/22/2021	189.0	189.0	189.0	189.0	189.0
Tue	2/23/2021	189.4	189.4	189.4	189.4	189.4
Wed	2/24/2021	190.6	190.6	190.6	190.6	190.6
Thu	2/25/2021	189.6	189.6	189.6	189.6	189.6
	Overall Average	189.1	135.1	189.1	188.7	189.2

FIGURE 5.30 Splitting a composite column.

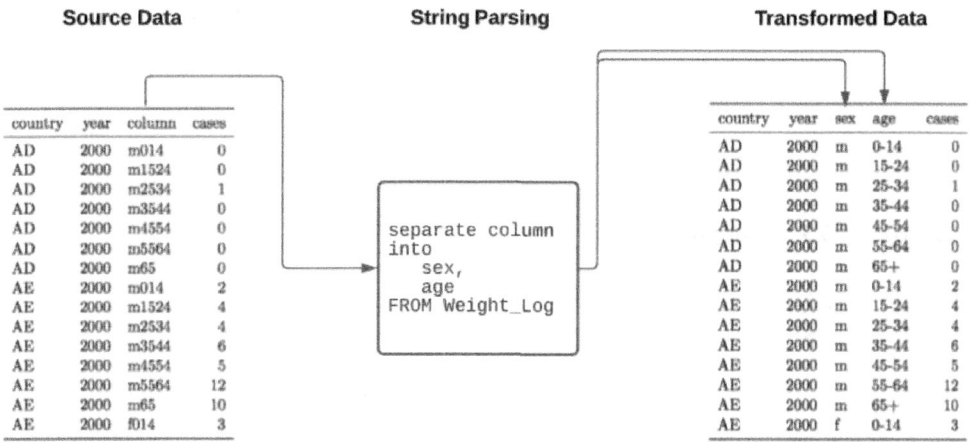

FIGURE 5.31 Combining multiple columns.

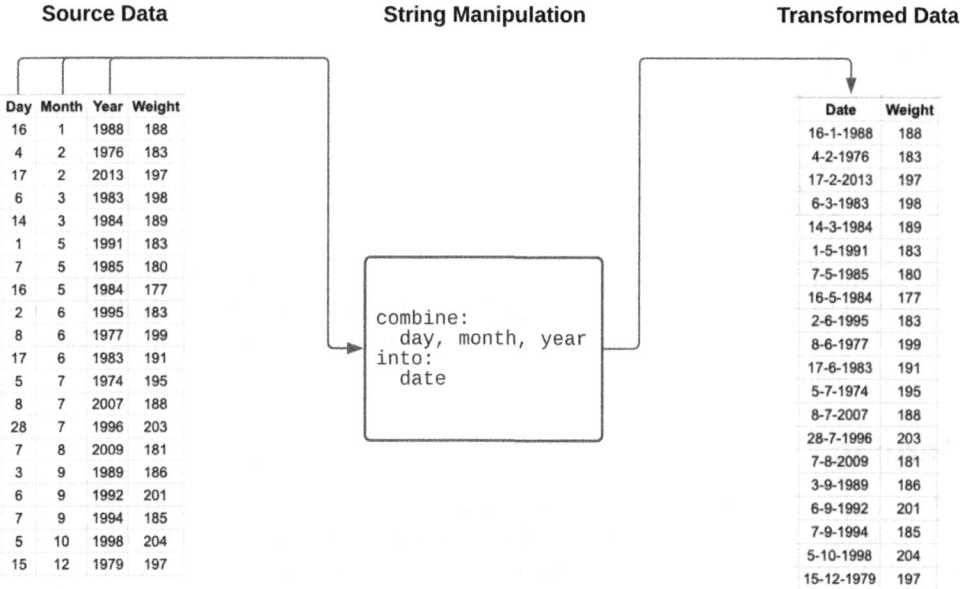

Examine the string concatenation process in Figure 5.31. The source data contains date elements in individual columns. To analyze the data by date, the string manipulation process combines the values from the Day, Month, and Year columns into a new Date column. Once you have a Date column, you can use programming functions to extract the day, month, and year if you need them.

FIGURE 5.32 Improving data quality with string manipulation.

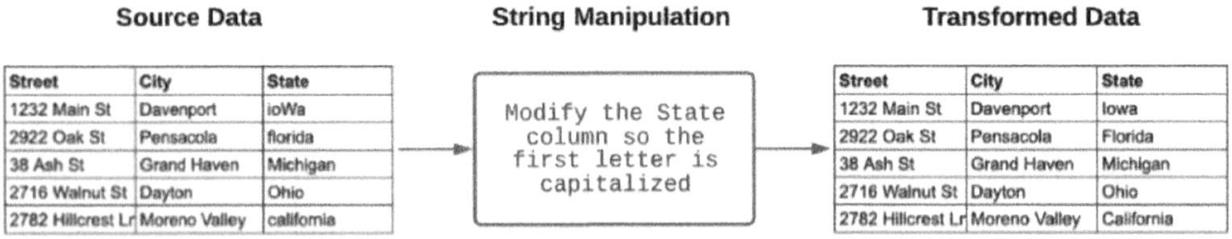

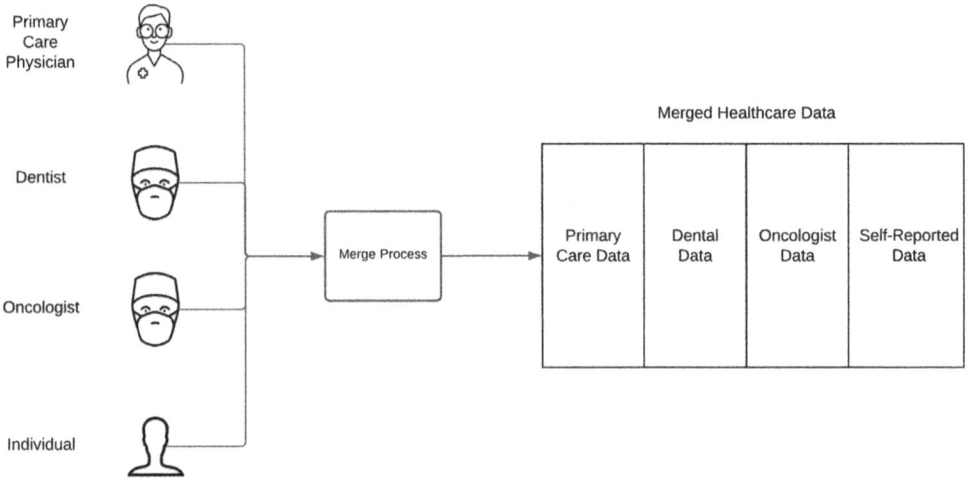

FIGURE 5.33 Merging disparate data.

You also may need to manipulate string data to improve data quality. For example, suppose you have a data source containing address information. Due to a lack of upstream data quality controls, the data you receive is inconsistent. Figure 5.32 illustrates a string transformation that brings consistency to the State data.

Merging

A *data merge* uses a common variable to combine multiple datasets with different structures into one dataset. Merging data improves data quality by adding new variables to your existing data. Additional variables make for a richer dataset, which positively impacts the quality of your analysis. ETL processes commonly append data while transforming data for use in analytical environments.

Since a data merge adds columns to a dataset, merging gives you additional data about a specific observation. Imagine you want to get an overall picture of a person's health. You obtain records from the person's primary care physician and other medical specialists to get the data. You also get self-reported dietary and exercise habits. Figure 5.33 illustrates the

FIGURE 5.34 ETL and the data merge approach.

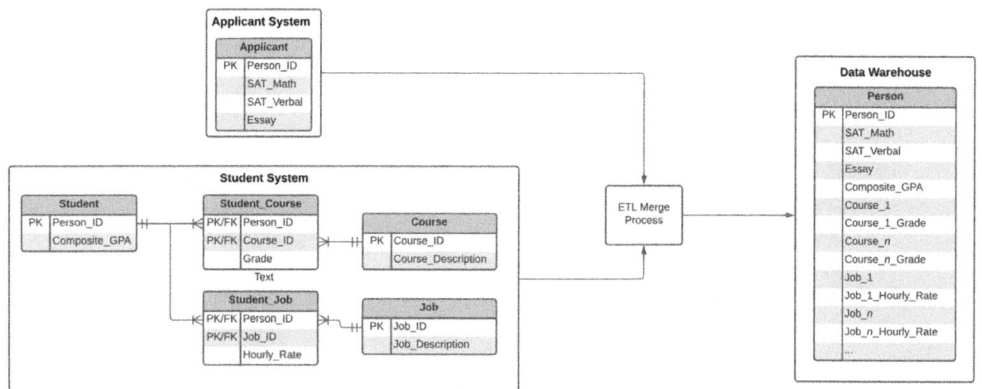

merging of these sources of data. You can imagine the resulting table as having additional columns, as you are augmenting the amount of data about each person in the population.

Consider the systems that support a university. When a person applies, the university stores data, including admissions essays, high school transcripts, letters of recommendation, and standardized test scores. Upon becoming a student, a person generates academic data, including course enrollment and grades. Some students have work-study jobs, which create payroll data, including hours worked and hourly rate.

Suppose you want to examine factors that contribute to academic success. To improve data quality, you decide to include applicant and admission data in addition to student data. You want all this data in a single table to facilitate advanced analytical techniques, so you perform a data append as part of the ETL process in Figure 5.34.

Appending

Appending data combines multiple data sources with the same structure, resulting in a new dataset containing all the rows from the original datasets. When appending data, you save the result as a new dataset for ongoing analysis.

Imagine you are a meteorologist working on a weather report for the evening national news. To improve the accuracy of your forecast, you want current data from as many locations across the country area as possible and rely on the National Weather Service (NWS) to provide this data.

In turn, the NWS appends data from multiple individual weather stations before making it available. A particular weather station collects weather data and transmits it via an API to an NWS server. The server appends the data, giving you a reliable source to develop your forecast. Figure 5.35 illustrates this append scenario.

Consider the needs of a franchisor with multiple franchisee locations. Although each franchise operates independently, they use the same point of sales system. When the franchisor

FIGURE 5.35 Appending weather data.

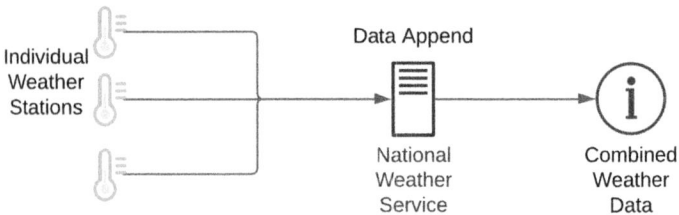

FIGURE 5.36 Patient pain data.

	A	B
1	Patient_ID	Reported_Pain
2	1054	3
3	1055	1
4	1056	5
5	1057	3
6	1058	2
7	1059	9
8	1060	10
9	1061	4
10	1062	9
11	1063	3

conducts aggregate sales analysis, it appends data from each franchisee's point of sales system into a single, unified table for ongoing analysis.

Recoding Data

Recoding data is a technique that maps original values for a variable into new values to facilitate analysis. Recoding groups data into multiple categories, creating a *categorical variable*. A categorical variable is either nominal or ordinal. *Nominal* variables are any variable with two or more categories without natural order, like hair or eye color. *Ordinal* variables are categories with an inherent rank. For example, T-shirt size is an ordinal variable, as sizes come in small, medium, large, and extra-large. Variable values fit into a fixed number of categories, similar to how lookup tables work in Chapter 4. Recoding is helpful when you have numeric data you want to analyze by category.

For example, suppose a hospital administrator gives you the data in Figure 5.36 and asks you to determine how many people entering an emergency room report moderate pain according to the pain scale in Figure 5.9. The pain levels on the scale belong to the categories No Pain, Mild Pain, Moderate Pain, and Severe Pain. Since these groupings exist, the pain scale is categorical. Your data is numeric, whereas the administrator wants to understand it by category.

To complete this analysis, you recode the numeric data and create a categorical variable. Recoding maps the numeric value to the appropriate category. You can implement recoding logic regardless of the programming language you use. Figure 5.37 illustrates the recoding process. Note that you create the Pain_Category column. With this new categorical variable, you are ready to inform the administrator that two people reported moderate pain.

Derived Variables

A *derived variable* is a new variable resulting from a calculation on an existing variable. In the case of the recoded data in Figure 5.37, the Pain_Category categorical variable is an example of a derived variable. However, derived variables don't have to be categorical. Consider the patient data in Figure 5.38 consisting of a unique identifier, first and last name, and date of birth.

You create a *calculated field* by applying a formula to a piece of data to create a new field. For example, a person's date of birth doesn't change over time. However, the person's

FIGURE 5.37 Recoded patient pain data.

FIGURE 5.38 Patient data.

	Patient_ID	First_Name	Last_Name	Date_of_Birth
1	Patient_ID	First_Name	Last_Name	Date_of_Birth
2	1054	Maurene	Easton	1/29/1994
3	1055	Stewart	Atterberry	4/10/2001
4	1056	Vince	Clifford	8/12/1978
5	1057	Diana	Ivers	10/30/1990
6	1058	Bruce	Hutson	9/13/2015
7	1059	Wilda	Duke	3/8/1970
8	1060	Darnell	Styles	11/25/1989
9	1061	Vance	Whitehead	12/2/2011
10	1062	Houston	Koop	1/17/1987
11	1063	Sarah	Babcock	7/26/1996

FIGURE 5.39 Deriving age.

	Original Data				Derivation Logic		New Derived Variable			

Patient_ID	First_Name	Last_Name	Date_of_Birth
1054	Maurene	Easton	1/29/1994
1055	Stewart	Atterberry	4/10/2001
1056	Vince	Clifford	8/12/1978
1057	Diana	Ivers	10/30/1990
1058	Bruce	Hutson	9/13/2015
1059	Wilda	Duke	3/8/1970
1060	Darnell	Styles	11/25/1989
1061	Vance	Whitehead	12/2/2011
1062	Houston	Koop	1/17/1987
1063	Sarah	Babcock	7/26/1996

Age = 1/1/2022 - Date_of_Birth

Patient_ID	First_Name	Last_Name	Date_of_Birth	Age
1054	Maurene	Easton	1/29/1994	28
1055	Stewart	Atterberry	4/10/2001	21
1056	Vince	Clifford	8/12/1978	44
1057	Diana	Ivers	10/30/1990	32
1058	Bruce	Hutson	9/13/2015	7
1059	Wilda	Duke	3/8/1970	52
1060	Darnell	Styles	11/25/1989	33
1061	Vance	Whitehead	12/2/2011	11
1062	Houston	Koop	1/17/1987	35
1063	Sarah	Babcock	7/26/1996	26

age is a function of the current date. Suppose you need to conduct an age-related analysis on patients as of January 1, 2022. Figure 5.39 illustrates deriving an Age variable using Date_of_Birth. Storing Age as a derived column is a bad practice, as it would need constant updates over time. Instead of keeping Age as a derived variable, you should write code that embeds the formula to calculate it using Date_of_Birth. That way, you derive the value of Age exactly when you need it, and you avoid potential age-related data errors.

Deletion

Deletion is the process of removing data from a dataset. There are times when you must get rid of data. You may delete data as a function of a regulatory requirement or because the cost of storing data no longer outweighs the data's value proposition.

In the United States, some regulations require banks to retain email for at least seven years. Suppose you work at a bank and want to minimize the data made available during any potential legal action. You can automate the deletion of data as soon as the legal obligation allows.

Imagine you are collaborating with a mobile telecommunications provider on a project aimed at identifying the features customers are willing to pay an additional fee for. You may explore the number of calls made, text messages sent, and cellular data consumed by each customer. Having the call detail record for each phone line doesn't advance your analysis, as call duration, time of day, and details about the number called are irrelevant in this context. You can create an ETL job that removes the extraneous information.

Data Blending

Data blending combines multiple sources of data into a single dataset at the reporting layer. While data blending is conceptually like the extract, transform, and load process in Chapter 4, there is a crucial difference. Recall that ETL processes operate on a schedule, copying data from source systems into analytics environments. Business requirements drive the scheduling, such as near real-time, hourly, daily, weekly, monthly, or annually. An organization's IT department typically designs, builds, operates, and maintains ETL processes.

Data blending differs from ETL in that it allows an analyst to combine datasets in an ad hoc manner without saving the blended dataset in a relational database. Instead of persisting over time, the blended dataset exists only at the reporting layer, not in the source databases.

For example, data visualization tools such as Tableau allow analysts to connect to different source systems and blend the data using a shared attribute. Data blending can reduce the burden on IT by allowing analysts to merge data.

One important consideration is the level of knowledge the analyst has to have to be productive. Consider the illustration in Figure 5.40. With the traditional ETL workflow, the analyst needs to understand the data warehouse's structure to create a visualization. For routine analysis, such as weekly profitability, the ETL approach works well.

Now suppose the analyst sees a dramatic shift in profitability, and leadership wants to understand the cause. The analyst can blend data from additional sources with the data warehouse to shed light on the profitability change, as shown in Figure 5.41. While this type of analysis does not modify ETL processes, the analyst must understand how data maps across systems. Where data warehouses enforce referential integrity, the accuracy of blended data depends on the analyst's domain knowledge.

FIGURE 5.40 Extract, transform, and load process.

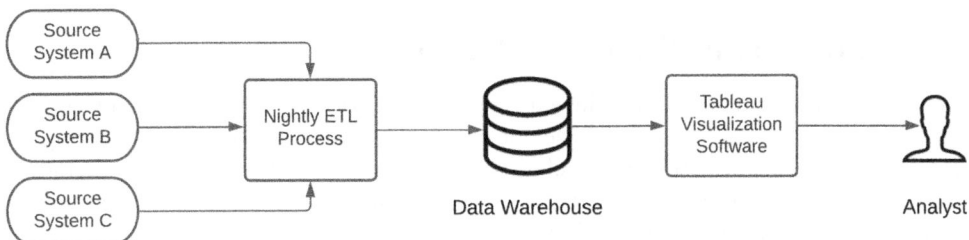

FIGURE 5.41 Data blending.

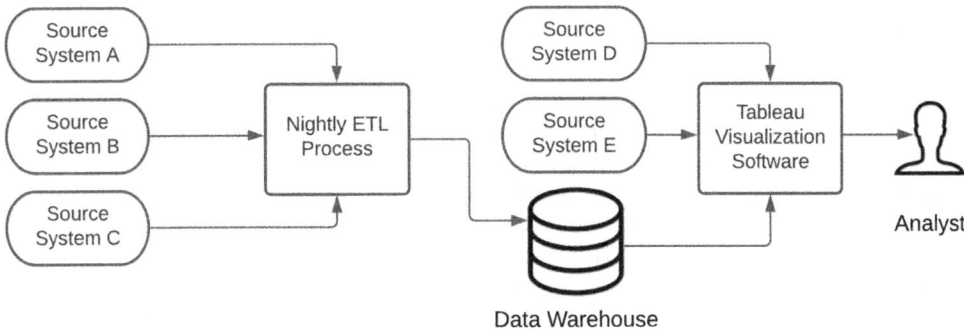

> **Exam Tip**
>
> As you prepare for the Data+ exam, remember that ETL/ELT processes are programmatic and operate on a schedule, resulting in a merged dataset that persists at the data layer. After creation, ETL/ELT processes perform the same action on a routine basis. While conceptually similar, data blending combines data at the visualization layer and allows an analyst to integrate additional data sources in an ad hoc, exploratory manner. ETL/ELT connects data to the database layer, whereas data blending connects data to the visualization layer.

Managing Data Quality

There are many techniques you can use to improve data quality. To be a successful analyst, you must recognize scenarios that create the conditions for data quality issues. To help you develop a mental data quality checklist, this section explores various situations and explains how different data quality controls apply.

Circumstances to Check for Quality

There are numerous circumstances where it is appropriate to implement data quality control checks. Every stop along the data lifecycle journey can impact data quality. Errors during data acquisition, transformation, manipulation, and visualization all contribute to degrading data quality. You should recognize the types of quality issues that can occur and have an overarching strategy to ensure the quality of your data.

Data Acquisition

The data acquisition process is one place to introduce data quality issues. Source systems inconsistencies can result in missing or invalid values. Especially when you are working with multiple data sources, you need to understand when to double-check for potential quality gaps.

For example, suppose you work with a major international logistics company to inform routing decisions. One of the impediments to shipping is sea ice. Since it would cost too much to implement your own network of satellites to monitor the planet's weather conditions, you look to see what federal and private data sources are available. Since it has "near-real-time" in its name, you identify the National Snow and Ice Data Center's Near-Real-Time Daily Global Ice Concentration and Snow Extent data as a potential source.

However, as Figure 5.42 illustrates, the metadata for this data clearly states that it is not for real-time navigation decisions. This limitation informs whether or not this data source will work for you. Although the data is valuable and provides insight into what is currently

FIGURE 5.42 Data source description.

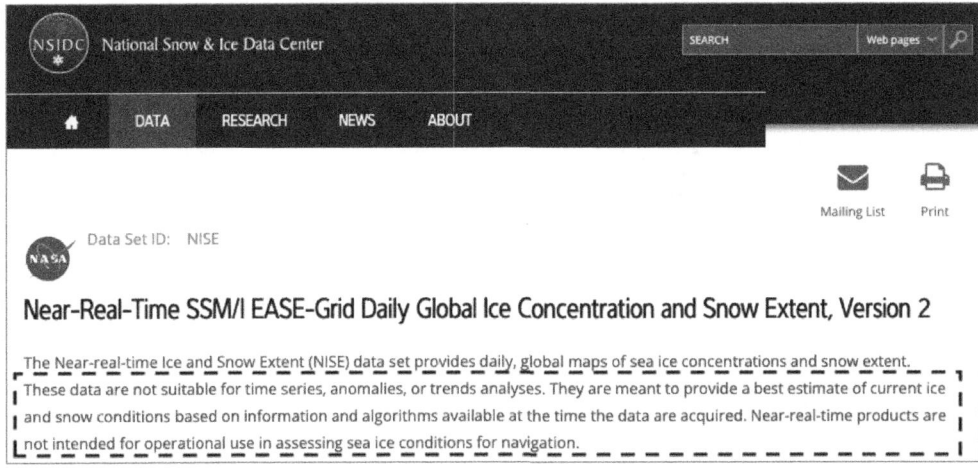

happening with sea ice, it's not appropriate for making real-time decisions about whether a specific part of the ocean is navigable. Understanding the limitations of source data is one way to ensure data quality.

You also have to consider your data source when evaluating data quality. For example, suppose you use a website to sell automotive parts. You typically require the year, make, and model to match the right parts with customer vehicles. An optimal way to ensure data quality is to present drop-down lists for the year, make, and model. If you allow the customer to type in values for these attributes, you will have data inconsistencies. In addition to "Chevrolet," you will end up with abbreviations like "Chevy" or misspellings like "Chevorlet." Positively influencing data quality as early as possible in the acquisition process will reduce your data cleaning efforts.

Data Manipulation

Recall that a data manipulation language defines table structures within a relational database. Data manipulation occurs when data is reshaped as part of an ETL process. Suppose that in Figure 5.27, the Analytics database has a snowflake schema while the Order, Billing, and Shipping databases are in third normal form. The ETL 3 process has to denormalize the transactional data in preparation for the analytics environment. As part of this manipulation, errors may be introduced.

Figure 5.43 illustrates two different ETL scenarios that focus exclusively on manipulating the ZIP code. In reality, ZIP code is just one of many attributes that are manipulated when moving from a normalized to denormalized schema. In the Bad ETL scenario, the last four digits of the ZIP code get dropped. Losing the last four digits could be due to various factors, including an error in the ETL code or a field-length limitation in the data warehouse.

FIGURE 5.43 Data manipulation issue.

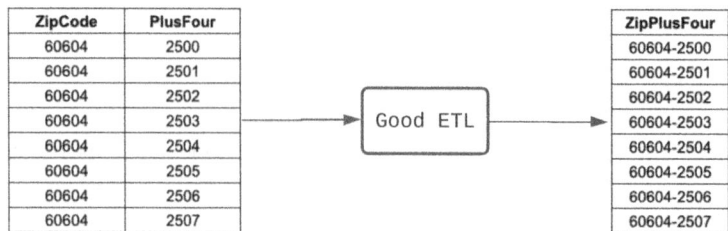

The process in Figure 5.27 ensures quality early in the process. However, as Figure 5.43 shows, a manipulation error can cause downstream data quality issues, even though the ETL does not have to verify the address data quality. Identifying when data is acquired and how it gets transformed and manipulated is an example of why it is crucial to consider acquisition and transformation when thinking about approaches to ensuring high-quality data.

Final Product Preparation

Data eventually gets packaged into reports and dashboards to help people make data-informed decisions. As part of the final data production process, it is possible to introduce data quality issues. For example, suppose you want to create a dashboard using a piece of data visualization software like Tableau. While designing the dashboard, it is possible to use Tableau to link multiple data sources together. If you don't understand the source data well, you may use the wrong join condition when linking data across systems. You learn more about data visualization in Chapter 7.

Automated Validation

Many data sources feed analytics environments. While some of these data sources are other computer systems, others depend directly on people. Whenever people interact with systems, it's possible to introduce data-related errors. Whether source data is machine- or human-generated, one way to prevent data entry mistakes from adversely impacting data quality is to automate data validation checks.

Before automatically validating input data, you need to understand how source data fields map to their corresponding database columns. When mapping input data, pay close attention to the data types in the database. For example, suppose you have a web form where customers supply phone numbers, and the destination database uses a numeric data type to store phone data. If the input form allows for free text entry, someone may enter *(312) 555–1212*. Attempting to insert parentheses and hyphens into a numeric column results in a database error due to a data type mismatch. Automating the data type validation before passing the data to the database prevents this from happening.

Another example of automation is verifying the number of data points. For example, suppose you are collecting hourly temperature data from a collection of sensors. For each sensor, you would expect to have 24 data points per day. If a sensor fails, it no longer reports data. Automating the verification of the number of data points instead of their values can help you identify a sensor failure. Early identification of sensor failure prevents missing data from flowing into your analytics environment.

Data Quality Dimensions

It is essential to consider multiple attributes of data when considering its quality. Six dimensions to take into account when assessing data quality are accuracy, completeness, consistency, timeliness, uniqueness, and validity. Understanding these dimensions and how they are related will help you improve data quality. The following sections take a closer look at each of these dimensions.

> **Exam Tip**
>
> As you prepare for the Data+ exam, make sure you understand the six dimensions of data quality and can determine their appropriate level based on situational objectives.

Data Accuracy

Data accuracy denotes how closely a given attribute matches its intended use. For example, when collecting address data in the United States, you need to determine whether the five-digit ZIP code meets your needs or if you need the complete nine-digit ZIP code. The answer depends on the context of what you are trying to do. If you are analyzing income by geography, the five-digit ZIP code is sufficient. If you are looking to reduce postage costs, you need the nine-digit ZIP code's improved accuracy.

Data Completeness

As explored earlier in this chapter, *data completeness* ensures that all required data is present and accounted for. For example, suppose you are collecting customer profile data. Your database design can accommodate storing a person's title, first name, middle name, last name, and suffix. You don't need all those attributes to communicate successfully with a customer since first and last names are sufficient to generate an email or personalize a web page. When considering completeness, consider database columns that can't have a null value. If a column is required, then it's something you need for minimum viable data completeness.

Data Consistency

Data consistency describes the reliability of an attribute. Data consistency typically comes into play in large organizations that store the same data in multiple systems. For example, a hotel may have separate systems to handle reservation and loyalty activity. Both of these systems need to share customers' names and addresses. Ideally, both the reservation and loyalty systems have access to a single source of customer data. If that isn't the case, the name information exists in both systems.

The challenge is to keep the data consistent. Figure 5.44 illustrates a customer making a change in the Reservation system. The Address Synchronization Process has to propagate the updated address information to the Loyalty system to ensure consistency.

Considering data consistency is especially important when designing a data warehouse, as it sources data from multiple systems. If a customer's address is different in the source systems, data quality in the warehouse suffers. Ensuring consistency as early as possible resolves potential data quality problems before they occur in a data warehouse.

FIGURE 5.44   Ensuring consistency.

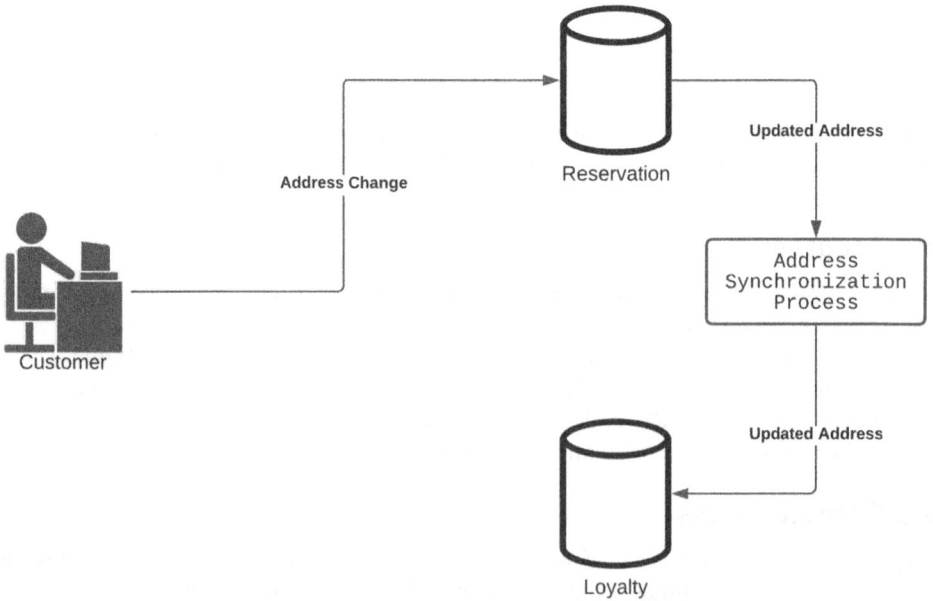

Data Timeliness

Data timeliness measures whether or not the data you need is available at the right time. For example, suppose you are running a marketing campaign and encouraging existing customers to buy additional products from your company. The success of that campaign depends on timely access to which of your products the customer already owns. Trying to sell a product to an existing customer who already owns it gives your company an uninformed appearance. With the abundance of data available in the world today, timeliness is essential to informing strategic decisions.

Data Uniqueness

Data uniqueness describes whether or not a data attribute exists in multiple places within your organization. Closely related to data consistency, the more unique your data is, the less you have to worry about replication and consistency. While you may aspire to have each attribute stored in its own location, the system complexities of modern organizations make that difficult to achieve.

Recall the challenge of a hotel having customer names and addresses in both the Reservation and Loyalty systems in Figure 5.44. Unless the Address Synchronization Process synchronizes changes as they occur, a loyalty statement can end up at the customer's old address. Figure 5.45 illustrates how improving the uniqueness of where name and address information is stored removes the need to make it consistent. In this figure, name and address data exist only in the Customer Profile database. Improving those attributes' uniqueness ensures consistent reservation and loyalty information delivery.

Data Validity

Data validity, also known as data integrity, indicates whether or not an attribute's value is within an expected range. One way to ensure data validity is to enforce referential integrity in the database. Consider Figure 5.46, which shows a customer trying to enter an address with an invalid value for the state.

Within the database, the state column has a character data type. A data type check is successful since "MM" is a character value. Without a validity check, this invalid value gets stored in the database. This situation illustrates the limitation of relying purely on data type attributes for data quality purposes.

However, the Validate State process takes the input value of "MM" and compares it to the database's list of valid state abbreviations. Since "MM" is not a valid state, the validity check fails, and the customer receives an error message and the option to fix the error. Checking data validity at the moment of creation improves the overall quality of your data.

Data Quality Rules and Metrics

With an understanding of data quality dimensions, you need to consider how to measure each of them in your quest to improve overall quality. This section considers data

FIGURE 5.45 Using uniqueness to improve consistency.

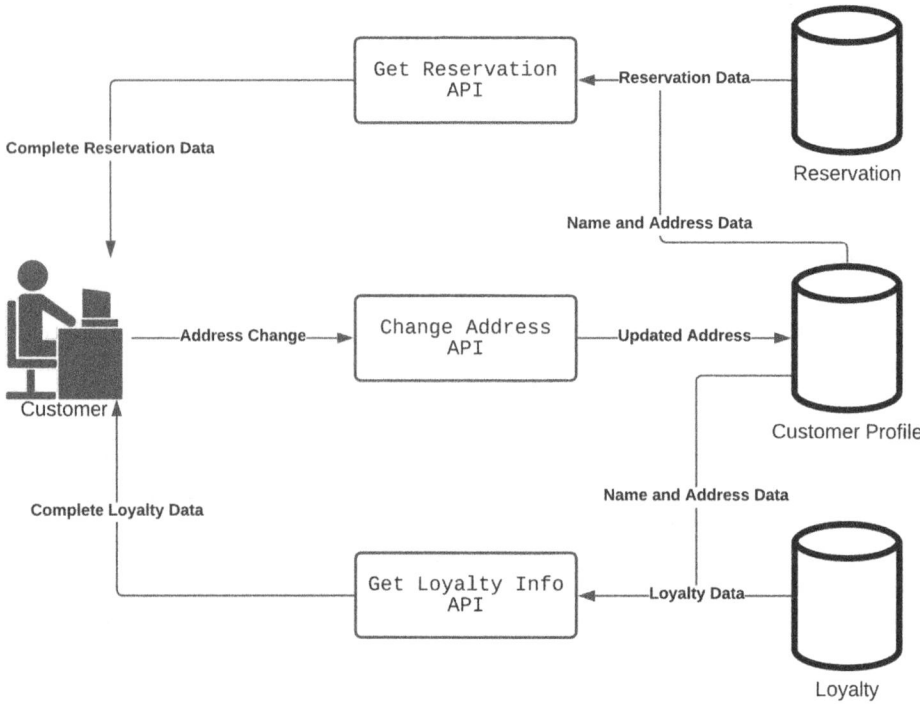

FIGURE 5.46 Referential integrity and data validity.

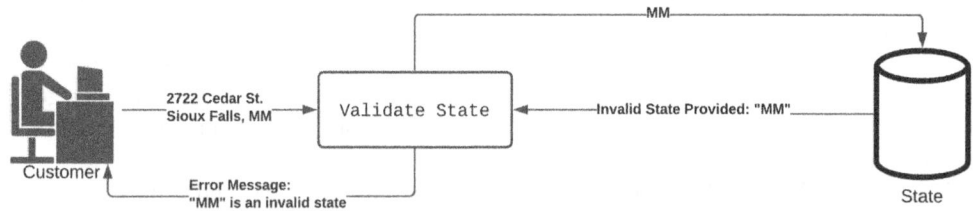

conformity, which encompasses elements of accuracy, consistency, uniqueness, and validity. When consolidating data from multiple source systems into an analytics environment, one factor you want to assess is the conformity or nonconformity of data. If source data does not match the destination data type size and format, you have nonconformity.

For example, consider the source systems in Figure 5.47. Since the Ordering, Billing, and Shipping databases are all distinct, customer information exists independently within these systems. The Warehouse Load ETL needs to ensure consistency as it propagates data from

FIGURE 5.47 Multiple source systems and the potential for nonconformity.

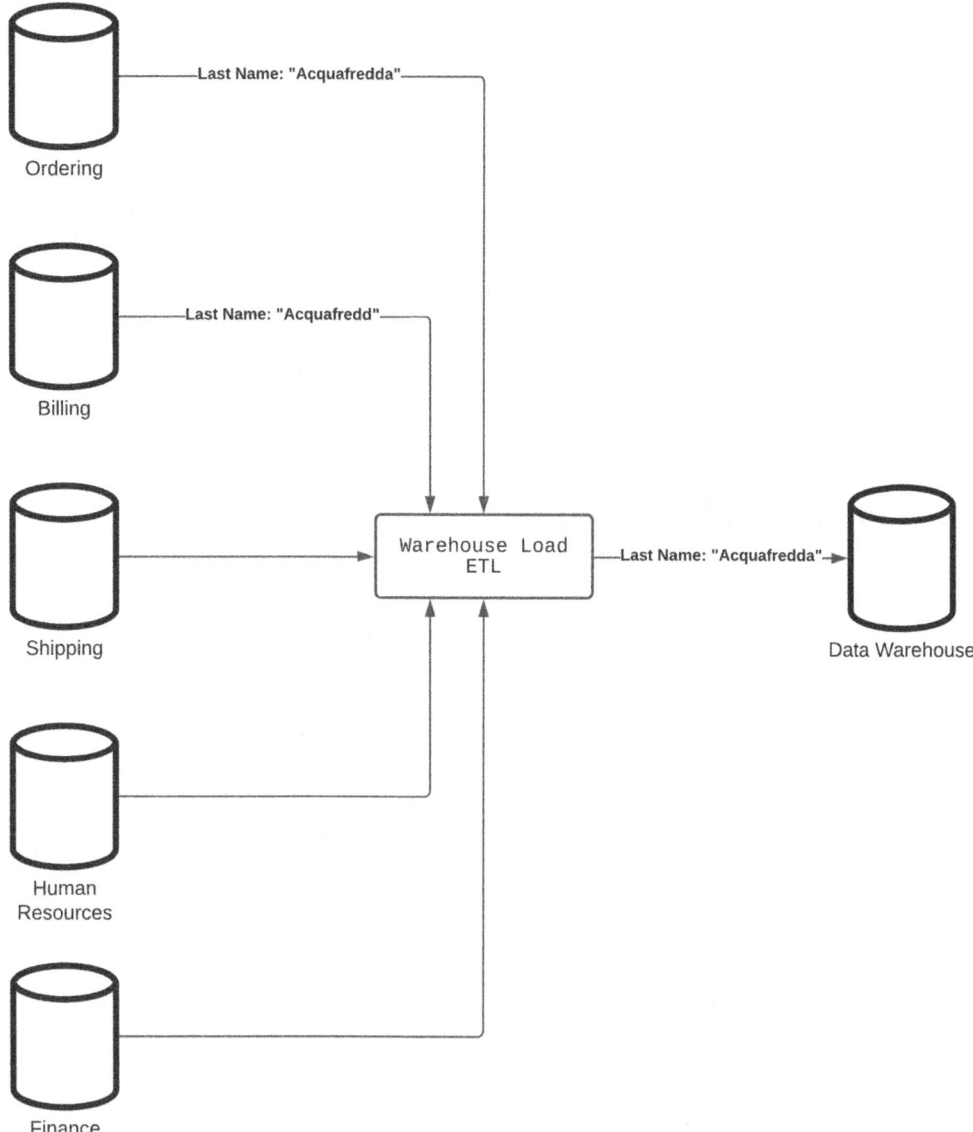

these source systems into the Data Warehouse to ensure data quality. As the source systems are from different vendors, they use different data types for similar attributes. For instance, the Ordering system has a 15-character field for storing a person's last name, whereas the Billing system only supports 10 characters.

This nonconformity presents an ETL challenge. Suppose a customer with an 11-character last name places an order, and the ETL propagates that order information into the Data Warehouse. After fulfilling an order, a bill is generated. However, the Billing system only supports a 10-character last name. Therefore, the ETL job needs to copy the bill details but not the last name field when loading the Data Warehouse. If the ETL overwrites an 11-character last name from the Ordering system with a 10-character last name from the Billing system, it creates a data quality issue in the Data Warehouse.

One way to validate data conformity issues is to confirm how many rows pass successfully to the target environment and how many fail. Suppose you have 1 million billing records to migrate into the Data Warehouse. Figure 5.48 shows what happens when only 900,000 rows are successful. Instead of aborting the entire data load, the Warehouse Load ETL job sends the 100,000 nonconforming rows to a Bad Data staging area. A data engineer then resolves the root cause of the data quality issue before sending the remediated data into the Data Warehouse. With this design, the nonconformity of a single row does not cause the entire load process to fail. By only reprocessing failed rows, this approach makes efficient use of resources as well as improving quality.

Methods to Validate Quality

Numerous methods are available for validating data quality. These methods range from whether or not your data passes reasonable expectations to statistical methods that look for irregular patterns within your data. A sound approach to ensuring and improving data quality is to combine these methods appropriately.

FIGURE 5.48 Reprocessing bad data.

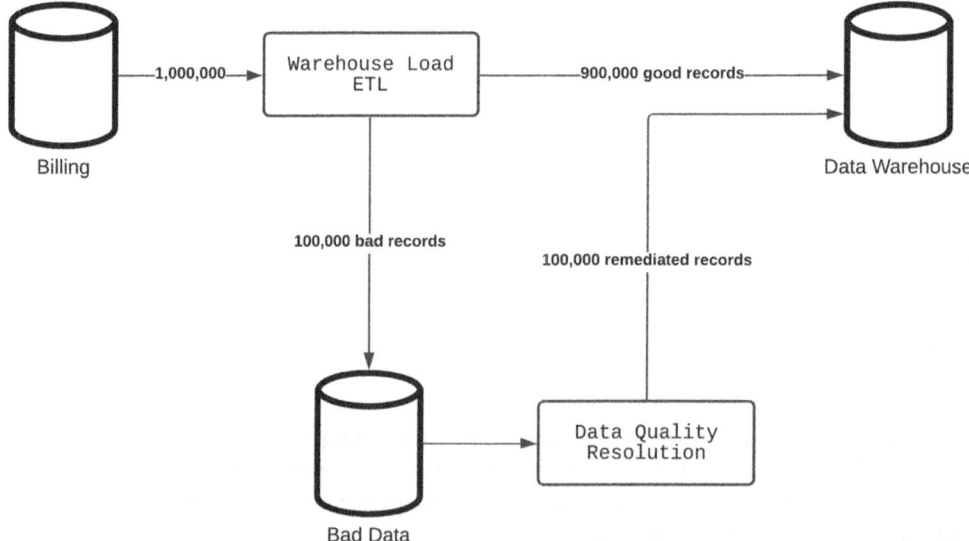

Reasonable Expectations

One approach is to determine whether or not the data in your analytics environment meets your reasonable expectations. For example, if your transactional systems process 10 million records per day, it is reasonable to expect an incremental 300 million records in your analytics environment at the end of 30 days. If, after 30 days, you only see an additional 20 million records, it is reasonable for you to presume that the data propagation ETL is failing.

It is worth spending time reflecting on what measures are reasonable for your environment. After defining how you want to measure your expectations, automate the reasonable expectation check by creating exception reports as part of your ETL processes. For example, if the number of successful rows is less than a large percentage of attempted rows, your internal alarm bells should start ringing. The root cause of the ETL load failure needs remediation to prevent ongoing issues with data quality.

Data Profiling

Another approach to improving quality is to profile your data. *Data profiling* uses statistical measures to check for data discrepancies, including missing values that occur infrequently or too frequently or should be eliminated. Profiling can also identify irregular patterns within your data.

For example, suppose you are trying to analyze customer engagement by examining the frequency with which customers log in to your website. On average, you see that customers log in once per day from one of four devices. However, profiling your data shows that a specific customer logs in 300 times daily from 300 unique devices. Further analysis shows that these logins originate from multiple different places around the globe.

The results of your data profiling activity fail the reasonable expectation test, as customers typically log in less frequently and from fewer devices. Instead of trusting this data, you proceed to investigate whether or not this activity is fraudulent.

Data Audits

Another method to keep in mind is auditing your data. *Data audits* look at your data and help you understand whether or not you have the data you need to operate your business. Data audits use data profiling techniques and can help identify data integrity and security issues.

For example, suppose you work with a large company that has relationships with numerous suppliers. To understand what is reasonable, you create a report to show the average payment amount by supplier. One day, you notice an unusually large supplier payment. Looking into the disbursement, you also discover that the payment was sent to a new financial institution.

As you continue your investigation, you learn that one of your employees fell victim to a social engineering scheme that commits financial fraud. As a result of your data audit, you work with the Federal Bureau of Investigation and your financial institution to investigate the fraud. You also develop a security awareness program to help your employees recognize fraudulent transfer requests.

Cross-validation

Analysts frequently use existing data to generate predictive models using a variety of statistical methods. *Cross-validation* is a statistical technique that evaluates how well predictive models perform. Cross-validation works by dividing data into two subsets. The first subset is the training set, and the second is the testing, or validation, set.

You use data from the training set to build a predictive model. You then cross-validate the model using the testing subset to determine how accurate the prediction is. Cross-validation is also helpful in identifying data sampling issues.

For example, suppose you want to predict overall automotive fastener quality using data from a sample. To generate the most accurate predictions, you want a random sample representing all of the fasteners in a shipment. However, instead of being random, you only test fasteners from one box in a shipment of 1,000. Using a single box is an example of sampling bias, where there is a systematic error in how you obtain a sample. Cross-validation can help identify sampling bias since predictions using biased data are inaccurate.

Summary

Having high-quality data is the foundation for all things analytical. A good analyst needs a firm understanding of why data needs to be cleaned, techniques for cleaning, and ways to verify data quality.

Remember that organizations with complex systems frequently encounter missing, duplicate, or redundant data when assessing data quality. When an organization integrates multiple systems, you need to be on the lookout for redundant data. Apart from duplication and redundancy, you need to check data values for inconsistencies. Inconsistencies can include missing data, falling outside an expected range of values, or not matching the target data type. Keep in mind that outliers have an outsized effect on statistical analysis. When initially exploring your data, it is imperative to identify, understand, and address any outliers in your data.

When preparing data for analysis, you can use numerous data transformation techniques. You will likely use regular expressions to identify patterns in character data that need replacing. You will also need to convert disparate data to be consistent before analysis begins. Techniques for grouping data include clustering and binning. Clustering creates groups using similarities within the data, while binning creates ranges using intervals you define. You may need to augment data with additional attributes for further analysis.

Analysts need a deep understanding of how your data sources will work together. You may have to merge or blend sources or concatenate or split columns within an individual source. Depending on your statistical technique of choice, you may end up recoding a categorical variable as numeric. In today's world, there is an overabundance of data. You may need to reduce the number of rows or columns to facilitate your analysis.

Invariably, you will want to compare the effects of different attributes. Recall that you need to normalize the data values when multiple columns use different measurement units. Normalizing avoids exaggerating the impact of a column based on the numeric values it contains.

Modern data analysts must recognize opportunities for data quality errors to occur. Data acquisition, transformation, conversion, manipulation, and visualization are steps in the analytical process where quality issues arise. Beyond recognizing when quality errors happen, an analyst needs to consider automatically injecting quality improvements into data collection and preparation processes.

When thinking about assessing quality, keep in mind the dimensions of data quality. It is essential to define your business objectives through the lenses of data accuracy, completeness, consistency, uniqueness, and validity. Having the right data at the right time improves your ability to make data-informed decisions.

Once you understand where your data comes from and how you are going to use it, be sure to define ways in which you will continuously assess its quality. Quality assessment methods include everything from reasonable expectations and audits to advanced statistical techniques.

Exam Essentials

Describe the unique challenge of missing data values. A missing value is the absence of a value. Regardless of the programming language you use to manipulate data, you need additional checks to account for the lack of a value. You cannot compare values to the absence of a value. Instead, you first have to determine whether or not a value exists before doing the comparison.

Describe why it is crucial to account for data outliers. An outlier is an observation whose value differs significantly from other observations of the same type. Leaving outliers in your data can negatively impact the quality of your analysis.

Describe the difference between data merging and data blending. Both data merging and data blending combine data sources. However, data merging combines sources programmatically, typically through an ETL operation. Data blending is when an analyst merges data temporarily while exploring or visualizing data.

Differentiate between dimensionality reduction and numerosity reduction. Dimensionality reduction is a technique for removing attributes that are not relevant to the analysis at hand. Numerosity reduction is a technique for reducing the overall size of a dataset to facilitate processing efficiency.

Describe how you can enforce data validity. Data validity is the data quality dimension that identifies whether a given value falls within an expected range. Combining referential integrity in the database with data type validation is a layered approach to ensuring only valid data gets into a system.

Review Questions

The following questions are designed to test your understanding of this chapter's material. You can find the answers in Appendix A.

1. Jackie is designing an ETL process that pulls data from four different source systems. Examining the source data, she sees that data about people exists in three of the four systems. What does she have to ensure that her ETL accounts for? Choose the best answer.

   A. Duplicate data

   B. Redundant data

   C. Invalid data

   D. Missing data

2. Diego is exploring daily rainfall data from weather stations in South America. Looking at the data, he sees one station is consistently reporting values of −10 over time. What is this an example of?

   A. Duplicate data

   B. Redundant data

   C. Invalid data

   D. Missing data

3. Tony is looking at a dataset about movies. One of the attributes is the genre a movie belongs to. For a specific science fiction movie, the genre is listed as "star." What is this an example of?

   A. Duplicate data

   B. Redundant data

   C. Invalid data

   D. Missing data

4. Josephine is exploring emergency room data from a set of regional hospitals. Using a Python script, she encounters an error when trying to get the average patient temperature at time of admittance. What is this a symptom of? Choose the best answer.

   A. Duplicate data

   B. Redundant data

   C. Invalid data

   D. Missing data

5. Larry is evaluating the price of concrete in the European Union (EU). When exploring the data, he sees that prices in Spain are ten times greater than the other countries in the EU. What is the price of concrete in Spain an example of?

   A. Nonparametric data

B. Specification mismatch
   C. Duplicate data
   D. Data outlier

6. Melinda is analyzing a movie dataset, where individual films have a star rating between 1 and 5. What type of data is this?
   A. Nonparametric data
   B. Redundant data
   C. Duplicate data
   D. Data outlier

7. Raphael is designing the ETL process to load a data warehouse. He notices that all the data is coming from a single, well-designed transactional system. To ensure a high success rate for the load process, what is the most important thing Raphael needs to account for?
   A. Data type validation
   B. Redundant data
   C. Duplicate data
   D. Data outlier

8. Jorge's company just acquired a competitor, and he is responsible for integrating the Human Resources systems. One of the things he needs to account for are employees who work at his current company who used to work at the acquired company, and vice versa. What is this an example of?
   A. Data type validation
   B. Redundant data
   C. Duplicate data
   D. Data outlier

9. Lars is analyzing storm wind speed data to understand the number of worldwide Category 5 hurricanes over a ten-year period. A storm reaches Category 5 when wind speed exceeds 157 miles per hour. What does Lars need to do to the wind speed data to proceed with his analysis?
   A. Merge the wind speed data with the Category data
   B. Recode the numeric wind speed data
   C. Impute the category based on wind speed data
   D. Parse the category from the wind speed data

10. Mauro is an oceanographer who wants to analyze the temperature trends in the Mediterranean and Aegean Seas. Mauro has access to data from 18,392 temperature sensors across these bodies of water. How should he manipulate this data to prepare for analysis?
    A. Convert the temperature data from Fahrenheit to Celsius
    B. Transpose water temperature and pressure data

C. Derive a new variable to indicate whether the water is "hot" or "cold"

D. Merge the data from these 18,392 sources together

11. Ashley works as a data analyst for a major retailer. While reviewing monthly website impressions, she notices that the current month has double the number of expected impressions. To help her understand why, Ashley brings in some additional data from the marketing system using a data visualization tool. What is this an example of? Choose the best answer.

   A. Modifying an ETL process
   B. Blending data
   C. Recoding data
   D. Concatenating data

12. Alex's company is about to launch a new product, and Alex is trying to identify customers who will want to and have the ability to purchase it. He needs data to join data from four systems together for his analysis. What has to happen during the ETL process? Choose the best answer.

   A. Data needs to be recoded as numeric.
   B. Data from the four systems needs to be appended into a wide table.
   C. Product IDs from past purchases need to be concatenated.
   D. Price needs to be numeric.

13. Maggie is working on pricing a new product. As part of her analysis, she is looking at the average sales price and volume for competitive products. Noticing that the average price and volume are significantly smaller for a region, Maggie suspects a data quality problem. What should she start looking to see if her hunch is correct?

   A. Check for null values in the source data for the affected region
   B. Verify that the average function is working correctly
   C. Search online for the correct price
   D. Escalate the issue to IT support

14. Sebastien is performing a geospatial analysis to understand household income across a geographic region. He wants to be able to zoom in to the street level and see income on a household-by-household basis. In addition to income, his source data contains demographic and psychographic data. To make his analysis more efficient, what should Sebastien do?

   A. Perform a numerosity reduction technique
   B. Perform an aggregation technique
   C. Perform a dimensionality reduction technique
   D. Normalize the income data

15. Kathy wants to look at sales volume across three product categories. Her source dataset consists of 3 million rows, with columns including product, sales price, region, and product category. How should she manipulate the data to facilitate her analysis? Choose the best answer.

   A. Transpose by sales price and summarize
   B. Transpose by region

C. Remove all rows with null values for product category

   D. Transpose by product category and summarize

16. Randall is designing an ETL process to map source data into a data warehouse. When reviewing the metadata for the source data, he sees that one of the columns consists of Full Name, e.g., "Robert L Cormier." What should he consider designing into his ETL? Choose the best answer.

   A. Drop all data with a missing Full Name

   B. Separate Full Name into First Name, Middle Name, and Last Name

   C. Aggregate the data based on Full Name

   D. Transpose the data based on Full Name

17. Edgar is developing a model to predict which new product feature will appeal to his existing customers. What can he do to validate the accuracy of his model? Choose the best answer.

   A. Cross-validate using a subset of data

   B. Aggregate the number of customers

   C. Trust his instincts and what he feels is a reasonable expectation

   D. Normalize any attributes that use different units of measure

18. Jane wants to conduct a marketing campaign. To be minimally successful, she needs the first name and a valid email address for each intended recipient. What quality dimension is most crucial for Jane to consider? Choose the best answer.

   A. Accuracy

   B. Completeness

   C. Consistency

   D. Validity

19. Ron's company is acquiring a competitor. Ron's original company and the one being acquired sell to the same clients. When integrating transactional data from both companies into a data warehouse, what dimension of quality should Ron be most concerned with? Choose the best answer.

   A. Accuracy

   B. Completeness

   C. Consistency

   D. Validity

20. Shelton works with the International Olympic Committee on analyzing the effect of javelin weight on athlete performance over the past ten Olympiads. Looking in the data warehouse, Shelton sees that javelin weight is recorded in kilograms and determines the data available to him is of insufficient quality to complete the analysis. On what dimension of quality is he basing his conclusion? Choose the best answer.

   A. Accuracy

   B. Completeness

   C. Consistency

   D. Validity

Chapter 6

Data Analysis and Statistics

THE COMPTIA DATA+ EXAM TOPICS COVERED IN THIS CHAPTER INCLUDE:

✓ **Domain 3.0: Data Analysis**

- 3.1. Given a set of requirements, determine the appropriate communication approach for data analysis
- 3.2. Given a scenario, select the appropriate statistical method or function
- 3.3. Given a scenario, troubleshoot basic issues using the appropriate tool or method

In Chapter 5, "Data Quality," you learned where data comes from, when quality issues crop up and how to mitigate them, and techniques to prepare data for analysis. Once you have good, clean data, you are ready to develop insights. An *insight* is a new piece of information you create from data that then influences a decision.

While it's possible to make decisions using intuition, it is preferable to be analytical and use data. An analytical approach applies statistical techniques to analyze data on your journey to create insights.

This chapter explores foundational statistical techniques that describe data and show why they are essential. You will also develop an understanding of how to generate and test hypotheses using statistics and whether or not you can make generalizations using your analysis. This chapter ends by exploring situations where statistical techniques are particularly helpful in developing context and influencing decisions.

Communication Approaches

One of an analyst's most significant challenges is developing an appropriate communication approach for socializing the results of a data analytics effort. An effective communication approach distills months of effort into a few salient nuggets of information that people can use immediately to make decisions. Effective communication combines art and science, requiring you to carefully craft a unique message for your audience.

Audience

An *audience* is the group of people who will consume your data artifact. Creating analytical artifacts depends on having a clear understanding of the composition of your audience. The more clearly you can define who will consume the results of your analysis, the more you can tailor any artifacts you create for your audience.

User Persona Types

A common approach when defining an audience is to create user persona types for the typical audience member. A *user persona type* is the abstract personification of a typical audience member. For example, you may be communicating the results of your analysis to the most senior executives of your organization, also known as the C-suite. These individuals have job titles including Chief Executive Officer, Chief Financial Officer, Chief Operating Officer, and Chief Information Officer. Alternatively, your audience may focus on divisional leaders, product managers, or individual contributors. Each of these user types has different data needs and desires.

Establishing a user persona lets you focus on the idea of the position instead of the person who occupies the position. It is essential to consider the technical capabilities of each persona you create. Here are some example personas and a description of their needs:

- **Individual contributors:** Need sufficient data to effectively and efficiently perform their roles.
- **Nontechnical managers:** Need operational details about their teams to enable tactical decisions; less concerned with the details of the analysis.
- **Technical managers:** Besides needing operational details about their teams to enable tactical decisions, technical managers have additional knowledge about data sources included in the analysis and the analytical methods in use. May want access to raw, unaggregated data.
- **Product leadership:** Need sufficient data to enable strategic decision-making about the products they own, including market size, customer desires, production details, and distribution information.
- **C-suite:** Need insights that enable strategic decision-making. Less likely to understand analytical methods, focusing instead on the insights of the analysis.
- **Board members:** Need insights that enable strategic corporate guidance, report on established goals, and create new goals. They favor aggregated and summarized data instead of raw data and may be less interested in analytical methods.

As you develop user personas, carefully consider the level of detail each persona requires. Highly technical personas may know how to interpret and manipulate raw data accurately. That tends to be the exception rather than the rule, as raw data exists without the context of business rules or application logic. Having nontechnical personas benefit from pre-aggregated, summarized data is much more common.

Personas also inform domain areas to include when considering what your analysis product contains. For example, a report detailing profitability across divisions is appropriate for the Chief Financial Officer. However, the Vice President of Human Resources doesn't necessarily need visibility into that data. Similarly, data you make available to the C-suite may be inappropriate for individual contributors. Having clearly defined personas helps you conform to internal data handling and accessibility standards, ensuring the right people have contextually appropriate analysis.

Constituents

Another crucial aspect to consider when defining your audience is whether they consist of internal or external constituents. Defining the makeup of your constituencies informs the data you use and how you present the results of your analysis. Invariably, whether your audience includes internal or external constituents directly impacts the information sensitivity of the data you incorporate into your analysis.

Information sensitivity is a discipline that determines which constituents should have access to what data. Organizations typically have a data classification matrix that identifies the sensitivity of individual data elements. For instance, aggregated corporate profit is not sensitive and is suitable for external constituents. Alternatively, payroll information is sensitive and only appropriate for a subset of internal constituents. Chapter 8, "Data Governance," explores a data classification matrix in greater detail.

For example, if the results of your analysis will be part of your corporate annual report, while the audience for the annual report includes internal constituents, its primary audience is external. As such, you would only include data that can be publicly accessible.

Alternatively, suppose your analysis supports an early retirement proposal for Human Resources. You include eligible employees' salary and benefit costs in your analysis. This data is sensitive and not suitable for public consumption. As you identify the composition of your audience, you'll need to verify that your constituents should be able to access the data and insights you provide.

Key Performance Indicators (KPIs)

A *key performance indicator (KPI)* is a metric that leadership agrees is crucial to understanding how the organization is performing. Each business unit within an organization likely has its own set of KPIs, in addition to KPIs for the entire organization. Typically, the Chief Financial Officer will use financial KPIs, including:

- Gross Profit Margin
- Cost of Goods Sold
- Net Profit Margin
- Working Capital
- Operating Cash Flow
- Debut-to-Equity Ratio
- Burn Rate
- Accounts Receivable
- Accounts Payable

Meanwhile, the Chief Marketing Officer has an entirely different set of marketing-specific KPIs, including:

- Brand Awareness
- Churn
- Customer Satisfaction
- Customer Lifetime Value
- Cost per Click
- Net Promotor Score
- Return on Marketing Investment

Human Resources has its own set of KPIs, including:

- Employee Satisfaction
- Turnover
- Cost per Hire
- Time to Hire

Other organizational divisions each have unique KPIs relevant to their specific domain. When creating an analytical product, knowing the target audience and expected KPIs is essential. When you know which KPIs your constituents want to see as part of an analysis, you can ensure you have all the raw data you need to create the expected KPIs accurately and repeatably.

Mock-up

A *mock-up* is a simplified visual prototype that lets people in your audience get a directionally correct feel for the final communication product. Creating a mock-up of any data visualization to get feedback before committing the time required to make a functional product is a good idea, as the feedback you receive can profoundly impact your design.

Since mock-ups are not functional, you can create them using your preferred tool for creating visuals. You can use presentation tools like Microsoft's PowerPoint or Apple's Keynote for a straightforward, high-level mock-up. If you want to create a more intricate mock-up, technical drawing software like Lucidchart and Microsoft Visio have features and icon libraries that help you add additional levels of detail. Figure 6.1 illustrates some shape libraries available within Lucidchart that accommodate the degree of granularity you want to represent in a mock-up.

Accessibility

Accessibility refers to presenting insights in a way that makes it possible for people to consume data regardless of any physical disability. To communicate effectively, consider your intended and unintended audiences from an accessibility point of view. Creating accessible artifacts provides a foundation for clear communication. While accessibility is an entire field of study, there are several key considerations when creating analytical artifacts.

When choosing a color palette, pick colors with enough contrast to make it possible for people with visual impairments to distinguish. The same logic applies when using grayscales, or shades of gray, instead of colors. Figure 6.2 illustrates both effective and ineffective color and grayscale contrasts.

Text selection is an essential element of accessibility. Ensure that you are using a font size that is large enough for your audience. From a font standpoint, use sans-serif fonts and avoid using italics. Figure 6.3 illustrates how font size and sans-serif fonts improve accessibility.

FIGURE 6.1 Lucidchart shape libraries.

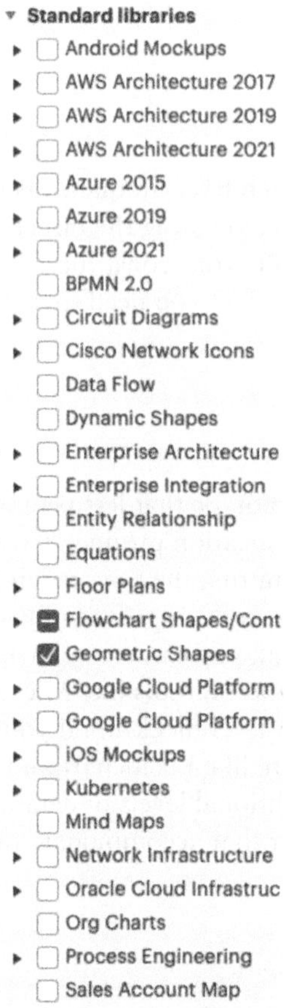

▼ **Standard libraries**
- ▶ ☐ Android Mockups
- ▶ ☐ AWS Architecture 2017
- ▶ ☐ AWS Architecture 2019
- ▶ ☐ AWS Architecture 2021
- ▶ ☐ Azure 2015
- ▶ ☐ Azure 2019
- ▶ ☐ Azure 2021
- ☐ BPMN 2.0
- ▶ ☐ Circuit Diagrams
- ▶ ☐ Cisco Network Icons
- ☐ Data Flow
- ☐ Dynamic Shapes
- ▶ ☐ Enterprise Architecture
- ▶ ☐ Enterprise Integration
- ☐ Entity Relationship
- ☐ Equations
- ▶ ☐ Floor Plans
- ▶ ⊟ Flowchart Shapes/Cont
- ☑ Geometric Shapes
- ▶ ☐ Google Cloud Platform
- ▶ ☐ Google Cloud Platform
- ▶ ☐ iOS Mockups
- ▶ ☐ Kubernetes
- ☐ Mind Maps
- ▶ ☐ Network Infrastructure
- ▶ ☐ Oracle Cloud Infrastruc
- ☐ Org Charts
- ▶ ☐ Process Engineering
- ☐ Sales Account Map

FIGURE 6.2 Color and grayscale contrast.

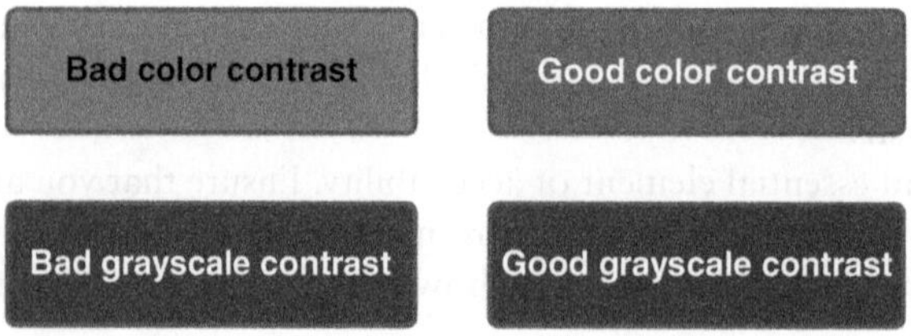

| Bad color contrast | Good color contrast |
| Bad grayscale contrast | Good grayscale contrast |

FIGURE 6.3 Font sizes and serifs.

Font Sizes	Serifs
This is a 10 point font	This is a font with serifs
This is a 16 point font	This is a sans-serif font

If you are creating an analysis product that will be web-accessible, ensure compatibility with screen readers. Ensuring people can use keystrokes for exploration instead of relying on a mouse increases the accessibility of your data artifact.

Fundamentals of Statistics

Knowledge of statistics is foundational for the modern data analyst. Before you explore the different branches of statistics, it is essential to understand some core statistical concepts.

One key concept is the definition of a population. A *population* represents all the data subjects you want to analyze. For example, suppose you are an analyst at the National Highway Traffic Safety Administration (NHTSA) and start to receive reports about a potential defect in Ford F-Series trucks. In this case, the population is all Ford F-Series trucks. If you want to examine all Ford F-Series vehicles, you'd have to conduct a census. A *census* is when you obtain data for every element of your population. Conducting a census is typically infeasible due to the effort involved and the scarcity of resources.

Collecting a sample is a cost-effective and time-effective alternative to gathering census data. A *sample* is a subset of the population. Suppose that further investigation into the potential defect identifies a batch of faulty third-party windshield wiper switches. Tracing the distribution of the defective component identifies F-Series vehicles made in Chicago between February 14, 2000, and August 4, 2000, as being potentially impacted. In this case, F-Series vehicles made in Chicago between February 14 and August 4, 2000, represent a sample. For this chapter, presume that you are working with sample data.

A *variable* is a unique attribute about a data subject. Recalling the definition of tabular data from Chapter 3, "Understanding Data," a variable corresponds to a column in a table. In this example, the serial number that uniquely identifies a wiper switch is a variable. *Univariate analysis* is when you explore the characteristics of a single variable, independent of the rest of the dataset.

An *observation* is an individual record in a dataset corresponding to a tabular data row. Continuing the example, whereas the serial number for a wiper switch is a variable, the serial number's unique value for a specific switch is an observation of the wiper switch variable.

When working with statistics, one thing to be mindful of is the sample size. Since it is unusual to have a full census for the population you are studying, you typically analyze data for a sample taken from the population. For example, suppose you want to discern the average height for females in the United States. Collecting that information about every female is infeasible. Instead, you would gather that data from a representative sample of females in the United States. The *sample size* is the number of observations you select from the population. For example, you may identify 1,000 females instead of measuring every female and obtain their heights. An *n* represents sample size in statistical formulas. The larger the sample size, the more confident you can be that the results of your analysis accurately describe the population.

You analyze samples in terms of statistics. A *statistic* is a numeric representation of a property of a sample. Considering the aforementioned sample of females, the average height is a statistic. You use statistics to infer estimates about the population as a whole.

You also use a sample statistic to estimate a population parameter. A *parameter* is a numeric representation of a property for the population. Continuing the example, you can use the average height of females from your sample to estimate the average height of all females. Just as statistics summarize sample information, parameters summarize the entire population.

When working with statistics, keep in mind that they depend entirely on the sample taken from the population. Every calculation you perform is specific to that sample. If you were to take a different sample from the same population, you'd have to recalculate all your statistics.

> **Common Symbols in Statistics**
>
> Statistics is all about exploring numbers and performing calculations. People use emojis when texting to symbolize emotions. Similarly, statisticians use symbols to convey meaning. To help provide context into some of the formulas in this chapter, use Table 6.1 as a guide.

Statistical Functions and Measures

Recall from Chapter 2, "Data Analytics Tools," that *descriptive statistics* is a branch of statistics that summarizes and describes data. As you explore a new dataset for the first time, you want to develop an initial understanding of the size and shape of the data. You use descriptive statistics as measures to help you understand the characteristics of your dataset.

TABLE 6.1 Common Symbols in Statistics

Symbol	Meaning
x	A variable
$|x|$	Absolute value of a variable The absolute value of a number is always positive, so $|-5| = 5$.
Σ	Summation For example, $\sum x_i$ denotes adding all observations of a variable together.
N	Population size
μ	Population mean
σ^2	Population variance
σ	Population standard deviation
n	Sample size
$\bar{x}$	Sample mean
$\tilde{x}$	Sample median
s^2	Sample variance
s	Sample standard deviation
C	Confidence level value
Z	Standardized score
α	Significance level
$Z_{\alpha/2}$	Critical value for a confidence interval level
r	Pearson correlation coefficient

When initially exploring a dataset, you may perform univariate analysis to answer questions about a variable's values. You also use descriptive measures to develop summary information about all of a variable's observations. This context helps orient you and informs the analytical techniques you use to continue your analysis.

Mathematical

Several mathematical functions are foundational when taking a statistical approach to analyzing data. Initially, applying these functions helps you understand the shape of a dataset and can inform the subsequent phases of your analysis. Mathematical functions exist to measure the frequency, central tendency, dispersion, and position of data.

FIGURE 6.4 Weight log.

ID	Date	Sex	Weight
993487	3/2/2003	Male	191
993488	3/2/2003	Male	233
993489	3/2/2003	Male	211
993490	3/2/2003	Male	232
993491	3/2/2003	Male	181
993492	3/2/2003	Male	248
993493	3/2/2003	Male	232
993494	3/2/2003	Male	225
993495	3/2/2003	Male	204
993496	3/2/2003	Male	199
993497	3/2/2003	Male	188
993498	3/2/2003	Male	250
993499	3/2/2003	Male	170
993500	3/2/2003	Male	218
993501	3/2/2003	Male	233
993502	3/2/2003	Male	244
993503	3/2/2003	Male	239
993504	3/2/2003	Male	176
993505	3/2/2003	Male	217

Measures of Frequency

Measures of frequency help you understand how often something happens. When encountering a dataset for the first time, you want to determine how much data you are working with to help guide your analysis. For example, suppose you are working with human performance data. One of the first things to understand is the size of the dataset. One way to accomplish this quickly is to count the number of observations.

Consider Figure 6.4, which has four variables. The first variable uniquely identifies an individual, the second is a date, the third is the person's sex, and the fourth is the person's weight on that date. Looking at this excerpt, you have no idea how many total observations exist. Understanding the total number helps influence the tools you use to explore the data. If there are 2 million observations, you can analyze the data on a laptop computer. If there are 2 billion observations, you will need more computing power than a laptop provides.

Count

The most straightforward way to understand how much data you're working with is to *count* the number of observations. Understanding the total number of observations is a frequently performed task. As such, there is a count function in everything from spreadsheets to programming languages. As Table 6.2 shows, you have to decide how to account for null values, then make sure you're using the appropriate function.

TABLE 6.2 Selected Implementations of Count

Technology	Count Implementation	Description
Google Sheet	`counta(cell range)`	Counts the number of values in a dataset, excluding null values
Google Sheet	`count(cell range)`	Counts the number of numeric values in a dataset
Microsoft Excel	`counta(cell range)`	Counts the number of values in a dataset, excluding null values
Microsoft Excel	`count(cell range)`	Counts the number of numeric values in a dataset
SQL	`count(*)`	Counts the number of rows in a table
SQL	`count(column)`	Counts the number of rows in the specified column, excluding null values
R	`nrow(data frame)`	Counts the number of rows in a data frame
R	`nrow(na.omit(data frame))`	Counts the number of rows in a data frame, excluding null values
Python	`len(data frame)`	Counts the number of rows in a data frame
Python	`len(data frame.dropna())`	Counts the number of rows in a data frame, excluding null values

Percentage

The *percentage* is a frequency measure that identifies the proportion of a given value for a variable with respect to the total number of rows in the dataset. To calculate a percentage, you need the total number of observations and the total number of observations for a specific value of a variable.

Table 6.3 illustrates the count of males and females for the sex variable in a dataset. Note that the total number of males and females together equals 200. You would use the following formula to calculate the percentage of females in the data:

$$Percentage\ Female = \frac{102}{200} = 0.51 * 100 = 51\%$$

Knowing that 51 percent of the sample is female helps you understand that the balance between males and females is pretty even.

TABLE 6.3 Sample Data

Count of Males	Count of Females
98	102

TABLE 6.4 Exploring Percentages

Male	Female
100%	0%

Understanding proportions across a dataset aids in determining how you proceed with your analysis. For example, suppose you are an analyst for the National Weather Service and receive a new dataset from a citizen-provided weather station. Using a count function, you determine it has 1 million observations. Upon further exploration, you observe that 95 percent of the observations for the temperature variable are null. With such a large percentage of the data not containing meaningful values, you would want to discuss this initial finding with the data provider to ensure something isn't wrong with the data extraction process.

Exploring percentages also gives you a better understanding of the composition of your data and can help identify any biases in your dataset. When data has a *bias*, your sample data isn't representative of the overall population you are studying. Suppose you are working with the complete dataset of which Figure 6.4 is an excerpt. Examining the Sex column, it takes you by surprise that all observations in the dataset are male, as Table 6.4 illustrates. To determine whether or not this is appropriate, you need to put it in context regarding the objective of your analysis.

For instance, if you are analyzing a men's collegiate athletic team, having 100 percent males in your data makes sense. However, suppose you are studying weight across all students at a coeducational university and the university's enrollment is evenly split between males and females. With this context, you would expect 50 percent of your data to be for males, with females representing the other 50 percent. An absence of data about females indicates a bias in the data and that your sample data doesn't accurately represent the population. To remediate the bias, you would want to understand the data collection methods to ensure equal male and female participation. After ensuring there is no collection bias, you would expect the proportion of males and females in your sample to align more appropriately with your knowledge about the population.

Apart from examining the static percentage for a variable in a dataset, looking at *percent change* gives you an understanding of how a measure changes over time. You can calculate the relative change by subtracting the initial value from the final value and then dividing by the absolute value of the initial value:

$$Percent\ Change = \frac{x_2 - x_1}{|x_1|} \times 100$$

For example, if a stock's price at the beginning of a trading day is 100 and its price at the end of the day is 90, there was a 10 percent decrease in its value.

Percent values are also applicable when comparing observations for a variable. The *percent difference* compares two values for a variable. You calculate the percent difference by subtracting the initial value from the final value and then dividing by the average of the two values:

$$Percent\ Difference = \frac{x_1 - x_2}{\left(\frac{x_1 + x_2}{2}\right)} \times 100$$

For example, suppose you receive two datasets. Each dataset is from a factory that creates automotive switches. Upon initial exploration, you find the first dataset has 4,000 observations while the second dataset has 6,000 observations, for a difference of 40 percent. You would want to understand why there is a discrepancy in the number of observations. If the factories are supposed to generate the same output, you are missing data, which will impact your ongoing analysis.

Frequency

Frequency describes how often a specific value for a variable occurs in a dataset. You typically explore frequency when conducting univariate analysis. The histogram is an optimal way to visualize frequency for continuous data. In Chapter 7, "Data Visualization with Reports and Dashboards," you will meet the bar chart. Bar charts are the visualization of choice for categorical data, as the values have no continuity.

In the United States, the Scholastic Aptitude Test (SAT) is an admissions test that some colleges and universities use to assess applicants. Figure 6.5 illustrates the average SAT score for admitted students at colleges and universities across the United States.

It is often helpful to compare frequency across values for an observation. For example, consider the histograms in Figure 6.6, which show the count of average SAT scores for private and public institutions. Since the histogram for private schools looks larger than the one for public schools, you might think that there are more private schools than public schools. To validate this conclusion, you can analyze the percentage of public and private schools, as shown in Table 6.5.

Returning your attention to the x-axis of Figure 6.6, you conclude that some private schools have an average SAT score of over 1400. Meanwhile, no public school in this sample has an average SAT score of over 1400.

210 Chapter 6 ▪ Data Analysis and Statistics

FIGURE 6.5 Histogram of average SAT score for U.S. institutions of higher education.

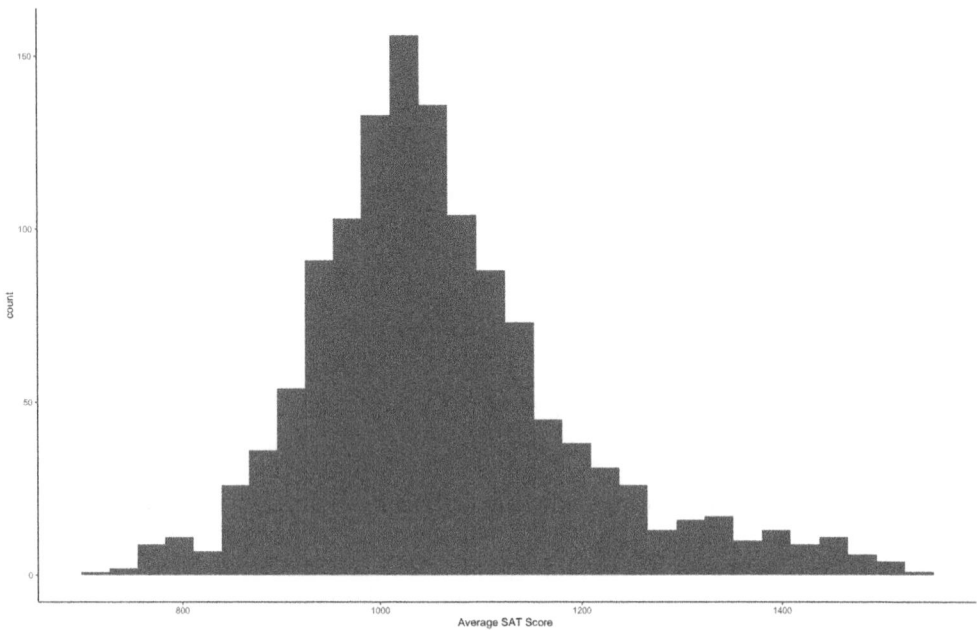

FIGURE 6.6 Histograms of SAT averages and institutional control.

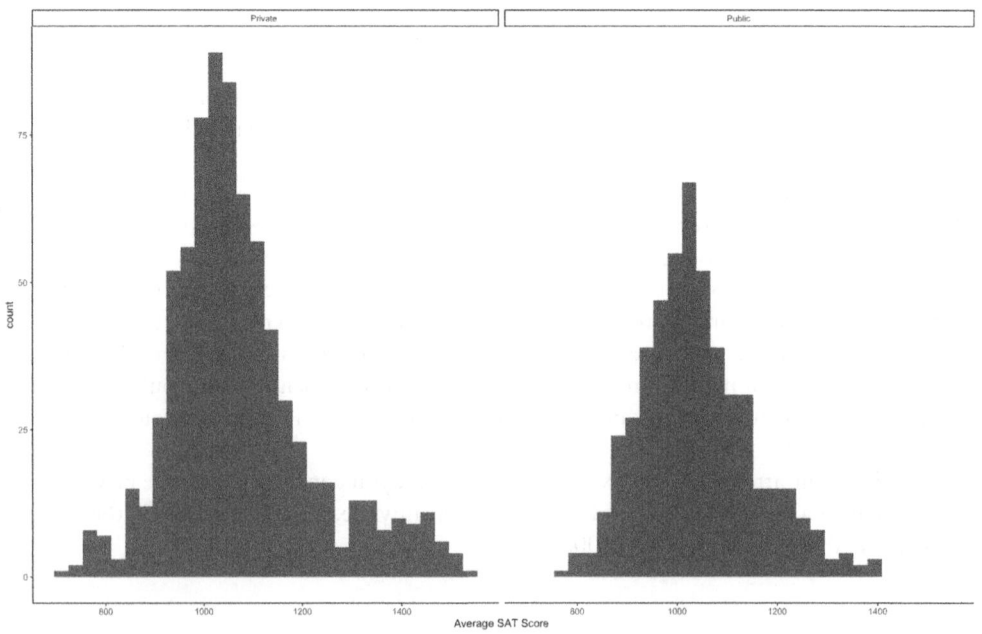

TABLE 6.5 Institutional Control Percentage

Private	Public
60%	40%

Measures of Central Tendency

An analyst explores various measures of central tendency to help establish an overall perspective on a given dataset. You use *measures of central tendency* to identify the central, or most typical, value in a dataset. There are numerous ways to measure central tendency, and you end up using them in conjunction with each other to understand the shape of your data. You learn about the different shape types when we discuss distributions later in this chapter.

Mean

The *mean*, or *average*, is a measurement of central tendency that computes the arithmetic average for a given set of numeric values. To calculate the mean, you take the sum of all values for an observation and divide by the number of observations. In the comparatively unlikely event that you have a complete census for your population, the following formula is the mathematical definition for calculating the mean of a population:

$$\mu = \frac{1}{N}\Sigma x_i$$

Although the formula for calculating the sample mean looks slightly different, the process is the same. You sum all sample observations for a variable and then divide by the number of observations:

$$\bar{x} = \frac{1}{n}\Sigma x_i$$

Data analysis tools, including spreadsheets, programming languages, and visualization tools, all have functions that calculate the mean.

While the mean is one of the most common measurements of central tendency, remember that you can only calculate a mean for quantitative data. You should also be mindful of the effect outliers have on the mean's value. An *outlier* is a value that differs significantly from the other values of the same observation. In Figure 6.7a, the mean salary for the 10 individuals is $90,600. In Figure 6.7b, ID 993496 has a salary of $1,080,000 instead of $80,000 in Figure 6.7a. The salary value for 993496 in Figure 6.7b is an outlier. The effect of the outlier on the mean is dramatic, increasing it by $100,000 to $190,600.

FIGURE 6.7a Mean salary data.

	ID	Salary
	993487	$72,000
	993488	$117,000
	993489	$138,999
	993490	$75,000
	993491	$124,000
	993492	$82,000
	993493	$81,000
	993494	$44,000
	993495	$92,000
	993496	$80,000
Average Salary		$90,600

FIGURE 6.7b Effect of an outlier on the mean.

	ID	Salary
	993487	$72,000
	993488	$117,000
	993489	$138,999
	993490	$75,000
	993491	$124,000
	993492	$82,000
	993493	$81,000
	993494	$44,000
	993495	$92,000
	993496	$1,080,000
Average Salary		$190,600

Exam Tip

As you prepare for the Data+ exam, keep in mind that you have to be wary of outliers when using the mean as a measure of central tendency. It is a best practice to check your data and account for outliers when using the mean.

Median

Another measurement of central tendency is the *median*, which identifies the midpoint value for all observations of a variable. The first step to calculating the median is sorting your data numerically. Once you have an ordered list of values, the next step depends on whether you have an even or an odd number of observations for a variable.

Identifying the median for an odd number of observations is straightforward—you just select the number in the middle of the ordered list of values. Mathematically, you add one to the total number of values, divide by 2, and retrieve the value for that observation. The formula for calculating the median for an odd number of values is as follows:

$$\tilde{x} = \left(\frac{n+1}{2}\right)$$

Suppose you have the following numbers: {1,3,5,7,9}. To find the median, you take the total number of values, add 1, divide by 2, and retrieve the corresponding value. In this case, there are five numbers in the dataset, so you retrieve the value for the third number in the ordered list, which is 5.

For datasets with an even number of observations, you need to take the average of the two observations closest to the midpoint of the ordered list. The following formula describes how to calculate the median:

$$\tilde{x} = \left(\frac{\left(\frac{n}{2}\right) + \left(\frac{n}{2}+1\right)}{2}\right)$$

Suppose you have the following numbers: {1,3,5,7,9,11}. Since there are six observations, the median is the mean of the values that surround the midpoint. In this case, you find the mean of 5 and 7, which is 6.

Outliers don't impact the median as dramatically as the mean. Consider the calculation for the mean in Figure 6.8a, which uses the same data as for Figure 6.7a. For this small dataset with 10 data points, the difference between the mean and median is 9,100.

Now consider Figure 6.8b, which calculates the median using the same data from Figure 6.7b. The difference between the mean and the median is 103,600. This gap is much more significant

FIGURE 6.8a Calculating median salary data.

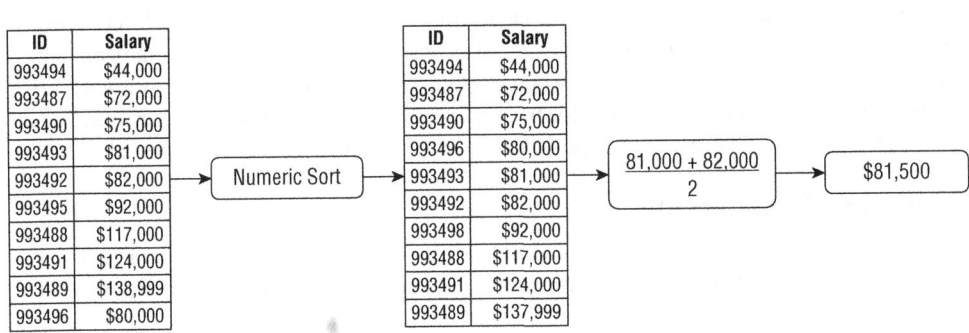

FIGURE 6.8b Effect of an outlier on the median.

ID	Salary
993487	$72,000
993488	$117,000
993489	$138,999
993490	$75,000
993491	$124,000
993492	$82,000
993493	$81,000
993494	$44,000
993495	$92,000
993496	$1,080,000

→ Numeric Sort →

ID	Salary
993494	$44,000
993487	$72,000
993490	$75,000
993496	$81,000
993493	$82,000
993492	$92,000
993498	$117,000
993488	$124,000
993491	$138,999
993489	$1,080,000

→ $\dfrac{82{,}000 + 92{,}000}{2}$ → $87,000

FIGURE 6.9 Categorical question.

than when there are no outliers present. Because of this effect, you should explore both the mean and median values when analyzing a dataset.

Mode

The *mode* is a variable's most frequently occurring observation. Depending on your data, you may not have a mode. For example, consider the salary data from Figure 6.7a. With only 10 values and no repeating value, there is no mode for this dataset. Depending on the level of precision and amount of data, the mode may not facilitate insight when working with numeric data.

However, the mode is more applicable when working with categorical data. For example, suppose you are collecting data about eye color from a group of people and use the survey question in Figure 6.9. Determining the mode of responses will identify the most commonly reported eye color.

Measures of Dispersion

In addition to central tendency, it is crucial to understand the spread of your data. You use *measures of dispersion* to create context around data spread. The following sections explore five common measures of dispersion.

Range

The *range* of a variable is the difference between its maximum and minimum values. Understanding the range helps put the data you are looking at into context and can help you determine what to do with outlier values. It can also identify invalid values in your data. Spreadsheets and programming languages have functions available to identify minimum and maximum values.

For example, suppose you are examining a group of people and their age in years. If the minimum value is a negative number, it indicates an invalid value, as it isn't possible to have a negative age. A maximum value of 140 is similarly invalid, as the maximum recorded lifespan of a human is less than 140 years.

If you are working with temperature data, expecting both positive and negative values is reasonable. To identify invalid temperature values, you need to establish additional context, such as location and time of year.

Distribution

In statistics, a *probability distribution*, or *distribution*, is a function that illustrates probable values for a variable and the frequency with which they occur. Histograms are an effective tool to visualize a distribution, because the shape provides additional insight into your data and how to proceed with analysis. Distributions have many shapes possible shapes, including normal, skewed, and bimodal.

Normal Distribution

The *normal distribution* is symmetrically dispersed around its mean, which gives it a distinctive bell-like shape. Due to its shape, the normal distribution is also known as a "bell curve." Figure 6.10 is a good example of normally distributed data with a high central peak and a high degree of symmetry.

The normal distribution is applicable across a number of disciplines due to the *central limit theorem* (*CLT*), a foundational theorem for statistical analysis. Recognizing that many different samples of a given sample size might be chosen for your data, the CLT tries to make sense of all the possible results you might obtain. According to the CLT, as sample size increases, it becomes increasingly likely that the sampling distribution of all those means will be normally distributed.

The sampling distribution of the mean will be normal regardless of sample size if the parent population is normal. However, if you have a skewed parent population, then having a "sufficiently large" sample size may be needed to get a normally distributed sampling distribution. Most people define sufficiently large as 30 or more observations in your sample. Because of the CLT, the normal distribution applies across a wide variety of attributes.

For example, suppose you are working with quantitative data about people. According to the CLT, you can expect the normal distribution to describe the people's height, weight, and shoe size. You can test the CLT at home by rolling a pair of dice at least 30 times to get a sufficiently large sample, then plotting the value and frequency of your rolls.

One way to use measures of central tendency to verify the normal distribution is to examine the proximity of the mean and median. When the mean and median are relatively close together, the distribution will be symmetrical. If the mean and median are far apart, the data is *skewed*, or asymmetrical.

FIGURE 6.10 Normal distribution.

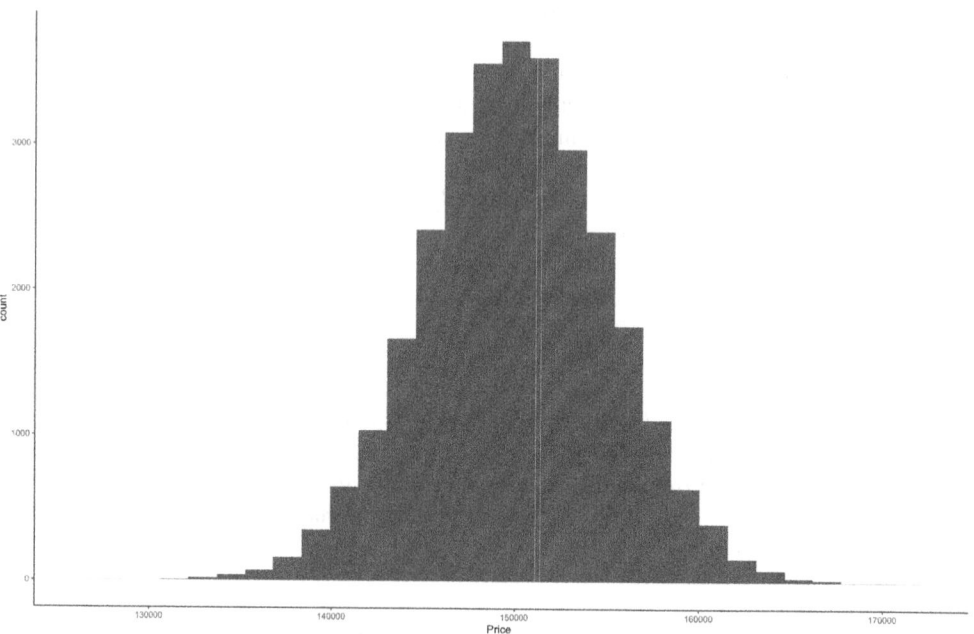

Skewed Distribution

A *skewed distribution* has an asymmetrical shape, with a single peak and a long tail on one side. Skewed distributions have either a right (positive) or left (negative) skew. When the skew is to the right, the mean is typically greater than the median. On the other hand, a distribution with a left skew typically has a mean less than the median.

Consider the histogram in Figure 6.11, which illustrates a distribution with a right skew. The long tail to the right of the peak shows that while most people have a salary of under $100,000, a large portion of the population earns significantly more. It is reasonable to expect that a right skew for income.

Sometimes, you would expect to see a left skew in the data. For example, imagine grades on a 100-point exam for students in a graduate statistics class. You would expect these students to have high intrinsic motivation and an innate desire to learn. While it is inevitable that some students perform poorly, it is reasonable to presume that most students would perform well. As such, you would expect the distribution to have a left skew, as Figure 6.12 illustrates.

Bimodal Distribution

A *bimodal distribution* has two distinct modes, whereas a multimodal distribution has multiple distinct modes. When you visualize a bimodal distribution, you see two separate peaks.

FIGURE 6.11 Right skewed distribution.

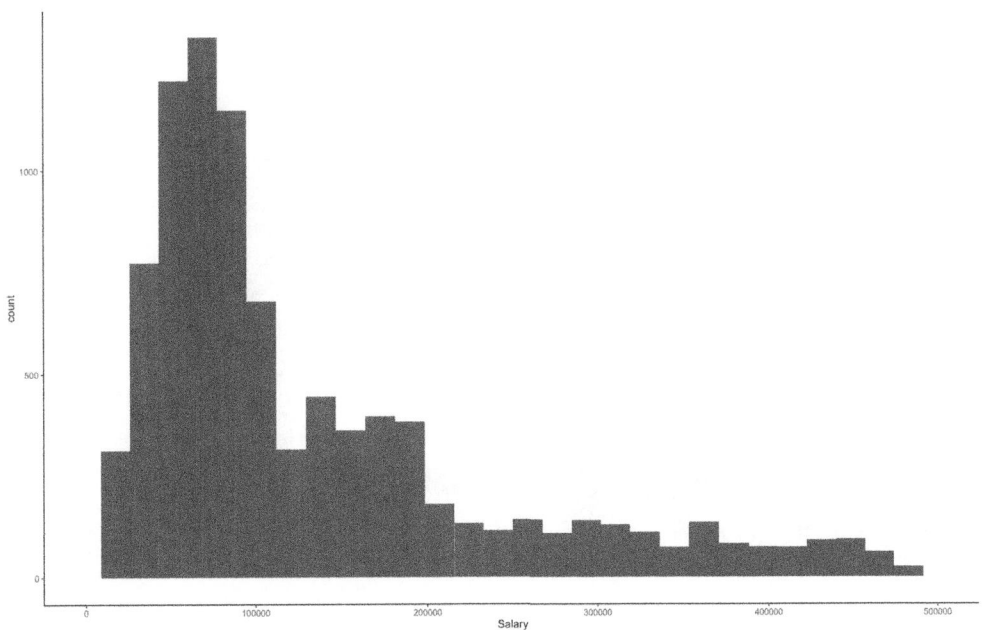

FIGURE 6.12 Left skewed distribution.

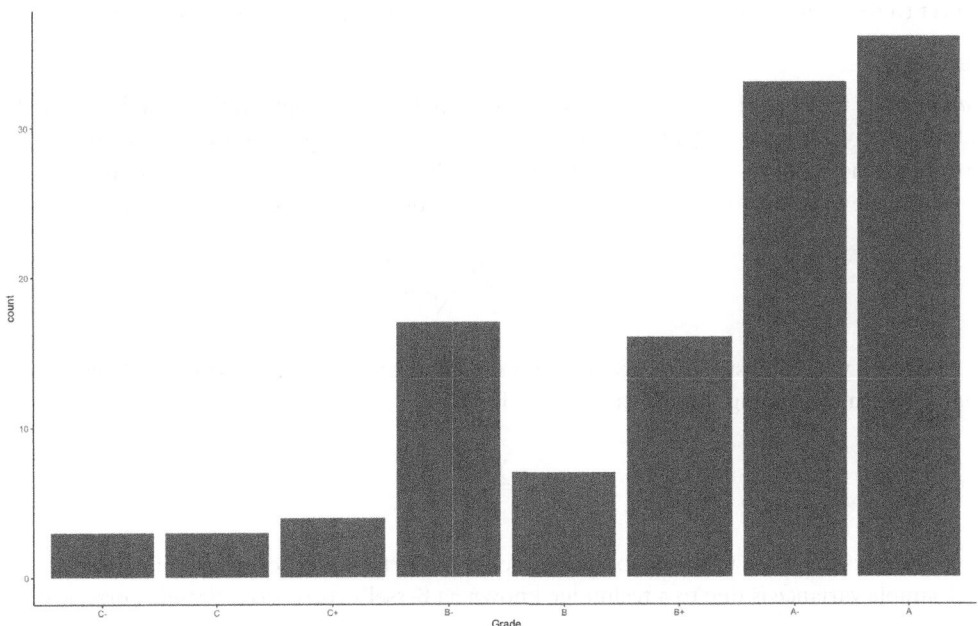

FIGURE 6.13 Bimodal distribution.

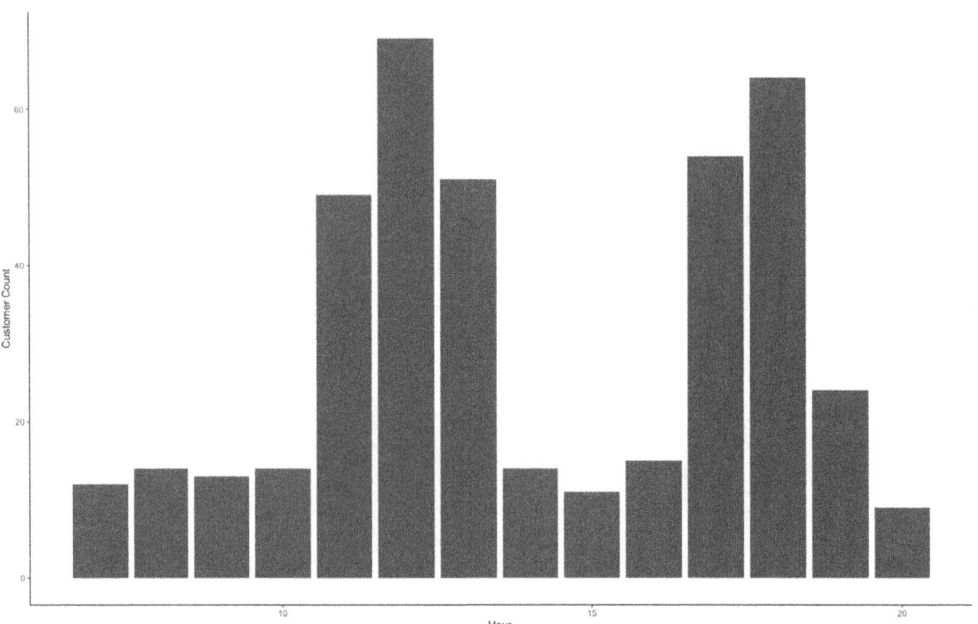

Suppose you are analyzing the number of customers at a restaurant over time. You would expect to see large numbers of customers at lunch and dinner, as Figure 6.13 illustrates.

Variance

Variance is a measure of dispersion that takes the values for each observation in a dataset and calculates how far away they are from the mean value. This dispersion measure indicates how spread out the data is in squared units. Mathematically, σ^2 signifies population variance, which you calculate by taking the average squared deviation of each value from the mean, as follows:

$$\sigma^2 = \frac{\sum(x_i - \mu)^2}{N}$$

However, you will usually be dealing with sample data. As such, the formula changes slightly when calculating sample variance, as follows:

$$s^2 = \frac{\sum(x_i - \bar{x})^2}{n - 1}$$

The slight difference in the denominator between the formulas for calculating population and sample variance is due to a technique known as Bessel's correction. *Bessel's correction*

FIGURE 6.14 Temperature variance.

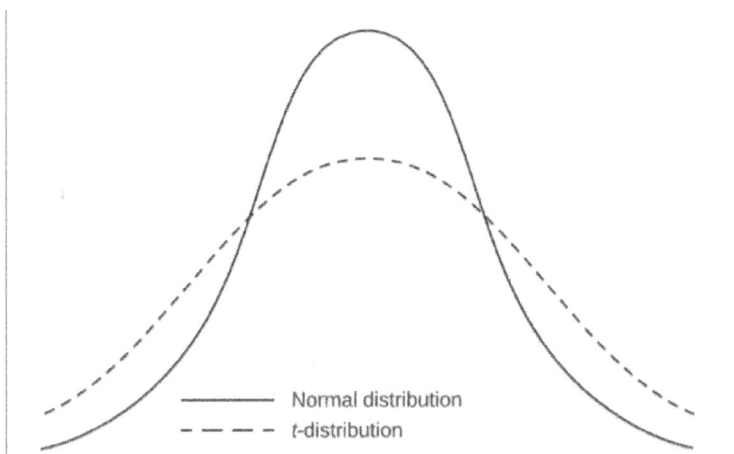

specifies that when calculating sample variance, you need to account for bias, or error, in your sample. Recall that a sample doesn't fully represent the overall population. When you have sample data and use $n - 1$ (the degrees of freedom) in the denominator, it provides an unbiased estimate of the variability.

When the variance is large, the observations' values are far from the mean and thus far from each other. Meanwhile, a small variance implies that the values are closer together.

Consider Figure 6.14, which shows histograms of temperature data for Chicago, Illinois, and San Diego, California. As a city in the Midwest, Chicago is known for having cold winters and hot summers. Meanwhile, San Diego has a much more stable climate with minor fluctuations in temperature. Using the data behind Figure 6.14, the variance for Chicago temperature is 517.8, while the variance for San Diego is 98.6.

Variance can be a useful measure when considering financial investments. For example, a mutual fund with a small variance in its price is likely to be a more stable investment vehicle than an individual stock with a large variance. However, since variance is measured in squared units, it is not presented as often as its sister statistic, the standard deviation, to describe the dispersion of values in a dataset.

Standard Deviation

Standard deviation is a statistic that measures dispersion in terms of how far the values of a variable are from its mean. Specifically, the standard deviation is the average deviation between individual values and the mean. Mathematically, σ signifies population standard deviation, which you calculate by taking the square root of the variance as follows:

$$\sigma = \sqrt{\sigma^2} = \sqrt{\frac{\sum(x_i - \mu)^2}{N}}$$

Similar to the difference between population and sample variance, the formula for sample standard deviation uses Bessel's correction:

$$s = \sqrt{s^2} = \sqrt{\frac{\sum(x_i - \bar{x})^2}{n-1}}$$

As you can see from these formulas, calculating variance is an important step on the way to determining standard deviation.

Similar to variance, the standard deviation is a measure of volatility, with a low value implying stability. Standard deviation is a popular statistic because of the empirical rule. Also known as the three-sigma rule, the *empirical rule* states that almost every observation falls within three standard deviations of the mean in a normal distribution. Specifically, the empirical rule states that approximately 68 percent of values are within one standard deviation of the mean, 95 percent of values fall within two standard deviations, and 99.7 percent fall within three standard deviations.

Combining the central limit theorem and the empirical rule makes standard deviation a common way of describing and discussing variability. For example, using the data behind Figure 6.14, the San Diego temperature mean is 64, and the standard deviation is 10. Using the empirical rule, this implies that 68 percent of the time, the temperature in San Diego is between 54 and 74 degrees. Similarly, using two standard deviations, the implication is that the temperature in San Diego is between 44 and 84 degrees 95 percent of the time.

Standard deviation is a widely accepted measure of quality control in manufacturing processes. Large manufacturers implement programs to improve the consistency of their manufacturing processes. The goal of these programs is to ensure that the processes operate within a certain number of standard deviations, or sigmas. Quality control literature frequently uses the word sigma instead of standard deviation due to sigma being the mathematical symbol for population standard deviation.

One quality control program is known as Six Sigma, which sets the goal for a production process to six standard deviations. Achieving that degree of consistency is difficult and expensive. However, considering the data in Table 6.6, achieving six standard deviations of consistency implies a process that has almost no defects.

TABLE 6.6 Standard Deviation Performance Levels

Standard Deviations	Defects per Million	Percent Correct
1	691,462	30.85
2	308,538	69.146
3	66,807	93.319
4	6,210	99.379
5	233	99.9767
6	3.4	99.9997

Each Sample Is Unique

Keep in mind that each sample from a population is unique. Suppose you take two different samples from a population. The variance and standard deviation for each sample will be different.

Special Normal Distributions

The Central Limit Theorem and empirical rule combine to make the normal distribution the most important distribution in statistics. There are two special normal distributions that have broad applicability and warrant a deeper understanding.

Standard Normal Distribution

The *standard normal distribution*, or *Z-distribution*, is a special normal distribution with a mean of 0 and a standard deviation of 1. You can standardize any normal distribution by converting its values into Z-scores. Converting to the standard normal lets you compare normal distributions with different means and standard deviations.

Calculating Standardized Scores

If you are curious about the math behind calculating the Z-score's value, the formula is as follows:

$$Z = \frac{x - \mu}{\sigma}$$

Student's *t*-distribution

The *Student's t-distribution*, commonly known as the *t-distribution*, is similar to the standard normal distribution in that it has a mean of 0 with a bell-like shape. One way the *t*-distribution differs from the standard normal distribution is how thick the tails are since you can use the *t*-distribution for sample sizes of less than 30. Consider Figure 6.15, which overlays a normal distribution and a *t*-distribution. Note that there is more area under the tails of the *t*-distribution than of the normal distribution.

It's crucial to note that the height of the bell and the thickness of the tails in *t*-distributions vary due to the number of degrees of freedom. Numerically, the value for *degrees of freedom* is one less than the number of observations in your sample data. The degrees of freedom represent the number of values that can vary when calculating a statistic.

For example, consider the data in Table 6.7. In each row, there are three observations, and the value of the mean calculates to 50. In this example, if the first two observations are known, the value of the third observation is not free to vary. It must be fixed in order to calculate a mean of 50.

FIGURE 6.15 Standard normal distribution and *t*-distribution.

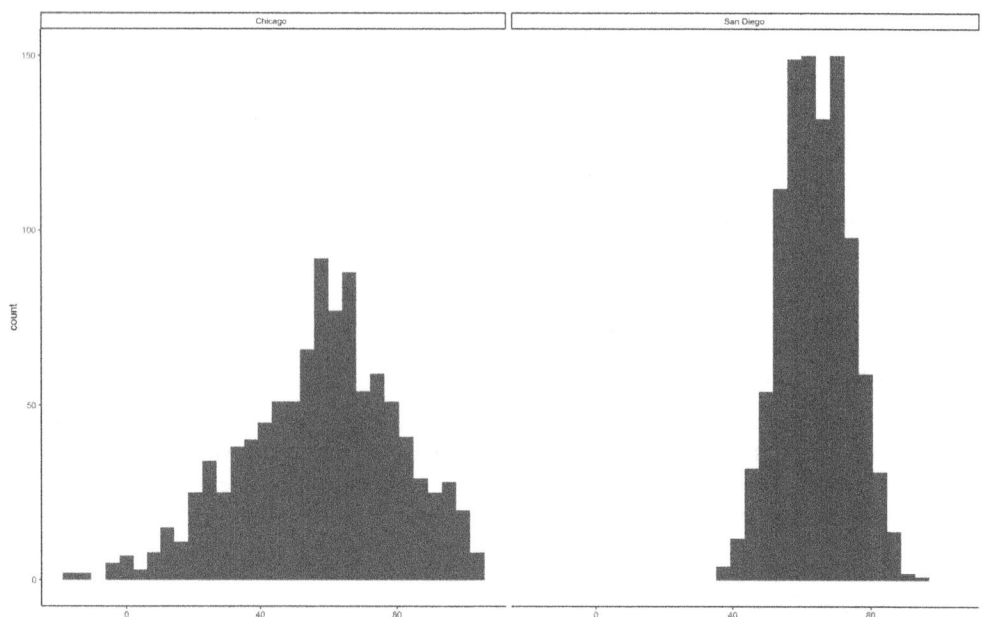

TABLE 6.7 Illustrating Degrees of Freedom

x_1	x_2	x_3	Mean
49	50	51	50
40	50	60	50
20	50	a	50
20	b	c	50

Consider the third row of Table 6.7. Since the mean is 50, the value of *a* must be 80:

Initial Equation: $\quad \dfrac{20 + 50 + a}{3} = 50$

Multiply both sides by 3: $\quad 20 + 50 + a = 150$

Subtract 70 from both sides: $\quad a = 80$

Now consider the last row of Table 6.7, where b and c represent unknown values:

Initial Equation: $\frac{20 + b + c}{3} = 50$

Multiply both sides by 3: $20 + b + c = 130$

Subtract 20 *from both sides*: $b + c = 130$

In this case, b and c can be any combination of values that add up to 130, meaning that the values are free to vary. Since there are two observations that can have variable values, this sample data has two degrees of freedom.

Recall that by definition, the number of degrees of freedom increases as the sample size goes up, affecting the shape of the curve. The greater the degrees of freedom, the more the t-distribution looks like the standard normal distribution.

Measures of Position

Understanding a specific value for a variable relative to the other values for that variable gives you an indication of the organization of your data. Statisticians commonly use quartiles to describe a specific observation's position. The process of obtaining quartiles is similar to that of determining the median. You first sort a numeric dataset from smallest to largest and divide it positionally into four equal groups. Each grouping is known as a *quartile*. The first quartile is the group that starts with the minimum value, whereas the fourth quartile is the group that ends with the maximum value.

Figure 6.16 visualizes a dataset containing the sales price for 30,000 homes. To better understand the specific values for this data, you calculate an initial set of summary statistics, including the minimum, median, and maximum values and the quartiles. Table 6.8 illustrates the summary statistics for this data.

Once you've calculated these summary statistics, you have a better understanding of the position of your data, as shown in Table 6.9.

The *interquartile range* (*IQR*) combines the second and third quartiles and contains the middle 50 percent of the values in the data. When exploring a dataset, recall that outliers can significantly impact the mean and range. Using the IQR as a dispersion indicator, in addition to the range, improves your perspective since the IQR excludes outliers.

Logical

A *logical function* evaluates whether a condition is true or false. While Chapter 4, "Databases and Data Acquisition," introduces how to combine multiple comparisons with a logical operation to filter data, it's worth exploring logical functions in greater detail. Table 6.10 details the most common logical operators.

One of the most common uses of logical functions is testing for existence instead of equality. Recall from Chapter 5 that a null value is the absence of a value. Consider the

FIGURE 6.16 Sales prices for 30,000 homes.

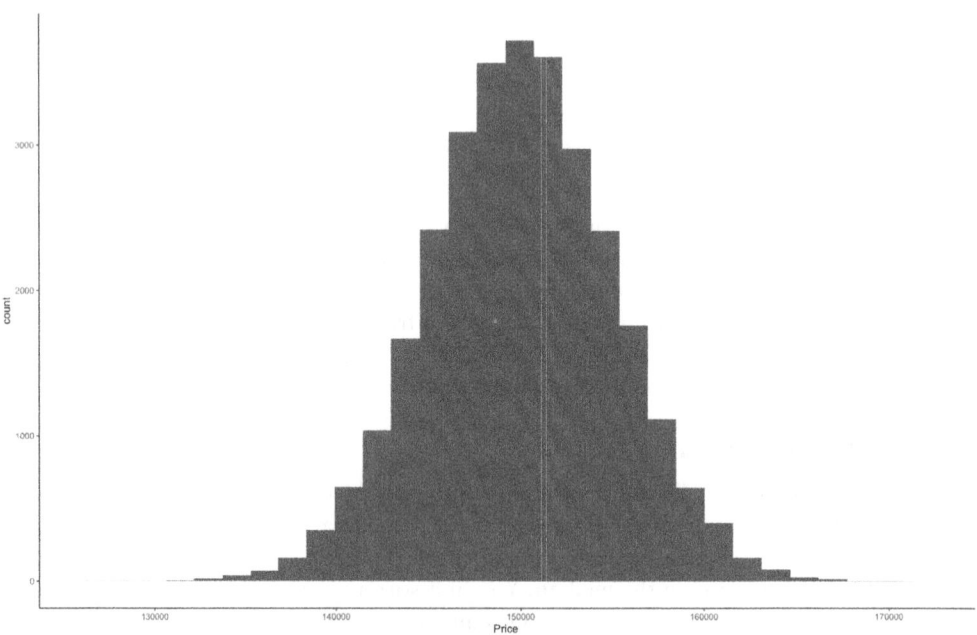

TABLE 6.8 Confidence Percentage and Level for Normally Distributed Data

Positional Statistic	Value
Minimum	128,246
First Quartile	146,657
Median	150,069
Third Quartile	153,420
Maximum	172,197

sample person data in Table 6.11. Note that the Middle_Name column is optional, and Amy and Tony don't have middle names. Since Amy and Tony don't have middle names, the value for the Middle_Name column for these two records is NULL.

To identify all records in Table 6.11 without a middle name, you need to match all records with a NULL middle name. You can't use an equality operator since NULL is the absence of a value. Instead, you need a logical operator to test for existence instead of

TABLE 6.9 Confidence Percentage and Level for Normally Distributed Data

Quartile	Lower Bound	Upper Bound	Range
First	128,246	146,657	18,411
Second	146,657	150,069	3,412
Third	150,069	153,420	3,351
Fourth	153,420	172,197	18,777

TABLE 6.10 Logical Operators

Operator	Description
IS	Returns true when a condition exists
IS NOT	Returns true when a condition does not exist
AND	Returns true when two comparison operations both return true
OR	Evaluates true when either of two comparison operations returns true

TABLE 6.11 Sample Person Data

ID	First_Name	Middle_Name	Last_Name
69	Karl	Joseph	Kamienski
70	Aaron	Stephan	Lettow
71	Amy		Olsen
72	Yvette	Stephan	Schilling
73	Tony		Conforti

equality. For example, the following SQL returns zero rows since you can't use equality to compare an unknown value with another:

```
SELECT *
FROM Sample_Person_Data
WHERE Middle_Name = NULL -- doesn't work, can't use an equality test
```

Instead, you need the IS logical function to test for existence. The following SQL retrieves all columns and all rows from Table 6.11 for Amy and Tony since they don't have a middle name:

```
SELECT *
FROM Sample_Person_Data
WHERE Middle_Name IS NULL -- works because of the logical existence operator
```

Similarly, using the IS NOT logical function following SQL identifies Karl, Aaron, and Yvette since they all have a middle name, regardless of the value of that middle name:

```
SELECT *
FROM Sample_Person_Data
WHERE Middle_Name IS NOT NULL
```

You can combine the OR and IS logical functions to identify people with either a middle name of "Stephan" or a blank last name. The following query returns all columns for Aaron, Amy, Yvette, and Tony, since Aaron and Yvette both have a middle name of Stephan and Amy and Tony don't have a middle name:

```
SELECT *
FROM Sample_Person_Data
WHERE Middle_Name = "Stephan"
   OR Middle_Name IS NOT NULL
```

Date

Date functions help you work with and manipulate date and time. Chapter 5 emphasizes the importance of data type validation to improve the data quality in a given column. Date functions help you extract components of a date from a column with a date or date time data type.

While philosophically aligned, the implementation of date manipulation functions is specific to individual database platforms. The syntax of date manipulation functions on Oracle differs from SQL Server, which differs from PostgreSQL or MySQL. While the functions vary by platform, date functions exist to extract a date's components from a column with a date data type. Date functions can retrieve only the day number, day name, day of year number, month number, month name, year number, and more.

Other date functions handle comparing dates. For example, functions exist to calculate the number of days, weeks, months, or years between two dates. Suppose a company grants an additional week of vacation time once its employees enter their fifth year of service. You can use date functions within a filter to ensure that employees with fewer than five years of service remain ineligible until they reach the fifth anniversary of their hire date.

One of the most challenging date-related manipulations relates to leap year. When calculating the number of days over three years, you can't simply multiply 365 days by three since one of those years could be a leap year. Combining creativity and the appropriate date functions helps you accurately account for the number of days.

For columns that support time, additional date functions can retrieve the hour, minute, second, millisecond, and more. Suppose you want to identify the time of day when the most component defects happen on a manufacturing line. Storing the time of component creation lets you summarize the number of defects. Using time manipulation functions, you can aggregate at the second, minute, quarter-hour, half-hour, hour, or whatever granularity is appropriate for the question you're trying to answer.

Time zone is a crucial concept when working with time data. Suppose you are trying to resolve an information security incident impacting an organization across multiple continents. Evaluating timestamps using the local time zone leads to confusion. It's best practice to convert the time from local time to *Coordinated Universal Time* (*UTC*) in situations like this.

String

Chapter 5 discusses string manipulation to improve data quality. You use string functions to clean and transform text data. Like date functions, how string functions work differs according to the database platform. Table 6.12 contains some of the most common string manipulation functions.

Consistency reduces variability while improving quality. Consistent handling of string data improves data quality. As part of an ETL job, suppose you have a CSV file containing the customer name data in Table 6.13.

During the transformation phase of your ETL job, you want to ensure consistent data in the database. How you ensure consistency is an organizational decision. Table 6.14 illustrates the effect of the UPPER(), LOWER(), and INITCAP() functions on the name data from Table 6.13.

For example, the United States Postal Service (USPS) address standard prefers address details in uppercase. You can use the UPPER() function to create a USPS standard-compliant address regardless of how you store address details in a database.

TABLE 6.12 String Functions

Function	Description
UPPER()	Converts a string to all uppercase
LOWER()	Converts a string to all lowercase
INITCAP()	Converts the first letter in a string to uppercase and all remaining letters to lowercase
TRIM()	Removes leading or trailing characters

TABLE 6.13 Sample Customer Data

Last_Name
singh
van blair
Melinauskas

TABLE 6.14 Effect of String Functions

UPPER()	LOWER()	INITCAP()
SINGH	singh	Singh
VAN BLAIR	van blair	Van Blair
MELINAUSKAS	melinauskas	Melinauskas

TABLE 6.15 Data with Whitespace

First_Name	TRIM(First_Name)
'Faris '	'Faris'
' Bruce'	'Bruce'
' Joaquin '	'Joaquin'

While you can use the TRIM() function to remove leading or trailing characters, the most common use of the TRIM() function is when there is whitespace in your data. Table 6.15 illustrates the impact of the TRIM() function on whitespace. The quotes are for emphasis only and are not part of the value for First_Name. Imagine you receive the data in the First_Name column. Note that the first entry in the table has a space trailing the name, the second entry has spaces preceding the name, and the third entry has both leading and trailing spaces. TRIM() can remove leading whitespace, trailing whitespace, or both depending on database platform and function parameters.

Each string column requires an independent approach to ensure consistency. However, all programming operations within an organization must handle strings consistently. If one ETL process uses UPPER() while a second ETL process uses UPPER(), it's possible to unintentionally create duplicate rows for the same record.

Troubleshooting

You will invariably encounter unexpected data errors during analysis. *Troubleshooting* is understanding why errors exist and where they come from. When troubleshooting, you identify an error, clean up existing data issues, determine the root cause of the error, and make changes to prevent the error from happening again.

Issues

Data analysts frequently encounter issues when working with data. Understanding some common causes of data issues will help you troubleshoot and resolve data quality challenges. Typical sources of data issues include inconsistent network connectivity, reports from data consumers, coding issues, and data corruption.

Connectivity-related

We live in a time of robust networks and highly distributed systems. Geographically distributed systems commonly send data to a single database for aggregation and analysis. One area where data collection continues to grow is in the automotive sector, with modern vehicles acting as Internet of Things (IoT) sensors. Figure 6.17 illustrates how today's connected cars send data to a corporate database for analysis. The location and diagnostic data are vital for product development, identifying maintenance trends, and even identifying potential recalls.

Some vehicles use cellular networks to transmit data back to the manufacturer regularly. Sometimes, owners use their vehicles beyond the range of a cellular network. If the vehicle was transferring data as it lost its cellular connection, you end up with missing or incomplete data in the database. Missing or incomplete data can happen whenever there is intermittent or inconsistent network connectivity.

FIGURE 6.17   IoT vehicles interacting with corporate database.

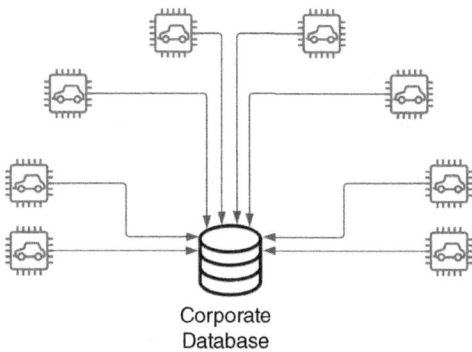

FIGURE 6.18 Customer and service desk interactions.

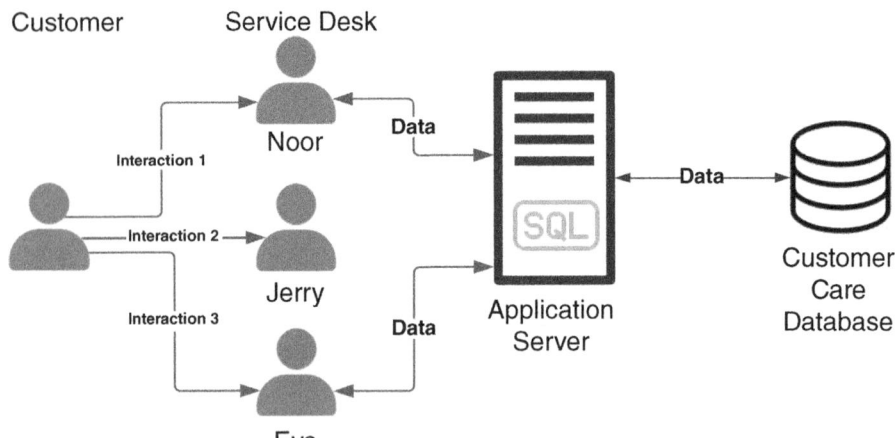

User-reported

One of the worst ways to learn about a data issue is when a user informs the service desk of an error. Ideally, you can identify and resolve errors before they impact users, but that doesn't always happen. While far from ideal, many situations could result in users reporting data errors.

For example, Figure 6.18 shows a customer working with three service desk representatives on the same issue. In the first interaction, the customer supplies data to Noor, who logs it into the customer care database. When the customer calls a second time, Jerry handles the interaction. However, Jerry neglects to put the updated customer information into the customer care database. When the customer calls a third time and speaks with Eva, Eva only has the customer's information from the interaction with Noor. Eva's lack of context embarrasses everyone, as the customer becomes angry that there is no record of the interaction with Jerry, making the company appear not to keep track of customer data.

Basic SQL Code

You'll run into SQL-related issues when data moves between systems in a complex, multi-system environment. As a data analyst, you'll have to get comfortable troubleshooting SQL-related errors. Consider the situation in Figure 6.19, where a financial analyst joins data from the Domestic Sales and International Sales databases in Tableau to understand total sales by sales region.

When executing the query, the analyst gets an error message when joining the data by sales region. The analyst discovers that region code is an integer data type in the Domestic Sales database, while the International Sales database stores region as a character data type.

FIGURE 6.19 Invalid JOIN due to data type issue.

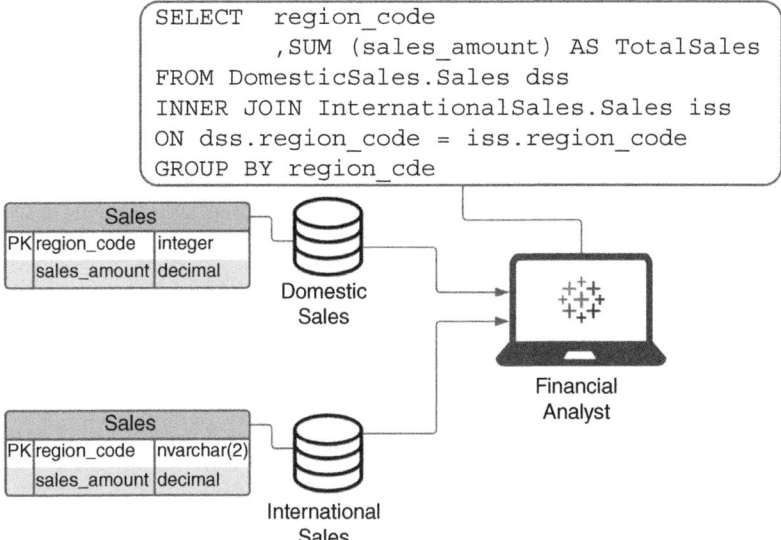

To resolve this situation, the analyst needs to verify that the region code contains the same data in the Domestic Sales and International Sales databases. If the region code contains the same data, the analyst must convert the region code to a common data type for the join to work correctly.

While it's possible to find poorly written SQL that does not work, SQL-related errors typically involve data-related errors. Data synchronization issues due to incomplete ETL jobs or duplicate data are a common source of data errors.

Corrupted Data

Data corruption is a leading cause of data-related issues. One situation in which corruption is likely to happen is when an organization has multiple external data sources and uses batch processes to exchange data files. Connectivity issues can result in an incomplete data file whenever you transmit data over a network connection. Loading an incomplete file can create incomplete records, contributing to data corruption.

It's also possible for real-time interface issues to create corrupt data. Figure 6.20 illustrates an address standardization process that relies on an external vendor to transform addresses in the United States to the United States Postal Service (USPS) standard format.

Under normal operations, the application server sends address data to the Address Standardization API, receives the standardized address data, and writes it to the database. The application design dictates that having the original user-provided address data is better than having no address data at all. If the API call times out, the application server writes the user-provided address to the database, which causes data corruption.

FIGURE 6.20 Address standardization.

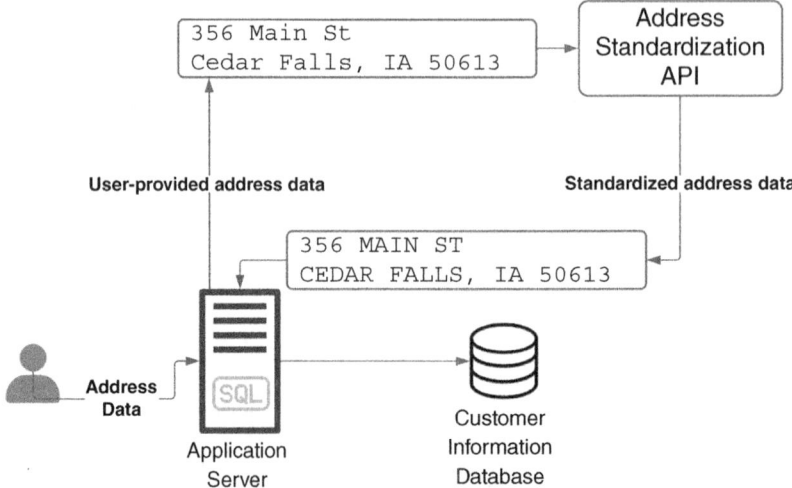

FIGURE 6.21 Primary key violation log entry.

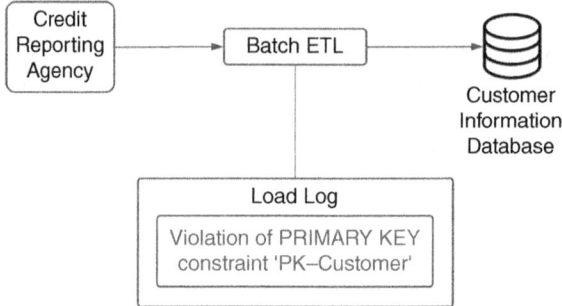

Tools and Methods

Many methods exist to help troubleshoot data corruption issues. No single tool or method will resolve all your troubleshooting issues. It's great to be aware of troubleshooting tools and techniques. Combining various approaches and methods will enhance your troubleshooting effectiveness.

Enable Logging

Whether you work with batch or real-time applications, log files are a source of additional information. Figure 6.21 shows an excerpt from a log file from a batch ETL process that loads customer credit rating data into a customer information database.

In this case, the log file contains an error message that one of the records violates the PK_Customer primary key constraint. Resolving this issue requires examining the initial ETL file to determine the root cause. Due to a transmission error, the file could have duplicate rows. Another possibility is that the batch ETL job mistakenly processes the same file twice. Regardless of the root cause, enable logging to give you additional information to assist with your troubleshooting efforts.

Examining log files is equally informative from a real-time standpoint. Consider the address standardization process from Figure 6.20. Ideally, you want to create a metric that examines the application log files for records indicating an API timeout. While it's likely to experience an occasional timeout, more than 20 timeouts in a minute are probable cause for concern. Raising an alert using the data from the log file helps you address the root cause before too much data corruption happens.

Validate Data Sources

Ensuring you have processes that validate data sources is essential to troubleshooting. There are many approaches to validating data sources when processing files. These approaches include:

- **Header record:** Having a header record with column names helps you verify the columns within a file.
- **Footer record:** Having a footer record that includes the number of lines in the file informs the destination table's expected row count.
- **Checksum:** Using a checksum to verify the size of a file before processing can help you identify corruption due to network transmission. If the file is not the same size as the transmitted file, it will have a different checksum value.
- **Network rules:** When migrating data between systems, ensure no firewall rules impede network traffic.

Most organizations have development, testing, and production environments. When validating your data sources, ensure the configuration for your production systems refers to their production counterparts. Feeding test data into a production system will surely generate data quality issues.

Consult Vendor Communities

An increasing number of organizations integrate internal and external systems for analytical purposes. Vendors usually operate communities for people who use their products. For example, suppose you are working on a data quality initiative to ensure postal address consistency for your organization's customers. Figure 6.22 shows an organization with an internal process for standardizing address information. This organization also uses Salesforce as its Customer Relationship Management (CRM) system. Customers interact directly with the organization using the application server, and customer care representatives maintain customer information in Salesforce.

Organizationally, you want the address standardization processes to be the same in Salesforce and the internal systems. If you need help understanding and configuring address standardization in Salesforce, posing a question on the vendor's community site may give you the help you need.

FIGURE 6.22 Address information in multiple systems.

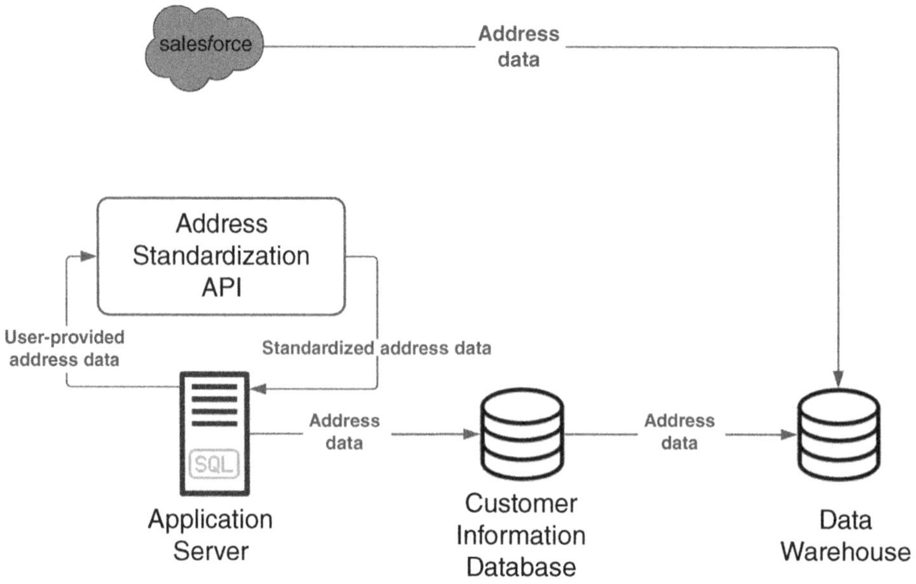

Consult Online Resources

Online resources are a good source of assistance beyond what you find in a vendor community. When using an online resource, keep in mind who operates the website. Vendors may monitor their online communities and remove noncomplimentary content. Open forums like Stack Overflow let you ask questions in an independent community where people may be more forthcoming than in a vendor-operated community.

People are increasingly turning to generative AI for technical solutions. While these responses can be remarkably effective, you should understand that, like people, generative AI isn't perfect. Generative AI functions by using its training data to predict the next most likely word. Since generative AI uses predictions, it's possible for it to predict incorrectly, causing errors in its output. These resulting errors are sometimes called hallucinations. A generative AI answer can be directionally, but not wholly, correct.

Analysis Techniques

Data analysts have an abundance of statistical tools available to explore data in the pursuit of insights. While you need to understand when to use the appropriate tool or statistical test, it is crucial to identify and apply techniques that help you structure your approach. When assessing techniques, you should identify and adopt frameworks that help improve the consistency of how you approach new data challenges.

Determine Type of Analysis

When embarking on a new analytics challenge, you need to understand the business objectives and desired outcomes. This understanding informs the type of analysis you will conduct. The first step to understanding the objectives is to ensure that you have clarity on the business questions at hand. Recall that the goal of answering a business question is to develop an insight that informs a business decision.

Business questions come in many forms. You may receive questions informally through hallway conversations, text messages, or emails. More significant initiatives should have written requirements documents defining the business questions that are in scope. Regardless of the form your requirements are in, you need to review the business questions and identify any points that require additional clarification. This clarity will help you identify the data you need as well as the data sources.

While reviewing requirements, develop a list of clarifying questions. This list can help define the scope of your analysis. Your clarification list can also identify any gaps between what is achievable given data source and time constraints. For example, one of the requirements may be to analyze sales data for the past 10 years. However, due to a change in the system that records sales, you only have access to seven years of historical information. The absence of data over a three-year period is a gap you need to discuss with your business partner.

Once you have your list of questions, review it with the business sponsor to ensure you agree on expectations. Recognize that reviewing and refining business questions is an iterative process. While you need to have initial clarity, you will likely have to return to your business leader for additional clarification as you conduct your analysis.

When you have consensus on the scope of your analysis, clarity about outstanding questions, and know what data you need and where it is coming from, you can proceed confidently with conducting your analysis. It's a good idea to maintain your requirements document as you go about your work. Use the document to track new issues that impact the project timeline and any adjustments to project scope or ultimate deliverables. A running log identifying any scope changes is a valuable aid that can help you make sure you deliver your analysis on time. It can also help you after your work is complete as you reflect on what went well and what would make future endeavors more successful.

Types of Analysis

With a clear scope and access to the data you need, you can get on with your analytical work. One of the types of analysis you may be asked to perform is trend analysis. *Trend analysis* seeks to identify patterns by comparing data over time. Suppose you work for a hospitality company with properties in the United States, and one of your goals is to evaluate corporate performance. To advance that goal, you examine the total sales for each state over the past five years. In conducting trend analysis, you can identify whether sales are declining, remaining consistent, or growing in every state. Understanding sales trends may influence the company to sell unprofitable properties and invest in areas that show signs of sustained growth.

In addition to trend analysis, you may also conduct performance analysis. *Performance analysis* examines defined goals and measures performance against them and can inform the development of future projections. Continuing with the hospitality example, the company may have average occupancy goals for each property in its portfolio. Performance analysis can identify whether properties are achieving those goals. Combining performance analysis with trend analysis can help develop projections for the future.

For example, suppose one of the company's properties is a hotel in Chicago. The sales trend for that property has been going up over the past five years. However, the data shows that this property has been inconsistent in achieving its occupancy target. The results of this analysis show that hotel management has found a way to grow sales despite inconsistent occupancy performance. The company could then follow up with local management to understand why this is true and if any local tactics are applicable to other properties.

Suppose another of the company's properties is a hotel in Des Moines, Iowa. The data shows that this property's sales and occupancy numbers are growing. With no obvious location factors influencing this growth, the company can follow up with local management to better understand this location's success. While past performance doesn't guarantee future success, the results of this analysis can help the company establish basic occupancy and sales projections for the coming year.

If you need to explore patterns in the connection between individual observations, it may be necessary to perform a link analysis. *Link analysis* is a technique that uses the relationships between data points to discover patterns. In 2015, the International Consortium of Investigative Journalists (ICIJ) received one of the most sizable data leaks in history, known as the Panama Papers. Over 11.5 million documents consisting of 40 years' worth of data are in this leak. By conducting a link analysis, the ICIJ analyzed these documents and uncovered patterns of illicit financial behavior, including tax evasion and money laundering.

Exploratory Data Analysis

At the onset of your analysis, you will encounter many datasets for the first time. When first exploring a dataset, it's a good idea to perform an exploratory data analysis. An *exploratory data analysis* (EDA) uses descriptive statistics to summarize the main characteristics of a dataset, identify outliers, and give you context for further analysis. While there are many approaches to conducting an EDA, they typically encompass the following steps:

- **Check data structure**: Ensure that data is in the correct format for analysis. Most analysis tools expect data to be in a tabular format, so you must confirm that your data has defined rows and columns.
- **Check data representation**: Become familiar with the data. In this step, you validate data types and ensure that variables contain the data you expect.

- **Check if data is missing:** Check to see if any data is missing from the dataset and determine what to do next. While checking for null values, calculate the proportion of each variable that is missing. If you discover that most of the data you need is missing, you need to either categorize it as missing or impute a value for the missing data. You can also return to the source and remediate any data extraction issues.
- **Identify outliers:** Recall from Chapter 4 that an outlier is an observation of a variable that deviates significantly from other observations of that variable. This chapter shows that outliers can dramatically impact some descriptive statistics, like the mean. It would be best to determine the cause of outliers and consider whether you want to leave them in the data before proceeding with any ongoing analysis.
- **Summarize statistics:** Calculate summary statistics for each variable. Examples of summary statistics for numeric variables include mean, median, variance, and standard deviation. Standard deviation is the best descriptive statistic for describing variable variability because it will be in the original metric of the values. For categorical data like eye color, you could develop a table showing the frequency with which each observation occurs.
- **Check assumptions:** Depending on the statistical method you are using, you need to understand the shape of the data. For example, if you are working with numeric data, you should choose a normal or t-distribution for drawing inferences.

Summary

Communication, statistical methods, and troubleshooting are key skills for the modern data analyst. Communication is a crucial component of the analysis process. Clearly defining your audience is fundamental to creating a good analysis product. You need to understand who you're addressing to appropriately tailor your message.

The process of developing personas further refines your audience composition. For example, the C-suite should have access to more sensitive data than the average individual contributor. Similarly, product managers may need a cross-section of marketing, manufacturing, and distribution data. However, data for a given product manager should be limited to only the data that directly impacts their product.

When identifying your audience composition, it's crucial to determine whether your constituents are external or internal. Internal constituents are privy to analysis that is not publicly available, while external constituents are limited to a subset of data that is publicly accessible.

Once you have the audience definitions you need, it's vital to define and validate the KPIs for each persona. Subject areas such as finance, marketing, and human resources have KPIs specific to their discipline, regardless of industry. You also will encounter organization-specific KPIs. Exhaustively defining expected KPIs helps ensure you can try to collect all the data you need to create those KPIs.

Mock-ups let you optimize your time by visualizing the final product, socializing it, and incorporating feedback. Having your business stakeholders sign off on your mock-up before investing time to create a finished product is a good idea. When creating any visual artifact, it's essential to ensure your work is accessible to all audiences, regardless of any physical disability.

Wielding statistical techniques to analyze data is a cornerstone ability of the modern data analyst. It is imperative to appreciate the difference between census and sample data. A census consists of an observation for every member of the population, whereas a sample is data about a specific subset. Since it is frequently prohibitive to obtain a census, analysts typically work with sample data. Whether you are working with census or sample data, you end up using statistics.

Descriptive statistics is a branch of statistics that describes a dataset. Descriptive statistics help you understand the data's characteristics and can help you understand events that have already happened. One category of descriptive statistics is measures of frequency. Measures of frequency shed light on recurring values in your data. Count is the most common measure of frequency. For example, one of the first things an analyst does when encountering a new table in a database is to get the total number of rows by issuing the following SQL statement:

```
SELECT COUNT(*) FROM <table_name>
```

Once you understand the total number of rows you are dealing with, exploring proportions in the data is typical to check for bias. For example, if the population you are studying is split evenly between men and women, you would expect that any random sample from the population would have an equal proportion of men and women.

Measures of central tendency are descriptive statistics that help you understand how tightly or widely distributed your data is. Mean, median, and mode are all measures of central tendency. Exploring how far apart the mean and median values are can tell you whether you are working with data that follows a normal distribution. If the mean and median are close, the distribution will likely be approximately normal. The data is skewed to one side if the mean and median are far apart.

Measures of dispersion help you understand how widely distributed your data is. The range, or difference between maximum and minimum values, establishes your data's upper and lower limits for numeric variables. Variance is a dispersion measure that calculates in squared units how far each observation in a dataset is from its mean value and is most often used as a path to calculating standard deviation. Standard deviation, or the square root of variance, is a more frequently referenced statistic due to the empirical rule, stating that almost every observation falls within three standard deviations of the mean in a normal distribution.

Measures of position help identify where a specific value for an observation is relative to other values. The interquartile range is a valuable measure of position, as it places all values of a variable into one of four quartiles, where the middle 50 percent of the values in a dataset are in the second and third quartiles.

You will use many functions when manipulating data. Logical functions test for the existence of a condition. Date functions help you work with dates and their components. For example, using aggregation with a date function lets you identify which days of the week and hours of the day are the busiest for a retail operation. String functions help you manipulate and compare string values. ETL jobs use string functions to ensure case consistency when data moves between systems.

Unexpected things happen whenever you work with data or move data between systems. A robust troubleshooting process is crucial to identifying an issue's root cause and subsequent remediation. Troubleshooting is also essential in identifying and fixing corrupted data. When you need additional insight into a data issue, use system and application log files to ensure nothing inhibits transmitting data. If you get stuck, look to broadly accessible and vendor-controlled online communities.

Regardless of the statistics you use, it is crucial to have a systematic approach when conducting an analysis. Having a clearly defined scope that the business representative agrees on is imperative. You also need to have access to good sources of data. With these two things in place, you initiate an analytics project by performing an exploratory data analysis (EDA). The EDA will inform you about the type of data you are working with and whether you have any missing data or outlier values, and it will provide summary statistics about each variable in your dataset.

Exam Essentials

Differentiate between technical and nontechnical audiences. Nontechnical audience members need aggregated and summarized data. While a technical audience may be able to analyze raw, unaggregated data, beware that the application and database context will be gone once data is in a CSV file.

Calculate measures of central tendency. Given a dataset, you should feel comfortable calculating the mean, median, and mode. Recall that the mean is the mathematical average. The median is the value that separates the lower and higher portions of an ordered set of numbers. The mode is the value that occurs most frequently. While mean and median are applicable for numeric data, evaluating the mode is particularly useful when describing categorical data.

Describe the normal distribution as a measure of dispersion. The normal distribution, with its bell-shaped curve, is typical in many disciplines due to the central limit theorem. Variance measures how far data is from the mean, with larger values indicating greater dispersion.

Describe how logical functions differ from string functions. Logical functions test for existence, while string functions test for equality. You can also use string functions to transform string data between lowercase and uppercase.

Identify tools and methods that enable troubleshooting. Enabling logging, validating data sources, consulting with vendor communities, and consulting with online resources are all valid approaches that simplify troubleshooting data quality issues.

Review Questions

The following questions are designed to test your understanding of this chapter's material. You can find the answers in Appendix A.

1. Sandy is studying silverback gorillas and wants to determine the average weight for males and females. What best describes the dataset she needs?
   A. Observation
   B. Population
   C. Sample
   D. Variable

2. James wants to understand dispersion in his dataset. Which statistic best matches his needs?
   A. Median
   B. Mode
   C. Mean
   D. Interquartile range

3. Yunqi is collecting data about people's preferred automotive color. Which statistic will help her identify the most popular color?
   A. Mean
   B. Median
   C. Mode
   D. Range

4. Jenna is a data analyst tasked with presenting the market analysis results to her company's C-suite. She knows that the executives prefer high-level insights with minimal technical details. Jenna needs to develop a communication approach tailored to their needs to ensure her report is effective and well-received. Which of the following strategies would be most appropriate for Jenna?
   A. Use detailed, raw data tables and include complex statistical methods in the report.
   B. Focus on aggregated data and highlight key performance indicators (KPIs) relevant to strategic decisions.
   C. Prepare a mock-up with low-contrast colors and small serif fonts for an elegant design.
   D. Include a deep dive into the analytical methods, with step-by-step explanations of the statistical techniques.

5. David is preparing a data visualization for a group of product managers to help them understand market trends and customer feedback. The product managers are not particularly technical but need enough detail to make informed strategic decisions about product features and improvements. How should David approach designing his communication artifact?

A. Use simple visualizations and focus on key insights without including raw data.

   B. Include raw, unprocessed data so the product managers can explore it themselves.

   C. Emphasize the statistical methods used in the analysis to build credibility.

   D. Present the data using technical jargon and highly detailed analytics.

6. Emma is a database analyst at a logistics company. She is working with a dataset that includes optional middle name fields for each employee and needs to filter the records to identify employees who did not provide a middle name. Which of the following SQL statements should Emma use to accurately retrieve these records?

   A. `SELECT * FROM Employee_Data WHERE Middle_Name = NULL`

   B. `SELECT * FROM Employee_Data WHERE Middle_Name IS NULL`

   C. `SELECT * FROM Employee_Data WHERE Middle_Name IS NOT NULL`

   D. `SELECT * FROM Employee_Data WHERE Middle_Name = ''`

7. What is the mean of the following numbers: 1, 1, 2, 3, 3, 4, 5, 6, 7, 8?

   A. 1

   B. 3

   C. 3.5

   D. 4

8. What is the range of the following numbers: 1, 1, 2, 3, 3, 4, 5, 6, 7, 8?

   A. 1

   B. 3

   C. 7

   D. 8

9. What is the median of the following numbers: 1, 1, 2, 3, 3, 4, 5, 6, 7, 8?

   A. 1

   B. 3

   C. 3.5

   D. 4

10. Alex is a database analyst at a logistics company. She is working with a dataset that includes optional middle name fields for each employee and needs to filter the records to identify employees who did provide a middle name. Which of the following SQL statements should Alex use to accurately retrieve these records?

    A. `SELECT * FROM Customer_Info WHERE Middle_Name IS NOT NULL`

    B. `SELECT * FROM Customer_Info WHERE Middle_Name = NULL`

    C. `SELECT * FROM Customer_Info WHERE Middle_Name = ''`

    D. `SELECT * FROM Customer_Info WHERE Middle_Name IS NULL`

11. Michael is a data engineer at a global company working on a report that analyzes timestamps from a security monitoring system. The timestamps are stored in various local time zones, but Michael needs to standardize them for accurate analysis across all regions. Which approach should Michael use to handle the timestamps correctly?

    A. Store the timestamps as is in local time zones and use string functions to convert them later.

    B. Use a date function to convert all timestamps to Coordinated Universal Time (UTC).

    C. Ignore time zone differences, as they do not impact the overall analysis.

    D. Multiply the hour component of each timestamp by a fixed factor to adjust for time zone differences.

12. Ari is a data analyst working on a customer database. She needs to standardize the customer names by ensuring each last name is stored with the first letter capitalized and all remaining letters in lowercase, regardless of how customers originally entered them. Which string manipulation function should Ari use?

    A. UPPER()

    B. LOWER()

    C. INITCAP()

    D. TRIM()

13. Katsuyuki is a data analyst at a logistics company, and his team has started noticing data inconsistencies in customer addresses across various systems. His organization uses a CRM system and has an internal application that processes and standardizes customer addresses. Katsuyuki needs to ensure that the address standardization process in Salesforce matches the one used internally. Where could Katsuyuki seek help to understand and configure address standardization in Salesforce? Choose the best answer.

    A. Ask his colleagues for guidance

    B. Consult the Salesforce vendor community

    C. Look for answers on social media

    D. Use trial and error to experiment with settings

14. Zach is interpreting a left skewed distribution of test scores. Enzo scored at the mean, Alfonso scored at the median, and Jezebel scored at the end of the tail. Who had the highest score?

    A. Zach

    B. Enzo

    C. Alfonso

    D. Jezebel

15. Gregory is examining the following sample data:

5, 12, 6, 8, 5, 9, 7, 5, 12, 4, 9, 8, 9, 10, 11, 11

What is the median?

- **A.** 8
- **B.** 8.5
- **C.** 8.125
- **D.** 9

16. Odin wants to understand patterns in a social network. Which is the most appropriate type of analysis technique to conduct this analysis?

- **A.** Trend
- **B.** Performance
- **C.** Exploratory data
- **D.** Link

17. Loki is studying global warming by examining temperature data. What type of analysis is Loki conducting? (Choose the best answer.)

- **A.** Trend
- **B.** Performance
- **C.** Exploratory data
- **D.** Link

18. Balder wants to understand how well his team measures up against corporate sales goals. What type of analysis will give Balder the perspective he needs?

- **A.** Trend
- **B.** Performance
- **C.** Exploratory data
- **D.** Link

19. Piper is a data analyst at a healthcare company and is troubleshooting an issue where patient information from an external system isn't syncing correctly with their internal database. The data transfer often fails partway, leading to incomplete patient records. She needs to identify the root cause of these incomplete records. What would be a helpful first step for Piper to take in her troubleshooting process?

- **A.** Consult the external system's manual for potential fixes
- **B.** Ask the patients to resubmit their information
- **C.** Enable logging to capture error details
- **D.** Manually update the missing data

20. Vidar has been asked to determine whether snowboard sales are trending higher over time. Vidar is given two datasets, one with 10 years of precipitation data, and the other with 10 years of snowboard sales from multiple manufacturers. What kind of analysis should he do next? (Choose the best answer.)

   A. Trend
   B. Performance
   C. Exploratory data
   D. Link

Chapter 7

Data Visualization with Reports and Dashboards

THE COMPTIA DATA+ EXAM TOPICS COVERED IN THIS CHAPTER INCLUDE:

✔ **Domain 4.0: Visualization and Reporting**

- 4.1. Given a scenario, use the appropriate visual elements
- 4.2. Given a scenario, use the appropriate delivery or consumption method
- 4.3. Given a scenario, troubleshoot issues using report validation techniques

In Chapter 6, "Data Analysis and Statistics," you learned about various techniques for analyzing data. In Chapter 2, "Data Analytics Tools," you explored a selection of software packages and programming languages that facilitate analysis. While the analytical process aims to derive insights from data, it is crucial to communicate those insights to the appropriate people at the right time. As raw data evolves into usable information, reports and dashboards are essential tools for sharing the results of analytical work.

Every day, businesses rely on data to inform decisions. While it is desirable to have beautiful, visually appealing reports and dashboards, the essence of visualizing data is to tell a story, giving the appropriate information to the right people at the right time. If a report or dashboard fails to facilitate effective communications, it will diminish the organizational impact of the analysis behind the visualization.

This chapter helps you develop an understanding of considerations to think through when translating business requirements into a visualization. You first learn understand why it is vital to understand the business needs before creating visualizations. You explore design considerations to keep in mind when creating reports and dashboards. You then explore considerations that influence dashboard development methods and the process to build a dashboard.

There are a wide variety of visualizations from which to choose. In this chapter, you learn about several different types of visualization and the considerations for their use. Finally, the chapter compares and contrasts different types of reports, always keeping in mind the needs of the business and the objective to communicate clearly and efficiently.

Exploring Visualization Elements

You have many options for presenting information visually. Selecting a visualization type that appropriately conveys the story you are telling with your data in a compelling format is vital. This section examines some of the most widely used shapes for visualizing information.

Charts

Charts are one of the foundational methods for visualizing both qualitative and quantitative data. There are many chart types, including line, pie, bar, stacked, scatter, and bubble charts. As you recall from Chapter 5, "Data Quality," histograms are particularly well suited to illustrating frequency and centrality. With so many options to choose from, it's crucial to know when to apply the appropriate chart shape to the data at hand.

Line Chart

A *line chart* shows the relationship of two variables along an x- and a y-axis. Line charts effectively visualize the relationship between time on the x-axis and a variable on the y-axis. Consider Figure 7.1, which illustrates how the average duration of Hollywood movies changes between 1927 and 2016. Interpreting the line, the range of the average duration varies significantly between 1927 and the late 1970s. After the late 1970s, the range for the average duration is smaller, converging to around 112 minutes.

Pie Chart

A *pie chart* gets its name from its circular shape where the circle represents 100 percent, and each slice of the pie is a proportion of the whole. A pie chart presents categorical, or discrete, data as individual slices of the pie. When using a pie chart, ensure that you label each pie slice appropriately, as shown in Figure 7.2. Without the percentage labels, it is a challenge to determine the relative proportions of the Crime and Adventure slices. While pie charts are an option, a bar chart illustrates the same information in a more easily interpreted format.

Bar Chart

Similar to a pie chart, a *bar chart* presents categorical data. Where a pie chart is circular, a bar chart uses rectangular bars to depict each proportion. Bar charts tend to be more interpretable

FIGURE 7.1 Line chart.

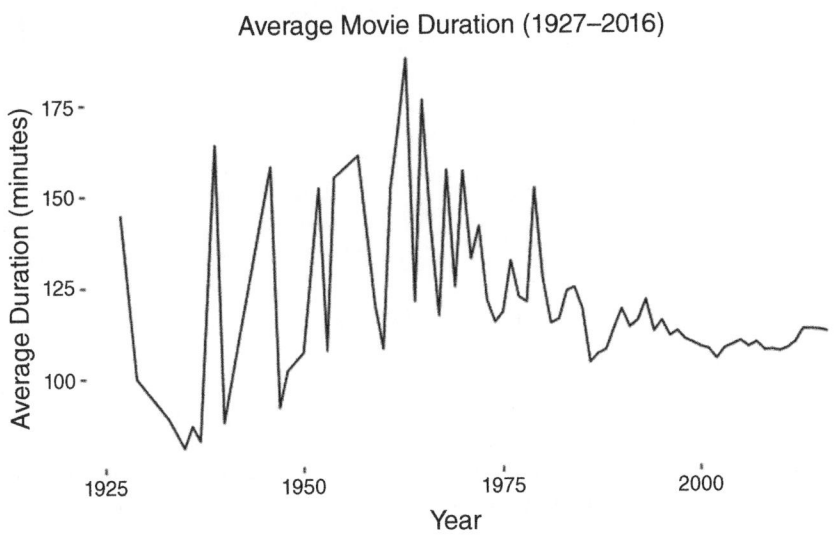

FIGURE 7.2 Pie chart.

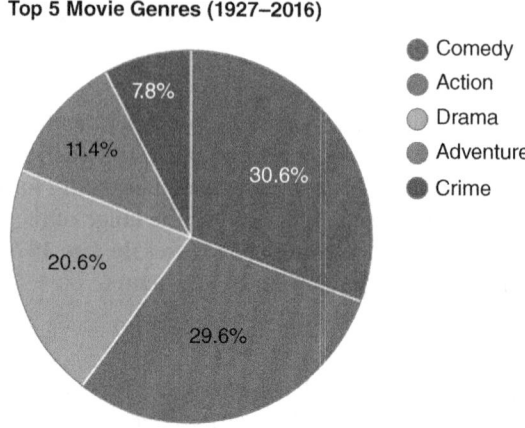

FIGURE 7.3 Bar chart by genre.

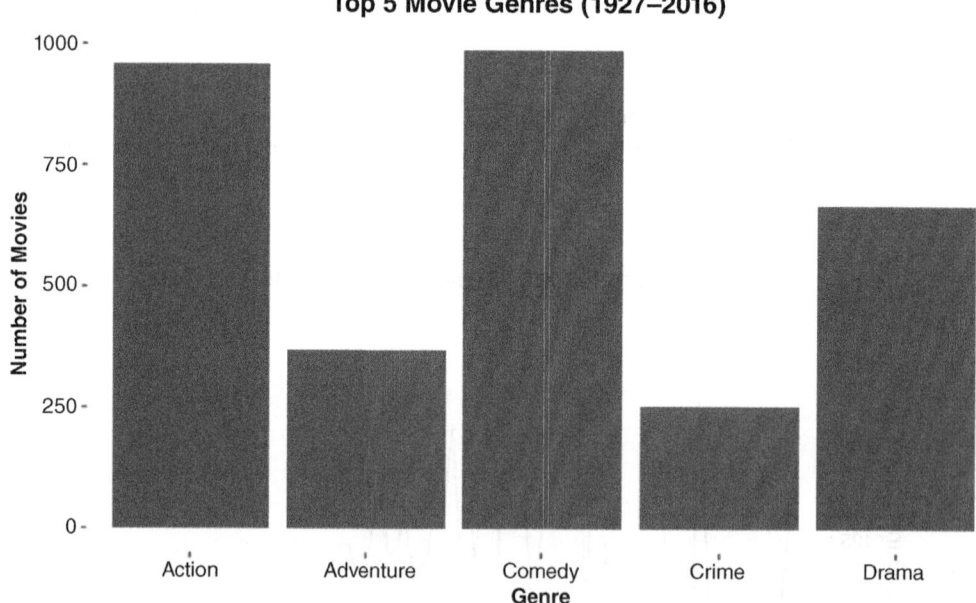

for people than pie charts. For example, Figure 7.3 illustrates the same data as Figure 7.2. Visually, it is straightforward for a person to compare the relative heights of each bar.

Keep in mind the information you are trying to convey when using bar charts. If the alphabetic order of the categories is a critical component that your audience will anchor to,

FIGURE 7.4 Bar chart by count.

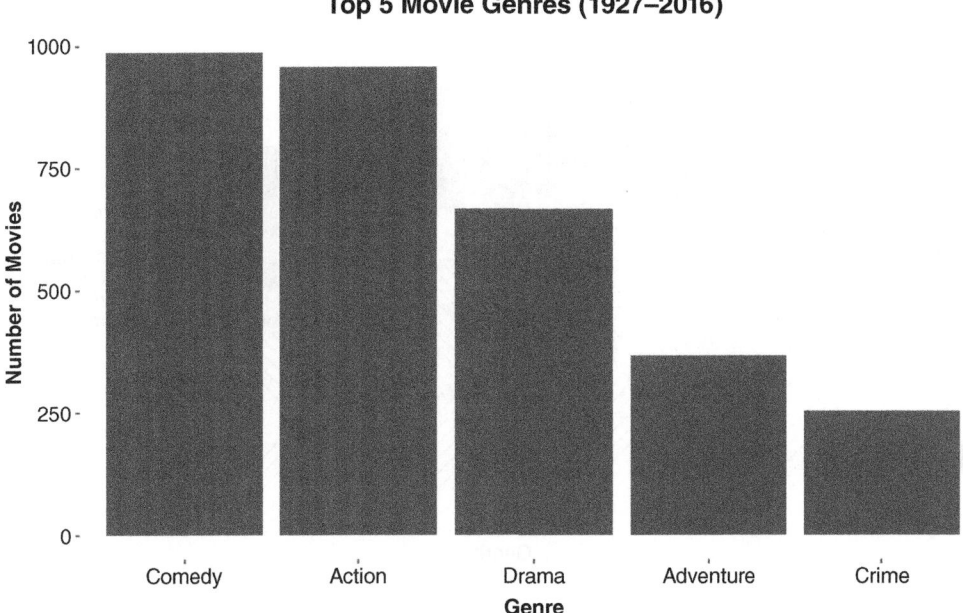

then Figure 7.3 is appropriate. However, as the title indicates, the intent is to show the top five movie genres between 1927 and 2016. Arranging the bars according to height is a better way to present the data, as the Pareto chart in Figure 7.4 illustrates.

Stacked Chart

A *stacked chart*, or *stacked bar chart*, starts with a bar chart and extends it by incorporating proportional segments on each bar for categorical data. Suppose that you identify the top movie genres, as shown in Figure 7.4, and want to explore the number of movies in each category over time. Figure 7.5 uses a stacked bar chart to visualize the proportional number of films made over 10 years.

Scatter Chart

A *scatter chart*, or *scatter plot*, uses a dot for each observation in a dataset to show the relationship between two numeric variables. Recall the line chart in Figure 7.1, which shows how the average duration for a film changes over the years. Since years are numeric, you can use a scatter plot to visualize the relationship between year and duration, as shown in Figure 7.6.

FIGURE 7.5 Stacked bar chart.

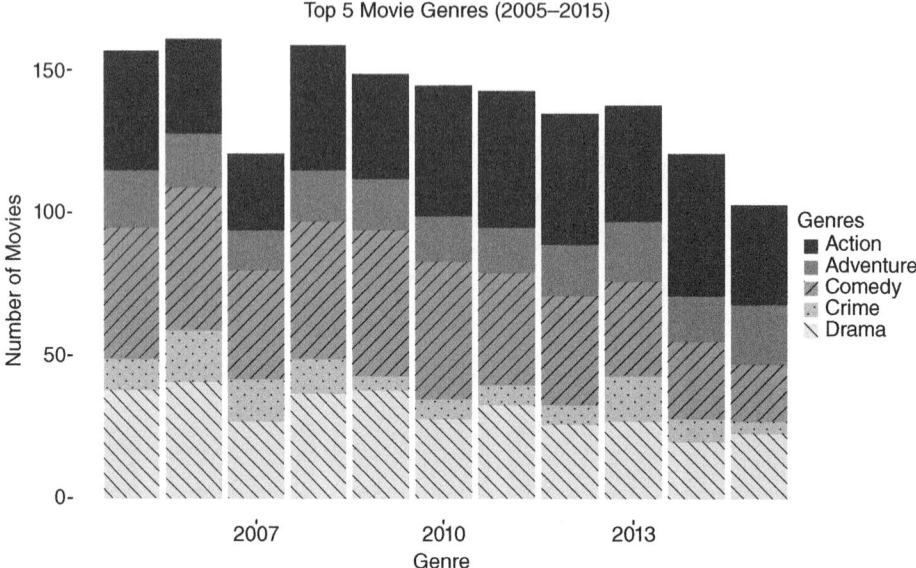

Suppose you are a pricing analyst for a movie studio and want to explore the relationship between a film's budget and its gross revenue. Since you can use dollars to measure both budget and revenue, you could use a scatter plot to visualize the relationship, as shown in Figure 7.7.

However, sometimes it makes sense to layer different charts together to increase a visualization's impact. Considering the scatterplot in Figure 7.7, it appears that the bigger a film's budget is, the higher the box office gross. By combining tools and visualizations, Figure 7.8 adds a linear regression line on top of the scatter plot. Adding a layer with the regression line facilitates conveying the message that there is a positive relationship between a film's budget and its box office gross.

Bubble Chart

A *bubble chart* is a scatter plot where the size of each dot is dependent on a third numeric variable. Consider the density of dots in Figure 7.8. One way to increase the visual appeal of that chart is to add aggregation. Converting the y-axis from actual gross to average gross gives us the graph in Figure 7.9. However, in aggregating this data, you lose the perspective of how many individual observations exist.

To illustrate the number of observations without cluttering the scatter chart, create a bubble chart, as shown in Figure 7.10. In this figure, the size of each dot represents

FIGURE 7.6 Average duration scatter plot.

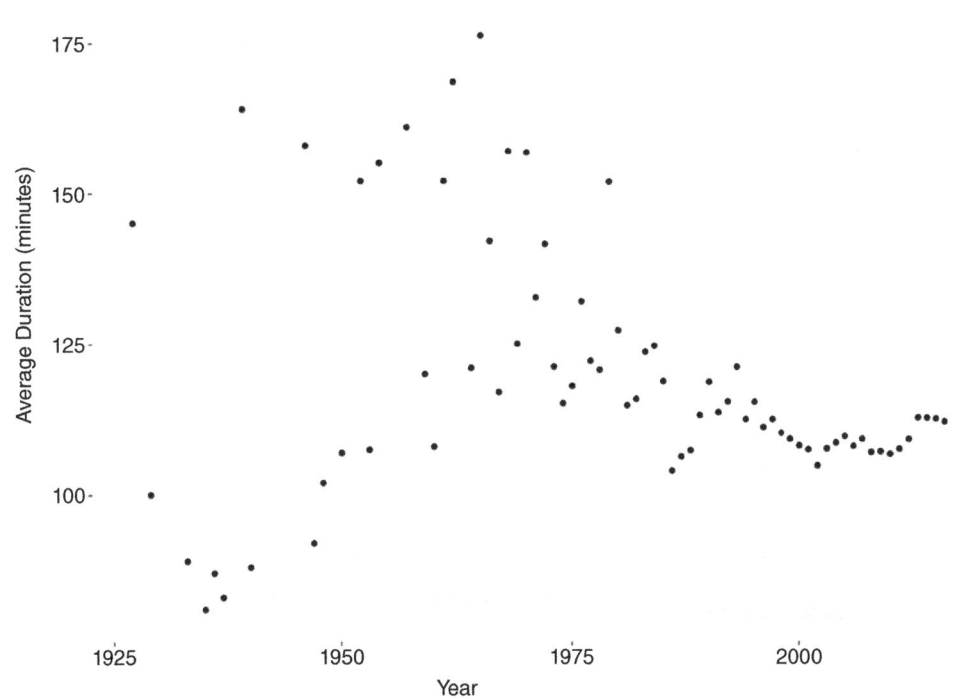

the number of movies at that budget level. Using dot size to represent the third numeric dimension of movie count lets you convey additional information without adding clutter.

Histogram

A *histogram* is a chart that shows a frequency distribution for numeric data. When performing an exploratory data analysis, create histograms for numeric data. These histograms illustrate the shape of the distribution and can inform the next stage of analysis. Histograms are also effective for communicating a distribution's shape to stakeholders.

Considering Figure 7.11, there is a considerable right skew to the distribution and the majority of movies have a box office gross of under $200 million. Meanwhile, Figure 7.12 shows that the duration of films during the same period as Figure 7.11 has a more normal distribution with a slight right skew.

FIGURE 7.7 Budget and box office gross scatterplot.

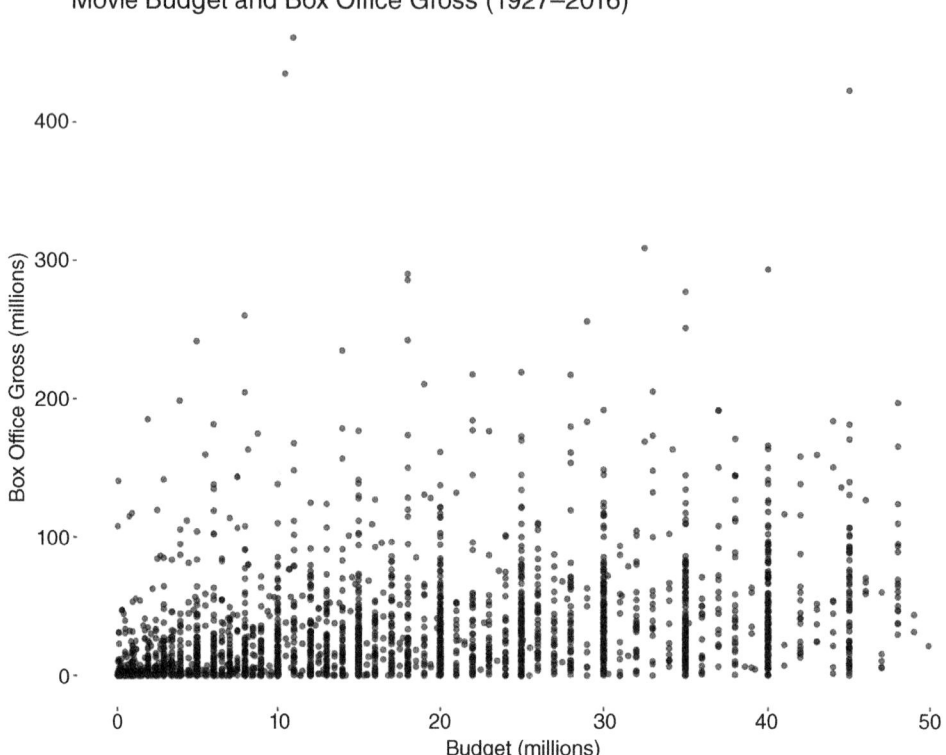

Maps

People frequently use maps to convey the location of a country, town, or individual address. Maps are effective methods orienting a person to a dataset. There are numerous types of maps available to visualize data, including geographic, heat, and tree maps.

Geographic Maps

Geographic maps are excellent for location-related data. For example, Figure 7.13 shows the location of higher education institutions in the United States where the undergraduate population exceeds 25,000 students. Use geographic maps when location is a component of your data.

Heat Maps

A *heat map* is a visualization that uses color and location to illustrate significance. Heat maps are versatile and apply in many different contexts. For example, a heat map can

FIGURE 7.8 Budget and box office gross scatter plot and line chart.

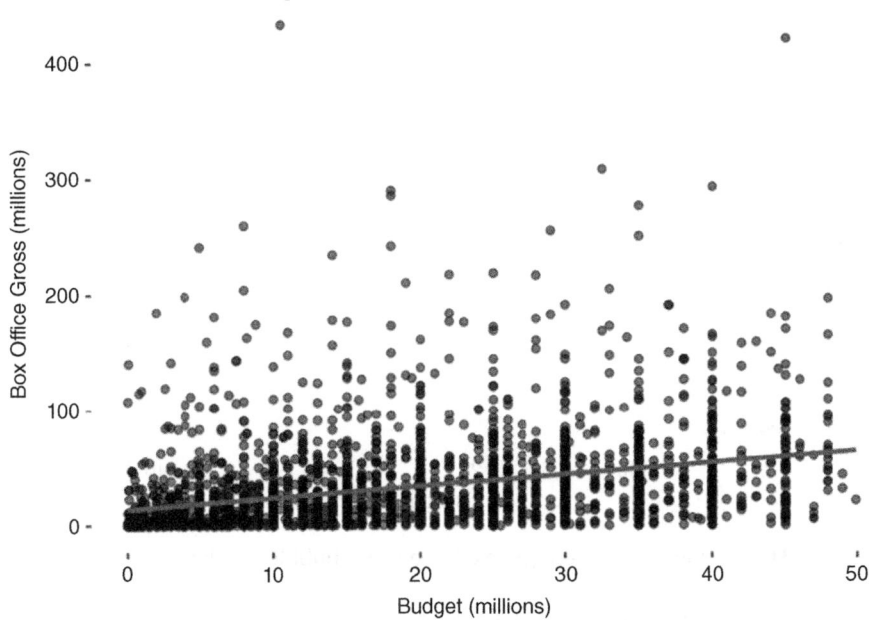

represent organizational risks, as shown in Figure 7.14. You first assign the risks facing your business a likelihood and impact score. After scoring, you put the risks on the heat map. The higher the probability and impact of a specific risk, the more an organization needs to develop a strategy to manage the risk. Risk heat maps help orient leaders to the challenges they face, especially during times of transition.

Heat maps can also illustrate the relationship between variables. Figure 7.15 shows the correlation between movie attributes. *Correlation* is a statistical measure describing the relationship between two variables. Correlation shows how changes in one variable are associated with changes in another.

At one extreme, cast_total_facebook_likes and actor_1_facebook_likes are highly correlated, while movie_facebook_likes and facenumber_in_poster are not. Understanding correlation impacts the variables you would consider for making predictions.

Tree Maps

A *tree map* uses rectangles whose area depicts a proportional representation of hierarchical data. Tree maps are effective at showing the distribution at levels within the hierarchy.

FIGURE 7.9 Budget and average box office gross plot and line chart.

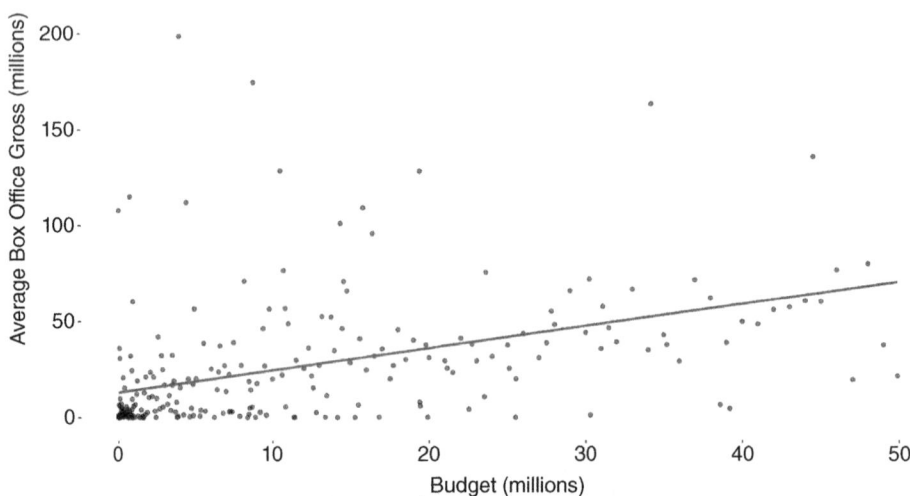

FIGURE 7.10 Budget and average box office gross bubble and line chart.

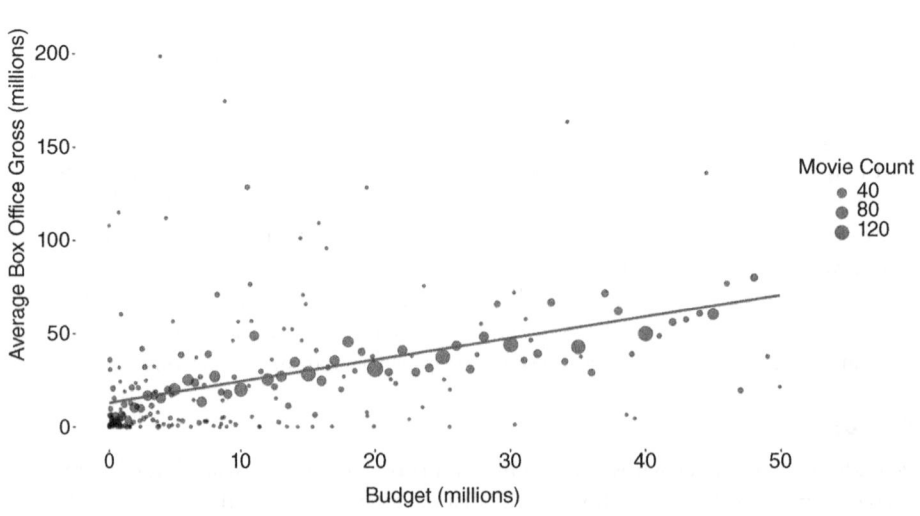

FIGURE 7.11 Histogram of box office gross.

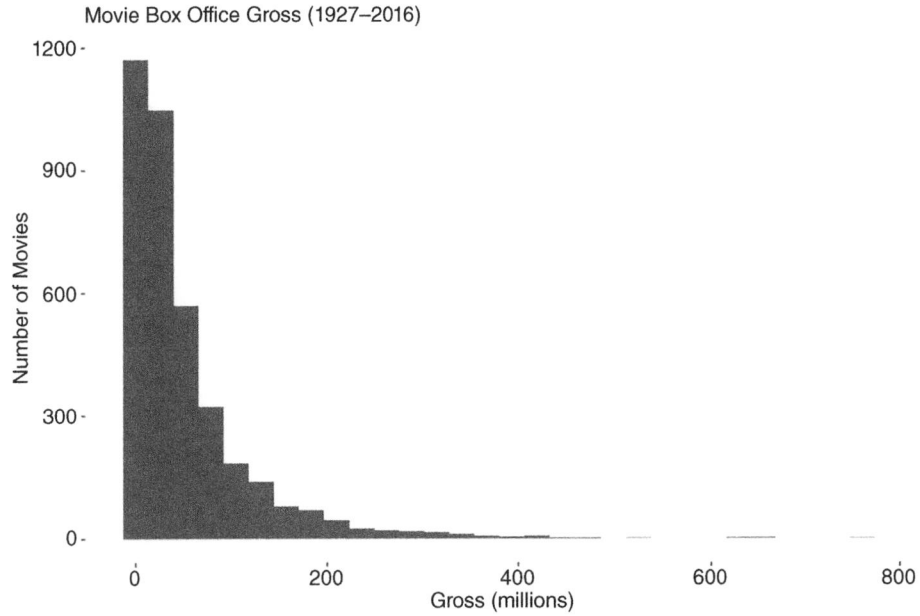

For example, Figure 7.16 shows aggregate movie genres from 1927 to 2016, with the area of each rectangle representing the number of films and the color indicating the genre. Looking at the size of the rectangles in Figure 7.16, the most prevalent genres are comedy and action. Figure 7.17 decomposes the comedy genre, where romantic comedies occupy the largest segment.

Consider tree maps when creating interactive visualizations. You can imagine a person opening the Comedy rectangle from Figure 7.16 to see the tree map in Figure 7.17.

Pivot Tables

A *pivot table* is a tool that summarizes data, allowing you to explore it from various perspectives. Pivot tables use aggregation functions, including SUM, COUNT, AVERAGE, MAX, and MIN, to reshape and aggregate data. Pivot tables are a great way to let people interact with data, and you can find pivot tables in personal spreadsheet tools, including Apple Numbers, Google Sheets, and Microsoft Excel. Business intelligence platforms like Tableau, Microsoft Power BI, and Qlick also have pivot table functionality. Suppose you work for a company that sells exhaust systems. Table 7.1 contains data about salespeople, the fiscal quarter of a sale, and some details about the exhaust system sold. While there's nothing incorrect about having the data in this format, pivot tables help you answer questions leadership may want to know.

FIGURE 7.12 Histogram of movie duration.

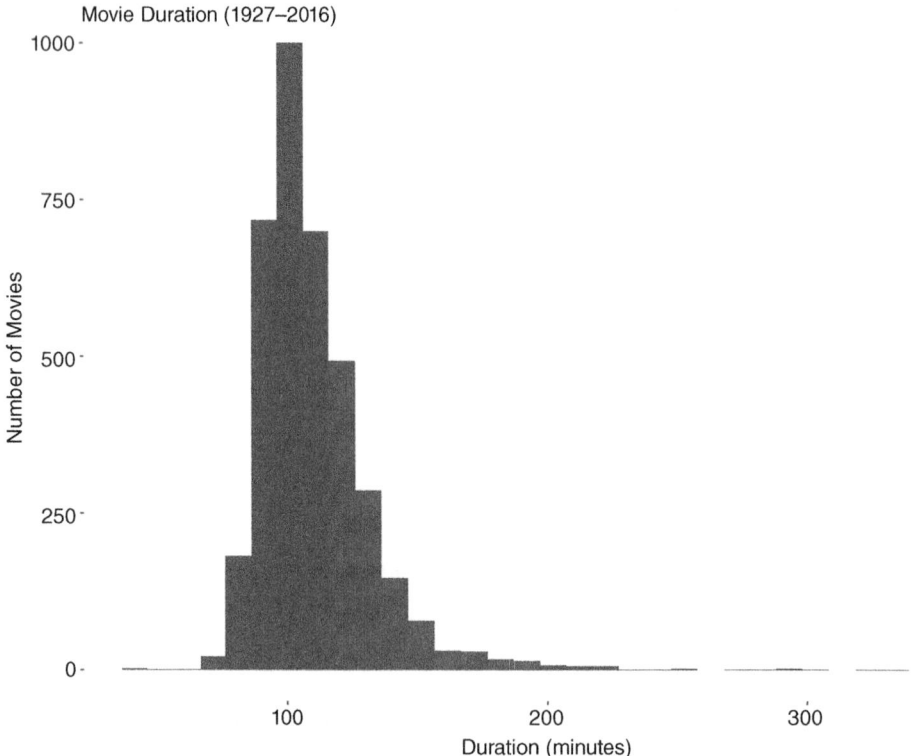

FIGURE 7.13 Large U.S. colleges and universities.

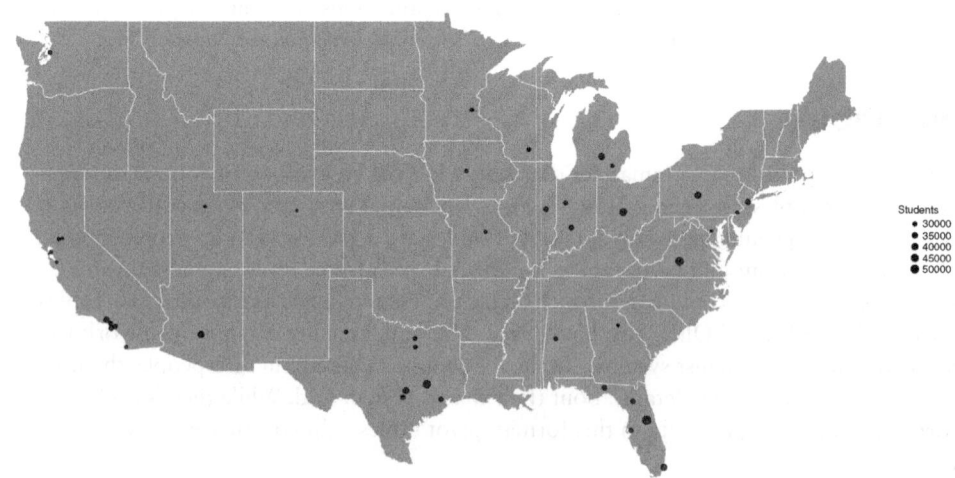

Source: US Department of Education

FIGURE 7.14 Risk heat map.

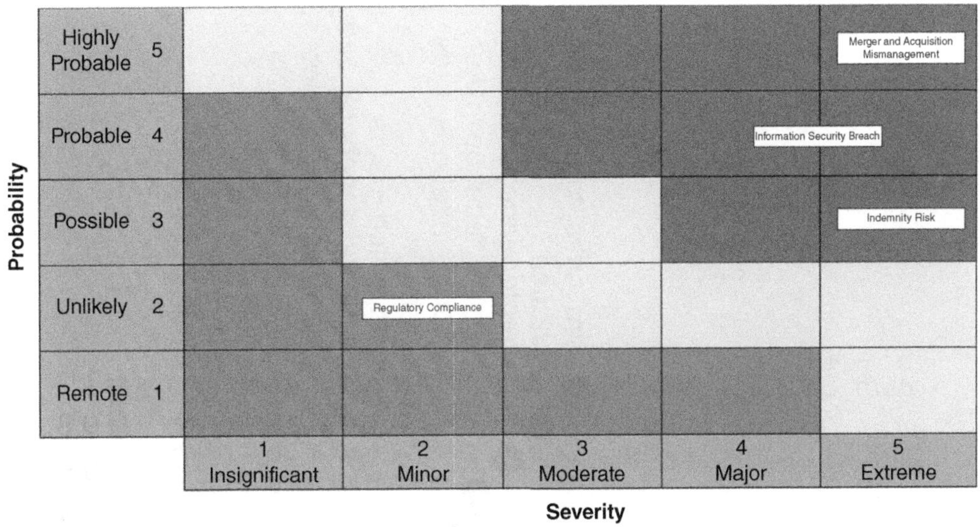

		1 Insignificant	2 Minor	3 Moderate	4 Major	5 Extreme
Highly Probable	5					Merger and Acquisition Mismanagement
Probable	4				Information Security Breach	
Possible	3					Indemnity Risk
Unlikely	2		Regulatory Compliance			
Remote	1					

Probability (y-axis) / Severity (x-axis)

The data in Table 7.1 is transactional, with one row per transaction. Frequently, business leaders need aggregated data. Using the data from Table 7.1, you can pivot it to reflect total sales, total sales by exhaust brand, total sales by vehicle type, total sales by fiscal quarter, or any combination of these aggregations. You could also use a pivot table to show the number of exhaust system sales by manufacturer or the average sale price by manufacturer and vehicle type. You can also use pivot tables to understand the productivity of your sales representatives.

You need to specify at least three things when creating pivot tables. First, you must identify the column from which you want to make rows. You also need to identify the column from which to create columns. Finally, you need to specify an aggregation function to create the values.

Figure 7.18 shows a pivot table aggregating quarterly sales by exhaust brand. In this case, the row values come from the unique values of the Exhaust Brand column in Table 7.1. The column values come from the unique values of the Fiscal Quarter column. Finally, the SUM aggregation function on the Sales Amount column calculates the values. Pivoting the data in this format shows that Kline generates the most overall sales.

Figure 7.19 pivots the data differently, showing total sales by vehicle type. In this case, row values come from the unique entries in the Vehicle Type column from Table 7.1, while the column and value data sources are the same as in Figure 7.18.

Figure 7.20 contains two pivot tables relating to employee productivity. These pivot tables use the Sales Representative column from Table 7.1 to create unique row entries and the Fiscal Quarter column to create unique columns. The first pivot table uses the SUM aggregation function to depict gross sales by sales representatives per quarter. In contrast,

FIGURE 7.15 Correlation heat map.

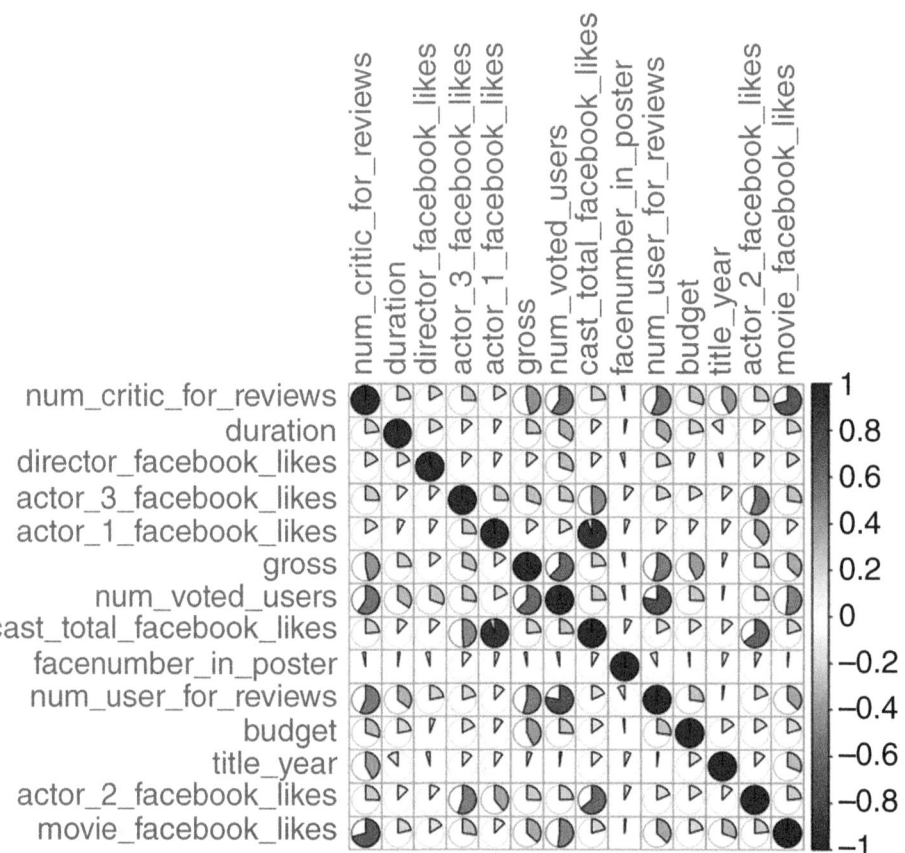

the second pivot table uses the COUNT function to illustrate the number of sales. You can use Table 7.1 and Google Sheets to replicate these pivot tables on your computer.

Infographic

An *infographic*, which gets its name from the words "information" and "graphic," is a visualization that presents information clearly and concisely. Infographics minimize text in favor of visual elements to represent a topic in a format that is easy to understand. The goal of an infographic is to convey an insight in a way that minimizes the time to comprehension.

Consider the infographic in Figure 7.21. This infographic conveys how advising and interventions combine to positively affect academic success. The central portion of the infographic illustrates how the design, build, capture, identify, notify, boost, evaluate, and

FIGURE 7.16 Tree map of movie genres.

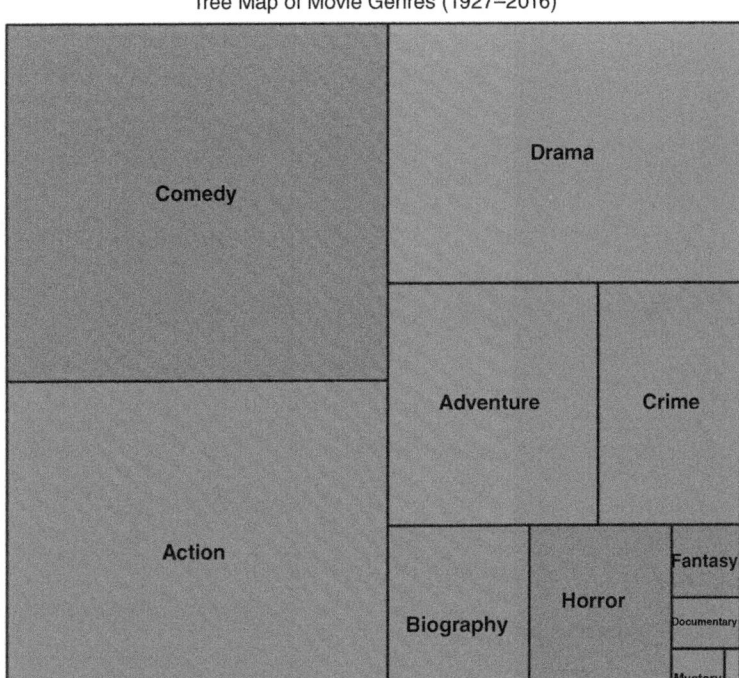

report processes flow together. The detailed phase descriptions on the edges of this infographic provide additional information about how data is collected, analyzed, and assessed. By combining graphics, text, and data, this infographic tells a compelling story about how one university is building the infrastructure and processes to help students realize their potential.

Waterfall

A *waterfall chart* displays the cumulative effect of numeric values over time. Waterfall charts facilitate an understanding of how a series of events impact an initial value. Use a waterfall chart any time you want to see how events affect a baseline value.

For example, Figure 7.22 shows the change in the number of employees over a calendar year. Comparing End of Year Headcount to Initial Headcount shows that this organization grew the number of employees. The rest of the bars illustrate how a variety of factors impacted employee count during the year. The color and position for both Internal and External Hires show that these are positive events, whereas Internal Moves, Separations, and Involuntary Separations have a negative impact.

FIGURE 7.17 Tree map of the comedy genre.

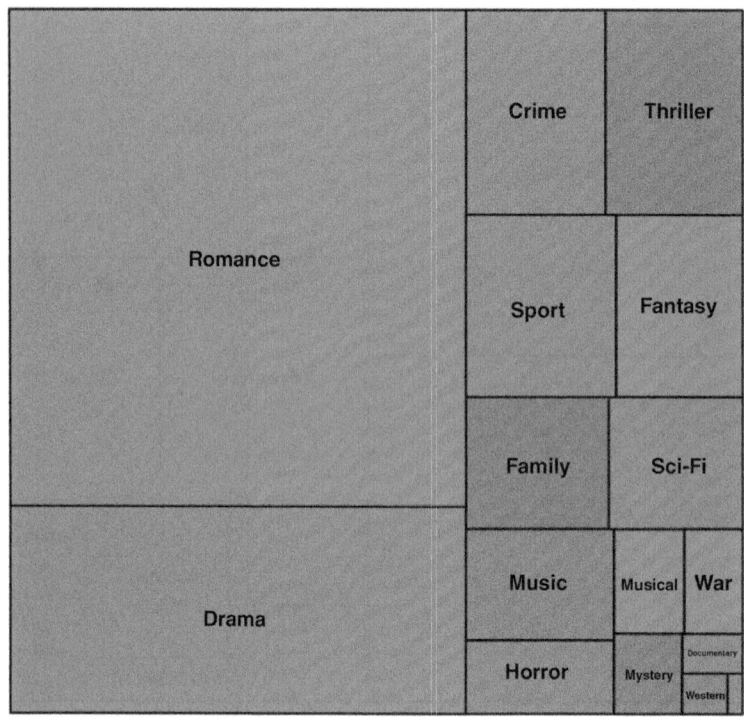

TABLE 7.1 Exhaust Sales Data

Sales Representative	Fiscal Quarter	Vehicle Type	Exhaust Brand	Sales Amount
Olivia	Q1	Porsche 911	TubiStyle	$3,760
Luca	Q1	Porsche 911	Akrapovič	$5,691
Olivia	Q4	Porsche 718	Akrapovič	$8,056
Madeline	Q1	Porsche 911	Kline	$4,468
Madeline	Q2	Porsche 718	TubiStyle	$5,320
Madeline	Q3	Porsche 718	Borla	$1,517
Luca	Q3	Porsche 718	Kline	$9,420
Olivia	Q4	Porsche 911	Fabspeed	$4,066
Olivia	Q2	Porsche 911	Borla	$3,078
Enzo	Q2	Porsche 718	Fabspeed	$3,736

FIGURE 7.18 Quarterly sales by exhaust brand.

SUM of Sales Amount	Fiscal Quarter				
Exhaust Brand	Q1	Q2	Q3	Q4	Grand Total
Akrapovič	$5,691.00			$8,056.00	$13,747.00
Borla		$3,078.00	$1,517.00		$4,595.00
Fabspeed		$3,736.00		$4,066.00	$7,802.00
Kline	$4,468.00		$9,420.00		$13,888.00
TubiStyle	$3,760.00	$5,320.00			$9,080.00
Grand Total	$13,919.00	$12,134.00	$10,937.00	$12,122.00	$49,112.00

FIGURE 7.19 Quarterly sales by vehicle type.

SUM of Sales Amount	Fiscal Quarter				
Vehicle Type	Q1	Q2	Q3	Q4	Grand Total
Porsche 718		$9,056.00	$10,937.00	$8,056.00	$28,049.00
Porsche 911	$13,919.00	$3,078.00		$4,066.00	$21,063.00
Grand Total	$13,919.00	$12,134.00	$10,937.00	$12,122.00	$49,112.00

FIGURE 7.20 Pivot tables for employee productivity.

SUM of Sales Amount	Fiscal Quarter				
Sales Representative	Q1	Q2	Q3	Q4	Grand Total
Enzo		$3,736.00			$3,736.00
Luca	$5,691.00		$9,420.00		$15,111.00
Madeline	$4,468.00	$5,320.00	$1,517.00		$11,305.00
Olivia	$3,760.00	$3,078.00		$12,122.00	$18,960.00
Grand Total	$13,919.00	$12,134.00	$10,937.00	$12,122.00	$49,112.00

COUNT of Sales Amount	Fiscal Quarter				
Sales Representative	Q1	Q2	Q3	Q4	Grand Total
Enzo		1			1
Luca	1		1		2
Madeline	1	1	1		3
Olivia	1	1		2	4
Grand Total	3	3	2	2	10

FIGURE 7.21 Infographic.

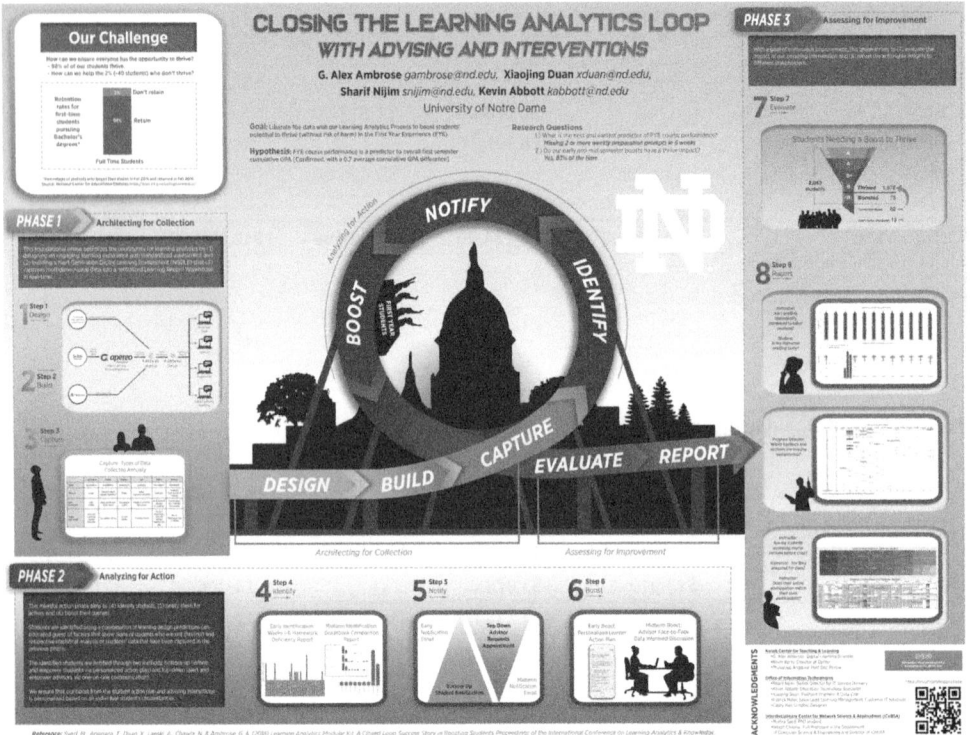

FIGURE 7.22 Headcount waterfall chart.

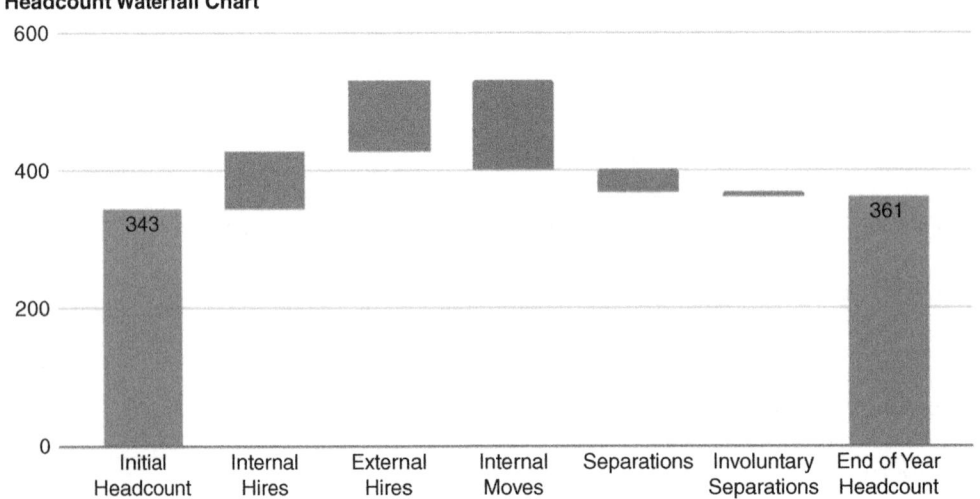

FIGURE 7.23 Positive word cloud.

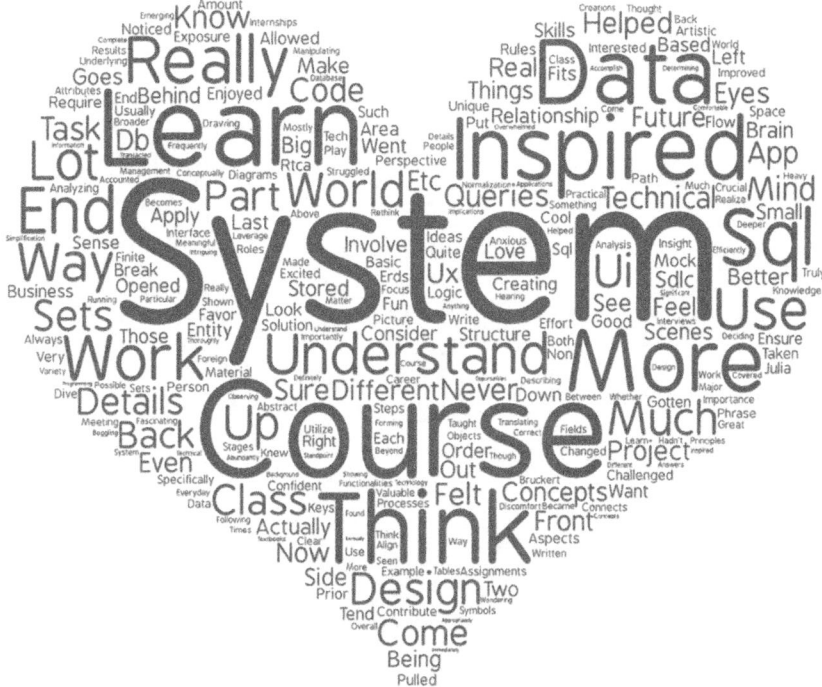

Word Cloud

A *word cloud* is a visualization that uses shape, font size, and color to signify the relative importance of words. Word clouds are effective at visualizing free-form text responses. When creating a word cloud, you eliminate common words and conjunctions as they occur frequently and don't add value in terms of meaning. The heart shape of Figure 7.23 conveys positivity, and the words *system, learn, data, inspired, course,* and *think* stand out.

Be deliberate when choosing a word cloud's shape, as it helps convey the overall sentiment. For example, the shape of Figure 7.24 establishes the context that responses about struggle form the basis of the word cloud, with *assignments* standing out as the most significant individual word.

Understanding Business Requirements

Reports and dashboards both summarize data for end users, but they distribute those summaries in different ways. A *report* is a static electronic or physical document that reflects information at a given point in time. On the other hand, a *dashboard* is an interactive

FIGURE 7.24 Negative word cloud.

visualization that encourages people to explore data dynamically. Both reports and dashboards are ideal tools for visualizing data content.

The most important thing to do when developing a report or dashboard is to answer the question, "Who is the audience?" For example, a custodial supervisor might want to track the remaining cleaning products' daily levels to inform restocking decisions. Alternatively, a chief executive officer (CEO) may want to understand revenue by brand and global region. You shouldn't begin creating a report or dashboard until you clearly understand who your audience is and how they will use the product.

Once you clearly understand the audience and their needs, you can turn your attention to identifying the data sources that will satisfy the requirements of your audience. For instance, you may need to combine data across multiple subject areas. If you are working with corporate executives, you may need to combine data from various divisions within the organization. Sourcing this data can be a challenge, as when a corporation grows inorganically through acquisition, it can end up with multiple redundant systems to accomplish a single business objective. As an analyst, your job is to ensure that you have access to the appropriate data sources.

As you identify data sources, you'll need to consider how old the data can be while satisfying the needs of your audience. Suppose you are working with the chief financial officer (CFO) of a consumer products company to develop a historical report on corporate sales revenue for the past five fiscal years. In that case, you don't need real-time sales information and can instead focus on obtaining high-quality historical data. It is most likely that views within a data warehouse or data mart, as described in Chapter 4, "Databases and Data Acquisition," would serve as the data source for this type of report, as Figure 7.25 illustrates.

As you consider the needs of the CFO, you will want to think through the parameters of the report and how that affects data sources and report design. Report parameters let you define data range limits for the data elements in your report. For instance, even if you think the CFO will want to see six years of historical sales, you'll want to avoid limiting the report to a specified number of years. Instead of restricting the report generation process, accommodate the ability to filter data by date range. Filtering data in this manner provides you with more flexibility down the road if the CFO later decides that they want to see 10 years of sales data.

In most reports, you'll want to filter by more than one parameter. For example, suppose the CFO wants to share eyecare-related sales data with the person who leads the eyecare division. In that case, you would want to enable the ability to filter the data by content so that the eyecare leader only sees the section of the report that is relevant to their operations.

Alternatively, suppose you are working with a regional sales manager in the dental division who wants to understand the progress of their staff against their sales goal. In this

FIGURE 7.25 Historical reporting.

scenario, you need to ask the sales manager how frequently they need the report updated. That frequency may change depending on the time of year. For example, the sales manager may only check this report every month for much of the year. However, as the end of a fiscal quarter approaches, they may want to see updates weekly, daily, hourly, or in real time. In this case, you want to design your report to accommodate when they need updates most frequently, which influences your data source. To satisfy the need for real-time data, you use the transactional system for recording dental sales instead of relying on older data from a data warehouse, as shown in Figure 7.26.

Once you identify who needs what data and when they need it, you can focus on how people access the report. If people will access the report digitally, one way to solve the distribution challenge is with a pull approach. With a *pull approach*, you publish a report to a known location, like a web page, and let people know the frequency and timing of when the report updates. With this approach, people can go to the website when they want to use the report.

Alternatively, you could implement a push approach. With a *push approach*, the report is automatically sent to the appropriate people as it becomes available. When designing a push approach, you need to think through distribution considerations. For example, a report may prove to be too large to distribute via email. In that case, you could use a blended distribution approach. With a *blended approach*, you store the report centrally and let people know when the report has been updated and is ready for use. With the blended approach, you inform people that the report is available while maintaining central control of the report itself.

FIGURE 7.26   Real-time reporting.

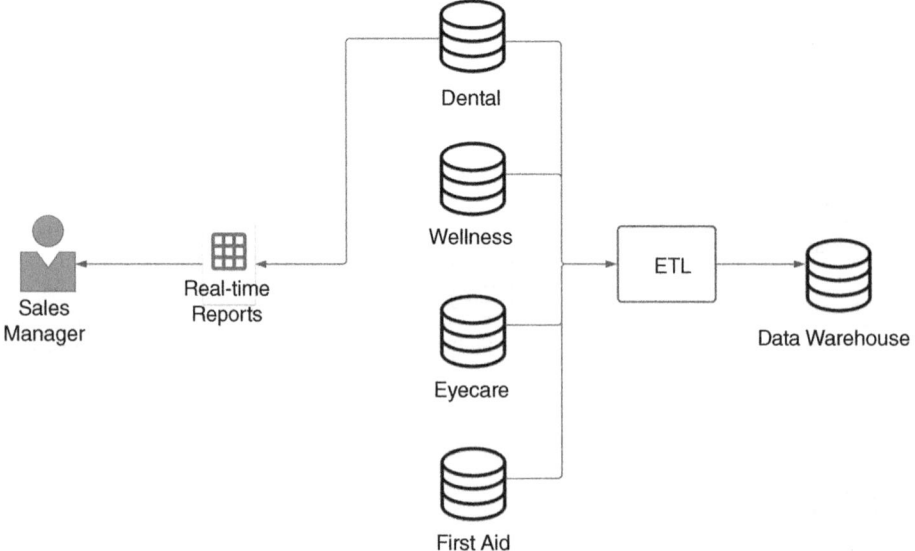

If you go with a push or blended approach for informing people about the readiness of a given report, be sure to think through the maintenance of the distribution list of people to notify. With all organizations, people rotate in and out of roles. As people transition out of a position, you want to ensure that they no longer receive notifications about reports that are no longer relevant to their job role. On the other hand, as a new person joins the organization, you need to get that person the reports they require to be effective in their role.

However, suppose you are creating a printed report that will be distributed physically to its recipients. In this case, the distribution challenge is entirely different. If the recipients are within your organization, you can use existing distribution channels to distribute the printed report. However, if the recipients are in other locations across the country, you need to ensure that you have the appropriate mailing address for each recipient. You also need to ensure you have enough lead time to send the report through the mail. Alternatively, you could speed up distribution by paying more for overnight delivery.

Understanding Design Elements

Whenever you give people a tool, it should be approachable and easy to use. When creating a report or a dashboard, you can use existing design principles as guideposts. These design principles, known as the "five Cs" of creating visualizations, help ensure that your reports and dashboards communicate clearly and efficiently. When thinking visually, the five Cs are control, correctness, clarity, consistency, and concentration.

Control has to do with how you focus the attention of your audience. When someone encounters a dashboard for the first time, one of your goals is to deliver the pertinent information quickly. For instance, if there is a place where people can adjust parameters and have the dashboard respond, use visual highlights to focus attention on this capability.

Correctness makes sure that your information is accurate and that there are no spelling mistakes. Pay close attention to correctness when using corporate names and logos. For example, Procter & Gamble is a large consumer goods corporation. Misspelling the company name as "Proctor & Gamble" is embarrassing as it displays a lack of correctness.

Clarity refers to selecting the right visualization tool for communicating your message, making sure the visualization is easy to interpret and visually crisp, and using fonts and sizes that are easy to read. For example, consider Figure 7.27, which uses an ornate font. While the diagram conveys the same information as Figure 7.26, the font compromises clarity and makes it hard to read.

Consistency refers to using the same design and documentation elements throughout your report or dashboard to give your visualization a cohesive and complete feel. Using the same font, page layout, and web page design are all techniques for ensuring consistency.

FIGURE 7.27 Poor font choice.

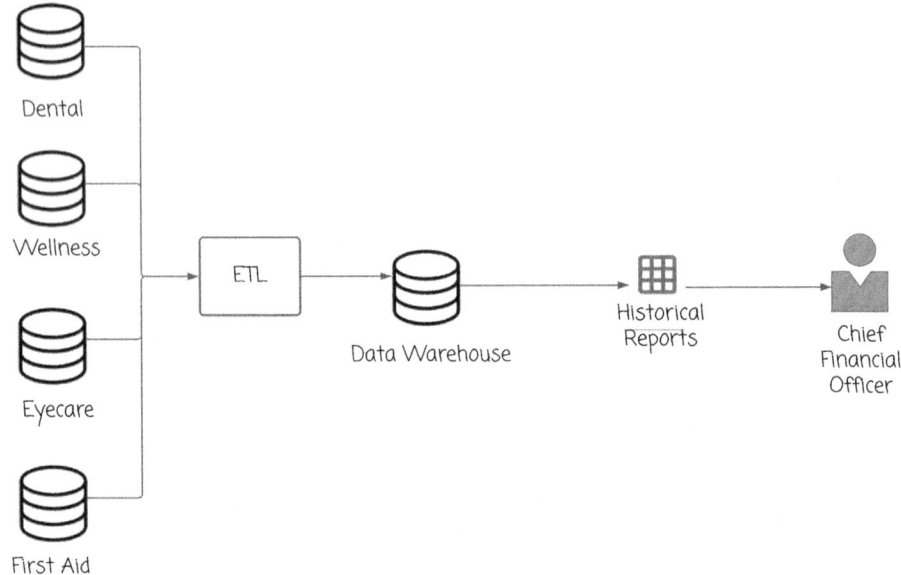

Concentration refers to using visuals to focus your audience's attention on the most relevant information without overwhelming them with details. Concentration, along with clarity and control, helps you focus your audience by reducing clutter and removing unnecessary details. Use a layout that increases concentration and removes distracting visual elements from charts. For example, suppose you are creating a report that summarizes quarterly sales performance. Only show the necessary summary statistics to improve concentration instead of including the raw daily sales data.

Cover Page

When developing a report, keep in mind that the first thing people see is the cover page. It is therefore vital that it sets expectations about the observations and insights the reader will find within. Effective cover pages have a concise title describing the report's contents. Ideally, a cover page will also communicate a significant insight from the report itself. As the saying goes, you never get a second chance to make a good first impression. In that vein, a cover page has to entice a person into turning the page and diving into the report. Figure 7.28 shows the cover page for the 2020 Porsche AG Annual Report. It incorporates product imagery with text on the right detailing what the reader can expect to find within.

Accompanying the title page should be clear instructions on how to use the report. For example, if the report analyzes five years' worth of data, the range of years should stand out on the cover. Excluding the range of years demonstrates a lack of clarity and control.

FIGURE 7.28 Porsche AG Annual Report cover page.

Source: Copyrighted by Dr. Ing. h. c. F. Porsche AG

Executive Summary

Following a report's cover page is an executive summary. The executive summary provides an overview of the report's contents. When crafting an executive summary, you should begin with the end in mind, summarizing crucial observations and insights. With time an executive's most precious resource, the summary needs to convey the big ideas, while the body of the report details the analysis that led to those ideas. Figure 7.29 illustrates a compelling executive summary taken from the 2020 Porsche AG Annual Report.

When developing a report or dashboard, you need to incorporate design elements into your thinking. Color schemes, page layout, font size and style, charts, and corporate standards are among the many design elements you should consider. These considerations apply if you enhance an existing report or create a new dashboard.

Branding

Following corporate branding standards is essential regardless of the data product you create. Adhering to brand standards ensures that the dashboards and reports you create feel

FIGURE 7.29 Porsche AG Annual Report executive summary.

Dear Reader,

The year 2020 was a very challenging year. The coronavirus pandemic has severely tested human co-existence. Meanwhile, the global economy was subjected to a stress test. Porsche too was affected. We were forced to halt production for six weeks in the spring, and our dealership operations also had to temporarily close.

Our response to these challenges was rapid, flexible and pragmatic. We introduced targeted measures to protect our workforce. And we engaged in systematic crisis management, successfully shoring up our liquidity and stabilising our results. In this way we steered Porsche strategically and robustly through the crisis.

With good results. With deliveries of new vehicles totalling 272,162, we were a mere three per cent down on the record figure set in 2019. Our company remains highly profitable. Operating profit: 4.2 billion euros. Return on sales: 14.6 per cent. Figures that are unmatched in our sector. Figures that represent a great success for our entire team. In a difficult environment, that team has remained united, shown fighting spirit, and been dedicated to the task at hand.

This success is founded on our fresh and attractive product range. 911 Turbo, 911 Targa, 718 GTS – thoroughbred sports cars, and the stuff of our customers' dreams. Then there are our attractive best-sellers: the Cayenne and the Macan. Not forgetting our powerful Gran Turismo, the Panamera.

Our electric mobility strategy has also provided a strong tailwind, noticeably gaining momentum in 2020. In Europe, one third of our new deliveries were already electrified, with an equal split between all-electric and hybrid vehicles. This figure will rise to 50 per cent by 2025. What this shows is that our electrification strategy is taking hold.

Our success is driven by our innovative power. The technological strength that has always set Porsche apart has been concentrated in the Taycan, our first all-electric sports car. Its innovative 800-volt architecture already has a proven track record, used in our winning race cars at Le Mans. This architecture means that it is not only fast on the road, but also quick to recharge. In a further success story, the Taycan was voted the most innovative vehicle in the world in 2020. Internationally, it has picked up more than 50 awards – more than any other Porsche model has ever achieved in the space of one year.

Porsche is clearly committed to the goals of the Paris Agreement, and is a trailblazer in this area. We are pursuing a consistent electrification and sustainability strategy. And we are setting ourselves ambitious decarbonisation targets, including in comparison with the rest of the industry. Porsche is also setting new standards in sustainable production.

Our original plant in Zuffenhausen has been CO_2-neutral since 2020, with the Leipzig plant following suit in January 2021. This is also where the all-electric Macan will come off the production line in future. This underlines our credentials as a sustainable mobility pioneer. Our goal is ambitious: Porsche will be completely CO_2-neutral as early as 2030.

We see ourselves as a partner in society and embrace the responsibilities that this involves – towards the environment, social issues and the economy. Porsche has, for example, supported countless social activities in 2020, the year of coronavirus. These have all been targeted and well coordinated, with a significantly increased volume of donations and a voluntary commitment from many employees.
In addition, we supported the state governments of Baden-Württemberg and Saxony in the procurement of Personal Protective Equipment and made our expertise available to the crisis teams. Porsche has also been involved in many aid activities with an international aspect. This has greatly advanced our understanding of sustainability and carries us into the future.

And we are also investing in our employees. Employees who work hard every day to inspire our customers – with pioneering spirit and passion. Last year, we signed works agreements to secure jobs at our locations until 2030, sending out a clear signal of our future intentions. Our team is highly motivated. With that team, we are successfully shaping the future of sustainable mobility.

The new Porsche Strategy 2030 shows us the way forward. This also applies to the further expansion of our digital capabilities: we are systematically stepping up the efficiency, precision and quality of our processes. Making us even faster and even more flexible. We are undertaking considerable efforts to succeed in our goals: between now and 2025, Porsche will be investing 15 billion euros in electromobility, sustainable production and digitalisation. This is money well spent, not least because it will strengthen our commercial success and profitability in the long term. Even in an age of transformation, we remain as focused as ever on our strategic return target of 15 per cent.

In 2020, Porsche showed impressively: our business model is robust and flexible. Our brand has never had such a positive appeal. Strategically, we remain firmly on course. Sustainability, innovation and digitalisation will determine our future path. We are also strongly and profitably positioned for the future. Our good performance in terms of return and capital value allows us to look to that future with confidence: we will embrace our opportunities with self-confidence and a down-to-earth approach.

The Executive Board of
Dr. Ing. h.c. F. Porsche AG

Letter from the Executive Board of Porsche AG The figures for fuel consumption, energy consumption and CO_2 emissions are found on pages 212 – 213. 5

Source: Copyrighted by Dr. Ing. h. c. F. Porsche AG.Design Elements

immediately familiar to your users. Your organization will inform you of the degree to which you incorporate various branding elements. For example, universities have overall brand standards, while a specific college within a university may have its sub-brand standards. Color schemes, layouts, font choices, and graphics are a few of the branding elements to incorporate when creating a data artifact.

Color Schemes

A *color scheme* is a limited selection of colors you use when creating a report or a dashboard. The first decision to make is whether you need to use a monochromatic color palette or have the flexibility to use more than one color. A *monochromatic* palette limits you to working with shades of a single color, as shown in Figure 7.30. One use case where a black monochromatic palette is an appropriate choice is creating physical reports. For example, suppose you are designing a less formal printed report for frequent, high-volume distribution. Given the distribution needs, printing in full color could be prohibitively expensive. When distributing electronically, consider whether the recipient has access to a color printer.

If you have the luxury of working with more than one color, selecting a complementary color palette is a sound choice. A *complementary* palette starts with two contrasting colors. Examples of complementary colors are orange and blue, yellow and purple, and red and green. Understanding your audience is crucial, as most people with partial color blindness have difficulty differentiating between red and green. Suppose you are creating a corporate annual report for broad distribution. This kind of report has a high impact and yearly distribution, making the cost of color printing insignificant. Whether working in monochrome or multiple colors, ensure that the font color contrasts with the background color to ensure readability.

Layouts

The *layout* of a report or dashboard determines the arrangement of its component parts. It is crucial to consider approachability when thinking about the design. When developing the layout for a report, begin with a summary before diving into the supporting detail. For a long, multipage report, use a table of contents so that the reader can efficiently navigate to a topic of interest, as well as headings for sections and subsections.

Use brief paragraphs and bullet points to focus the reader's attention. Ensure parallel construction when developing bullet points. *Parallel construction* is when all bullet points use the same form and have the same style and approximate length. Figure 7.31 shows nonparallel construction, where the second bullet point has a different format than the other three. Figure 7.32 fixes the construction issue by changing the phrasing of the second bullet point.

FIGURE 7.30 Black monochromatic color palette.

FIGURE 7.31   Nonparallel construction.

Considerations for managing data
- Structure
- How easy it is to integrate
- Quality
- Access

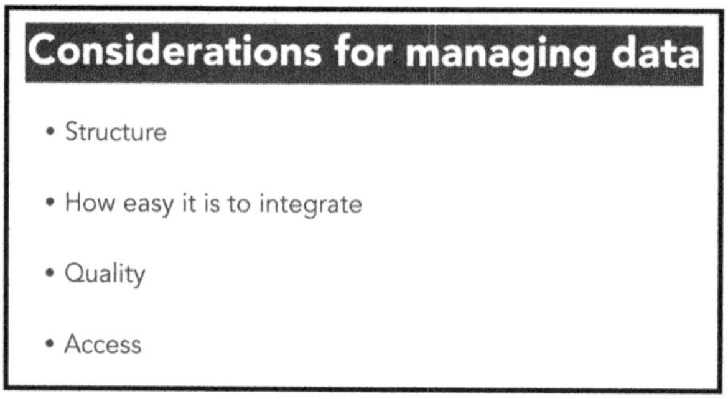

FIGURE 7.32   Parallel construction.

Considerations for managing data
- Structure
- Integration
- Quality
- Access

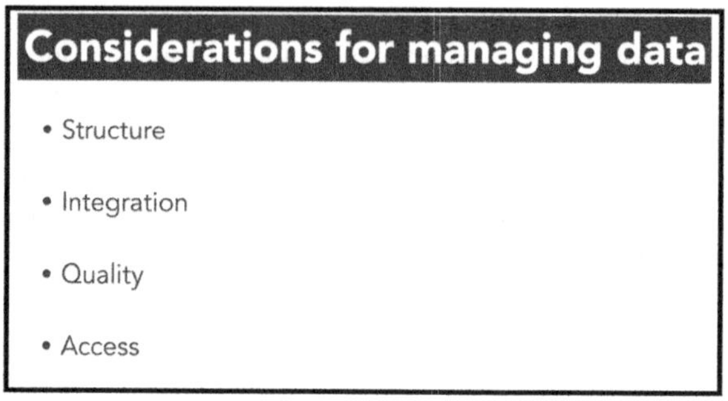

Fonts

When choosing a font style, pick one that is easy for people to read by avoiding ornate fonts. After excluding ornate options, you need to decide between a serif or sans serif font style. In typography, a *serif* is a finishing detail for each letter in a typeface. A *serif font style* includes serifs, whereas a *sans serif font style* does not. Consider the capital T at the start of each sentence in Figure 7.33. For all the sans serif font styles, the horizontal component of the capital T is a straight line. On the other hand, all serif style fonts have a finishing flourish at either end of the horizontal line.

While sans serif fonts work well digitally, studies show that serif fonts work well for printed text. Times New Roman, Garamond, and Courier New are all examples of serif fonts, while Helvetica, Arial, and Geneva do not have serifs. Spend some time studying all the letters in Figure 7.33 to compare these popular fonts and see the stylistic difference for each serif and sans serif letter.

FIGURE 7.33 Serif and sans serif fonts.

Serif	Sans Serif
Times New Roman: The quick brown fox jumped over the lazy dog.	**Helvetica:** The quick brown fox jumped over the lazy dog.
Garamond: The quick brown fox jumped over the lazy dog.	**Arial:** The quick brown fox jumped over the lazy dog.
`Courier New:` `The quick brown fox jumped over the lazy dog.`	**Geneva:** The quick brown fox jumped over the lazy dog.

FIGURE 7.34 Sample layout elements and font sizes.

Layout Element	Font Size
Title	30 points
Heading Level 1	26 points
Heading Level 2	20 points
Heading Level 3	16 points
Body Text	13 points

After selecting a font style, determine the appropriate font size for your title, table of contents, headings, subheadings, and body text. You measure font sizes in points, with each point representing 1/72 of an inch. Start with your body text when determining font sizes. The body text makes up most of what a person reads, so you want to ensure you don't pick a font size that is too small. It is common for body text to range between 12 and 14 points. After selecting a font size for your body text, use progressively larger sizes for subheadings, headings, and titles. Figure 7.34 illustrates a sample style guide that specifies layout elements and their font size.

Remember that selecting an appropriate font size is crucial for printed reports, as the size becomes fixed during printing. However, font size is less critical when distributing electronically, as recipients may adjust the overall font size on a computer, tablet, or mobile device.

Graphics

Using graphics to present summary information is a practical choice, whether creating a report or developing a dashboard. As the saying goes, a picture is worth a thousand words, and visually conveying information with charts helps focus your audience's attention. Think through the key chart elements when designing charts, including the chart's title, labels, and legends.

When developing a chart, make sure you specify a chart title. A *chart title* uses a large font size and concise wording to clearly describe what the chart depicts. If necessary, you can use a subtitle to supplement your title with additional information to add clarity.

When using a chart, be sure to use labels appropriately. In a chart with an x-axis and a y-axis, a *label* describes what each axis represents. Consider Figure 7.35, which shows

FIGURE 7.35   Sample chart with labeled axes.

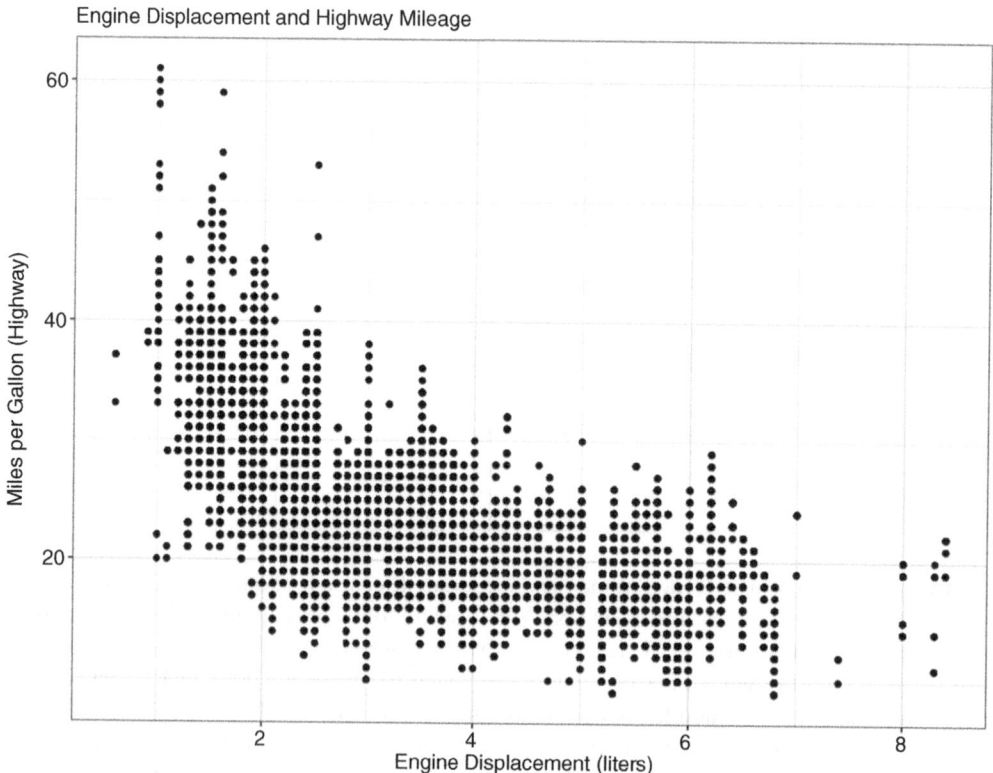

Source: Environmental Protection Agency National Vehicle and Fuel Emissions Laboratory

how a vehicle's engine displacement on the x-axis relates to its highway efficiency in miles per gallon on the y-axis. If the axes did not have labels and the title was missing, a person wouldn't know what information the chart conveys.

When a chart shows multiple categories, use a *legend* to help the reader distinguish between categories. For example, consider Figure 7.36, which shows Ford's and Volkswagen's corporate average highway fuel economy in miles per gallon. The legend indicates that the data in the chart for Ford uses circles, whereas the data for Volkswagen uses triangles.

Corporate Reporting Standards

When developing any type of visualization, be mindful of any existing corporate reporting standards. For instance, your organization may have a style guide for reporting. A *style guide* is a set of standards that drives consistency in communication. As a means of enforcing structure and consistency, style guides define the use of a variety of branding elements, including page layout, font selection, corporate color codes, logos, and trademarks.

Imagine that you work for General Electric and are developing a new visualization. Figure 7.37 shows the logo for General Electric. The logo is quite recognizable.

FIGURE 7.36   Sample chart with a legend.

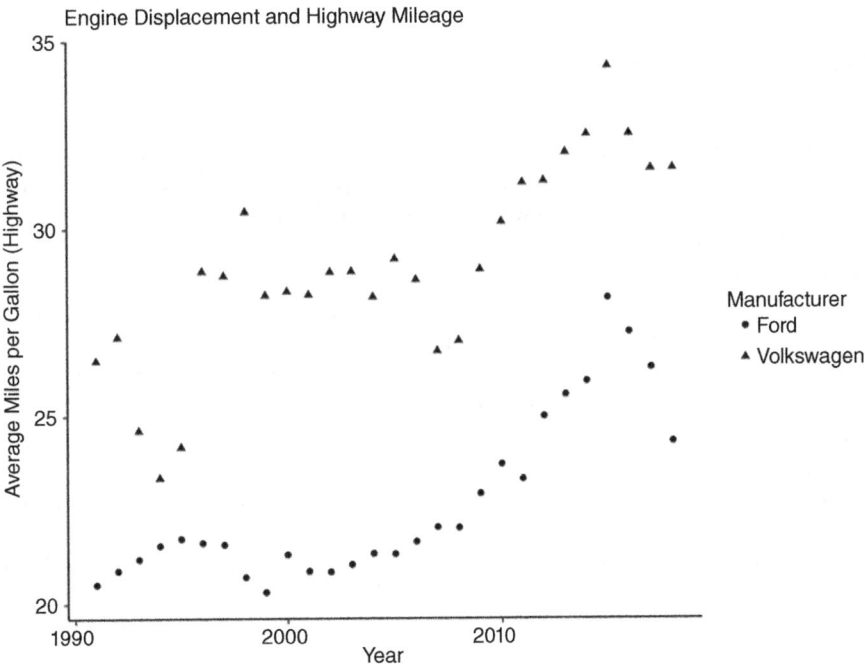

Source: Environmental Protection Agency National Vehicle and Fuel Emissions Laboratory

FIGURE 7.37 General Electric logo.

TABLE 7.2 Color Codes for General Electric Blue

Format	Value
Pantone	PMS 4151 C
HEX Color	#026CB6
Red Green Blue (RGB)	(2, 108, 182)
Cyan Magenta Yellow Key (CMYK)	(89, 56, 0, 0)

Incorporating the logo into a report or dashboard communicates an association with the brand. If you are working in color, you also want the appropriate color code from Table 7.2 to use the "General Electric Blue" elsewhere in your visualization. Using consistent colors is one way to give your visualizations a cohesive look.

Style guides can also incorporate watermarks. Typically text or a logo, a *watermark* is superimposed over a report or web page. If you do not want people to share your visualization outside your organization, you could use an "INTERNAL USE ONLY" watermark, as shown in Figure 7.38. Watermarks are especially important during the development process. For example, using a "DRAFT" watermark allows you to circulate a report to ensure it meets expectations while letting people know it is a work in progress.

Larger organizations have a communications department responsible for developing brand standards. When creating visualizations, make sure you work with your communications colleagues to ensure you are doing your part to project your organization's brand consistently.

FIGURE 7.38 Sample chart with watermark.

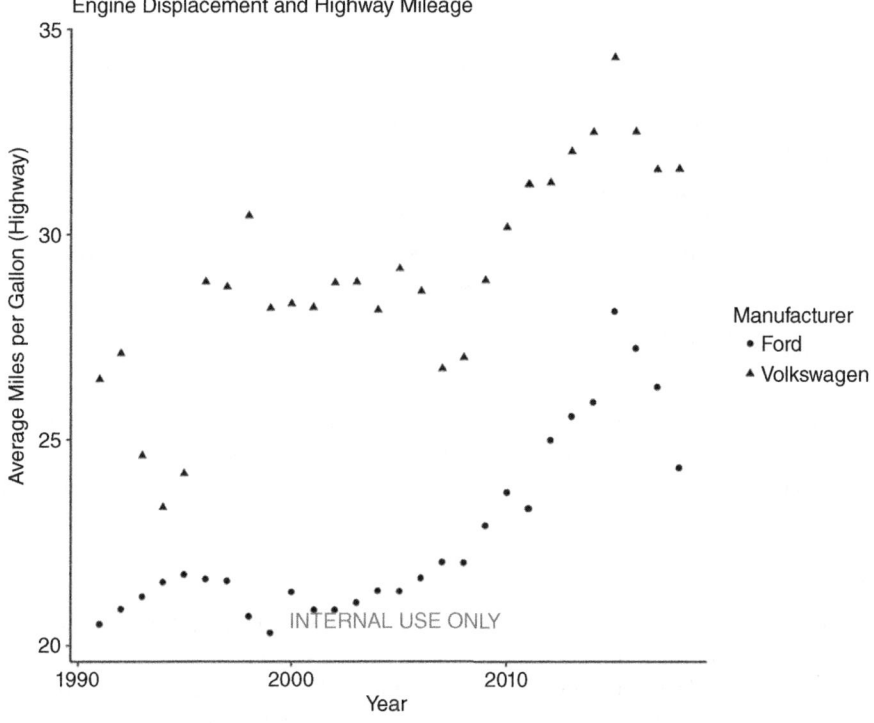

Source: Environmental Protection Agency National Vehicle and Fuel Emissions Laboratory

Documentation Elements

People must trust the information in your visualizations. To help establish trust, you can incorporate documentation elements, including version numbers, reference data sources, and reference dates. Reference dates include the initial creation date, report run date, and data refresh date.

Version Number

A version number is a numeric value that refers to a specific version of a report. Version numbers help you keep track of changes to content and layout over time. Reference data sources identify where data in the report originates. For example, if you are using a data mart to create a visualization for colleagues in the finance division, specify the name of the data mart.

Reference Data Sources

Reference dates help people understand what to expect in terms of data recency. For example, if a report has a daily refresh cycle, the report run date helps people realize when the last data refresh date was. If they see that the refresh date is from a week ago, they know the report is missing a week's worth of data.

Consider the version history for a daily sales report, as shown in Table 7.3. Note that a significant change happens on January 12, 2022. The source for this report becomes the Sales Data Mart, replacing the Corporate Data Warehouse. Note that the version numbering scheme changes to acknowledge the significance of using a different data source. With this level of transparency about the report's origins, people's level of trust in the report increases. It also underscores the integrity of the data sources.

Frequently Asked Questions

When developing a report or a dashboard, it is good to maintain a set of frequently asked questions (FAQs). A FAQ provides answers to people's most common questions. If the dashboard is available online, the FAQ can contain links to a glossary of unique terms, cross-references to other dashboards or reports, and contact information if there are additional questions.

Appendix

When developing a report, use an appendix to include supporting details that are inappropriate to include in the main body. For example, suppose you use statistical analysis to derive the central insight for a report. Recall that one of the goals of creating a report is to convey insights. Instead of detailing each calculation in the main report body, move them to

TABLE 7.3 Sample Daily Sales Report Version History

Data Sources	Version	Data Refresh Date	Initial Creation Date
Sales Data Mart	2.3	January 14, 2022	January 7, 2022
Sales Data Mart	2.2	January 13, 2022	January 7, 2022
Sales Data Mart	2.1	January 12, 2022	January 7, 2022
Corporate Data Warehouse	1.5	January 11, 2022	January 7, 2022
Corporate Data Warehouse	1.4	January 10, 2022	January 7, 2022
Corporate Data Warehouse	1.3	January 9, 2022	January 7, 2022
Corporate Data Warehouse	1.2	January 8, 2022	January 7, 2022
Corporate Data Warehouse	1.1	January 7, 2022	January 7, 2022

an appendix. That way, the general reader will not feel overwhelmed by the details, while the informed reader can explore the calculations in detail.

Understanding Dashboard Development Methods

Recall that dashboards are dynamic tools that help people explore data to inform their decision-making. Since dashboards are dynamic, their design, development, and delivery mechanisms are more complex than the considerations for developing reports. This section explores the dashboard considerations that you should keep in mind.

Consumer Types

As with developing a report, it is crucial to identify who will be interacting with the dashboard you create. For example, *C-level executives*, with titles like chief executive officer and chief financial officer, have the most senior leadership positions in an organization. Your dashboard needs to consolidate critical performance metrics with the ability to get additional detail on an as-needed basis to assist people with C-level responsibilities in making strategic decisions. Ensure you spend sufficient time identifying the *key performance indicators* (*KPIs*) crucial to senior leaders. A KPI is a metric that leadership agrees is crucial to achieving the organization's business objectives. As you identify *what* leaders want to see, you can locate *where* to get the relevant data.

A large organization typically has external stakeholders who serve on its board of directors. While the board's needs closely align with the needs of C-level executives, you need to incorporate any of the board's unique requirements in your dashboard so that board members can fulfill their oversight and corporate management duties effectively.

Lower levels of management focus on a different set of metrics than senior leadership. Although the information needs differ from the C-suite, they are no less critical to organizational success. To ensure your dashboard will add value, make sure to work with managers to identify the KPIs that provide the information they need to lead their portion of the organization effectively.

You may be developing dashboards for people external to your organization. Your organization may enter into a *service level agreement (SLA)* that describes the level of service an external vendor or partner can expect. Violating an SLA can result in financial and reputational damages. To help communicate clearly and with transparency, a dashboard that is available to the general public provides a single source of information for anyone interested in the status of your services. For example, Figure 7.39 shows a publicly accessible dashboard for Amazon Web Services, one of the world's leading cloud service providers. This dashboard shows a list of services and their operational status. In addition to showing the current status, you can opt into receiving status updates for a particular service.

FIGURE 7.39 Sample public-facing dashboard.

Current Status - Oct 1, 2021 PDT		
Amazon Web Services publishes our most up-to-the-minute information on service availability in the table below. Check back here any time to get current status information, or subscribe to an RSS feed to be notified of interruptions to each individual service. If you are experiencing a real-time, operational issue with one of our services that is not described below, please inform us by clicking on the "Contact Us" link to submit a service issue report. All dates and times are Pacific Time (PST/PDT).		
North America South America Europe Africa Asia Pacific Middle East		Contact Us
Recent Events	**Details**	**RSS**
✓ No recent events.		
Remaining Services	**Details**	**RSS**
✓ Alexa for Business (N. Virginia)	Service is operating normally	🔊
✓ Amazon API Gateway (Montreal)	Service is operating normally	🔊
✓ Amazon API Gateway (N. California)	Service is operating normally	🔊
✓ Amazon API Gateway (N. Virginia)	Service is operating normally	🔊
✓ Amazon API Gateway (Ohio)	Service is operating normally	🔊
✓ Amazon API Gateway (Oregon)	Service is operating normally	🔊
✓ Amazon AppFlow (Montreal)	Service is operating normally	🔊
✓ Amazon AppFlow (N. California)	Service is operating normally	🔊
✓ Amazon AppFlow (N. Virginia)	Service is operating normally	🔊
✓ Amazon AppFlow (Ohio)	Service is operating normally	🔊
✓ Amazon AppFlow (Oregon)	Service is operating normally	🔊
✓ Amazon AppStream 2.0 (N. Virginia)	Service is operating normally	🔊
✓ Amazon AppStream 2.0 (Oregon)	Service is operating normally	🔊

You may need to develop a dashboard for technical experts. For instance, the people who use the dashboard in Figure 7.15 could have functional or technical responsibilities. A person with financial responsibility might only want to know when the outage violates an SLA, which triggers a service credit. However, a technical expert using the service wants to learn more about the specifics of an outage and how that impacts the services they provide.

Data Source Considerations

With clarity on what your dashboard needs to contain, you can proceed with identifying data sources. The most vital determination you make about data sources hinges on whether or not the dashboard needs to incorporate live data. *Static data* is data that refreshes at some regular interval. A typical design pattern is for operational databases to update a data warehouse every night. *Continuous data*, also known as *live data*, typically comes directly from an operational database that people use to perform their daily duties. The operational database provides a *live data feed* to the dashboard.

For example, a CFO has many needs as the senior leader responsible for an organization's finances. Since people are among an organization's most expensive assets, one of the KPIs a CFO tracks is employee count. Suppose the CFO expects their dashboard to reflect how many employees an organization has up to the minute. In that case, you need to source data directly from the operational human resources database.

However, if it is sufficient to have the employee count updated at the end of each business day, you can pull data from a data warehouse. Figure 7.40 visualizes the process for determining whether you need to connect with an operational database. Depending on the needs of the dashboard consumer, you may end up with connections to both operational and reporting databases.

Data Type Considerations

One thing that differentiates dashboards and reports is the fact that dashboards use software as the delivery mechanism. As such, you have to have a deeper understanding of your source data than when you are creating a report. Whether you use packaged software like Tableau or Qlik or write your own visualization using a programming language like Python or R, you need to ensure you can handle the data type of each attribute.

When creating a dashboard, you use qualitative data to create dimensions. A *dimension* is an attribute that you use to divide your data into categories or segments. To make sure you are representing the source data categories entirely, map the field definitions from the source data to your visualization tool. For example, a geographic dimension lets you look at your data by geographic region. A date dimension enables you to explore data at various levels of time-related granularity. For example, suppose you are creating a sales dashboard and want to allow the flexibility to look at sales by day of the week, week, month, quarter, year, fiscal quarter, and fiscal year. Each date increment is a value within the time dimension.

A *measure* is a numeric, quantitative value that a dashboard user is curious about. For example, a sales executive may want to examine regional sales of a specific product over time. In this case, the number and dollar value of sales are measures, and region and time

FIGURE 7.40 Data sourcing flowchart.

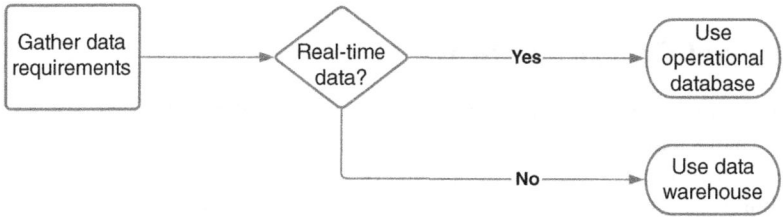

are dimensions. When in doubt, recall that a measure contains what a user wants to look at, while a dimension provides ways to segment or subdivide the data.

Development Process

After you identify the data sources that will power your dashboard, you must turn your attention to developing the dashboard itself. Use wireframes and mockups to help build and refine the dashboard's design. A *wireframe* is a blueprint for an application that defines the basic design and functions of a dashboard. Think of a wireframe like a blueprint for a building. Architects develop blueprints to describe the internal structure of a building. Similarly, a wireframe defines the basic structure, functionality, and content of a dashboard. Use wireframes to define the presentation layout and navigation flow to guide how people will interact with the dashboard.

A *mockup* extends a wireframe by providing details about the visual elements of the dashboard, including fonts, colors, logos, graphics, and page styles. While a wireframe is conceptually similar to a blueprint, a mockup is closer to an architectural rendering. The goal of a mockup is to give people a perspective as to the dashboard's final user interface. Use mockups to ensure your dashboard is consistent with your organizational communication standards.

As you develop a dashboard, keep in mind the story you want to tell with the data. For example, data story planning often begins with aggregated data that answers straightforward questions like "How many people work here?" While the answer to that question is a number, you should anticipate follow-on questions, including "How many men and women work here?" and "What is the average tenure and age distribution of our workforce?" The latter question can help inform succession planning. Incorporating wireframes, mockups, and a data story plan help design an optimal *web interface*.

Keep in mind that creating a dashboard is an iterative process. As you develop wireframes and mockups, be sure you deliberately incorporate steps to obtain approval to proceed. One way to ensure you don't lose sight of crucial requirements is to include the voice of the customer during feedback sessions. In these sessions, show your mockups to the people who will be using your dashboard. Most often, people think of additional features and voice other requirements when reacting to the design of a mockup. Document and incorporate this feedback to improve the quality and usefulness of your dashboard. At the end of the development process, the goal is to have a dashboard that informs and delights its users.

Operational Considerations

Once you have final approval, you proceed with developing the dashboard. Similar to the design stage, make sure you include frequent opportunities to gather feedback. Once dashboard development is complete, test it thoroughly to verify its functionality.

As you build a dashboard, make sure you clearly define the access permissions. *Access permissions* define the data that a given person can access. When defining access permissions, do so in terms of roles instead of people. For example, suppose Megan Trotter is a promising regional sales leader. In that role, Megan needs access to sales performance data in her region but doesn't need access to sales data for other regions. To give Megan only the data she needs, assign access permissions to the regional sales leader role instead of Megan directly since a person can switch roles over time. Suppose that Megan ends up in the chief sales officer (CSO) role. In that case, she needs access to all sales data. However, if Megan pivots and ends up with a role in Human Resources, she no longer needs access to sales-related data.

As you confirm that the dashboard will serve its intended purpose, you are ready to deploy it to production. Once the dashboard is in active use, your work is not over. You need to ensure the dashboard continues to answer leadership's questions while performing well. As the person responsible for the dashboard, you must pursue ongoing *dashboard optimizations*. A given optimization may improve the performance of a dashboard component or may include a new data source to enable answering new sets of questions.

Delivery Considerations

There are several delivery considerations to incorporate when creating dashboards and reports. Remember to identify the audience and their needs when embarking on any project that creates a data artifact like a report or dashboard. After clarifying who will consume your report and what information they need to see, it is crucial to determine when they need it.

Static and Dynamic Delivery

Identifying whether a dashboard or report needs to be static or dynamic is imperative, as that difference impacts where and how you get your data. *Static reports* and *static dashboards* pull data from various sources to reflect data at a specific point in time. Suppose you work in a financial services firm and develop a five-year trend report for securities in the automotive sector, including Ford, Volkswagen, and Tesla. You need the daily price for each security over five years to feed your trend report. Data marts and data warehouses are typical sources for this type of data.

Dynamic reports and *dynamic dashboards* give people real-time access to information. Using your five-year trend report to inform their analysis, a financial analyst in your company may want to execute a trade. For the analyst to determine the price they are willing to pay for a given security, they need access to real-time pricing data. Data marts and data warehouses are insufficient for providing real-time information. In this case, you require current pricing information from the exchange where the security is actively traded, like the New York Stock Exchange or the Nasdaq. This type of real-time access typically uses an application programming interface (API).

Self-service portals provide on-demand access to aggregated data, allowing individuals to answer questions that are specific to them at a time of their choosing. Instead of having data pushed to them, an attribute of self-service reporting is that individuals can refresh the report's underlying data when they need it. For instance, consider an organization with 200 salespeople. Each one of those 200 people has a unique sales goal. A self-service progress-to-goal report lets the salespeople check the current state of their sales against their sales objectives. Self-service reports can source data from transactional or analytical systems depending on how current the data needs to be.

Frequency

Delivery considerations are a crucial part of the development process. Accounting for how you will refresh data is one of the many things to consider. As you document requirements and develop mockups, you need to determine whether people can subscribe to changes. If *subscription* capability is required, you need a system where people can opt in to receive a notification when the underlying data changes.

In addition to offering a subscription service, another delivery consideration is *scheduled delivery*. Suppose a portion of your dashboard consists of daily production figures. The leader of a manufacturing facility wants to subscribe to data refresh notifications. However, they also want the daily number of defects to be delivered to their mobile device at six o'clock in the morning to help them prepare for their daily quality control meeting. In this case, you can schedule a notification to provide a link to the relevant data at the appropriate time.

A crucial detail you need to identify as part of the development process is how interactive the dashboard needs to be. The level of interactivity needs to accommodate requirements from the data story plan. Once again, consider an executive's questions about the composition of the organization's employees. As dashboards convey aggregated data, you need to understand the dimensions where people interacting with the dashboard will want to explore additional details. Defining the dimensions will help you design a dashboard that lets people *drill down* into deeper levels of detail. For example, suppose the dashboard landing page for a CSO shows total corporate global sales. The CSO may want to see more detail for a given region, country, or metropolitan area. When the CSO drills down into a specific region, the dashboard filters data to only show details for that region. Similarly, if the CSO further drills into a country, the dashboard only shows the sales data for that country.

Some requirements dictate the ability to *roll up* data. For example, regional managers want to know about total sales in their region. In contrast, the CSO wants to roll up, or aggregate, sales activity across all regions. A well-designed dashboard gives the regional managers the data they need while accommodating the needs of the CSO.

Suppose that as the CSO explores sales activity across regions, they become concerned about a specific region. A good dashboard will allow *filtering* on the appropriate dimension to limit the data to only that region.

A CSO pays close attention to the sales funnel, where people progress from lead to customer. A well-designed dashboard provides the number of people at each level in the funnel, as shown in Figure 7.41. However, the CSO may want to see individual details for prospects

FIGURE 7.41   Sales funnel.

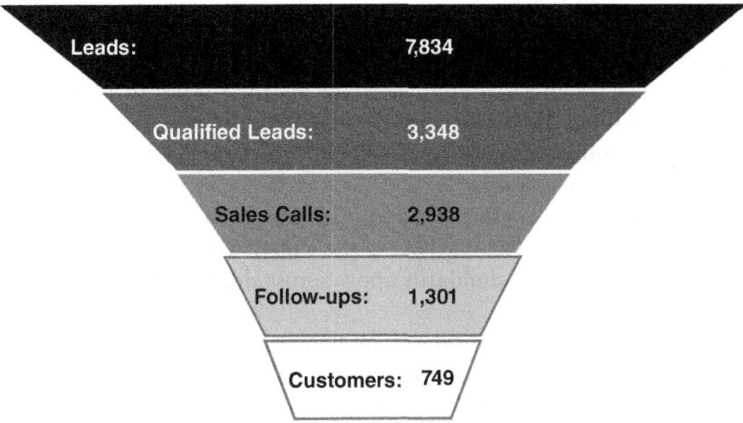

in the Follow-ups category, as they are one step away from becoming customers. Instead of searching for this information, a well-designed dashboard allows the CSO to create *saved search* criteria. Once saved, they can re-execute their search as data updates over time without having to reinput the original search criteria. As you can imagine, the dashboard translates this type of search into an SQL query against a database.

Ad Hoc

Ad hoc reports, or *one-time reports*, use existing data to meet a unique need at a specific point in time. For example, suppose a hospital suffers an information security breach. As a result of the breach, some of their patient data is posted publicly on the Internet. In reaction to this one-time event, hospital administrators commission an ad hoc report to identify the patients they need to notify.

Recurring Reports

Recurring reports provide summary information on a regularly scheduled basis. Typically, recurring reports get delivered to their audience immediately after creation. For example, a company's sales leader will want monthly, quarterly, and annual sales numbers available regularly.

Organizations use numerous types of recurring operational reports to monitor organizational health and performance. Operational reports typically show the KPIs for an organization. For example, logistics organizations monitor the total number of packages and whether or not they are on time. Airlines monitor on-time departures and arrivals. Manufacturing companies keep track of daily defect rates. Financial KPIs, like the debt-to-equity ratio, apply to virtually every type of organization.

Compliance reports detail how your organization meets its compliance obligations. Depending on where your organization operates, country-specific compliance requirements exist for various business functions, including financial, health, information technology, and safety.

From a *financial compliance reporting* standpoint, if you are a public company in the United States, you need to document annual compliance with the Sarbanes–Oxley Act (SOX). SOX compliance ensures that your company provides proof of accurate financial reporting. To comply with SOX, you need to document access controls, security controls, your data backup methodology, and the processes by which people become authorized to make financially significant changes.

From a *safety compliance reporting* standpoint, you need to comply with the Occupational Safety and Health Act (OSHA) in the United States to ensure the safety of your employees. General industry standards apply across the manufacturing, retail, and wholesale sectors.

If you process health-related data in the United States, you must meet *health compliance reporting* obligations. These obligations are subject to the U.S. Health Insurance Portability and Accountability Act of 1996 (HIPAA). HIPAA protects sensitive patient health information from being disclosed without a patient's knowledge or consent.

Organizations develop *risk compliance reports* to engender trust. For example, System and Organization Controls (SOC) reports document how an organization maintains its IT systems' security, availability, and confidentiality in the information technology space. These reports also demonstrate how an organization collects, uses, retains, discloses, and disposes of data.

Each industry has its own set of unique regulatory requirements. *Regulatory compliance reports* document how an organization meets those compliance burdens. For example, if you process credit card payments, you must comply with the Payment Card Industry Data Security Standard (PCI DSS). This standard documents rules for storing, processing, or transmitting cardholder or sensitive authentication data.

These compliance obligations are a mere subset of the regulations that exist. Regardless of the type of compliance obligation, you need to produce the appropriate compliance report regularly.

Data Versioning Techniques

Data versioning is a technique that helps people use the same data when making decisions. Data versioning is vital when producing static or on-demand reports and dashboards. Attaching the date and time to a report or dashboard is a typical approach to uniquely identify its version. For example, suppose salespeople and sales managers use a static progress-to-goal sales report to track activity. If the manager refers to a two-week-old version of the report while their salesperson uses a version including the previous week's sales, the sales manager necessarily has a different perspective on total sales than their salesperson. Data versioning refers to labeling reports and dashboards with an indicator of the last date.

A snapshot is a copy of data at a specific point in time. Operationally, database administrators use snapshots to protect data in case of a system failure. Similarly, it is common to use data snapshots when creating static reports. Attaching the date and time to any static data product helps people establish context for decision-making. For example, Figure 7.42

FIGURE 7.42   Date-stamped data.

```
┌─────────────────────────────────────┐
│          Report Title               │
│                                     │
│          Report details             │
│                                     │
│                                     │
│                                     │
│                                     │
├─────────────────────────────────────┤
│  Last Updated: 1/3/2025  3:43:38 PM │
└─────────────────────────────────────┘
```

illustrates a date stamp and timestamp in the report's footer. With the date and time prominently displayed, you immediately understand how recently the report was generated.

Just as snapshots provide context for data freshness, setting expectations for real-time data is essential. For example, when driving a car, you expect the speedometer to reflect your current speed. It may be prohibitive to provide up-to-the-minute freshness when data volume or velocity is high. Business processes can also complicate the real-time aspect of a dashboard. For example, when booking a flight, there is a short period when the seat is held, but the purchase still needs to be completed. A real-time dashboard showing available seats could get around this complication by showing unreserved seats in green, reserved seats in red, and seats currently being reserved in yellow.

Tactical and Research

Identifying whether the report you create is for tactical or strategic purposes is vital. *Tactical reports* provide information to inform an organization's short-term decisions. Tactical information helps organizations accomplish initiatives like constructing a building, opening a manufacturing plant, or shipping products from one location to another. Enabling operational decisions, the data for tactical reports come from various sources, including operational and analytical systems.

A *research report* helps an organization make strategic decisions. To achieve strategic objectives, an organization executes multiple tactical initiatives. Where a tactical report informs a decision with a finite scope and duration, research reports inform the development of an overarching strategy. The implications of strategic decisions are broad, including whether to acquire a competitor, how many component suppliers an organization needs, and whether to diversify and enter an entirely new market. Since the decision implications are broad, strategic reports take longer to create than tactical reports. Strategic reports often combine internal data about an organization's operational performance and risks with data about external forces.

Report Validation Techniques

Organizations depend on reliable, accurate reports to inform decision-making. Organizations can make suboptimal decisions when reports contain incorrect data. When reports are late, decision-making gets delayed. Even worse, organizations can't make data-informed decisions when reports are absent. Reliably accurate reports are essential for maintaining organizational trust.

Even well-designed reports in a robust operational environment occasionally fail. Understanding the potential root causes of these failures and remediation techniques will help you reduce the time needed to fix these errors.

Issues

A typical issue affecting timely report delivery is excessive load times. *Excessive load times* occur when the Extract, Transform, and Load (ETL) jobs that populate a data warehouse take longer than their designed batch window. Consider a retail scenario where transactional data from point-of-sale systems flows into a data warehouse daily. The expected batch window for these ETL processes is between one and five in the morning.

After a particularly effective marketing campaign, there is a corresponding surge in transaction volume due to the *large data size*. When large data sizes occur, you have more transactions than the system typically processes, which could cause the ETL processes to keep operating past the five o'clock hour. With the ETL processes running late, the reports that depend on those processes will also be late.

Slow data refresh rates contribute to invalidating reports. A *slow refresh rate* happens when data changes take longer than expected before being reflected in a report. Slow refreshes can result from system design. Suppose a user provisioning system generates new user accounts twice daily. Due to the design limitation, the provisioning system could never give an accurate hourly count of new users. Beyond design considerations, irregularities like a missing index on a table can cause poor query performance, resulting in slow data refresh rates.

Another issue impacting report availability is when a data filter is not working correctly. For example, suppose a regional sales manager wants to analyze the performance of her salespeople during the fourth quarter of 2024. However, a misconfigured filter includes details for 2024 instead of just the fourth quarter. As a result, the report displays sales data from the entire year of 2024 instead of the fourth quarter. The impact of this misconfigured filter can lead to an incorrect interpretation of sales performance.

Reports are invalid when based on stale data. While *stale data* is accurate to a point in time, it lacks data that reflects any changes after that point in time. Suppose you were responsible for real-time aircraft utilization reports for an airline. If you use ticket data that reflects occupancy an hour before departure, you are working with stale data. In the hour up until departure, there might be an extra ticket sale, movement on the standby list, or a seat taken by an employee. In this case, you must solve the data currency problem to fix the stale data problem.

Data corruption directly impacts the validity of reports. *Corrupt data* is when inaccurate or incomplete data enters the reporting infrastructure. In addition to human error, common root causes for data corruption include transmission errors, load failures, and underlying media failures.

Techniques

There are many ways to mitigate and resolve issues that impact the validity of reports. Combining techniques and operational experience will help you troubleshoot problems when they occur to ensure a robust reporting environment.

Data Filtering

Data filtering refers to creating a subset from an existing dataset. Recall from Chapter 4 that the WHERE clause in a SQL statement filters data. Accurate data filtering is crucial for interactive reports where users can aggregate or subset data.

Understanding user requirements helps you ensure you are surfacing data filters appropriately. For example, suppose a regional sales manager wants to look at yearly, quarterly, monthly, and daily sales performance. In that case, you must ensure sales managers can access the appropriate data filters to meet these requirements.

Reviews

A robust review system during the report development lifecycle surfaces potential issues before they make it into production. A *code review* is when someone other than the author looks through the code for a report to identify logic errors, ensure appropriate error handling, and identify performance impediments. Senior engineers, senior developers, and team leaders commonly conduct code reviews.

A *peer review* is like a code review but broader in scope. In addition to code, peer reviews can include technical documentation, automation processes, and report design elements. While senior technical staff conduct code reviews, nontechnical subject matter experts can participate in peer reviews. Peer reviews aim to ensure you have the business context captured accurately, while code reviews focus specifically on software components.

Calculation reviews are a third type of review. A *calculation review* focuses on verifying the correct use of underlying mathematical formulas and their results. Suppose you work with an Internet service provider (ISP) and want to exclude bandwidth bursts three standard deviations above the mean. A calculation review ensures the correct mean and standard deviation calculation implementation. Frequently, calculation reviews happen concurrently with code reviews.

Source Validation

Validating data sources goes a long way to ensuring valid reports. *Source validation* ensures that the data powering a report is accurate, complete, and free from formatting anomalies. For example, suppose you are working on a report that includes data from a mainframe as one of its sources. Some mainframe files have header and footer lines. While the header line may define the file layout, the footer line typically includes a row count. Ensuring that the ETL job responsible for loading this data compares the row count from the file with the total number of rows in the footer record.

Data Structures

Data structure changes can result from database schema changes, interface file changes, and modifications to API behavior. When the underlying data structures change, it can break any reports that rely on them. For example, consider the Customer table in Figure 7.43.

To construct a report including customer name and email information, you write an SQL statement against the Customer table as follows:

```
SELECT  First_Name
       ,Last_Name
       ,Email_Addr
FROM    Customer
```

Over time, your company gets feedback from its customers that they want to use one email address for primary communications and a different one for marketing-related activities. To address this new requirement, you change the schema to allow multiple email addresses per customer, as shown in Figure 7.44.

FIGURE 7.43 Customer table.

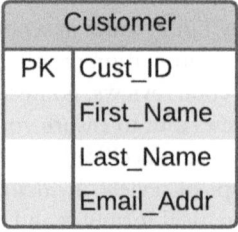

FIGURE 7.44 Customer and Email tables.

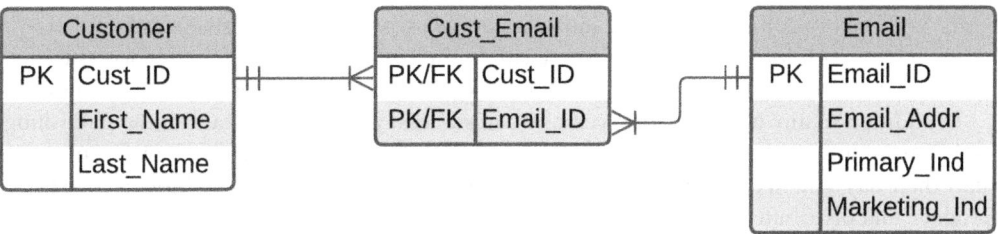

An unfortunate result of the schema change is that the original SQL no longer works to retrieve customer names and email information. To address this data structure change, you must rewrite the query to retrieve the data you need from the new Customer, Cust_Email, and Email tables.

Monitoring Alerts

Creating appropriate monitoring alerts is essential to maintaining a robust, reliable operational environment that fosters confidence in the validity of reports. *Monitoring alerts* raise exceptions when ETL jobs or data refresh processes fail, and interfaces or APIs are unavailable. You and your team must carefully construct and monitor error-related alerts so you can promptly respond to and resolve the underlying issue.

For example, suppose you receive an alert that an ETL job between a source system and a data warehouse exits in an error state. As part of your troubleshooting, you examine the error log created by the ETL job. Going through the log, you discover that unexpected data in a source system is the root cause. At that point, you have all the information you need to work with the appropriate developers and system operators to resolve the data issue and maintain valid reports.

Summary

Communicating data visually is one of the most impactful activities an analyst performs. It is imperative to understand the audience of your visualization clearly. Senior leaders have different information requirements than individual salespeople, and you need to understand what decisions people make using your visualization.

You also need to clarify the business objectives for each visualization and the appropriate vehicle for distribution. If the situation requires static information, a report is a suitable choice. However, if people need to interact with the data, you need to create a dynamic dashboard that enables exploration.

As you identify requirements, make sure that you understand the limitations of the data or its use. If someone wants to look at 10 years' worth of data but you only have data for seven years, you need to communicate that shortcoming and work with the business user to determine a viable path forward. Similarly, some circumstances require you to restrict access to specific data elements. Take data sensitivity into account as you consider distribution options.

In addition to any unique data-specific circumstances, you need to establish the publishing and distribution frequency. For instance, if people need a report in their email by 7 a.m. to start their day, you need to ensure that you have updated data sources and enough time to produce and distribute the report.

There are numerous visual elements to consider when designing a report. More formal reports need a cover page with instructions for use and an executive summary that provides a synopsis of insights. In the body of the report, ensure you use consistent, legible font sizes and styles. Make sure the chart titles, axes, and legends have clear labels. If you work with a large organization, work with corporate communications to incorporate corporate branding and style guides as appropriate.

From a change management perspective, make sure you update the publish date, version number, data sources, and refresh date when distributing a report. Careful change management helps ensure that people have the same data when contemplating decisions.

Dashboards are more complex than reports, as they are interactive and can reflect real-time information. When building a dashboard, keep dimensional modeling in mind when gathering business requirements. Understanding the dimensions that people want to use for segmenting data helps ensure you bring in the appropriate data sources. Keep in mind that the objective is to communicate essential information while minimizing clutter.

The key to an impactful dashboard is an iterative development process. Use wireframes to define the structure of your dashboard, and get mockups of the interface into the hands of the dashboard consumers as early as possible. If you have access to user experience professionals, tap into their knowledge to create a dashboard design that is intuitive and easy to use.

Just as you have different recipients for different reports, consider the types of roles that will access your dashboard. Work with your information security and application administration teams to identify the best way to implement role-based permissions.

There are many different types of charts that can help convey information visually. Keep in mind the situation where different chart types apply. For example, when presenting categorical data, you should choose between a bar, stacked bar, and pie chart, and histograms are ideal for showing a frequency distribution.

Make sure you can compare and contrast the different types of reports. For example, static reports provide a snapshot of information at a point in time, whereas dynamic reports incorporate real-time data. Ad hoc reports tend to be tactical and helpful for a limited time, whereas research reports take longer to compile, include more data sources, and are valuable for a longer time.

Organizations have many different reporting obligations. These recurring reports can address internal and external audiences and satisfy compliance, risk, regulatory, and operational commitments.

From an information delivery standpoint, tailor the design of dashboards and reports to your audience and its needs. Delivery considerations include whether reports statically capture data at a specific point or dynamically reflect real-time data. For example, static dashboards use data warehouses for historical analysis, while dynamic dashboards leverage APIs for live data.

Data refresh frequency is another essential delivery consideration. Determine a data refresh schedule that lets you meet specific business objectives, such as daily defect rates or quarterly sales performance.

Flexibility in design helps you meet ad hoc reporting needs for one-time reports, while recurring reports power key performance indicators and help meet compliance obligations.

Data versioning improves trust and provides context by attaching timestamps to reports. Version numbers and timestamps are among the tactics to successfully version reports.

Troubleshooting is vital for resolving issues and maintaining the validity of your reports. Excessive load times, slow refresh rates, misconfigured filters, stale or corrupted data, and schema changes can impact report validity. A robust code, calculation, and peer review system helps ensure quality and can help solve reporting issues before they occur. Once operational, appropriately configured monitoring alerts, automated validation of source data, and an awareness of when data structures change combine to keep your reporting environment reliable.

Exam Essentials

Describe the most crucial first steps when developing a visualization. The most important first steps when developing a visualization are identifying the audience and understanding their needs. If you don't know who will use a visualization or understand its purpose, your creation will have a limited impact.

Compare reports and dashboards. Reports are static documents that get distributed physically or electronically. As static documents, they reflect data at the time of creation. Dashboards are dynamic and encourage data exploration. Typically delivered as a web interface, dashboards can integrate real-time data and enable users to explore segment data along multiple dimensions.

Identify the best type of chart for a given scenario. Given a specific scenario, select the type of chart that is most appropriate. Bar and pie charts work well for categorical data, whereas line charts are excellent for illustrating the relationship between two variables. Scatter charts show all of the points in a dataset, whereas bubble charts use size to show the effect of a third numeric attribute. Maps are good for spatial data, waterfall charts show positive and negative impacts over time, and infographics convey a message. A word cloud is an optimal choice for displaying the relative significance of words when dealing with unstructured data.

Identify the type of report that should be used in a given scenario. Given a specific scenario, identify the type of report that would meet the requirement. For example, you need a recurring report on a regular schedule to meet various compliance objectives. On the other hand, self-service reports enable individuals to answer a specific question at the time of their choosing.

Describe troubleshooting techniques that help ensure valid reports. Validating data filters and conducting code, calculation, and peer reviews can help identify reporting issues before the reports are in production. Ensuring you and your team know when data structures change can help identify impacted reports. Monitoring alerts that raise exceptions when data sources are invalid or unavailable reduces the time required to troubleshoot reporting issues.

Review Questions

The following questions are designed to test your understanding of this chapter's material. You can find the answers in Appendix A.

1. Igor is creating an inventory report for the manager of a local convenience store. On average, replacement items are delivered within three days after the manager places an order. What is the most appropriate frequency for this report? (Choose the best answer.)
   A. Real time
   B. Hourly
   C. Daily
   D. Weekly

2. Jasmine is a data analyst for a retail company. After a successful marketing campaign, she noticed that the daily sales report was unavailable at the usual time. Upon investigation, she discovered that the ETL job processing transactional data exceeded its batch window due to a significant increase in transaction volume. Which of the following is the most likely cause of the delayed report delivery?
   A. Data corruption in the transactional database
   B. A misconfigured filter in the sales report
   C. Excessive load times in the ETL process
   D. Stale data being used in the report

3. Bowen is developing a report that explores how consumer sentiment about his company's products changes over time. Where should he put a paragraph describing the most profound insight in the report? (Choose the best answer.)
   A. Title page
   B. Executive summary
   C. Report body
   D. Appendix

4. Javier wants to illustrate the relationship between height and weight. What type of chart should he use?
   A. Bar
   B. Scatter
   C. Line
   D. Histogram

5. John's CEO wants to be able to explore how retail sales have been changing over time. What is the best way to present the information to the CEO? (Choose the best answer.)
   A. Historical report
   B. Recurring report
   C. One-time report
   D. Interactive dashboard

6. Ron is a recent hire at a large organization and is developing his first report. What should he do first? (Choose the best answer.)
   A. Check with the communications division to see whether any corporate style guides exist.
   B. Work with his supervisor to identify distribution mechanisms.
   C. Work with operations to develop a delivery schedule.
   D. Check with his colleagues to determine the best way to get his completed report to the appropriate people.

7. Kelly wants to get feedback on the final draft of a strategic report that has taken her six months to develop. What can she do to get prevent confusion as she seeks feedback before publishing the report? (Choose the best answer.)
   A. Distribute the report to the appropriate stakeholders via email.
   B. Use a watermark to identify the report as a draft.
   C. Show the report to her immediate supervisor.
   D. Publish the report on an internally facing website.

8. Maggie is a new analyst tasked with developing a dashboard. What should she focus on to obtain an understanding of requirements for internal senior leaders? (Choose the best answer.)
   A. Service credits
   B. Service level agreements
   C. Key performance indicators
   D. Defect rate

9. Cian is mapping dashboard requirements to data sources. What should he use to ensure the structure is in place to deliver the dashboard successfully?
   A. Mockup
   B. Wireframe
   C. Data warehouse
   D. Data mart

10. Zakir wants to visualize aggregate sales data over time. What type of chart should he select?
    A. Pie chart
    B. Tree map
    C. Histogram
    D. Line chart

11. Celine wants to visualize annual precipitation in South America. What type of chart would create the greatest impact?
    A. Geographic heat map
    B. Stacked bar chart
    C. Word cloud
    D. Waterfall chart

12. Piper is an analyst for a sporting venue. She wants to distill post-event free-response survey data to inform leadership what respondents have on their minds. What type of visualization should she choose?
    A. Pie chart
    B. Bar chart
    C. Word cloud
    D. Dashboard

13. Aubree wants to visualize the correlation between 15 different variables. What type of chart should she select?
    A. Tree map
    B. Bar chart
    C. Infographic
    D. Heat map

14. Appa wants to tell a story about the effect of climate change on coastal cities with a single, static visualization. Which of the following should he choose?
    A. Tree map
    B. Bar chart
    C. Infographic
    D. Heat map

15. Jeremiyah is a project manager at a software company. To assess resource allocation, he wants to analyze employee hours worked on different projects by department and month. Additionally, he needs to adjust his view dynamically to focus on specific teams or projects without creating separate reports for each query. Which visualization tool would best meet Jeremiyah's needs?
    A. Line chart
    B. Scatter plot
    C. Pivot table
    D. Stacked bar chart

16. Rita wants to illustrate the relationship between per capita GDP, life expectancy, and population size. What type of visualization should she choose?
    A. Bubble chart
    B. Bar chart
    C. Infographic
    D. Heat map

17. Sanjay's company has three primary brands that drive corporate profitability. If Sanjay wants to visualize the contribution of each brand over time, what type of chart should he choose?
    A. Bubble chart
    B. Stacked bar chart
    C. Infographic
    D. Heat map

18. Adeline is developing a poster to raise awareness about climate change. What type of visualization should she use?
    A. Bubble chart
    B. Stacked bar chart
    C. Infographic
    D. Heat map

19. Abbas's CFO wants to drill down on cost centers across the organization. What type of visualization should Abbas create?
    A. Bubble chart
    B. Stacked bar chart
    C. Infographic
    D. Dashboard

20. Marcus is an operations manager at a logistics company responsible for forecasting truck availability. He relies on a real-time truck utilization report to track daily capacity. However, he notices that last-minute pallet additions are missing from his report, inaccurately reflecting available capacity and negatively impacting his forecast. Which of the following is the most likely cause of this issue?
    A. Data corruption in the truck availability system
    B. Stale data in the report
    C. A misconfigured filter excluding recent data
    D. Excessive ETL load times

Chapter 8

Data Governance

THE COMPTIA DATA+ EXAM TOPICS COVERED IN THIS CHAPTER INCLUDE:

✔ **Domain 5.0: Data Governance**
  - 5.1. Explain data management concepts
  - 5.2. Summarize concepts related to data compliance
  - 5.3. Compare and contrast data privacy and protection practices
  - 5.4. Compare and contrast data quality assurance practices

Recall from Chapter 5, "Data Quality," that high-quality data is the foundation for all things analytical. In Chapter 5, you learned about methods for assessing data quality. That chapter also explored various manipulation techniques for improving data quality. While the tactical approaches in Chapter 5 are vital to ensuring high-quality data, this chapter examines the procedural and regulatory constraints that organizations face when safeguarding data.

This chapter explores foundational data quality concepts. It explores how regulatory requirements directly impact data governance, especially how those requirements drive the need for data classification standards. Legal or contractual requirements also impact organizational obligations in the event of a data breach.

The chapter then explores considerations and controls available for using, storing, transmitting, and sharing data. To conclude, this chapter explores how testing and automation can continuously improve data quality in an operational environment.

Data Management Concepts

Data management is the collection of architectures, policies, practices, and procedures defining how an organization manages data over its entire lifecycle. From the moment of creation until no longer adding organizational value, organizations must deliberately create frameworks for managing data. Governments have a method for creating, interpreting, and enforcing laws. Part of this process ensures that these laws are known to the citizenry. For organizations, data management is an umbrella term covering how to manage data throughout its lifecycle.

Organizations develop numerous policies to manage their data. These policies promote data quality, specify the use of data attributes, and define access to different data domains. Additional data management policies identify how to integrate disparate data sources, secure data, comply with regulations, protect data privacy, and manage data versions over time. Just as countries enforce laws, organizations implement procedural and technical controls to comply with data management standards.

Data governance is the set of policies, procedures, and controls an organization develops to safeguard its information while making it useful for transactional and analytic purposes. As the name implies, data governance is primarily a business function. Strong executive support is vital to any data governance effort.

An organization invests significant time and resources to define, develop, implement, and control access to data. For a data management effort to succeed, all levels of an organization must appreciate the importance of well-governed data. While technology is critical to facilitating policy adherence, an information technology organization can't drive data governance efforts on its own. You need executive support across the organization for data governance efforts to succeed.

Integration

Integration is the practice of consolidating data from disparate sources to improve organizational decision-making. Modern enterprises typically use internal databases fed by transactional systems to store their core operational data. Batch processes migrate data from transactional to analytical systems, and enterprises augment internally managed data with external sources in either a real-time or batch manner. Figure 8.1 shows how an airline uses both real-time and batch integrations.

A *real-time integration* provides an organization with the most currently available data. For example, Figure 8.1 illustrates how an airline can combine internal flight occupancy data with weather data from an API to develop real-time flight operation forecasts to predict the likelihood of on-time departures.

A *batch integration* provides a snapshot of data at a point in time. While real-time weather data impacts on-time flight operations, real-time data is unnecessary when performing a monthly analysis of on-time performance. Figure 8.1 shows how operational flight data, including departure and arrival details, moves from the transactional flight operations system into a data warehouse using flat files created by a nightly extract, transform, and load (ETL) batch process. When working with batch integrations, understanding the timing of the batch process is vital. For instance, when looking at January data, you must be confident that the most recent batch process includes data from January 31. If the last batch run is on January 30, you miss a day's worth of data, which can lead to uninformed conclusions about January's performance figures.

FIGURE 8.1 Real-time and batch integrations.

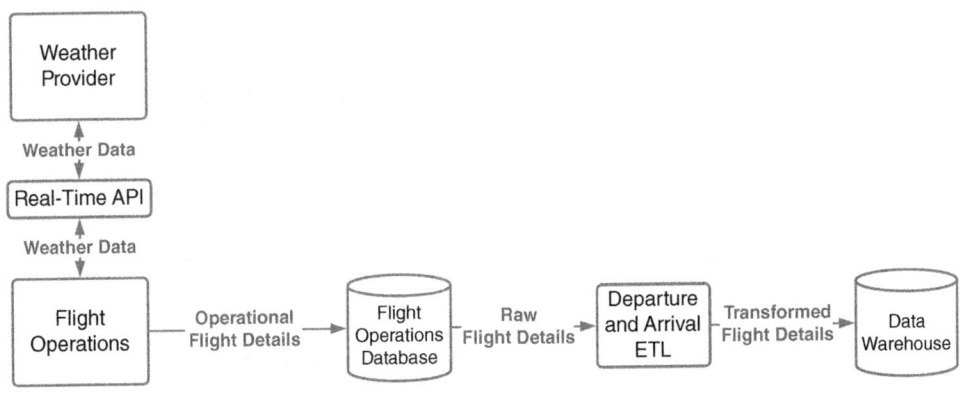

Documentation

For all organizations, accurate and up-to-date documentation is essential to managing knowledge. When people use accurate documentation to resolve issues promptly, operational stability and organizational confidence increase. Documentation is also vital when getting new employees up to speed, as it helps orient people to how an organization manages its data.

Data Flow Diagram

A *Data Flow Diagram* (DFD) is a drawing of how data flows within a system. DFDs show external entities that either source or consume data, processes that modify data, data flowing throughout the system, and data stores for maintaining data at rest. DFDs are common system-level artifacts that help people understand how data flows throughout a system. Figure 8.2 illustrates the symbols that comprise DFDs.

DFDs have multiple levels that correspond to levels of abstraction. A context diagram, or Level 0 diagram, is a DFD with a single process that illustrates a system and its external interfaces. Figure 8.3 is a sample context diagram for an airline reservation system.

Examining Figure 8.3, the Airline Reservation System exists as a single process. The Customer and Payment Processor are both external entities, and the arrows represent data flowing between the external entities and the system. While the context diagram provides an overview of the system, you need additional detail to understand how the system works. You must decompose a context diagram into a Level 1 DFD to see the additional details you require. You can think of decomposition as opening up the single process from the context diagram and seeing what is inside. Figure 8.4 is a sample Level 1 decomposition of the context diagram.

FIGURE 8.2 Data flow diagram symbols.

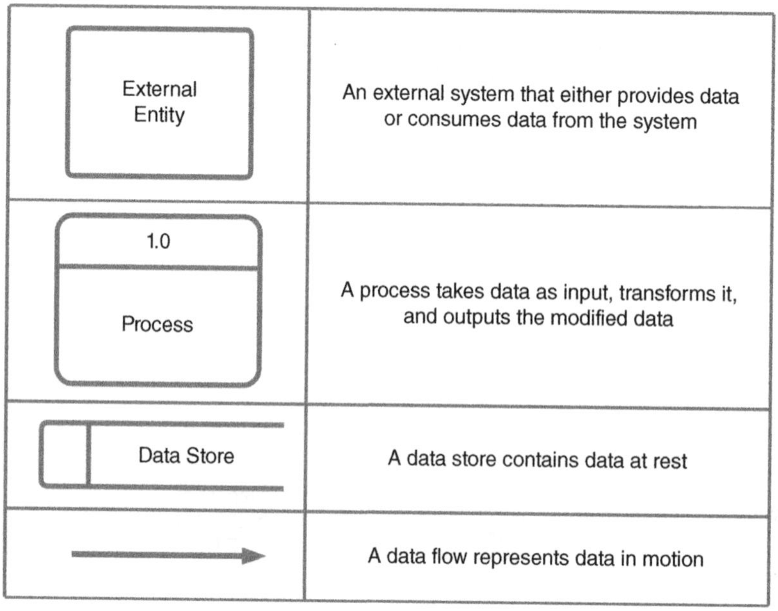

External Entity	An external system that either provides data or consumes data from the system
1.0 Process	A process takes data as input, transforms it, and outputs the modified data
Data Store	A data store contains data at rest
→	A data flow represents data in motion

Data Management Concepts   303

FIGURE 8.3 Sample context diagram.

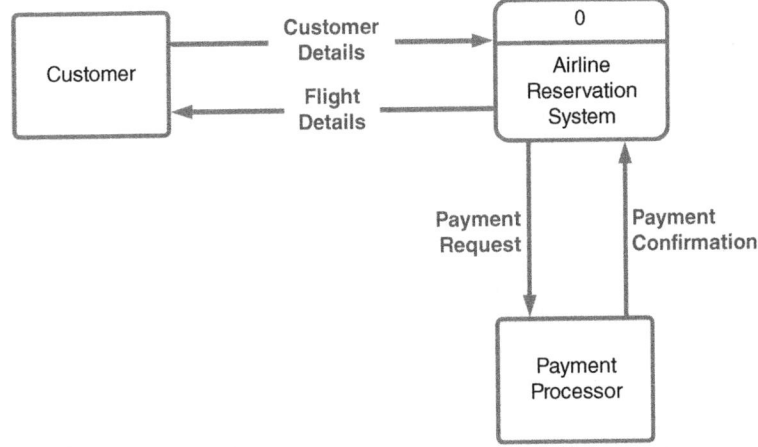

FIGURE 8.4 Level 1 data flow diagram.

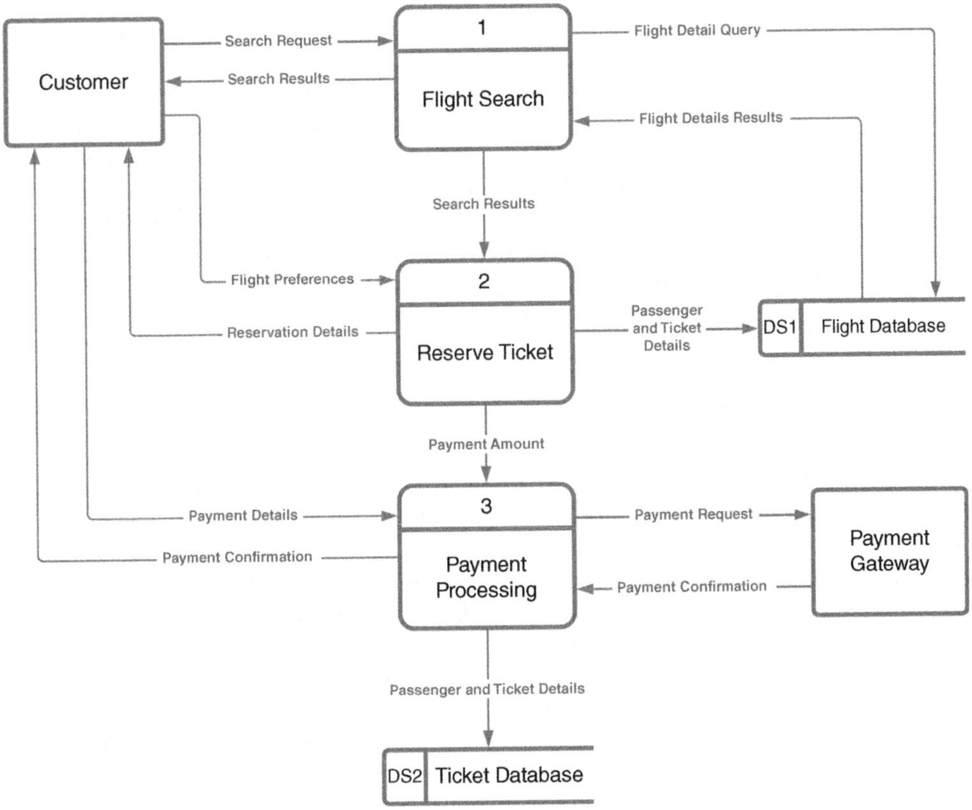

While the Customer and Payment Gateway external entities from the context diagram remain, Figure 8.4 replaces the single Airline Reservation System process with separate processes for Flight Search, Reserve Ticket, and Payment Processing. This Level 1 DFD also shows two data stores for information at rest: the Flight Database and the Ticket Database. Each process within a Level 1 DFD identifies a key business logic within the system. It's possible to further decompose Level 1 DFD processes into a Level 2 DFD. For example, to show the additional steps within the Flight Search process, you can create a Level 2 diagram showing the business subprocesses that comprise Flight Search.

Data Lineage

Data lineage describes the complete lifecycle of data from the moment of creation until its final destination. Tracing the lineage for a specific piece of data includes identifying its system of origin, any extract, transformation, and load (ETL) processes that act on it, and its movement across systems. You can use Figure 8.5 to trace a customer's address information lineage.

In Figure 8.5, the customer first inputs address data into the Customer Loyalty Application when initially creating an account. The Customer Loyalty Application then sends the raw address data through the Address Standardization process, which transforms the address to comply with U.S. postal standards. The standardized address returns to the Customer Loyalty Application, which places the address into its Customer Information Database.

The ETL process runs regularly, extracting the normalized address data from the Customer Information Database, transforming it, and storing the denormalized data in the Customer Data Warehouse. The Customer Data Warehouse stores the address data without additional modification and contains additional customer-centric data elements.

Identifying data consumers is another aspect of data lineage. In Figure 8.5, the Marketing Application and the Customer Analytics Application source address data from the Customer Data Warehouse. Data lineage gives you a comprehensive understanding of how data flows and greatly aids debugging when physical components break or processes exit with errors.

Data Explainability Report

A *data explainability report* describes where data originates, its unique attributes, and what processing is applied when creating an artifact to inform decisions. Data explainability reports provide data transparency and traceability, which are vital to ensuring confidence when building machine learning models. While data explainability reports describe data, model explainability reports describe how the algorithms applied to data function. For example, a data explainability report details the data used when training a large language model like OpenAI's ChatGPT or Google's Gemini. In contrast, a *model explainability report* describes the functioning of the algorithms within those models.

While there is no global standard for constructing a data explainability report, it typically starts with an overview of the dataset. The overview includes which system the data comes

FIGURE 8.5 Address data lineage.

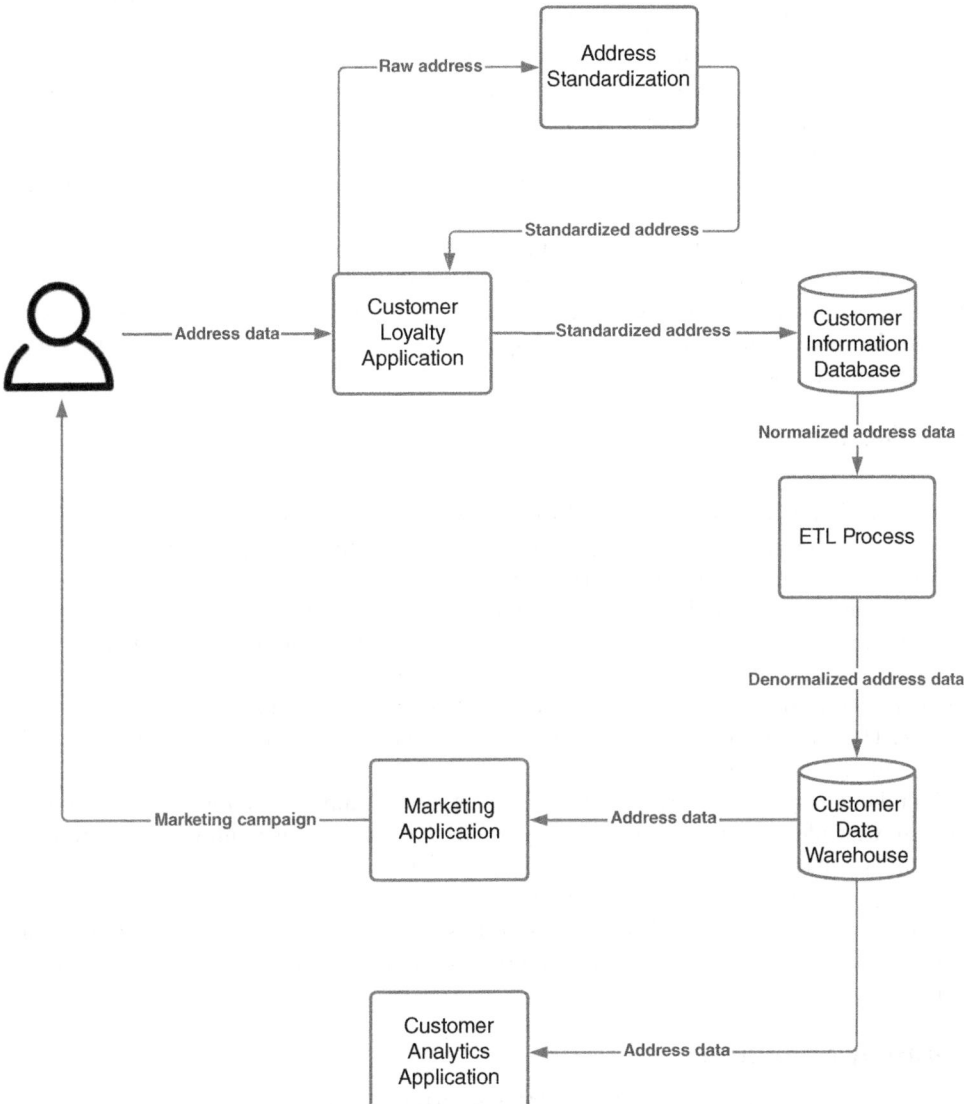

from, and metadata describing the data, its size, and its structure. The overview also provides context clues to orient consumers of the data. Suppose you are developing a dashboard that explores on-time delivery for a logistics company. The data overview includes context unique to a logistics operation.

Data explainability reports also include a data lineage section describing the preprocessing and steps taken to clean and transform the data. Data explainability reports also describe handling missing and outlier values and feature engineering techniques. An example of feature engineering is the scaling approach from Chapter 5. Data explainability reports also include an exploratory data analysis, first seen in Chapter 6, "Data Analysis and Statistics," to help orient people to the data.

Depending on data sensitivity and applicable compliance obligations, data explainability reports aid traceability by referencing log files with details about who accessed or modified a specific piece of data.

Assumptions and limitations are essential to using data appropriately. For example, suppose you want to perform a ten-year historical analysis on a dataset. Upon reading the limitations section of the data explainability report, you learn that it contains eight years of data. At that point, you either add an assumption to your analysis or find a source for the missing two years of data.

Data Dictionary

A *data dictionary* is a document detailing the specifics of objects within a relational database, including tables, indexes, and views. Data dictionary entries provide details about each database object, helping orient people to the context surrounding each object.

Consider the sample data dictionary entry in Table 8.1. This entry is for a database table, showing its name and a lengthy description of its purpose. It also includes indicators for columns participating in the table's primary key and if the column is a foreign key referencing a different table. This entry also includes column names, if the column is required, each column's data type, and a long text description defining each column's purpose. The sample entry in Table 8.1 also includes the names of indexes on the table and the column the index covers.

Data dictionary entries vary by database object. For example, a dictionary entry for a database view identifies the column, data type, and if the column is required. In addition, the data dictionary entry identifies the source table for each column in the view. Dictionary entries for stored procedures describe input parameters, expected output, and the tables the stored procedure uses. While dictionary entries for database functions are like those for stored procedures, the table description section is optional, as not every function operates on a table.

Hierarchy Structure

A *hierarchy structure* organizes data in a tree-like arrangement, representing parent-child relationships between database objects. Hierarchical structures have a top-down organization, with higher levels (parents) defining broad categories and lower levels (children) providing additional detail. You can use hierarchical structures to show the organization of a relational database and access control levels.

TABLE 8.1 Sample Data Dictionary Entry

Table Name	Addr_Type					
Table Description	Table for maintaining the type of an associated address, such as home, work, etc.					
Primary Key	Foreign Key	Column	Data Type	Nullable	Default	Description
X		Addr_Type_Cd	varchar2(4)	No		Contains the address type code value.
		Cd_Nm	varchar2(50)	No		Long text description for the code value, e.g., Home.
		Cd_Descr	varchar2(250)	Yes		Additional description of the address type.
		Cd_Eff_Start_Dt	Date	No	Current Date	The date on which addresses can first be given this address type.
		Cd_Eff_End_Dt	Date	Yes		The date after which addresses can no longer use this address type.
		Last_Updt_Sys_ID	Varchar2(16)	No		System identifier of the upstream system that made the last update for a given row.
		Last_Updt_Dt_Tm	Date	No		Date of the last update for a given row.

Indexes:

Index Name	Index Column
PK_Addr_Type_ATC	Addr_Type_Cd

FIGURE 8.6 Hierarchical depiction of a relational database.

```
                    Customer
                    Information
                    Database
                        |
                    Customer
                    Schema
         _____|_____
        |                   |                   |
     Address             Addr_Type            Customer
      Table                Table               Table
                            |
    _____|_____
   |        |        |           |              |             |             |
Addr_Type_Cd  Cd_Nm  Cd_Descr  Cd_Eff_Start_Dt  Cd_Eff_End_Dt  Cd_Eff_End_Dt  Cd_Eff_End_Dt
   (PK)
```

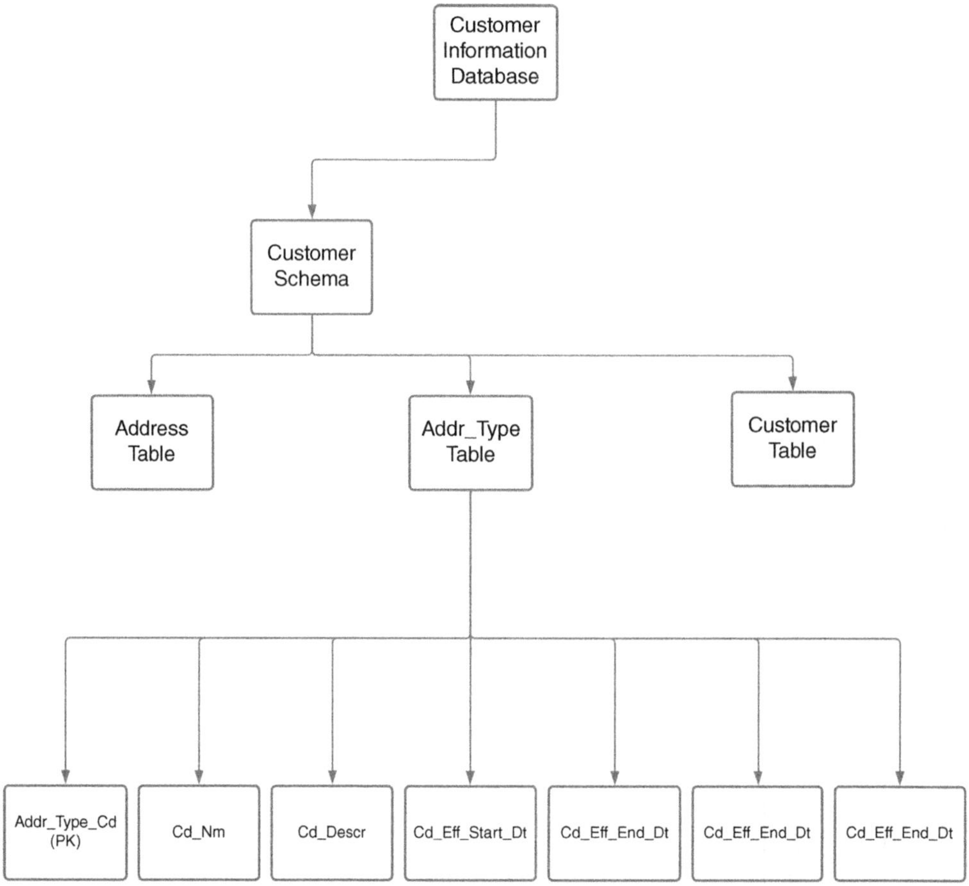

While hierarchical databases exist specifically for storing hierarchical data, you can use a hierarchy structure to define the organization of a relational database. Figure 8.6 depicts the Addr_Type table from Table 8.1 in a hierarchical context.

In Figure 8.6, the tree structure's root, or parent, node is the Customer Information Database. The Customer Schema is a child of the Customer Information Database. Likewise, the Address, Addr_Type, and Customer tables are children of the Customer schema. At the bottom of Figure 8.6 are the child columns of the Addr_Type table. While it's possible to represent the organization of a relational database hierarchically, the Entity Relationship Diagram (ERD) from Chapter 4, "Databases and Data Acquisition," is more space efficient.

FIGURE 8.7 Hierarchical depiction of access controls.

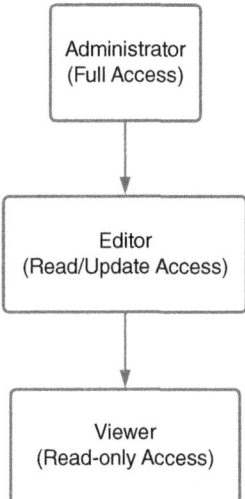

A hierarchy structure is particularly effective for illustrating access control. Figure 8.7 shows how the Administrator level has full access to the system, including inserting, reading, updating, and deleting records. The Editor level has read and update access, while the Viewer level can only read.

Hierarchy structures also appear in storage formats. For example, Figure 8.8 illustrates a hierarchy structure, and Figure 8.9 shows data in an Extensible Markup Language (XML) representation of the structure from Figure 8.8. Other file formats, including JavaScript Object Notation (JSON), support hierarchical data.

Source of Truth

A *source of truth* is the authoritative system of record for data within an organization. It's vital to understand which system is the source of truth for each data element when building data warehouses, reports, and dashboards. An absence of an authoritative source of truth for each data element reduces organizational confidence in data, undermining the trust in decisions made using that data.

Figure 8.10 shows four independent transactional systems that all process customer data for an airline. Data from these systems flows into a data warehouse for reporting and analytics. In this scenario, customer data has no transactional source of truth. If a customer updates their address in the reservation system, the new address does not exist in the other transactional systems. Depending on how the ETL jobs work, the data warehouse may contain obsolete customer addresses.

FIGURE 8.8 Hierarchy structure for automotive data.

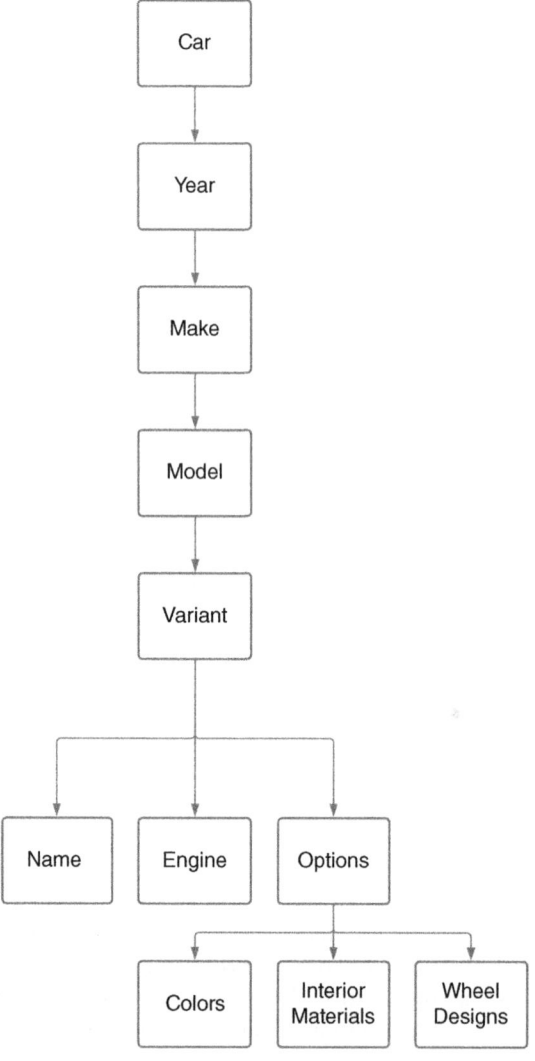

Figure 8.11 creates a source of truth for customer data by establishing the Customer Information Database. With this design, the transactional systems store customer data in a centralized source of truth. Having the Customer Information Database as the authoritative source of truth for customer data improves the airline's confidence in the consistency and accuracy of customer data in its data warehouse.

FIGURE 8.9 Hierarchical depiction of access controls.

```xml
<?xml version="1.0" encoding="UTF-8"?>
<car>
    <year>
        <value>2024</value>
        <make>
            <name>Porsche</name>
            <model>911</model>
            <variants>
                <variant>
                    <name>Carrera</name>
                    <engine>
                        <type>3.0L Twin-Turbo Flat-6</type>
                        <horsepower>379</horsepower>
                        <torque>331</torque>
                        <transmission>
                            <type>8-Speed PDK Automatic</type>
                            <manual_option>true</manual_option>
                        </transmission>
                    </engine>
                    <options>
                        <colors>
                            <color>Schwarz Black</color>
                            <color>Carrara White Metallic</color>
                            <color>Jet Black Metallic</color>
                        </colors>
                        <interior_materials>
                            <material>Leather</material>
                            <material>Alcantara</material>
                        </interior_materials>
                        <wheel_designs>
                            <wheel>Standard</wheel>
                            <wheel>Turbo</wheel>
                            <wheel>Exclusive Design</wheel>
                        </wheel_designs>
                    </options>
                </variant>
                <variant>
                    <name>Turbo S</name>
                    <engine>
                        <type>3.8L Twin-Turbo Flat-6</type>
                        <horsepower>640</horsepower>
                        <torque>590</torque>
                        <transmission>
                            <type>8-Speed PDK Automatic</type>
                            <manual_option>false</manual_option>
                        </transmission>
                    </engine>
                    <options>
                        <colors>
                            <color>Guards Red</color>
                            <color>Gentian Blue Metallic</color>
                            <color>GT Silver Metallic</color>
                        </colors>
                        <interior_materials>
                            <material>Leather</material>
                            <material>Full Leather</material>
                            <material>Carbon Fiber</material>
                        </interior_materials>
                        <wheel_designs>
                            <wheel>Turbo S</wheel>
                            <wheel>RS Spyder</wheel>
                            <wheel>Exclusive Design</wheel>
                        </wheel_designs>
                    </options>
                </variant>
            </variants>
        </make>
    </year>
</car>
```

FIGURE 8.10 Customer data in separate transactional systems.

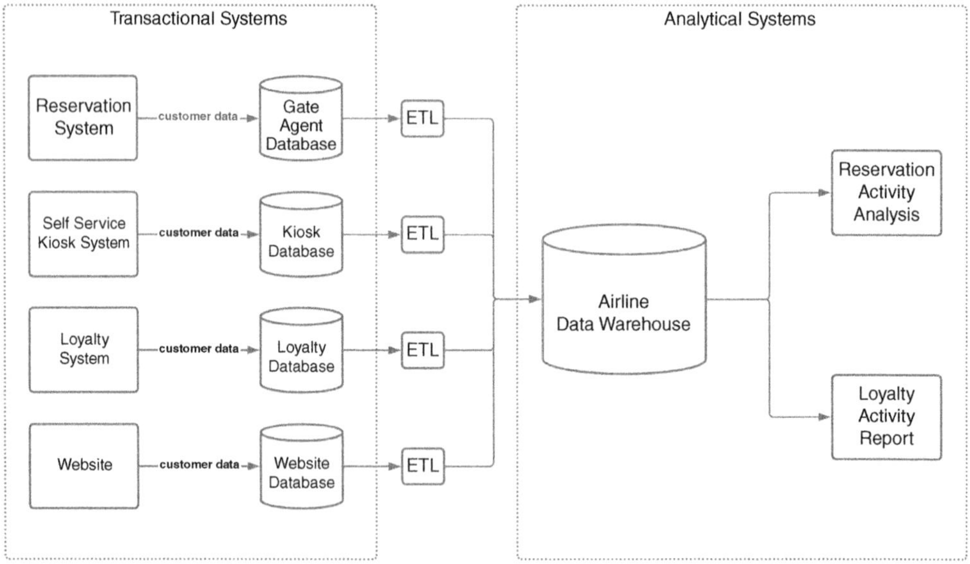

FIGURE 8.11 Centralized customer data in a source of truth.

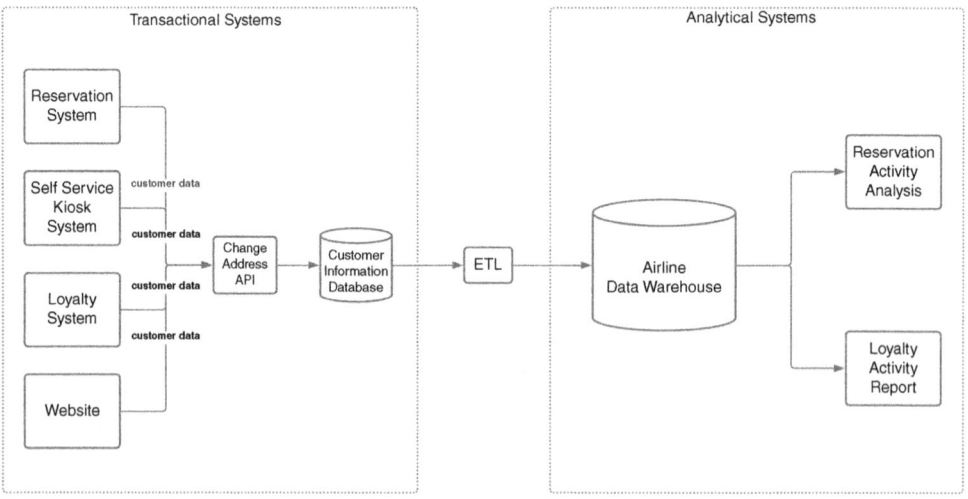

It is common for complex organizations to have multiple sources of truth for different data domains. An organization likely has independent sources of truth for customer, employee, and financial data.

Data Versioning

Data versioning systematically tracks and manages dataset changes over time by uniquely identifying each version. You can establish uniqueness with a unique number, character string, or timestamp. Associating a report or dashboard with a specific dataset version lets people make insights using data from a known moment in time.

Unless a report requires real-time data, it uses data from a snapshot. A *snapshot* is a copy of a dataset at a specific time. As snapshots represent data frozen in time, you need to consider the business requirements for data freshness when determining refresh intervals for datasets. A *refresh interval* is the rate at which snapshots happen. For instance, it is common for ETL jobs to copy data from transactional systems into data warehouses on a nightly basis. As long as the ETL processes function as expected, data consumers know they are working with data from the previous day. If the ETL jobs fail, you must alert data consumers that the previous day's data is missing.

Metadata

Metadata is data that describes data, providing business context that you do not have by examining the data itself. In Table 8.1, the description column is an example of metadata, as it describes the contents of the actual table column. Metadata is instrumental in data lineage efforts because it contains information that helps document how data flows from systems of origin into downstream systems. Metadata is equally essential for documenting sources of truth.

Since metadata is data about data, it provides the context to inform access control decisions. For example, the metadata for a column containing Social Security numbers (SSNs) should specify that only people with legitimate business needs can access the Social Security number column, with other users seeing only redacted data.

Similarly, metadata can impact how you work through compliance obligations. For example, metadata about columns containing sensitive medical data should specify that access be periodically reviewed and updated to meet the appropriate compliance obligations.

Data Governance Roles

It takes multiple people in a variety of roles for data governance to thrive. A crucial concept relating to data governance is data stewardship. Stewardship denotes looking after something, like an organization or property. *Data stewardship* is the act of developing the policies and procedures for looking after an organization's data quality, security, privacy, and regulatory compliance. The most vital role for effective data stewardship is that of the organizational data steward. An *organizational data steward*, or *data steward*, is the person responsible for data stewardship.

The data steward is responsible for leading an organization's data governance activities. As the link between the technical and nontechnical divisions within an organization, a data steward works with many people, from senior leaders to individual technologists. To establish policies, a data steward works with various data owners.

A *data owner* is a senior business leader with overall responsibility for a specific data domain. A *data domain*, or *data subject area*, contains data about a particular operational division within an organization. Finance, human resources, and the physical plant are all examples of operational divisions. Data owners work with the data steward to establish policies and procedures for their data domain.

In large, complex organizations, data owners may choose to delegate day-to-day governance activities to subject area data stewards. A *subject area data steward* works in the data owner's organization and understands the nuances that apply within that organizational unit. A subject area data steward works on behalf of their data owner to handle daily tasks. For example, processing access requests as people rotate in and out of roles is a responsibility a data owner may delegate to their subject area data steward. The need for subject area data stewards arises from the intricacies of different data domains. To implement data governance policies, data stewards work with data custodians.

A *data custodian* is a role given to someone who implements technical controls that execute data governance policies. Data custodians are frequently information technology employees who configure applications, dashboards, and databases.

For example, unique laws govern an organization's finances, people, and physical plant. Figure 8.12 visualizes how an organizational data steward works both vertically and

FIGURE 8.12 Organizational example.

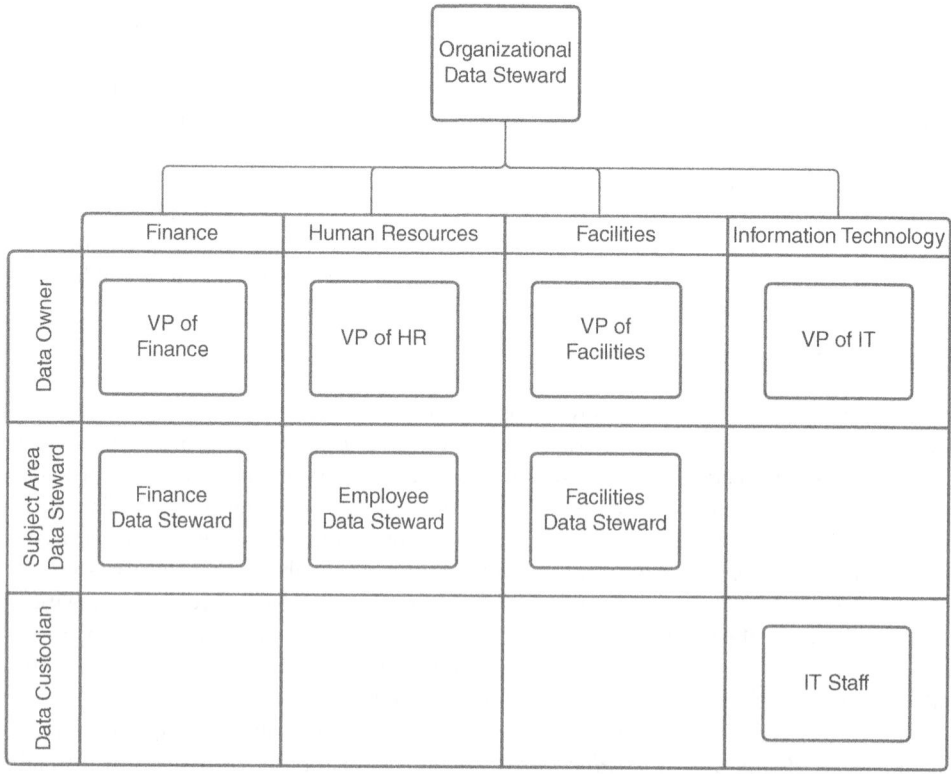

horizontally with the various data owners, subject area data stewards, and data custodians to actively steward, or take care of, the organization's data.

Data Compliance Concepts

Data compliance ensures that organizations handle, process, and store data while adhering to legal, regulatory, and industry-specific standards. Data compliance is a domain-specific activity, as regulations differ across industries. For example, providers of medical services, credit card processors, and universities all have unique compliance objectives.

National Institute of Standards and Technology (NIST)

The *National Institute of Standards and Technology (NIST)* is a nonregulatory agency in the U.S. Department of Commerce that promotes innovation. While NIST performs many functions, one area of responsibility is the creation of industry standards and guidelines for various subject areas, including cybersecurity, cryptography, and risk management. Formed in 1901, NIST directly impacts data governance and compliance with its cybersecurity and data protection standards. Adopted by public and private sector organizations, NIST's guidelines help improve organizational security controls and risk management. These guidelines also ensure compliance with federal regulations.

One of NIST's most influential contributions is the NIST Cybersecurity Framework. The Cybersecurity Framework is a nonregulatory framework that provides organizations with guidelines for identifying, protecting, detecting, responding to, and recovering from cybersecurity threats. This voluntary framework is broadly adopted across many industries to improve cybersecurity postures.

NIST also publishes the Special Publication (SP) 800 series. The SP series of documents provides specialized security guidelines. SP 800-53 is a foundational SP series document that defines security and privacy controls for federal information systems. SP 800-171 documents requirements for protecting Controlled Unclassified Information (CUI) in non-federal systems. The Cybersecurity Maturity Model Certification (CMMC), a requirement for Department of Defense (DoD) contractors, is based on SP 800-171. Other notable documents include SP 800-37, which introduces the Risk Management Framework (RMF) for assessing and mitigating cybersecurity risks. SP 800-61 provides best practices for incident response and security incident handling.

In cryptography, NIST maintains widely used standards like the Advanced Encryption Standard (AES) for data encryption. NIST also maintains the Secure Hash Algorithm (SHA) series for hashing and digital signatures. As an example of supporting innovation, NIST is working on cryptographic algorithms to resist the threat of quantum computing.

Federal laws and compliance regulations commonly refer to NIST guidelines. The Federal Information Security Modernization Act (FISMA) requires U.S. federal agencies to follow NIST security standards. Many industry regulations specify NIST data protection recommendations. In healthcare, the Health Insurance Portability and Accountability Act (HIPAA) adopts NIST standards, as does the Gramm-Leach-Bliley Act (GLBA) in the financial services sector.

As a data analyst, you will undoubtedly encounter NIST-related standards as you help your organization meet its compliance obligations.

Retention

Retention is a policy-driven process that defines how long to store data. Retention policies consider legal, regulatory, and business requirements as a function of compliance. Effective retention policies ensure that data is available when needed and disposed of after its retention period expires to minimize organizational risk.

Retention requirements specify collecting, processing, using, storing, retaining, and removing data. You need to consider retention requirements at each stage of the data lifecycle, from the moment you create data until the point at which it is removed or archived. Determining and documenting retention requirements at each stage of the data lifecycle facilitates meeting your data compliance objectives.

As you develop retention policies, consider the organizational value of a given piece of data. For instance, if you work with a logistics operation, you may want to keep an archive of the transaction details for each package you deliver forever. While the value of these details diminishes with time, you might derive additional value by applying statistical methods to identify patterns and trends.

Include data deletion requirements as part of your retention policies. Once you determine that the cost of keeping data exceeds its value to the organization, your retention policies should specify its removal. For example, suppose you have a system that stores job applications for your organization. Eventually, it no longer creates value for your organization to keep applications for filled positions. While the length of relevance differs per organization, you ultimately want to delete old applicant data.

Jurisdictional Requirements

As you think through different compliance scenarios, you must understand the impact of industry and governmental regulations on your organization. There are four categories for you to consider when thinking through regulatory and legal compliance obligations. These categories include criminal law, civil law, administrative law, and private regulations.

The goal of *criminal law* is to discourage people from acting in a way that negatively impacts society. A legislative body creates national, state, or local criminal laws. Legislative bodies include the U.S. Congress and state legislatures. There is a broad range of criminal offenses, including hacking, insider trading, espionage, robbery, and murder. One exclusive characteristic of criminal law is that punishment can include depriving liberty, such as a jail sentence or probation.

Civil law aims to resolve disputes between individuals, organizations, and government agencies. Like criminal laws, a legislative body creates civil laws, encompassing almost anything not addressed by criminal law. For instance, civil law covers contractual disputes and liability claims. Instead of jail time, outcomes from civil lawsuits are typically monetary damages or orders by the court to perform or refrain from a specific action.

Administrative law aims to enable effective government operations by allowing government administrative agencies to propagate regulations. Administrative regulations frequently provide details missing from criminal or civil law. For example, civil laws in the United States enable individuals with disabilities to receive government assistance. The Social Security Administration (SSA) is the administrative agency that implements Social Security and disability laws. Federally, in the United States, the Code of Federal Regulations (CFR) defines administrative law.

Private industry regulations aim to govern the activities of individuals and organizations without the force of law. However, it is common for contracts to specify compliance with nongovernmental regulations. For example, the Payment Card Industry has a Data Security Standard (PCI DSS) detailing how to process electronic payments securely. If you work with an external partner to process electronic card payments, you will find language that ensures compliance with PCI DSS as part of the contract.

Especially for organizations that operate internationally, it is vital to understand the government with jurisdiction over your operations. Jurisdiction influences how and where to handle regulatory, administrative, civil, or criminal disputes. For example, the European Union has the *General Data Protection Regulation (GDPR)* law. GDPR aims to give individuals control over how their personal data is collected, stored, and used. GDPR is one of the strictest privacy and security laws in the world. If you have operations in Europe, GDPR applies. However, if you only operate within the United States, there is no legal obligation to comply with GDPR.

It is essential to approach data retention from a policy perspective. In the United States, businesses and corporations should keep tax-related data for seven years. Suppose you operate in the United States and terminate an employee. In that case, the U.S. Equal Employment Opportunity Commission (EEOC) specifies that you must retain personnel and employment records for one year from the employee's termination date.

Replication

Replication copies data from one environment to another. You can use replication to copy production data into test environments in the same physical location, and you can use replication to synchronize data across multiple locations to ensure availability. Since you can use replication to copy data between separate physical locations, it can help organizations meet data protection and disaster recovery compliance objectives.

You must consider data jurisdiction requirements when developing a replication strategy, especially when using public cloud providers like Amazon Web Services (AWS), Microsoft Azure, and Google Cloud Platform (GCP). Suppose you use AWS for your storage needs and are working with data that, from a compliance standpoint, must physically exist within the United States. If you replicate data from AWS' Ohio region to its region in central Canada, you would be facing a compliance violation.

Replication can help you meet industry-specific regulations. In the United States, regulations require financial firms to maintain unalterable copies of financial transactions. Configuring replication that copies data from a transactional environment into a read-only archive can help meet this type of regulation.

Storage

Storage refers to a durable location that holds data at rest. The two primary types of storage are block storage and object storage. *Block storage* is directly accessible by operating systems. From a personal device standpoint, smartphones and laptops use block storage. Enterprises frequently use a Storage Area Network (SAN) to connect servers and petabyte-scale storage devices. A SAN enables access to large volumes of centralized, high-speed storage. SANs are a crucial component when designing the storage architecture for high-performance database systems.

Object storage stores data as individual objects. Each object has a unique identifier, metadata, and associated data. Unlike block storage, which you access directly through an operating system, you access object storage using APIs. S3 is the AWS object storage service, first launched in 2006. Microsoft offers Azure Blob Storage, and Cloud Storage is GCP's service in the object storage space. Operating systems need helper software to interact with object storage. While block storage has a speed advantage, object storage is typically cheaper.

Organizations use both block and object storage. While block storage has its place powering relational databases, object storage is a more cost-effective choice when building a data lake.

Data Ethics

Data ethics focuses on the moral principles guiding the responsible collection, use, and sharing of data. Data ethics serves as the moral compass for an organization. Organizations have various compliance obligations that compel action. The ethical use of data compels action because it is the right thing to do.

There are many ethical considerations to take into account when using data. One ethical subject is informed consent. Informed consent makes people aware of how their data is collected and used. For example, an organization with European operations must seek informed consent when using website cookies due to the European Union's GDPR. While no current law in the United States requires this action, companies can gather user consent for website cookies because protecting people's privacy and transparently communicating data use is the right thing to do.

Bias and fairness are also ethical considerations. Bias and fairness seek to avoid discrimination when making data-informed decisions. In addition to evaluating business processes for bias, ensure that machine learning data and algorithms do not reinforce bias when influencing hiring, lending, and law enforcement decisions.

Another ethical consideration is data minimization. An organization incorporating data minimization collects the fewest possible data elements when automating a business process.

You can identify a person with their Social Security number in the United States. While an organization may have a compelling need to store SSNs, minimizing who has access aids compliance efforts, and it is the right thing to do.

It takes effort to ensure the ethical use of data. Organizations implement privacy-by-design when designing systems. Once operational, regularly audit algorithms for bias and fairness. In the context of informed consent, data minimization, and transparency, design systems that provide clear opt-in and opt-out options when collecting data.

Payment Card Industry (PCI)

The *Payment Card Industry (PCI)* is a nongovernmental body that governs card-based financial payments. To protect the integrity of card-based financial transactions and prevent fraud, leading financial service companies, including MasterCard, Visa, Discover, American Express, and the Japan Credit Bureau, created the *PCI Security Standards Council (PCI SSC)*. The PCI SSC develops policies to govern electronic payment processing, transmission, and storage.

The *PCI Data Security Standard (PCI DSS)* is the industry's core information security standard. The following six principles encompass the objectives set out by the PCI DSS:

- Building and maintaining a secure network
- Protecting cardholder data
- Maintaining a vulnerability management program
- Implementing strong access controls
- Regularly monitoring and testing networks
- Maintaining an information security policy

While all the PCI DSS objectives ensure the security of financial transactions, understanding what it means to protect cardholder data is vital from a data governance point of view. In terms of data classification, there are two primary categories, according to PCI DSS. The first category is *cardholder data (CHD)*. Cardholder data includes data from the front of a card, including the cardholder's name, primary account number, and expiration date. The service code, a three- or four-digit number encoded on the magnetic stripe, is also cardholder data.

The second category is *sensitive authentication data (SAD)*. SAD includes complete track data from the magnetic stripe or embedded chip, Personal Identification Number (PIN), and the Card Verification Value (typically three digits on the back of a card).

From a data compliance perspective, the crucial thing to understand is that under PCI DSS, you can store cardholder data but cannot store sensitive authentication data. Complying with the PCI DSS is complex. If you need to process, transmit, or store electronic payment information, you must have a comprehensive understanding of PCI DSS. It is best to work with PCI DSS specialists if you have any doubts about complying with the PCI DSS objectives.

Personally Identifiable Information (PII)

Personally Identifiable Information (PII) is any data that uniquely identifies a person. In the United States, the National Institute of Standards and Technology (NIST) defines PII as follows:

> PII is any information about an individual maintained by an agency, including (1) any information that can be used to distinguish or trace an individual's identity, such as name, Social Security number, date and place of birth, mother's maiden name, or biometric records; and (2) any other information that is linked or linkable to an individual, such as medical, educational, financial, and employment information.

According to NIST, PII falls into two categories: linked and linkable. *Linked PII* is data that you can use to uniquely identify someone, including:

- Full name
- Social Security number
- Date and place of birth
- Driver's license number
- Passport number
- Credit card numbers
- Addresses
- Telephone numbers
- Email addresses
- Login credentials and passwords

NIST goes on to identify *linkable PII*, which is information that you can use in combination with other identifying information to identify, trace, or locate an individual. For example, suppose you can access medical, educational, financial, or employment information. Data elements like country, state, city, ZIP code, gender, and race are all examples of linkable PII since you can join that data to identify a person.

Protected Health Information (PHI)

In the United States, the Health Insurance Portability and Accountability Act (HIPAA) is a comprehensive healthcare law that regulates the security and privacy of health data. HIPAA applies to two categories of information.

Under HIPAA, *Protected Health Information (PHI)* is the broad category of data elements identifying an individual's health information. This information can be about the individual's past, current, or future health status and covers providing healthcare, processing healthcare payments, or processing insurance claims. Alternatively, *Electronic Protected Health Information*, or *e-PHI*, is any PHI you store or transmit digitally.

> **Exam Tip**
>
> The CompTIA exam objectives use the acronym PHI to mean "personal health information." However, HIPAA and common usage define it as "protected health information." This difference doesn't alter the meaning or intent of the rules governing this information, so you should treat them as having the same meaning if you see either one on the exam.

While HIPAA is a broad regulation, under the privacy rule provision, it identifies 18 data elements as PHI:

- Names
- All geographic identifiers smaller than a state, including street address, city, county, precinct, and ZIP code
- Dates other than year that relate to an individual, including birth date, admission date, date of treatment, and so on
- Telephone numbers
- Fax numbers
- Email addresses
- Social Security number
- Medical record numbers
- Health plan beneficiary numbers
- Account numbers
- Certificate or license numbers
- Vehicle identifiers and serial numbers, including license plate
- Device identifiers and serial numbers
- Web Uniform Resource Locators (URLs)
- Internet Protocol (IP) address numbers
- Biometric identifiers, including finger, retinal, voice, and facial prints
- Full-face photographs and any comparable images
- Any other unique identifying number, characteristic, or code, unless otherwise permitted by the privacy rule for reidentification

The rules around ZIP codes are slightly more complex. The first three digits of a ZIP code are not PHI. However, if all ZIP code combinations with the same first three digits contain fewer than 20,000 people, according to the Bureau of Census, then the first three digits are PHI.

As you can tell by the list of data elements, PHI has a broad scope by design. However, two provisions are in place if you need to share medical data without patient consent. The first is *expert determination*, where you use statistical and scientific principles or methods to make the risk of identifying an individual very small. The second is *safe harbor*, where you de-identify a dataset by removing any PHI data elements.

Another aspect of HIPAA to be aware of is the *security rule*, which applies solely to e-PHI. While the privacy rule focuses on protecting patient privacy, the objective of the security rule is to ensure the confidentiality, integrity, and availability of e-PHI data. The security rule exists to ensure that digital records are in a secure location, that access is limited to authorized parties, and that systems and processes are in place to prevent unauthorized access or accidental disclosure.

The PHI provisions of HIPAA apply only to covered entities. A *covered entity* is an organization legally obligated under HIPAA to protect the privacy and security of health information. There are three types of covered entities under HIPAA:

- Healthcare providers (physicians, hospitals, clinics, etc.)
- Health insurance plans
- Healthcare information clearinghouses

Under HIPAA, several electronic transactions qualify as e-PHI. If a provider engages in any of these transactions in electronic form, they are a covered entity. These transactions include:

- Payment and remittance advice
- Claims status
- Eligibility
- Coordination of benefits
- Claims and encounter information
- Enrollment and disenrollment
- Referrals and authorizations
- Premium payment

Since this list has a broad scope, most medical facilities are considered covered entities.

HIPAA also extends beyond covered entities to business partners who handle PHI on the covered entity's behalf. HIPAA requires that covered entities enter into special agreements known as business associate agreements with their partners. A *business associate agreement* (*BAA*) requires the business partner to comply with HIPAA provisions. For example, if you use cloud-based storage, your provider is a business partner under HIPAA.

It is vital to understand that information about an individual's health does not automatically imply that the data is governed by HIPAA, as there are three important exceptions:

- Employment records
- Student educational records that are covered by the Family Educational Rights and Privacy Act (FERPA)
- De-identified data

The laws surrounding PHI are complex. If you work in healthcare or with health-related data, you must deeply understand the privacy rule and security rule. It is best to work with attorneys specializing in the field if you have any doubts about PHI, processing, storing, and protecting e-PHI, or working with partners that require a BAA.

Audit

An *audit* examines an organization's data management practices, security controls, and regulatory compliance. Audits verify that policies, procedures, and technical controls comply with your compliance obligations for handling, storing, and protecting data.

There are various types of audits, including an internal audit, an external audit, and a regulatory audit. In an internal audit, an organization's internal team works with functional teams to verify corporate policy and control adherence. Internal audits help identify vulnerabilities before an external audit.

As implied by the name, third parties perform external audits. Several regulatory and consortia requirements require external audits. For example, PCI DSS compliance requires periodic external audits for the unbiased evaluation of security and compliance practices.

Jurisdictional requirements can specify regulatory audits. Industry regulators or the government mandates regulatory audits to ensure adherence to regulations and laws. For example, healthcare providers in the United States must undergo a regulatory audit to comply with HIPAA.

The scope of an audit encompasses several subject areas, regardless of who is performing the audit. Typical audit subject areas include data access controls that restrict access to sensitive data, data protection measures, system logs, system monitoring, incident reporting, regulatory compliance checks, data retention, and data disposal.

With regular audits as a cornerstone of your data governance effort, your organization can proactively manage risks, maintain compliance, and uphold the integrity of its data.

Classification

Classification is a vital subject area concerning compliance. *Classification* assigns a risk-based category to data based on its level of sensitivity, value, and relevant regulatory requirements. Appropriately classifying data informs data access requirements, access permissions, group permissions, and how you share data with external parties.

One crucial component of data governance defines the access requirements for data. *Data access requirements* determine which people need access to what data. Access requirements differ by data subject area and can be as granular as a single field. For example, managers need access to details about their employees, including their names and contact information. Since managers are responsible for providing feedback, they also need access to performance data. However, no manager has a compelling need to view their employees' Social Security number. While SSNs are necessary for payroll and tax purposes, malicious actors can also use them for identity theft.

When you're determining access requirements, it is essential to develop a data classification matrix. A *data classification matrix* defines categories, descriptions, and disclosure implications for data. Table 8.2 is an example of a data classification matrix. It is vital to consider data classification when considering access requirements to ensure proper data stewardship.

A data steward works with a data owner to establish broad classifications, with subject area data stewards to develop procedures for granting access to information, and with data custodians to ensure the appropriate technical controls are in place to protect information.

Classifying data is appropriate for both structured and unstructured data. When classifying data, you put data elements into one of four classifications, similar to those in the data classification matrix found in Table 8.2. Note that the category names may differ. Instead of Public, Internal, Sensitive, and Highly Sensitive, you may come across Public, Internal-Only, Confidential, and Restricted. Regardless of the category names, it is vital to understand the attributes for each category so that you can make the appropriate category assignment.

Classifying data elements can feel like an overwhelming task. Fortunately, there are a variety of standards in place that simplify the classification process, enforce consistency, and protect privacy.

TABLE 8.2 Sample Data Classification Matrix

Classification Term	Classification Description
Public	Data intended for public consumption. For example, anything on a public-facing website meets this classification. No disclosure implications.
Internal	Data intended for use within an organization. For example, a comprehensive organization chart including names. Disclosure compromises an organization's reputation or operations, but not its privacy or confidentiality obligations.
Sensitive	Data intended for limited use within an organization. For example, a list of employees and their compensation. Disclosure implies a violation of privacy or confidentiality.
Highly Sensitive	Data intended for restricted use, typically due to compliance obligations. Examples include Social Security numbers and bank account numbers. Disclosure implies a legal obligation in the event of a data breach.

Incident Reporting

Incident reporting is the process that documents how to respond to security events that compromise data integrity, confidentiality, or availability. An incident report is an artifact of the incident reporting process. Incident reports describe the compromise, including when it occurred, how it was detected, remediation steps, the root cause, an impact assessment, and an associated communication plan.

Data breaches result in an incident report. A *data breach* is an incident that results in unauthorized access to an organization's data. Whenever you have a security compromise that includes a data breach, it is necessary to understand the root cause and develop steps to prevent similar breaches from happening again.

Despite people's best efforts, data breaches do occur. From a data governance standpoint, it is essential to understand how to react to a breach. You also need to understand the reporting obligations to which you are legally or contractually bound. While there are many frameworks to handle breaches, they generally include the following steps:

1. Verify the breach.
2. Stop the breach.
3. Assess the impact of the breach.
4. Notify the impacted parties.
5. Correct the cause of the breach.
6. Conduct a comprehensive review.

Breach reporting requirements vary by data classification. As you can imagine, if an unsecured laptop containing public data is lost or stolen, there is no obligation to report the event. However, if the breach involves PII, PHI, or payment data, you must escalate to the appropriate authority and notify impacted parties. Of particular note is the *Breach Notification Rule* for HIPAA, which provides a breach definition and notification requirements for individuals, the media, and the Secretary of Health and Human Services.

Within the United States, breach notifications are subject to state-level laws. Laws differ in the number of affected individuals that trigger a breach and the maximum number of days that can elapse before notifying people of the breach. On the other hand, there is greater consistency in the European Union, as the GDPR specifies a maximum 72-hour limit for violation notifications. Understanding the classification of your data, the laws and regulations you are bound to, and the jurisdiction for litigation is crucial to ensuring data compliance.

Data Privacy and Protection

Data is one of an organization's most precious assets. Safeguarding and protecting that data is of paramount importance. Fortunately, there is an abundance of technical and procedural controls to help protect an organization's data and the privacy of individuals who entrust an organization with their data.

Role-based Access Control (RBAC)

It is a best practice to use role-based access control to manage data access permissions for people. *Role-based access control* (RBAC) centers on the principle of granting access to the roles people occupy instead of granting access to people individually. When you define roles and then assign people to those roles, it simplifies how you manage permissions.

For example, it is common for people to switch jobs within an organization, as it allows for developing new skills and a more comprehensive understanding of the overall business. Figure 8.13 illustrates how the jobs of a specific employee change over time. In the first year, Ralph works in Finance. During his time in Finance, Ralph has access to data about the organization's finances.

In the second year, Ralph takes a new position in Facilities. Ralph needs access to facilities-related data for his new position and doesn't need to retain access to the Finance system. A data custodian removes Ralph's finance role and assigns him a facilities role to reflect that change.

In the third year, Ralph takes a position in Human Resources. Ralph needs access to human resources data in this new job and no longer needs to see the facilities-related data. A data custodian implements the change to Ralph's access permissions.

A role-based access approach facilitates permissions maintenance and improves consistency. This approach also ensures that Ralph has access only to the data he needs to perform his current duties. Managing permissions with roles also pays dividends when auditing permissions for compliance.

FIGURE 8.13 Access roles over time.

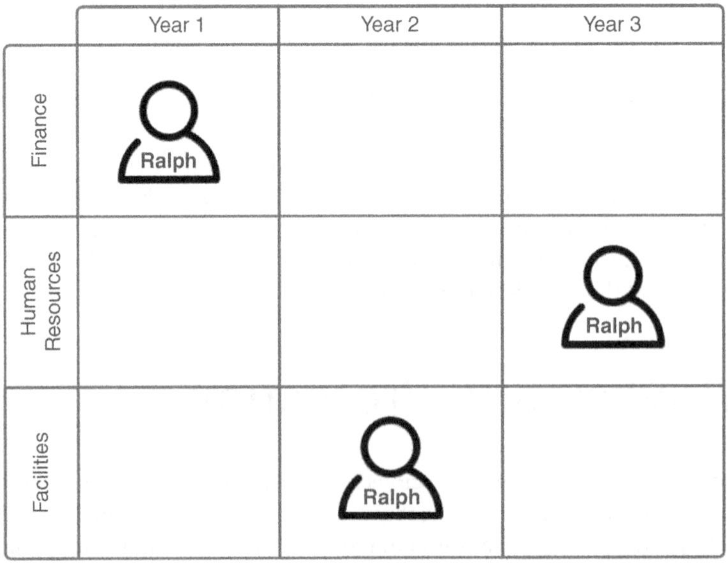

	Year 1	Year 2	Year 3
Finance	Ralph		
Human Resources			Ralph
Facilities		Ralph	

FIGURE 8.14 Danger of user-based access.

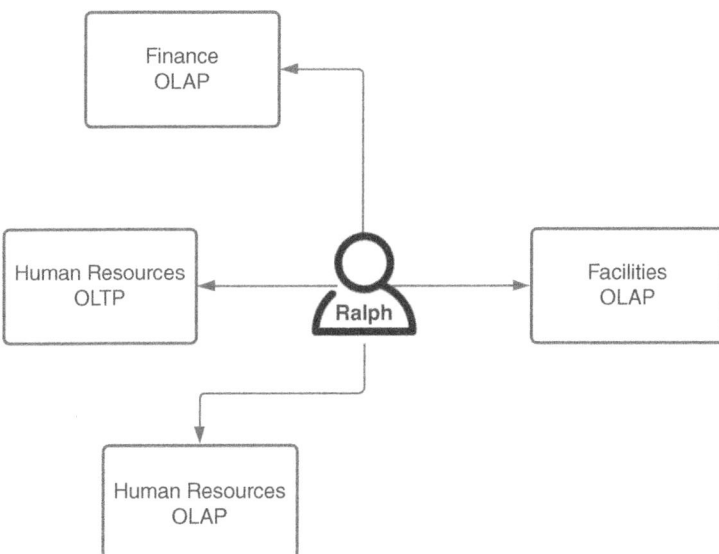

The alternative to role-based access is *user-based access*, which assigns permissions directly to individuals. User-based access is a dangerous practice, as it increases operational complexity and the potential for mistakes. Suppose there are both OLTP and OLAP environments for each data subject area. Figure 8.14 illustrates what could happen at the end of Year 3 if the data custodian forgets to remove OLAP permissions at each role transition. In this scenario, Ralph winds up with too much access by the end of Year 3.

Group Permissions

It's best to start by visualizing people within an organization when creating data access roles. An organization chart documents the reporting structure within an organization. Looking at an organization chart, like the example in Figure 8.15, informs how you develop roles.

When developing a role-based access strategy, it is common to implement user group–based permissions. Considering the sample organization chart from Figure 8.15, you can imagine vice presidents having broadly permissive access to data within their area of responsibility. Progressing down the organization chart reduces the scope of what someone in that role can access. Figure 8.16 illustrates how roles form naturally around groups of people.

Encryption

Encryption is a fundamental tool that facilitates improving data privacy and data protection. As you establish data classifications, define user roles, and determine data access requirements, you need to include encryption as part of your technical control suite for

FIGURE 8.15 Sample organization chart.

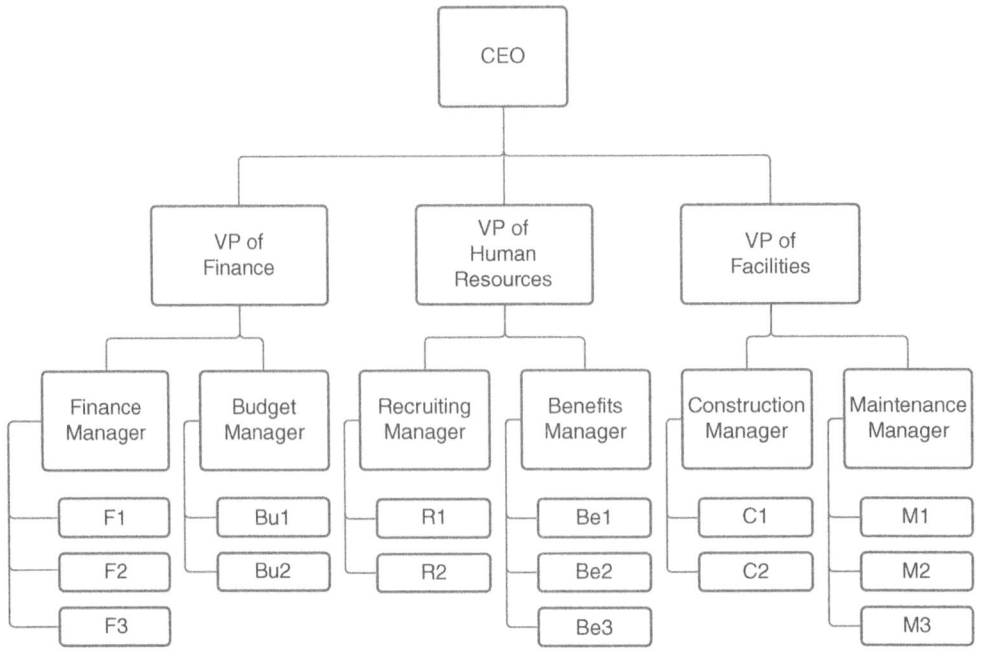

FIGURE 8.16 Sample user group–based roles.

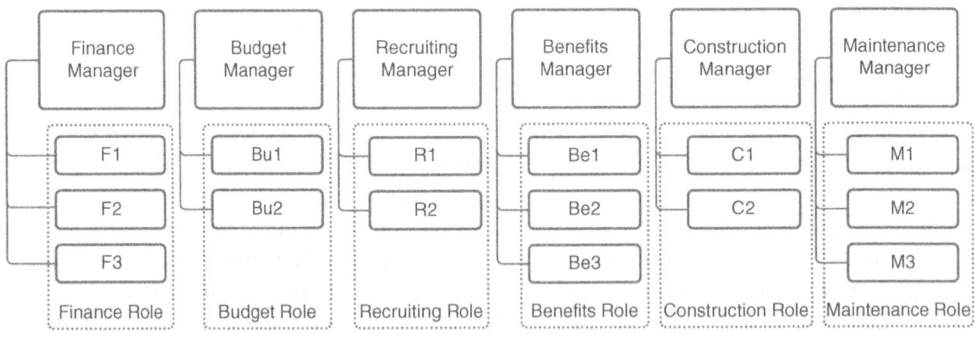

protecting data. In cryptography, *encryption* is the process of encoding data with a key so that only authorized parties can read it. Data encryption is one of the fundamental components of data protection, as the data is unusable without the key to decrypt it. An *encryption key* is a series of letters, numbers, and symbols used during the encoding process to make data unreadable. Once the data is encrypted, you can only access it by decrypting it with a valid key. If you lose the encryption key, any data encrypted with that key becomes useless.

Data at Rest

To keep data secure, you must encrypt data at rest and in transit. *Data at rest* is data that exists in permanent storage. The two most common locations for data at rest are databases and flat files. Databases have sophisticated access control mechanisms as part of the database software. Since databases centralize data and require a team of technologists to operate, they are comparatively easy to secure.

For example, Oracle and Microsoft have *Transparent Data Encryption* (*TDE*) as part of their database offering. TDE ensures the database files and log files are encrypted. With TDE, even if an unauthorized party gains access to the database server, the database files themselves are encrypted.

The chance of someone picking up a database server and walking away with it is slight. However, securing flat files is much more challenging as you can put them on any device that stores electronic data. Desktop computers, laptops, tablets, mobile phones, USB thumb drives, and cloud storage are all examples of devices that store flat files. Since many of these devices are portable, there is a good chance that one will be lost or stolen. If you lose an encrypted physical device, your information is safe. Gaining access to the data on a lost device requires decrypting it with the original encryption key.

Local storage is the storage media on an individual device, such as a hard drive in a laptop. Encrypting local storage is straightforward, regardless of the operating system you use. The steps, visualized in Figure 8.17, are as follows:

1. Create a password for encrypting the local storage.
2. Determine the operating system.
3. Use the encryption tool appropriate for the chosen operating system.

While encrypting local storage is straightforward and practical, remember that the encryption key is the only thing protecting the data. Make sure you store the encryption key in a secure location, for if the key is lost, you can no longer decrypt and access your data.

FIGURE 8.17 Local encryption process flow.

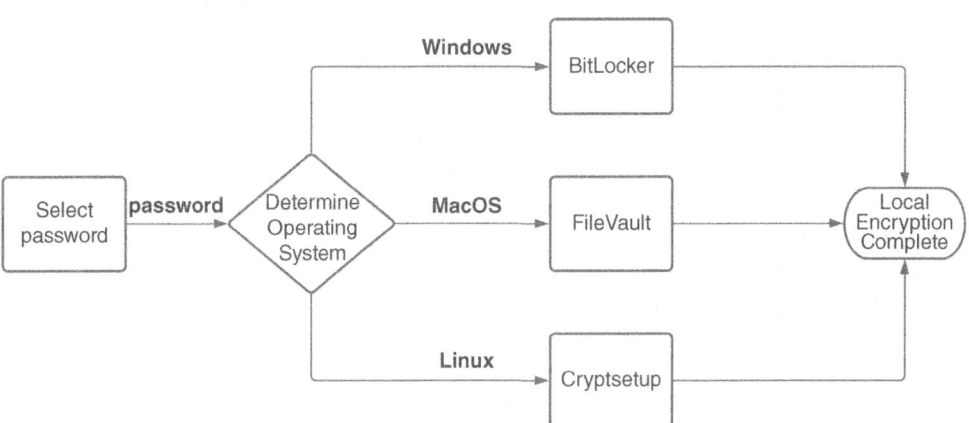

When using a shared drive, the security requirements are slightly more complex than with local storage. A *shared drive* is where groups of people can collaborate on shared documents. Apart from encrypting the physical media, you need to consider who needs access to the share and the type of access they need. When considering people, it's best to think in terms of groups. You must consider reading, creating, updating, and deleting content when considering access.

For example, suppose a hiring committee uses a shared drive to store candidates' cover letters and resumes. Only the search leader responsible for collecting and distributing the documents needs to create access to the shared drive, whereas everyone on the hiring committee needs read access.

Shared drive permissions can get very complicated since each file and folder has its own set of permissions. The safest way to manage shared drive permissions is by identifying groups of people and assigning them the appropriate roles. Every exception is an opportunity for a security compromise.

User-facing *cloud-based storage* is like a shared drive, except that the contents reside on computers run by the cloud provider instead of an internal IT team. By default, cloud storage offerings like Microsoft OneDrive, Google Drive, Box, and Dropbox all automatically encrypt files at rest using your login credentials. The same considerations about groups, roles, and permissions you use for shared drives apply to cloud storage.

Cloud storage offerings enable collaboration by design and offer advanced features like simultaneous editing in Google Docs. However, this collaboration by design philosophy means that the ability to share documents resides with the individual by default. When evaluating cloud storage offerings, an organization needs to assess the available administrative controls to minimize the risk of unintended data sharing.

Some organizations use cloud infrastructure to operate their enterprise computing environments. Amazon Web Services, Microsoft, and Google are three large cloud infrastructure providers. When using infrastructure in the cloud, it is essential to ensure encryption at rest. Recall that if you have access to an encryption key, you can access the data it encrypts. To ensure that only authorized people can access your data, consider using a customer-managed encryption key. With a customer-managed key, the cloud service provider can't decrypt and use your data.

Data in Transit

Data in transit is data that is actively moving between one location and another. During data transmission, you must encrypt the connection between the locations to ensure the data's security. When considering data in transit, you need to account for people interacting with computers and computers interacting with other computers.

Transmitting data over the Internet typically uses the Hypertext Transfer Protocol (HTTP). To ensure data security, use *Transport Layer Security* (*TLS*) as the cryptographic protocol for encrypting the connection. Adding TLS on top of HTTP results in *Hypertext Transfer Protocol Secure* (*HTTPS*), as seen in Figure 8.18.

When a person navigates the Internet using a web browser, a padlock shows up in the address bar to indicate an encrypted HTTPS connection. Figure 8.19 illustrates the padlock

FIGURE 8.18 Encrypted network connection.

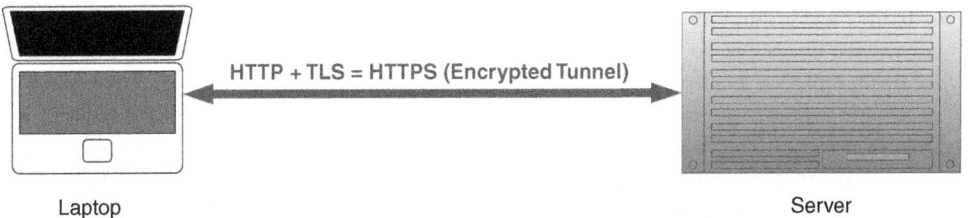

FIGURE 8.19 HTTPS padlock.

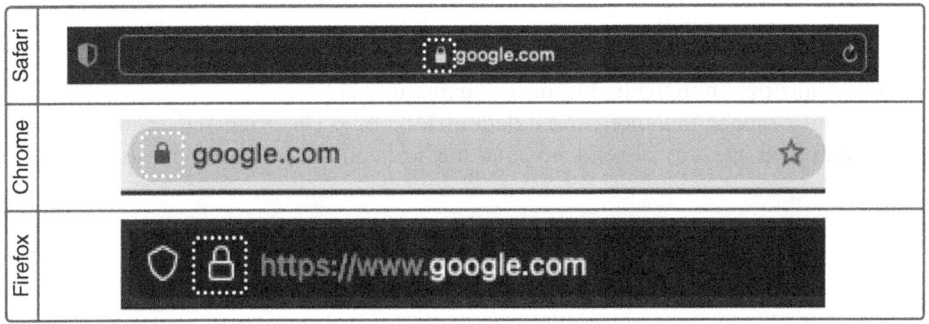

FIGURE 8.20 Encrypted ETL process.

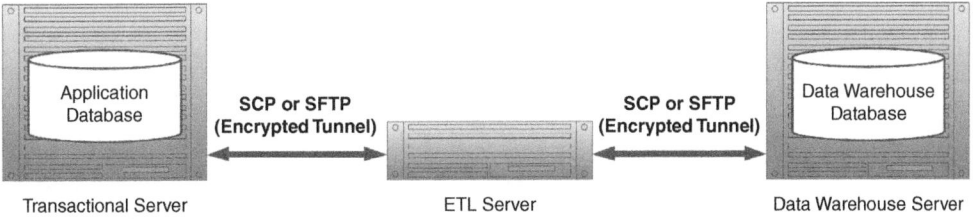

in three common web browsers. As part of amplifying the security message in the context of data governance, part of your training should include reminders to look for the padlock when putting sensitive information into a browser.

ETL processes copy data between transactional and analytical systems. When copying files between the transactional and analytical servers, use the *Secure Copy Protocol* (*SCP*) or the *Secure File Transfer Protocol* (*SFTP*). As their names imply, both SCP and SFTP establish an encrypted tunnel to copy data, as shown in Figure 8.20.

Masking

Apart from encryption, you also need to consider whether there is a reason for sensitive data elements, like SSNs, to exist in a nonproduction environment. *Data masking*, or *data obfuscation*, replaces sensitive information with a synthetic version. For example, you may use production data to populate your testing and training environments. While testing or training, using a simulated instead of an actual SSN doesn't diminish the testing or training use case. To protect individual privacy and minimize organizational risk, you can implement a data-masking strategy for sensitive information, as shown in Figure 8.21.

Anonymization

Depending on the use case, you can anonymize sensitive data to improve security. *Anonymization* alters, removes, or redacts personal data, making it impossible to identify an individual. Anonymization is a one-way process. Once anonymized, it should theoretically be impossible to identify an individual using anonymized data.

Consider the original and anonymized data in Table 8.3. The original data identifies an individual and their age, city of residence, and medical condition. However, it is impossible

FIGURE 8.21 Data-masking ETL process.

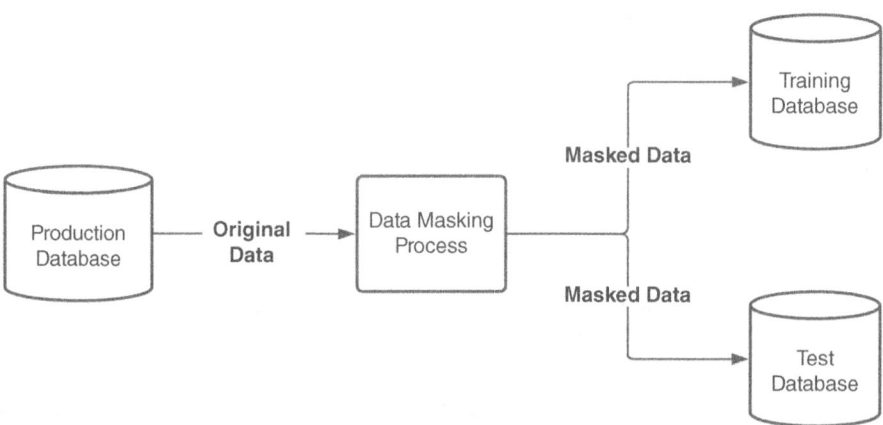

TABLE 8.3 Anonymization Example

Original Data	Anonymized Data
Giuseppe Rossi, aged 46, lives in Iowa City, Iowa, and has yellow fever.	Patient A, 40–50 years old, lives in the Midwest and has a medical condition.

FIGURE 8.22 Reidentification by combining datasets.

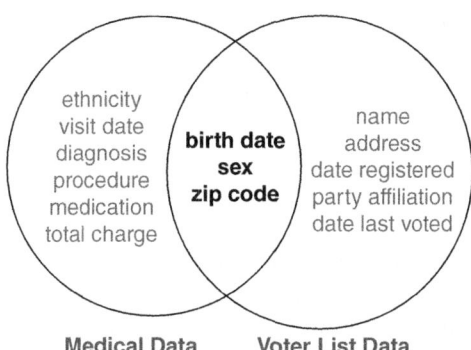

to determine the person, age, place, or medical condition using the anonymized data since many people between the ages of 40 and 50 live in the Midwest and have medical conditions. When you anonymize data, you necessarily lose details.

While de-identification is conceptually similar to anonymization, reidentification can reverse it. *De-identifying data* is the process of removing identifiers that can compromise individual privacy. How you de-identify depends on your use case. One way of de-identifying data is to share only aggregated or summarized data. Another way is to remove variables from the data.

Reidentifying data happens when you take de-identified datasets and join them in a way that establishes the identity of individuals. For example, you can identify most Americans by combining their birth date, sex, and ZIP code. Figure 8.22 illustrates the danger of reidentification, as it shows two separate datasets that share three data elements: birth date, sex, and ZIP code. Although the medical dataset is de-identified, you can reidentify individuals by combining the two datasets using the shared data elements. If the values for those three variables aren't essential to ongoing analysis, the most straightforward path to ensuring the de-identification of the dataset is to remove the variables you don't need. It is especially vital to consider reidentification possibilities when sharing data with an external party.

Data Usage

As data becomes increasingly important, employees must know how to use it appropriately. An *acceptable use policy* (AUP) defines an individual's responsibilities when accessing, using, sharing, and removing organizational data. While an AUP is a document with a broad scope, it has provisions for each type of data in an organization's data classification matrix. AUPs describe acceptable locations for storing proprietary information, what to do in the event of theft, loss, or unauthorized disclosure, and disposal methods.

For example, suppose you are crafting an AUP using the classification matrix in Table 8.2. For the Public classification, a reasonable policy specifies that using any device to work with Public data is acceptable, and any loss or theft doesn't warrant escalation or reporting.

At the most sensitive end of the data classification spectrum, a reasonable policy might require an organizationally owned, encrypted device to access Highly Sensitive data. The policy may also specify that reporting a loss, theft, or disclosure event requires an internal escalation and response.

Data Sharing

Defining, documenting, and circulating rules for data sharing is an essential data governance concept. Individuals in an organization must know what data can be shared, how to share it, and how to transmit it. A *data use agreement* (*DUA*) is a contractual document for transferring private data between organizations. You should establish a DUA before sharing data with an outside party. It is essential to understand the classification for each piece of data when crafting a DUA. The more sensitive a data element is, the more critical it is to prepare appropriate sharing-related language. Considering the sample classification matrix from Table 8.2, the data sensitivity level should inform your DUA needs.

A DUA provides details governing the data's transfer, use, and disclosure reporting protocols. Some of these details include:

- Identifying who will receive the data
- Identifying how the third party can use the data
- Prohibiting the further distribution of the data
- Establishing the method of transfer
- Identifying how the recipient will protect the data

Each organization may define its unique procedures for reviewing and approving DUAs. However, some organizations may need to consider legal and regulatory requirements when reviewing DUAs. In the United States, the Food and Drug Administration specifies that you need an Institutional Review Board when conducting research on human subjects. An *Institutional Review Board* (*IRB*) is a body that formally reviews and approves any sharing of this data. Similarly, healthcare providers subject to HIPAA must follow a formal process before sharing protected health information.

Data Quality Assurance Practices

Ensuring data quality is one of the most vital aspects of an analyst's job. Without high-quality data, an organization's ability to make appropriately data-informed decisions diminishes. Fortunately, data quality is a topic that humanity has spent years defining and refining, so you don't have to start from scratch.

International Organization for Standardization (ISO)

The *International Organization for Standardization (ISO)* is an independent organization that develops and publishes global standards. Founded in 1947, the ISO is headquartered in Geneva, Switzerland, and it includes national standards bodies from over 160 countries. While ISO standards are nonregulatory, various industries incorporate these standards to help an organization ensure quality, safety, and efficiency.

The ISO develops standards through an international consensus process. With broad, global representation, governments, businesses, and experts from different industries collaborate to create standards representing industry best practices. These standards cover various sectors, including information technology, cybersecurity, and data security.

ISO 9001 is one of the most widely recognized ISO standards related to data quality and security. ISO 9001 defines the principles of a Quality Management System (QMS). ISO 9001 core concepts include continuous improvement, customer satisfaction, and process efficiency. Broadly adopted, ISO 9001 is a foundational framework for maintaining data integrity within an organization.

The ISO collaborates with other standards-creating organizations like the *International Electrotechnical Commission (IEC)*. Founded in 1906 and headquartered in Geneva, Switzerland, the IEC includes more than 80 member countries. The IEC's primary focus is on standards for electrical technology.

Specific to the information security domain, the ISO and IEC created the ISO/IEC 27001, which provides guidelines for an Information Security Management System (ISMS). This standard helps organizations identify, assess, and mitigate security risks related to data storage, access, and processing.

As a data analyst, you should familiarize yourself with ISO 8000 and ISO 31000. ISO 8000 describes data quality and master data management, while ISO 31000 provides a risk management framework.

As a data analyst, you should be familiar with ISO's data-centric standards, as many organizations use ISO certification to demonstrate commitment to high-quality data management, security, and operational excellence.

Source Control

Source control refers to the combination of technologies and processes for managing change. Managing change is an essential part of ensuring data quality. There are many systems in an organization's data ecosystem. Systems that ingest, transform, and store data are core components of the data ecosystem, as is the software that makes data available to internal and external constituents.

Source Code Control

Software is an essential part of each component within a data ecosystem. Each transactional system, ETL job, database, report, and dashboard uses software to encode business logic.

Additionally, software packages require configuration files to facilitate integrations and operations. Using source control to manage configuration and software changes is essential for continuous improvement and high-quality data.

From a technology perspective, you need a *source code control* tool. While *git* is the most popular source code control tool, you may encounter older tools like *subversion*. These tools help software development teams make concurrent changes to source code. Source code control tools help developers avoid conflicts when multiple people need to make changes in the same file.

Beyond facilitating work, source code control tools help you manage software releases. Suppose an ETL job fails in a production environment and requires an immediate fix. Meanwhile, the file that needs changing to resolve the issue has already been modified to accommodate a new data feed. You can use source code control to retrieve the production version of the code, fix the problem, and verify that the issue won't reappear when the already-modified version of the file moves to production.

Similarly, source code control tools help manage configuration changes. Different versions of database software have different configuration settings. Using source code control to store the configuration files allows you to track configuration changes over time.

Issue Tracking

In addition to source code control technology, an issue-tracking system and the associated organizational processes help manage when software changes occur. Issue tracking systems like *Jira, monday.com,* and *GitHub* let you track requirements from idea generation to production. Issue-tracking systems integrate with source code control tools to associate issues with source code.

An organizational *Change Control Board* (CCB) governs when to deploy configuration and software changes in an environment. The CCB approves changes, schedules them, and keeps an associated maintenance calendar. While the frequency of change varies with each organization, communicating the change calendar lets people know when to expect changes and details about each change.

Unit Test

Developers need to test software changes before releasing them to production. The *unit test* is the most granular test a developer performs. The goal of a unit test is to ensure individual components or functions of a program work as expected.

Unit tests focus on a single function or stored procedure. Unit testing aims to catch errors as early as possible in the development cycle, resolving defects when they have the least organizational impact. Organizations want to identify and resolve defects as early as possible since the earlier you catch a defect, the cheaper it is to fix. After a successful unit test, the individual components, such as a Python function or database stored procedure, are ready for integration into a broader system.

Automating unit tests is a best practice that facilitates regression tests. A regression test ensures that new changes don't break existing functionality. Suppose you are working on a single function in a file that contains 20 functions. Running an automated unit test gives you confidence that your change does not impact the functionality of the other 19 functions. Since manual testing takes time and effort, automated unit tests increase software quality while improving the organizational efficiency of making changes.

Requirement Testing

Requirement testing ensures that a system meets its designed business requirements. Where unit tests focus on individual components, a requirement test validates a specific functional requirement. Suppose you work in the hospitality industry. An example unit test verifies that the query to retrieve available room inventory functions appropriately. Meanwhile, requirement tests verify the actions a user makes in the system. For example, individual requirement tests would check the ability to reserve a hotel room, change an existing reservation, and manage an individual's loyalty profile information.

Requirement testing also includes technical objectives like response time. Suppose you validate that the hotel room reservation requirement works as intended. However, if it takes five minutes of processing to complete the reservation, the requirement test fails, as people are unlikely to wait that long when the system is in production.

Incorporating technical requirements when creating requirement test cases is particularly important when working with applications that traverse or aggregate large volumes of data. For example, suppose you have a report that will scan 1 billion rows of data in production. Testing the report with ten rows in the database is insufficient, as you need to verify it also works with 1 billion rows.

Stress Test

Every system has its limits. *Stress testing* determines a system's breaking point by putting a load on the system that exceeds its design limits. The primary objective of conducting a stress test is to identify the bottleneck that ultimately causes a system to fail. Systems ultimately fail due to insufficient processing power, memory, storage, or network capacity.

You place load on the system in question to perform a stress test. This load can take the form of extraordinarily high transaction volumes. Suppose the system's original design is to handle 1,000 transactions per second. During a stress test, you progressively increase the load, exceeding 1,000 *transactions per second (tps)*, until performance degrades and the system fails. The reasons for failure will ultimately relate to processing power, memory, storage, or network capacity. If your organizational risk tolerance dictates that the system should be able to handle double its expected load, you iteratively drive load, identify the bottleneck, and resolve it until you reach the 2,000 tps objective.

You can also stress a system by increasing the number of concurrent users. Suppose a reporting environment handles 20 concurrent sessions by design. As with increasing the transaction volume, you increase the number of concurrent sessions until you identify a bottleneck. The bottleneck may manifest as the reporting server running out of memory to handle the additional sessions or the database running out of processing power to handle the extra workload.

As you conduct a stress test, make sure you have established metrics to identify what failure looks like. Apart from coarse metrics like memory consumption, include response times for the system's most common business transactions. Incorporating business transaction-derived metrics can identify bottlenecks like insufficient database indexes and insufficient storage bandwidth.

In addition to identifying why a system fails, stress testing also exposes how a system fails. For instance, a lack of processing power may cause a cascading failure that renders the entire system inoperable. Alternatively, resource contention may result in a gradual degradation of performance. Ideally, you design self-healing systems that can recover from the extra load with limited human intervention.

Another crucial discovery is to determine how a system recovers from stress. Ideally, the system gracefully recovers from stress without data corruption. However, if the database crashes due to a stress test, you must focus on how long it will take to recover the database and how many in-flight transactions will be lost.

The ability to cost-effectively replicate a production environment using public cloud resources lowers the barriers to stress testing. Don't be tempted to bypass stress testing due to cost or time considerations. By identifying weaknesses before deployment, organizations can understand when their systems will fail and can develop a plan to handle outlier load events.

User Acceptance Testing (UAT)

User Acceptance Testing (UAT) is when end users validate that a system meets business requirements and is ready for deployment. While technical staff perform stress tests, functional users conduct tests during UAT in collaboration with technical staff. The main objective of UAT is to ensure that the system handles functional use cases and meets user expectations before the system goes live. Since UAT is frequently the last step in the testing lifecycle, it happens after unit and requirement testing.

During UAT, subject matter experts verify that the system handles the business requirements for their functional unit. Suppose an organizational policy requires two people to approve expenditures exceeding $100,000. A member of the expense processing team would verify this test case during UAT.

Validation of workflow processes is another crucial aspect of UAT. Business users validate that data ingestion, routing, and decision-making happen according to expectations. For instance, a business user would validate the complete equipment request workflow in Figure 8.23, with test cases under, at, and above the $100,000 threshold.

In addition to business functionality, UAT examines the system's usability. Usability considerations like color, screen layout, and button placement are among the items in scope during UAT. As with unit testing, it is more cost-effective for an organization to resolve an issue during UAT than it is in production.

FIGURE 8.23 Equipment approval decision flowchart.

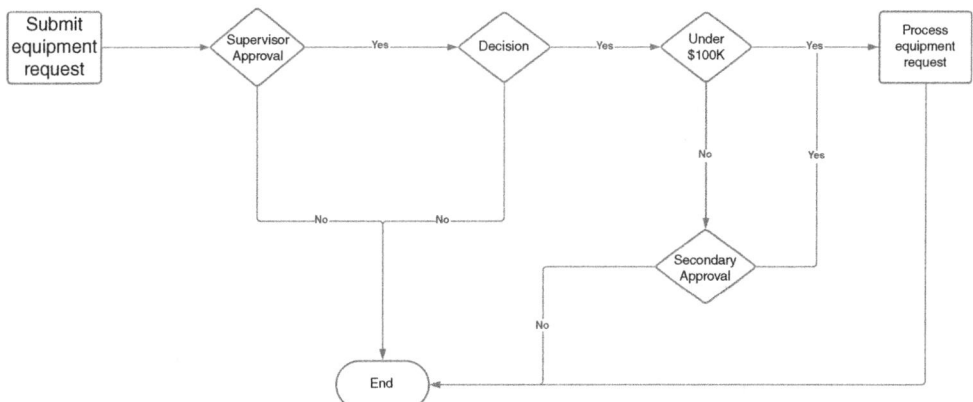

Data Health Check

A data health check is a routine dataset evaluation to detect inconsistencies, outliers, or other inaccuracies negatively impacting data integrity. Data health checks can identify missing values, duplicate records, outdated information, and format inconsistencies. A health check in a customer database can reveal multiple entries for the same customer with slight name variations.

In Figure 8.24, customer information comes from a credit agency, a bank, and the company's website. Without a data health check that resolves this duplication, the customer may receive multiple copies of a marketing campaign at 123 Walnut St with slightly different names. This duplication confuses the customer and puts the organization in a bad light. Meanwhile, health checks in a financial system can highlight data ingestion errors by detecting incorrectly formatted account numbers.

Data drift happens when data patterns change over time. The most significant impact of data drift is when past statistical distributions don't reflect current data. For example, databases maintain internal statistics that the optimizer uses to determine the most efficient way to execute a query. When data drift occurs due to changes in the data, database statistics grow stale, leading to inefficient query execution. Specifically, a query that typically uses an index may no longer use the index if the statistics are outdated. Database administrators regularly recompute database statistics to compensate for this eventual drift as part of their operational duties.

Automated Data Quality Monitoring

Maintaining data quality is imperative for making good data-informed decisions. Automated data quality monitoring extends the concept of data health checks by performing real-time checks as part of routine operations. By automating health checks, you proactively improve data quality instead of waiting for users to report atypical results.

FIGURE 8.24 Upstream systems causing duplicate data.

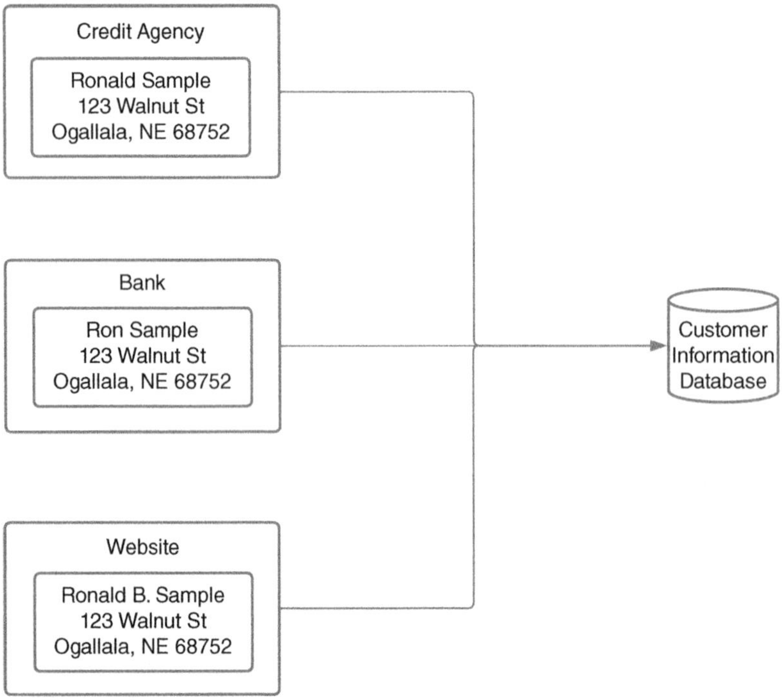

```
┌─────────────────────┐
│   Credit Agency     │
│  ┌───────────────┐  │
│  │ Ronald Sample │  │
│  │ 123 Walnut St │  │
│  │Ogallala, NE 68752│
│  └───────────────┘  │
└─────────────────────┘

┌─────────────────────┐
│        Bank         │          ┌──────────┐
│  ┌───────────────┐  │          │ Customer │
│  │  Ron Sample   │  │─────────▶│Information│
│  │ 123 Walnut St │  │          │ Database │
│  │Ogallala, NE 68752│          └──────────┘
│  └───────────────┘  │
└─────────────────────┘

┌─────────────────────┐
│       Website       │
│  ┌───────────────┐  │
│  │Ronald B. Sample│ │
│  │ 123 Walnut St │  │
│  │Ogallala, NE 68752│
│  └───────────────┘  │
└─────────────────────┘
```

Since automated data quality monitoring performs its checks programmatically, you reduce the amount of manual intervention and risk of human error. You also improve the speed and accuracy of decisions that rely on accurate data. From an algorithmic standpoint, you can use automated data quality monitoring to improve machine learning model accuracy by preventing outliers or corrupt data from degrading predictions.

You can use automated quality monitoring to validate data. For example, banking systems can process thousands of transactions per second. Automated data quality monitoring can validate incorrect account numbers, either rejecting transactions in real time or flagging them for human review. You can also programmatically verify the details of wire transfers and prevent the wire's completion if any details are missing.

Automated data quality monitoring can improve efficiency and consistency in the healthcare space by validating patient details and treatment codes. Validating patient details can reduce duplicates, as duplication similar to Figure 8.24 can happen when a patient visits multiple specialists within a single hospital system. Ensuring the accuracy of treatment codes minimizes the time spent working through insurance claims and the associated billing complications.

Data Profiling

Data profiling analyzes a dataset to understand its structure, quality, and content. When profiling, you summarize the underlying data to identify patterns, statistical distributions, and the relationships they contain. Data profiling is a necessary activity when preparing to integrate data from disparate systems or when migrating data from one system to another.

Quality metrics like column statistics are especially relevant when working with big data, as they give insight into the range of values in the column. When working with numeric data, obtaining the mean and median provides insight into common values while plotting the distribution helps you understand the data's shape. When working with text data, understanding the distinct values and the number of occurrences enables you to identify outliers and malformed data.

Suppose you are migrating customer data to a new electronic commerce platform. Data profiling helps determine the effort required to transform data from one system to another. In terms of postal addresses, it is more cost-effective to send mail to a U.S. address using the United States Postal Service standard for that address. Profiling the address columns can identify variations in the abbreviations for street (e.g., Street, St, and St.). Similarly, you can use profiling to identify the records that use only the first five digits of a ZIP code instead of the complete nine digits.

Data profiling can help you identify and formally define relationships when combining disparate datasets. Suppose you work in the hospitality industry and are executing a merger between two hotel chains. Profiling the data from both chains reveals the need to establish a common customer identifier to integrate existing customers while eliminating duplicates.

Master Data Management

Master data management (*MDM*) is a data governance discipline that combines processes and technologies to ensure that data assets across an organization have a single source of truth. Successfully implementing MDM is a challenge regardless of industry or organizational size. As organizational complexity increases, identifying and maintaining an accurate, consistent, well-governed single source of truth becomes more challenging.

For example, consider the complexities of automobile manufacturers. Customers purchase vehicles from the manufacturer through a network of independently owned and operated dealerships. The manufacturer receives customer information from the dealership that lets it track ownership of its cars. Getting this data from dealerships is vital to the manufacturer's warranty and recall obligations over the vehicle's life.

At some point, customers sell their vehicles. Each vehicle may have many subsequent owners in the used market. The manufacturer's likelihood of receiving a sales transaction record diminishes each time the vehicle changes owners. The lack of sales notification can cause the manufacturer to lose track of who owns its vehicles over time.

Automotive service shops also have a relationship with the manufacturer. For instance, repair shops need to acquire factory parts when performing a repair. If a manufacturer's warranty covers the repair, the shop may feed information about who the customer is back to the manufacturer.

Manufacturers' marketing teams purchase mailing lists of prospects to acquire new customers. Marketing teams keep track of the people with whom they interact. Some of those people may be existing customers, past customers, employees, or entirely new customers.

When a car is ten years old, the information about a vehicle, its previous owners, its service history, and its current owner exist in multiple operational systems. While the manufacturer owns some of these systems, others belong to dealers and repair shops. In addition, the quality of some data, like ownership status, degrades with time.

Each of these activities generates and collects data about customers. Since all of that data exists in separate systems, maintaining that data over time is challenging because different systems have different data, with no inherent mechanism for accuracy or consistency. A complex data lineage problem like this is the type of data challenge that MDM seeks to address.

Summary

Data is one of an organization's most important assets. Modern organizations have numerous systems that capture, process, transmit, and store data. Organizations also have a complex structure in terms of roles and responsibilities. Data governance is a discipline that takes an ordered, systematic approach to thinking about, organizing, managing, and using data. Data governance is vital to using data consistently and efficiently.

Organizations frequently need to integrate data from different systems. Integration can happen in a batch or a real-time fashion, depending on the business's needs. Documentation, including data flow diagrams, lineage tracking, and explainability reports, helps maintain transparency and troubleshoot issues. A data dictionary defines database structures, while data versioning tracks changes over time for historical accuracy. A source of truth establishes the authoritative system for data consistency. Having clearly documented sources of truth for each data element helps establish the lineage for that element.

Metadata provides context for data usage and compliance. Governance roles include data stewards, owners, and custodians, all of whom play a role in developing policies. After development, this team is responsible for implementing and enforcing these policies across the organization.

One of the prime objectives of data governance is ensuring that the right people have access to the right data at the right time. Data stewards use organizational structure and groupings within that structure to guide the creation of access controls. Access control policies describe the data subject area and access type, including reading, creating, updating, and deleting data. For example, while the leaders of Sales and Marketing both need access to financial systems for budgeting purposes, they shouldn't have access to each other's financial details. Additionally, people's roles change over time. Instead of granting data access to individuals, assigning role-based access to groups of people is best.

Protecting an organization's data is vitally important to an organization. Creating policies that mandate data encryption at rest and in transit is a data governance principle that accomplishes information security objectives. Using encryption technology appropriately helps ensure the safety of your data.

There are times when organizations need to share data, both internally and externally. For example, it is a common practice to use production data in test and training environments. However, people in the test and training environments don't need the actual production data. Instead, use simulated data in these environments. Data masking, or obfuscation, is one way to remove sensitive data from nonproduction environments.

When sharing data externally, consider de-identifying data to avoid compromising individual privacy. When de-identifying data, you remove identifiers that can uniquely identify a person. Strong data governance is a boon to maintaining a list of identifiers to remove during de-identification.

In a modern organization, data exists on local devices, shared drives, and the cloud. Each of these storage environments has its own unique set of considerations. Encrypting data at rest is foundational for all storage environments. If a physical device containing data is lost or stolen, encryption helps protect the data on that device. While this scenario is most likely with a local machine, encryption protects against that possibility regardless of the storage environment.

For shared drives and the cloud, it is crucial to implement group-based administrative controls. Just as data governance uses groups, departments, and divisions from an organizational chart to inform the creation of data access roles, the same process applies to defining role-based access to storage locations. When using user-facing cloud services, consider what controls you can implement to inhibit unintended external sharing.

Another aspect of data governance is to make it easy for people to accomplish their work while making it challenging to make mistakes. In addition to access controls, an acceptable use policy helps people understand how they can and cannot use the data they can access. Data use requirements define how to process data and how long to retain it. Use requirements also inform the decision to archive or delete data once it is no longer transactionally valuable.

The handling of certain data types has legal implications. Published standards define specific identifiers as PII and PHI, impacting how you handle the data internally, any necessary modifications before sharing, jurisdiction requirements, and data breach reporting timeframes. Other data types are subject to private regulations, like the PCI DSS. While private regulations don't have the force of law, seeing them as part of a contract between two organizations is common.

Using industry best practices for maintaining quality is essential to having robust, trustworthy data. Implementing issue tracking software to track business needs and source control to manage software and configuration helps you take a consistent approach to managing change. A crucial part of change is ensuring your changes have the desired effect. Unit testing validates changes at a local level, while requirement and user testing validate from the perspective of a functional user. Stress testing helps ensure your systems perform under their intended load targets.

Maintaining quality doesn't stop when your systems are operational. Using automated data quality monitoring to perform health checks programmatically maintains data quality continuously. Data profiling is essential when merging disparate datasets, helping identify the effort you will expend resolving duplicates and other quality-related data issues.

Exam Essentials

Describe the four primary data classification categories. Public is the most permissive category and applies to data intended for public consumption. Internal data applies to data for use within an organization. Sensitive data is for limited use within an organization, while Highly Sensitive data is the most restricted category. Certain PHI or PII identifiers fall within the Highly Sensitive category.

Describe the two types of integration. Integration connects systems together. Batch integration happens periodically. When data needs to move from the source system to the destination system immediately, you need real-time integration.

Describe the difference between person-based and role-based access. With person-based access, you give individuals access to data. Person-based access is inefficient and prone to people having permissions linger after transitioning to a new area of responsibility. Role-based access assigns permissions to job roles. As people transition in and out of job roles, their access to data adjusts accordingly.

Describe the difference between requirements testing and User Acceptance Testing. Requirements testing validates that a system successfully fulfills the requirements defined by functional users. While technical staff can perform requirements testing, functional subject matter experts conduct User Acceptance Testing as a final verification that a system meets user expectations before going live.

Describe the difference between anonymization and de-identification. Anonymization and de-identification both remove Personally Identifiable Information (PII) from a dataset. Anonymization irrevocably alters the data, making it impossible to reverse the process and identify specific individuals. Since de-identification removes individually identifying attributes, it is possible to reidentify individuals by combining the de-identified data with another data source.

Review Questions

The following questions are designed to test your understanding of this chapter's material. You can find the answers in Appendix A.

1. Which of these roles is directly responsible for an organization's data governance?
   A. Data owner
   B. Data custodian
   C. Data janitor
   D. Data steward

2. Which of these roles is assigned to a senior functional leader?
   A. Data owner
   B. Data custodian
   C. Data janitor
   D. Data steward

3. Which of these roles is assigned to an information technology professional who implements technical controls to further data governance objectives?
   A. Data owner
   B. Data custodian
   C. Data janitor
   D. Data steward

4. Eve is classifying data that is part of the interface between her organization and their health insurance provider. One of the fields in the dataset is Social Security number. What data classification is most appropriate?
   A. Public
   B. Internal
   C. Sensitive
   D. Highly Sensitive

5. Silas works in communications and has been asked to classify the assets on the organization's externally facing website. What data classification is most appropriate?
   A. Public
   B. Internal
   C. Sensitive
   D. Highly Sensitive

6. Ian has a new job as a chemist at Guinness & Co. As part of his new job, he is given the chemical formula for Guinness Extra Stout. What is the most appropriate data classification for this chemical formula?

    A. Public
    B. Internal
    C. Sensitive
    D. Highly Sensitive

7. Deondre has a new job with the Coca-Cola Company. As part of his role, Deondre has access to a list of logistics suppliers and pricing information. What is the most appropriate classification for this data?

    A. Public
    B. Internal
    C. Sensitive
    D. Highly Sensitive

8. Clarence is developing a data access strategy for his organization which consists of 150 people across five groups, with three roles in each group. How many roles should Clarence expect to create to appropriately safeguard the data?

    A. 3
    B. 5
    C. 15
    D. 150

9. Zeke wants to protect his organization's data. What precautions should he take for cloud-based storage?

    A. Encryption at rest
    B. Encryption in transit
    C. Encryption at rest and in transit
    D. User-based encryption

10. Maxine is completing some new-hire paperwork using a form on the web. What should she do to ensure the connection is encrypted?

    A. Use HTTP
    B. Use the Chrome browser
    C. Check for the padlock icon is open
    D. Check that the padlock icon is closed

11. Zaid needs to share medical imagery data with a partner who is developing a machine learning model to identify cancer. What does Zaid need to do to ensure privacy? Choose the best answer.
    A. De-identify the data
    B. Sort the data in random order
    C. Encrypt the data
    D. Aggregate the data

12. What is the primary goal of unit testing?
    A. To determine the system's breaking point
    B. To validate business requirements
    C. To ensure individual components work as expected
    D. To test the system's usability

13. What is a key reason for performing stress testing?
    A. To validate that individual software functions work correctly
    B. To determine how a system fails under extreme conditions
    C. To check that business users are satisfied with a system's functionality
    D. To ensure the system meets specific business requirements

14. Cindy wants to use production data in a training environment for new human resources employees and wants to protect the privacy of the production data. What should she do?
    A. Use SFTP
    B. Use SCP
    C. Implement data masking
    D. Implement HTTPS

15. Fred has two de-identified datasets. The first contains medical treatment data, and the other contains biographic information. The ZIP code, sex, and birth date exist in both datasets. Is personal privacy at risk? Choose the best answer.
    A. No, the data is de-identified.
    B. No, the datasets are separate.
    C. Yes, reidentification is possible using ZIP code, sex, and birth date.
    D. Yes, reidentification is possible because one of the datasets has biographic information.

16. Which of the following is not considered PII?
    A. Passport number
    B. Favorite food
    C. Address
    D. Credit card number

17. Which of the following is not considered PHI?
    A. Account number
    B. Fingerprint
    C. Email address
    D. Color preference

18. Which of the following has the shortest maximum breach notification requirement?
    A. PCI
    B. PII
    C. GDPR
    D. PHI

19. Which of the following is considered Sensitive Authentication Data by the PCI DSS?
    A. PIN
    B. Name
    C. Account number
    D. Expiration date

20. What does data lineage help organizations understand?
    A. The number of users accessing a database at a given time
    B. The complete lifecycle of data from its origin to its final destination
    C. The design of an application's user interface
    D. The financial cost of storing data in the cloud

Appendix

Answers to the Review Questions

Chapter 2: Data Analytics Tools

1. **D.** R is a programming language that is focused on solving analytics problems and is well known for its ease of learning. Python, Ruby, and C++ are all general-purpose programming languages that are not focused on analytics and have a steeper learning curve.

2. **C.** The SELECT command is used to retrieve information from a database. It's the most commonly used command in SQL as it is used to pose queries to the database and retrieve the data that you're interested in working with. The INSERT command is used to add new records to a database table. The UPDATE command is used to modify rows in the database. The CREATE command is used to create a new table within your database or a new database on your server.

3. **C.** Spreadsheets are indeed widely used because they are easy to use and available on most modern business computers. The most commonly used spreadsheet is Microsoft Excel. Spreadsheets do not, however, provide powerful machine learning capabilities.

4. **B.** SAS is a professional statistical analysis package and is the most likely choice of a professional statistician of the options presented. Excel is a spreadsheet that does not offer the powerful statistical tools offered by SAS. Tableau is a data visualization package. Looker is a fully functional analytics suite and would not be installed on a single user's computer.

5. **D.** This is an example of an infrastructure as a service (IaaS) cloud offering because the service provider is offering you virtual server instances (a core infrastructure component), and then you are configuring those server instances to meet the needs of your organization. In a software as a service (SaaS) approach, the provider would sell you a complete application that runs in the cloud, and you would not configure any of the underlying infrastructure yourself. In a platform as a service (PaaS) approach, the provider would allow you to run your own application code on a platform that they manage. You still would not manage any of the underlying infrastructure. Finally, in a desktop as a service (DaaS) offering, the cloud provider offers end user productivity desktops that users can use in place of personal computers. That is not the situation described in this scenario.

6. **B.** Anaconda natively supports Python and R, which are integral to its purpose as a distribution for data science and analytics. However, Scala is not natively supported by Anaconda, as it primarily focuses on languages and tools widely used in scientific computing and machine learning, while Scala is more associated with big data processing through frameworks like Apache Spark.

7. **A.** Jupyter supports Python, R, and Julia as they are among the most commonly used languages for data science and analytics, with well-established kernels available. Scala, however, is not natively supported by Jupyter. While it is possible to use Scala with Jupyter by installing additional tools like the Apache Toree kernel, it is not included as a default supported language. Python, R, and Julia are fully supported with dedicated kernels, making Scala the exception.

8. **C.** Power BI Report Builder is a desktop tool that developers can use to create paginated reports. Report Server is a server-based tool where developers may publish those reports. Power BI Desktop is also a desktop tool, but it does not create paginated reports. The Power BI service is a SaaS offering of Power BI that would not be installed on an analyst's computer.

9. **A.** Tableau is arguably the most popular data visualization tool available in the market today. The focus of this tool is on the easy ingestion of data from a wide variety of sources and powerful visualization capabilities that allow analysts and business leaders to quickly identify trends in their data and drill down into specific details. Excel is a spreadsheet that offers only limited visualization capabilities. Anaconda is a package and environment management platform for R and Python developers. The Tidyverse is a collection of packages used to manage the analytics workflow in R code.

10. **B.** Compass is the best tool for Bob's needs because it is specifically designed as a graphical interface for MongoDB, providing a user-friendly way to interact with and analyze MongoDB databases. MySQL Workbench is designed for MySQL, not MongoDB, and is therefore not compatible. DBeaver is a multi-database tool that can support MongoDB, but it lacks the deep integration and features tailored specifically for MongoDB that Compass offers. Toad is primarily focused on relational databases and does not provide native support for MongoDB.

11. **A.** Amazon EKS is a commonly used cloud-based containerization service because it is a managed Kubernetes service that allows users to run and scale containerized applications on AWS. Azure SQL is a cloud-based relational database service, not related to containerization. Google BigQuery is a serverless data warehouse designed for analytics, not for containerized applications. Google Vertex AI is a machine learning platform for building and deploying models but does not specifically focus on containerization.

12. **D.** The DROP command is used to remove an entire database or table from a database. The DELETE command is used to remove rows from a table but does not remove the table itself. The UPDATE command is used to modify rows within a table, while the ALTER command is used to modify the structure of a database or table.

13. **D.** Object storage best describes AWS S3 because it stores data as objects, which include the data itself, the metadata, and a unique identifier. This type of storage is ideal for unstructured data in a data lake, such as Ty's customer relationship management data. Block storage is used for structured data and low-latency access in applications like databases. Local storage refers to data stored on physical devices directly attached to a server, which is not relevant to cloud-based S3. Shared storage typically involves network-attached storage systems, which differ from the object storage approach used in S3.

14. **C.** The Python Data Analysis Library (pandas) provides a set of tools for structuring and analyzing data. The NumPy package is used for numerical analysis. TensorFlow is used for high-performance numerical calculations. Keras is used for artificial intelligence applications.

15. C. Relational databases do not natively understand natural language queries. Any queries sent to a relational database must be written in SQL. This SQL may be written directly by an end user, created by an end user within a graphical interface, or written by software created in any other programming language. Natural language query applications seeking to retrieve data from a relational database must first translate that query into SQL before sending it to the database.

16. C. Minitab, SAS, and Stata are all statistical analysis packages that are unlikely to produce any reporting fit for consumption by a business leader. Power BI, on the other hand, is an analytics suite that produces highly visual reports that would be ideal for sharing with a business leader.

17. B. Public cloud is most commonly associated with a consistently multitenant architecture because it is designed to share resources among multiple organizations or users, leveraging a shared infrastructure to maximize efficiency and cost-effectiveness. Private cloud, on the other hand, operates on a dedicated infrastructure for a single organization, avoiding multitenancy. Hybrid cloud combines elements of both public and private clouds, so multitenancy may apply only to the public cloud portion. IaaS cloud refers to a service model and can be implemented in public, private, or hybrid clouds, meaning multitenancy is not a consistent characteristic of IaaS itself.

18. D. The ALTER command is used to modify the structure of an existing database or database table. The UPDATE command is used to modify the data contained within a table, but not the table itself. The DROP command is used to delete an entire table or database. The MODIFY command does not exist.

19. D. Scala is the most suitable language for analysts working with Apache Spark because Spark itself is written in Scala, and it offers the most seamless integration and access to all Spark features. Python is also widely used with Spark due to its simplicity and the availability of PySpark, but it may not provide the same performance or access to advanced Spark features as Scala. Java is supported by Spark but is more complex and less user-friendly for analysts. R is the least suitable because its integration with Spark is limited and less commonly used in Spark-based workflows.

20. D. The data manipulation language (DML) contains the commands used to work with the data contained within a database. DML includes the SELECT, INSERT, UPDATE, and DELETE commands. The CREATE command is used to create a new database or table and is a component of the Data Definition Language (DDL).

Chapter 3: Understanding Data

1. D. While UA 769 contains numeric and text components, selecting an alphanumeric data type is the best option if you store this information in a single field. Since there is no date information contained in UA 769, the date data type is not appropriate.

2. C. Voice transcripts are unstructured digital audio files. As such, the BLOB data type is the only viable choice. The alphanumeric, numeric, and date data types are all structured data types.

3. D. In order to facilitate precise mathematical operations on financial data, a numeric data type is the most appropriate choice. Smallmoney does not support values in excess of $1 million. Both smallmoney and money are subject to rounding errors. While alphanumeric could be used to store financial records, the data would have to be converted to numeric in order to facilitate mathematical operations.

4. B. At 45 minutes in length with an average of 102,400 KB per minute, each session would consume in excess of 4 GB of data ((45 * 102400) / 1024 / 1024). Only the BLOB data type in Oracle can accommodate binary data of that size. Microsoft SQL Server has a maximum size of 2 GB in the varbinary data type. The CLOB data type is limited to character data, and the numeric data type is limited to numeric data.

5. B. Alexander should select a CLOB. The text of 1,168 pages greatly exceeds 4,000 bytes, so varchar is not an option. The numeric data type holds only numeric data, whereas the BLOB data type is used for binary objects.

6. A. While defective or functional is categorical, the *number* of defects represent a count of an occurrence. As such, it is an example of discrete data. Since it is not possible to produce half a control arm, continuous is an inappropriate choice.

7. A. Since shoes are only available in half-size increments, shoe size is considered discrete.

8. B. As it is a measurement, Amdee's foot size is continuous. Shoe size is discrete, and categorical and alphanumeric are not appropriate in this case.

9. D. The range of values and degree of precision for measuring temperature are virtually infinite, making temperature a continuous variable. As such, a numeric data type is preferred when compared with integer.

10. B. Opinions are not numeric, so quantitative is not an option. Opinions vary widely, so they are not categorical. An opinion is an unstructured piece of text, so it is not dimensional. By definition, the text put into an open-ended response is qualitative.

11. C. Spreadsheets are designed to manage structured data. Each of the data elements (check number, date, recipient, and amount) fit easily into appropriately titled columns. As such, this scenario describes structured data.

12. A. A comma-separated values option supplies columnar structure with minimal overhead and is easy to ingest into Python. Plain-text or XML files would be harder to parse, and HTML is what is used to display the account export screen.

13. A. Based on the name-value pairing, the absence of tabs or commas as delimiters, and the lack of tags, the API is expecting data to be formatted as JSON.

14. A. Based on the name-value pairing, the absence of tabs or commas as delimiters, and the lack of tags, the API is expecting data to be formatted as JSON.

15. A. A comma-separated values file can be imported natively into a Microsoft Excel spreadsheet. While Excel is capable of reading the other listed file formats, the data would not be processed into neatly organized rows and columns.

16. C. In order for a person to interact with a web page, the web page needs to be packaged as HTML. While a web browser is capable of opening the other file types, Claire's JavaScript needs to be wrapped in HTML in order to function appropriately.

17. C. Examining the data, you can see the curly braces containing key-value pairs. This is JSON data that can be rearranged to be more pleasing to the eye, as follows:

    ```
    [
      {
        "eventType": "start",
        "sessionOffsetMs": 0,
        "mediaOffsetMs": 0
      },
      {
        "eventType": "playing",
        "sessionOffsetMs": 3153,
        "mediaOffsetMs": 0
      },
      {
        "eventType": "stopped",
        "sessionOffsetMs": 4818,
        "mediaOffsetMs": 559
      }
    ]
    ```

18. D. Google Sheets can import tab- and comma-separated files but cannot process a composite delimiter.

19. A. Since web server logs are generated automatically by a machine, this qualifies as machine data.

20. B. Since Dave's data has both structured (client name, date of commission) and unstructured (thumbnail image) elements, it is semi-structured. Since Dave is creating the website on his own, this is not an example of machine data.

Chapter 4: Databases and Data Acquisition

1. D. Removing the personalization features disservices customers. While talking with a DBA or verifying the existence of the index on Customer_ID is useful, parameterizing the query will reduce parsing and improve performance.

2. A. The correct answer is A, as an INNER JOIN uses a join condition to match related rows between tables. In this case, a LEFT OUTER JOIN retrieves all customers, and if they have orders, the associated orders. A RIGHT OUTER JOIN retrieves all orders, and if they have customers, the associated customer information. A CROSS JOIN matches every single customer to every single order.

3. B. Key-value, column family, and relational are not optimized for quickly identifying patterns in connected data, making a graph database the best choice.

4. B. Foreign keys enforce referential integrity. A primary key uniquely identifies a row in a table. A synthetic primary key is system-generated.

5. C. A data mart is too narrow, because Taylor needs data from across multiple divisions. OLAP is a broad term for analytical processing, and OLTP systems are transactional and not ideal for this task.

6. D. Initial and delta loads describe how much data is moving. Although ETL is a reasonable choice, ELT is optimal.

7. A. Both start date and end date are necessary to understand when something happened. Middle date is not a valid design criteria.

8. B. A star schema is a data warehousing approach that minimizes query complexity. Avalanche and Quasar are not common design patterns. A snowflake schema is more normalized than a star schema and increases query complexity.

9. B. Static dimensions don't change over time. Counties are infrequently created, making C and D invalid choices.

10. C. A snowflake approach is more normalized, has more complicated queries, and requires less space than a star approach.

11. A. While she may need to parse JSON to load the data into an OLAP environment, she is in danger of getting blocked if the terms of service prohibit programmatic data collection.

12. B. Python is a versatile language well-suited to transforming data. The extract and load phases typically use database-centric utilities. Purging data also uses database-centric tools.

13. D. Surveys are completed by people, and public databases are unlikely to have information about a proprietary process. While Ellen may use sampling during her analysis, observation is the best approach for data collection.

14. C. Manually checking for updated data is error-prone and not sustainable. While an API would be nice, it is not necessary for data that is updated monthly. Since the data changes once per month, George should not be satisfied with the initial data load.

15. B. A complete purge and load removes historical data. ELT just changes the order in which data is loaded and transformed. While Martha may work with an ETL product, it is not necessary.

16. C. A survey would include any bias the production staff has. Testing a sample of finished goods does not inform Bob of what is happening during quality control, and historical trends would not account for any changes in the production process.

17. C. COUNT will return the number of rows. MAX will return the largest value, while AVG will return the average of a numeric column.

18. A. Since Elena focuses on transactions in Italy, she does not need data from the entire European Union. Creating a province-specific subset may make sense after her initial analysis is complete.

19. B. While ensuring an index on the county column is valid, it will not directly inform Jeff's analysis. Effective data logic may be necessary and would have to be to understand profitability over time—not just the profitability. Aggregating data at the county level does not inform analysis at the state or regional levels.

20. A. The ORDER BY clause sorts data. SELECT identifies columns, FROM identifies tables, and WHERE filters the results.

Chapter 5: Data Quality

1. A. While invalid, redundant, or missing data are all valid concerns, data about people exists in three of the four systems. As such, Jackie needs to be on the lookout for duplicate data issues.

2. C. Since the value –10 exists, this is not a case of missing data. With the data coming from a single source, it is not duplicate data. As the values exist over time, the data is not redundant.

3. C. Since the data is for a single movie and comes from a single dataset, it is neither redundant nor duplicate. Since the data exists, it is not missing.

4. D. Since the data comes from multiple hospitals, the possibility of duplicate or redundant data exists. Although invalid data is certainly possible, the fact that an aggregation function in a programming language returned an error indicates that some values are missing.

5. D. There is no specification that dictates the price of concrete, so this is not a specification mismatch. The order of concrete pricing doesn't matter, which eliminates nonparametric data, and duplicate data doesn't make sense in this context.

6. A. There may be duplicate or redundant data in the dataset, and an individual film might be an outlier. However, this scenario describes nonparametric data.

7. A. Since the data is coming from a single, well-designed system, redundant or duplicate data are unlikely. While outliers may exist, they do not cause database loads to fail.

8. C. The choice here is between redundant and duplicate data. In this case, Jorge is sourcing data from multiple systems, and redundant data comes from a single system, so duplicate is the correct answer.

9. B. Since Lars has numeric data and categorical definitions, there is no need to merge, impute, or parse the wind speed data.

10. D. Conversion and transposition are not necessary. While deriving an indicator may be beneficial, it is less valuable than merging the data from multiple sources.

11. B. As a data analyst, Ashley needs to work with IT to modify an ETL process. While she may be recoding or concatenating as part of this temporal work, Ashley is actively blending data.

12. B. It doesn't make sense to concatenate product IDs together, because you lose the ability to identify individual products. While some data may need recoding as numeric and price should be numeric, the ETL should append data from the four systems into a single, wide table.

13. A. Calculating an average is a single function call that produces unexpected results only when there is an underlying issue with the data. While looking online for the correct price may be useful to verify her hunch, checking for nulls herself is the best approach.

14. C. Since Sebastian wants to retain granular data, neither reducing the number of observations nor aggregating the data is the best approach. There is no need to normalize the income data.

15. D. While removing rows will nulls is appropriate, she needs to transpose by product category and summarize. Transposing by sales price or region will not help her current analytical goal.

16. B. Aggregation comes into play if there is a need to summarize the data by person. It is unlikely that a new column is needed for each Full Name. Dropping all missing values is a possibility, but not the best choice.

17. A. Aggregation is a good way to summarize data. Trusting his instincts does not help with model accuracy. Edgar may have normalized attributes during model creation.

18. B. Accuracy denotes how closely a given attribute matches its intended use. Consistency measures an attribute's value across systems. Validity ensures an attribute's value falls within an expected range. While all of these dimensions are important, completeness is foundational to Jane's campaign.

19. C. Accuracy denotes how closely a given attribute matches its intended use. Completeness measures the minimum viable data necessary for a business objective. Validity ensures an attribute's value falls within an expected range. While all of these dimensions are important, ensuring the consistency of customer data across two different source systems is crucial to Ron's work.

20. A. Completeness measures the minimum viable data necessary for a business objective. Consistency measures an attribute's value across systems. Validity ensures an attribute's value falls within an expected range. While all of these dimensions are relevant, measuring a javelin in kilograms indicates a lack of accuracy.

Chapter 6: Data Analysis and Statistics

1. C. Sandy needs sample data. An observation is the weight of a single gorilla, and the population is all silverback gorillas, which Sandy will be unable to weigh. A specific weight, like 369 pounds, is an observation of the weight variable.

2. D. The interquartile range is a dispersion measure that includes the second and third quartiles, which contains the middle 50 percent of the values in the dataset. The median represents the value in the middle of a sorted numeric list, the mode is the most frequently occurring value, and the mean is the average of all values. Median, mode, and mean are all measures of central tendency.

3. C. The mode is the most frequently occurring value, which is useful when working with categorical data like automotive color. The mean is the arithmetic average, the median represents the value in the middle of a sorted numeric list, and the range is the measure from minimum to maximum, which includes any outliers in the data.

4. B. Jenna should focus on aggregated data and highlight key performance indicators (KPIs) relevant to strategic decisions, as the C-suite generally requires high-level insights presented clearly and concisely. Emphasizing aggregated data and KPIs, Jenna can deliver the needed information without overwhelming them with unnecessary details.

   Raw data tables and complex statistical details are too granular for the C-suite and could detract from the main insights. Using low-contrast colors and small, serif fonts would hinder readability and accessibility, making the presentation difficult to consume. A detailed explanation of analytical methods is more suitable for a technical audience, not for senior executives interested in outcomes and actionable insights.

5. A. Product managers require clear, actionable insights presented in an easy-to-digest format. Simple visualizations highlighting the main trends and insights allow them to make strategic decisions without being bogged down by complex data or technical details. Raw data is overwhelming for nontechnical audiences and can obscure the key insights that product managers need. Discussing statistical methods is unnecessary and may confuse the audience, while using technical jargon and excessive detail would hinder understanding and lead to confusion, making the presentation ineffective for a nontechnical audience.

6. B. The IS NULL logical function is used to check for the existence of a NULL value. Since NULL represents the absence of a value and cannot be compared using an equality operator, Emma needs to use IS NULL to identify records where the Middle_Name field is NULL. Middle _ Name = NULL does not work because you cannot use an equality operator to compare a NULL value. Middle _ Name IS NOT NULL would return the opposite result, retrieving records where a middle name is present. Middle _ Name = `` '' checks for an empty string, not a NULL value. NULL and an empty string are different, so this would not identify the records Emma is looking for.

7. D. To get the mean, you add all the numbers of the dataset together and divide by the number of observations:
$$\frac{1+1+2+3+3+4+5+6+7+8}{10} = 4$$
1 is the minimum, 1 and 3 are the mode, and 3.5 is the median.

8. C. To calculate range, subtract the minimum (1) from the maximum (8).

9. C. Recall that for a sample with even numbers, you calculate the median using the following formula:
$$\tilde{x} = \left(\frac{\left(\frac{n}{2}\right) + \left(\frac{n}{2}+1\right)}{2}\right)$$
In this case, $\frac{n}{2} = 3$ and $\frac{n}{2} + 1 = 4$. With those two numbers, you can proceed with calculating the median as follows: $\frac{3+4}{2} = 3.5$.

10. A. The IS NOT NULL logical function is used to check for the presence of a value in the Middle_Name field, which is appropriate since Alex needs to find records where the middle name exists. Middle _ Name = NULL does not work because you cannot use an equality operator to check for NULL values. Middle _ Name = `` checks for an empty string, unlike NULL. An empty string means a value is present but is blank, while NULL means no value exists. Middle _ Name IS NULL would return customers without a middle name, which is the opposite of what Alex needs.

11. B. Converting timestamps to UTC ensures that time data is standardized. String functions aren't designed to handle time data or time zone conversions. Ignoring time zone differences would lead to incorrect analysis, especially in a global context where events need accurate time alignment. Multiplying the hour component by a fixed factor is not a valid method for adjusting time zones, as time zone differences are not uniform and can involve fractional offsets or changes due to daylight saving time.

12. C. The INITCAP() function capitalizes the first letter of each word and makes all remaining letters lowercase, which Ari needs to standardize the customer names. UPPER() converts the entire string to uppercase, LOWER() converts the entire string to lowercase, and TRIM() removes trailing or leading whitespace or characters without affecting the capitalization of letters within the string.

13. B. Vendor communities are a reliable resource for understanding and configuring features within specific software systems. The Salesforce community would likely have answers or advice from users with similar challenges and experiences. Asking colleagues may provide some guidance, but it's less likely to yield specific advice on Salesforce configuration. Social media can sometimes provide answers, but it lacks the specialized focus of a vendor community. Trial and error may be risky, especially in a live CRM environment, and can be time-consuming without guaranteed results.

14. C. A left skewed distribution typically has a mean less than the median, with the tail representing the lowest score.

15. B. Recall that the for a sample with even numbers, you calculate the median using the following formula:

$$\tilde{x} = \left(\frac{\left(\frac{n}{2}\right) + \left(\frac{n}{2}+1\right)}{2} \right)$$

After putting the numbers in numerical order, you have an n of 16, $\frac{n}{2} = 8$ and $\frac{n}{2}+1 = 9$. With those two numbers, you can proceed with calculating the median as follows: $\frac{8+9}{2} = 8.5$.

16. D. Link analysis explores connections patterns between data points, making it ideal for social network analysis. Trend analysis compares data over time, performance analysis assesses measurements against defined goals, and exploratory data analysis uses descriptive statistics to summarize data and provide context for ongoing analysis.

17. A. Trend analysis compares data over time. Performance analysis assesses measurements against defined goals, exploratory data analysis uses descriptive statistics to summarize data and provide context for ongoing analysis, and link analysis explores connection patterns between data points.

18. B. Performance analysis assesses measurements against defined goals. Trend analysis compares data over time, exploratory data analysis uses descriptive statistics to summarize data and provide context for ongoing analysis, and link analysis explores connection patterns between data points.

19. C. Enabling logging can help Piper capture specific error messages and identify the point of failure in the data transfer, allowing her to understand why the transfer is incomplete. Asking patients to resubmit information is impractical and doesn't address the root cause of the incomplete records. Consulting the manual might provide general information, but without specific error details, it may not help identify the exact issue. Manually updating the data does not resolve the underlying problem and is inefficient for a long-term solution.

20. C. Exploratory data analysis can help orient Vidar to the data, including summary statistics and identification of outliers across datasets. Trend analysis compares data over time, performance analysis assesses measurements against defined goals, and link analysis explores connection patterns between data points. As Vidar is encountering this data for the first time, he should check for outliers as part of his orientation process.

Chapter 7: Data Visualization with Reports and Dashboards

1. C. Real-time reports reflect data at the moment the report runs. Hourly reports update every hour. Weekly reports update every week. Since the manager needs three days of lead time, a daily report is the best option.

2. C. Excessive load times occur when the ETL process takes longer than expected. Long load times can be due to increased data volumes, as seen after the successful marketing campaign. The additional data volume delays report delivery because the ETL process must finish before the data is available for reporting.

   While data corruption can impact report validity, it does not directly impact ETL processing time. A misconfigured filter can result in incorrect report data but does not necessarily explain the ETL delay. Stale data refers to outdated information in a report, not a delay in delivery due to ETL processes running longer than anticipated.

3. B. The title page describes the title of the report and isn't appropriate for a paragraph. The appendix contains details that aren't necessarily relevant to the reader. While the report body could contains this kind of paragraph, it should be highlighted in the executive summary.

4. B. A scatter chart is an effective way to visualize the relationship between two numeric variables.

5. D. Since John's CEO wants to explore retail sales data, that rules out any type of static report.

6. A. As Ron is new to the organization, he needs to familiarize himself with corporate brand standards and any existing templates prior to working on distribution.

7. B. While Kelly needs feedback from the appropriate stakeholders, doing so without a watermark could lead them to believe the report they receive is the final product.

8. C. While all of the answers are relevant to determining requirements, Maggie should focus on key performance indicators for the organization as a whole.

9. B. Wireframes define the basic structure and content of a dashboard. A mockup provides details about the visual elements of a dashboard. Data marts and data warehouses are source systems.

10. D. A line chart effectively visualizes the relationship between time on the x-axis and a variable on the y-axis. A pie chart is best for categorical data, a tree map is for hierarchical data, and a histogram is for frequency data.

11. A. Since Celine is looking at South America, a geographic heat map is the best choice to contextualize precipitation.

12. C. Using a word cloud to signify the relative importance and commonality of words is the best approach.

13. D. Using color and location, a heat map is a great choice to visualize the correlation between multiple variables. A tree map is best for hierarchical data, a bar chart works well for categorical data, and an infographic is an effective tool for telling a story.

14. C. As an infographic conveys insights in a way that minimizes the time to comprehension, it is the best choice when telling Appa's story. A tree map is best for hierarchical data, a bar chart works well for categorical data, and a heat map works well in a spatial context.

15. C. A pivot table is the best choice for Jeremiyah because it allows him to dynamically group, filter, and aggregate data. While a line chart could show trends over time, it cannot dynamically adjust to group data by department or project as needed for Jeremiyah's analysis. Scatter plots show relationships between two numeric variables, which does not fit Jeremiyah's need for analyzing categorical data like departments and projects. Although stacked bar charts can represent proportions by category, they are static and do not provide the dynamic interactivity Jeremiyah requires for exploring his data.

16. A. Rita can use a bubble chart, having the size of each bubble correspond to the values of the variables she's visualizing. A bar chart works well for categorical data, an infographic is an effective tool for telling a story, and a heat map works well in a spatial context.

17. B. Since Sanjay is incorporating brand categories into his visualization, a stacked bar chart is the best approach; it incorporates proportional segments on each bar for categorical data. A bubble chart works well for showing the relationship between three variables, an infographic is an effective tool for telling a story, and a heat map works well in a spatial context.

18. C. As an infographic conveys insights in a way that minimizes the time to comprehension, it is the best choice when creating a poster to tell Adeline's story. A bubble chart works well for showing the relationship between three variables, a stacked bar chart is useful for showing proportional segments for categorical data, and a heat map works well in a spatial context.

19. D. A bubble chart works well for showing the relationship between three variables, a stacked bar chart is useful for showing proportional segments for categorical data, and an infographic is for telling a story. Since the CFO wants to drill into data, that necessitates an interactive dashboard.

20. B. Stale data is the most likely culprit since last-minute additions are missing from Marcus' report. Data corruption involves inaccurate or incomplete data due to errors. A misconfigured filter could exclude relevant data, but it would not specifically explain missing updates caused by a lack of real-time data. Delayed ETL processes could cause late report delivery, but they do not account for missing real-time updates in this scenario.

Chapter 8: Data Governance

1. D. A data owner is a senior leader over a functional unit, a data custodian is someone who implements technical controls, and a data janitor is not a valid role.

2. A. A data steward is responsible for looking after an organization's data, a data custodian is someone who implements technical controls, and a data janitor is not a valid role.

Chapter 8: Data Governance

3. **B.** A data steward is responsible for looking after an organization's data, a data owner is a senior leader over a functional unit, and a data janitor is not a valid role.

4. **D.** Highly Sensitive data is reserved for restricted use. Public applies to data intended for public consumption, Internal applies to data for use within an organization, and Sensitive applies to data that is for limited use within an organization.

5. **A.** Public applies to data intended for public consumption. Internal applies to data for use within an organization, Sensitive applies to data that is for limited use within an organization, and Highly Sensitive data is reserved for restricted use.

6. **C.** Sensitive applies to data that is for limited use within an organization. Public applies to data intended for public consumption, Internal applies to data for use within an organization, and Highly Sensitive data is reserved for restricted use.

7. **B.** Internal applies to data for use within an organization. Public applies to data intended for public consumption, Sensitive applies to data that is for limited use within an organization, and Highly Sensitive data is reserved for restricted use.

8. **C.** With role-based access, Clarence should create a data access role that allows each person in a group to perform their job function. Five groups with three roles per group comes out at 15 roles.

9. **C.** To keep his organizational data secure, Zeke needs to encrypt his data at rest as well as during transmission.

10. **D.** Maxine wants to ensure she is using HTTPS, which browsers illustrate with a closed padlock.

11. **A.** While aggregation is an option, it's not viable for individual images. While the data need to be encrypted, especially in transit, it is more important to de-identify it. The sort order does not matter.

12. **C.** Unit testing ensures that individual components or functions of a program work correctly, catching errors early in the development cycle when they are the cheapest to fix. It focuses on single functions or stored procedures rather than the entire system. Determining a system's breaking point is the goal of stress testing, which assesses performance under extreme conditions. Validating business requirements is the purpose of requirement testing, which ensures the system meets functional needs. Testing a system's usability falls under user acceptance testing (UAT), where business users check for ease of use and workflow correctness before deployment.

13. **B.** Stress testing determines a system's breaking point by applying loads beyond its design limits, helping to identify bottlenecks and assess how the system fails and recovers. It does not focus on verifying individual software functions, which is the role of unit testing. User Acceptance Testing (UAT) is when business users ensure the system meets their needs. Ensuring a system meets business requirements falls under requirement testing, which checks whether the software functions align with business needs rather than how it handles extreme loads.

14. C. Data masking replaces sensitive data with a synthetic version so the original data is no longer in the dataset. SFTP and SCP are encrypted transfer protocols, whereas HTTPS is encrypted web traffic.

15. C. The point of this question is that by using ZIP code, sex, and birth date, it is possible to reidentify individuals, thus making personal privacy at risk.

16. B. Passport number, credit card number, and address are all considered PII.

17. D. Account number, fingerprint, and email address are all considered PHI.

18. C. PCI has no notification requirement. PII is jurisdiction-dependent, PHI has a 60-day requirement, and GDPR has a 72-hour requirement.

19. A. The PIN is considered to be Sensitive Authentication Data under PCI DSS. Name, account number, and expiration date are all classified as Cardholder Data under PCI DSS.

20. B. Data lineage provides a comprehensive view of how data moves through an organization, from its point of creation to its final destination, including transformations and storage locations. It does not track real-time user access to a database, which is more of a security or monitoring function. An application's user interface design is unrelated to data lineage, as UI design focuses on user experience rather than data movement. While cloud storage costs are a consideration for data management, data lineage is concerned with tracking data flow rather than cost analysis.

Index

1NF (first normal form), 99
2NF (second normal form), 99
3NF (third normal form), 99

A

accessibility, 201–203
aggregate functions, 127–128
aggregation, 166–167
AI (artificial intelligence), 11–12
Ajax (Asynchronous JavaScript and XML), 74–75
AKS (Azure Kubernetes Service), 34
Anaconda, 24
analysis
 EDA (exploratory data analysis), 7, 236–237
 link analysis, 236
 performance analysis, 236
 trend analysis, 235–236
analytics
 AI (artificial intelligence), 11–12
 analysis, 7
 career opportunities, 5–6
 cleaning and manipulation, 7
 computing power, 5
 data, 2–3
 ata acquisition, 7
 deep learning, 11–12
 descriptive analytics, 10
 GenAI (generative AI), 12–13
 governance and, 3
 inferential analytics, 10
 iteration, 9–10
 Microsoft Excel, 14
 ML (machine learning), 11–12
 predictive analytics, 10–11
 prescriptive analytics, 11
 reporting and communication, 9
 RStudio, 15
 storage, 3–5
 visualization, 8–9
anonymization, 332–333
Apache Spark, Scala, 24
APIs (application programming interfaces), 109–110
appending, 175–176
audience, 198–201
audio, 60
augmentation, 160
AUP (acceptable use policy), 333
automated data quality monitoring, 339–340
average, 211–212
AWS (Amazon Web Services), 33
 public cloud computing, 36
Azure, 33
 AKS (Azure Kubernetes Service), 34
 Data Studio, 27–28
 public cloud computing, 36

B

bar charts, 247–249
Bessel's correction, 218–219
BI (business intelligence), 29–31
bimodal distribution, 216, 218
binary data, 58–59
binning data, 163
block storage, 34, 318
Boolean values, 50, 52
bots, RPA (robotic process automation), 13
bridge tables, 66
bubble charts, 250–251

C

career opportunities, 5–6
categorical data, 65
categorical variables, 176

character sets, 48–49
character strings, 46–49
charts, 246–247
    bar charts, 247–249
    bubble charts, 250–251
    histograms, 251, 255, 256
    line charts, 247, 253, 254
    pie charts, 247, 248
    scatter charts, 249–250, 251, 252, 253
    stacked charts, 249, 250
    waterfall charts, 259, 262
cleaning and manipulation, 7
CLOB (character large object) data type, 62
cloud computing
    drivers, 32–33
    hybrid clouds, 36
    IaaS (infrastructure as a service), 33–35
    on-premises clouds, 35
    PaaS (platform as a service), 35
    private clouds, 35
    public clouds, 35–36
    SaaS (software as a service), 33
cloud-based storage, 330
CLT (central limit theorem), 215
clustering data, 162
coding environments, 25–26
color palette, 201
column family databases, 95
communication, 9
    accessibility, 201–203
    audience, 198–201
    mock-ups, 201
Compass, 27
compliance
    audits, 323
    classification, 323–324
    data ethics, 318–319
    incident reporting, 325
    jurisdictional requirements, 316–317
    NIST (National Institute of Standards and Technology), 315–316
    PCI (Payment Card Industry), 319
    PHI (Protected Health Information), 320–323
    PII (Personally Identifiable Information), 320
    replication, 317–318
    retention requirements, 316
    storage, 318
computing power, 5
concatenation, 128–129
connectivity, troubleshooting, 229
continuous data, 64, 280–281
conversion, 158–159
correlation, 253
corrupt data, troubleshooting, 231–232
costs, storage costs, 3–5
count function, 206–207
CRAN (Comprehensive R Archive Network), 22
CRM (customer relationship management), 13
cross-validation, 190
CSV (comma-separated values), 70–72
currency data type, 54–57

D

dashboards, 9, 263–264
    consumers, 279–280
    continuous data, 280–281
    data sources, 280–281
    data types, 281–282
    development, 282
    dimensions, 281
    KPIs (key performance indicators), 279
    live data, 280–281
    measures, 281–282
    mockups, 282
    operational considerations, 282–283
    static data, 280
    wireframes, 282
data, 2–3
    categorical, 65
    continuous, 64
    dimensional, 65–66
    discrete, 64
    qualitative, 63

quantitative, 63
semi-structured data, 69–70
structured data, 66–68
tabular data, 45–46
unstructured data, 68–69
data acquisition, 7
    data quality check, 180–181
data analysis. *See* analysis
data analysts, 2
data analytics. *See* analytics
data audits, 189
data blending, 178–180
data completeness, 156
data custodians, 314
data dictionary, 306
data domains, 313–314
data duplication, 146–147
data elements, 44
data ethics, 318–319
data explainability report, 304–306
data governance. *See* governance
data health checks, 339
data lakehouses, 117
data lakes, 117
data management, 300
  data versioning, 313
  documentation
    data dictionary, 306
    data explainability report, 304–306
    data lineage, 304
    DFD, 302–304
    hierarchy structure, 306, 308–309, 310, 311
  integration, 301
  metadata, 313
  source of truth, 309–310, 312
data manipulation
  aggregate functions, 127–128
  concatenation, 128–129
  CRUD (Create, Read, Update, Delete), 121
  data quality check, 181–182
  date functions, 124–125
  execution plan, 138–139
  filtering, 123–124
  grouping, 130
  logical functions, 125–127
  queries
    full table scans, 137–138
    indexing, 137–138
    parameterization, 136–137
  sorting, 124
  SQL considerations, 121–123
  subsets, 138
  system functions, 135–136
  tables
    multiple, 131–135
    temporary, 138
data marts, 101, 115–116
data outliers, 153–154
data owners, 313–314
data profiling, 189, 341
data quality
  accuracy, 183
  acquisition, 180–181
  completeness, 183–184
  consistency, 184
  data manipulation, 181–182
  rules and metrics, 185–188
  timeliness, 185
  uniqueness, 185
  validity, 185, 188–190
    automated, 182–183
data redundancy, 147–150
data sharing, 334
data silos, 114–115
data sources
  APIs, 109–110
  dashboards, 280–281
  files, 113
  logs, 113–114
  observation, 120
  repositories
    data lakehouses, 117
    data lakes, 117
    data marts, 115–116
    data silos, 114–115
    data warehouses, 115
  sampling, 120

data sources (*Cont.*)
    surveys, 118–119
    validating, 233
    web scraping, 112
    web services, 110–112
data stewardship, 313, 314
data subject area, 313–314
data transformation
    aggregation, 166–167
    appending, 175–176
    augmentation, 160
    conversion, 158–159
    data blending, 178–180
    deletion, 178
    derived variables, 177–178
    exploding, 168
    grouping, 162–163
    imputation, 171–172
    merging, 174–175
    parsing, 172–174
    recoding data, 176–177
    reduction, 163–166
    scaling, 160–161
    standardization, 168–170
    string manipulation, 156–158
    transposition, 167–168
data types, 44
    audio, 60
    binary, 58–59
    Boolean values, 50, 52
    character sets, 48–49
    character strings, 46–49
    CLOB (character large object) data type, 62
    currency, 54–57
    dashboards, 281–282
    date, 52–53
    images, 60–61
    large text, 62–63
    numeric, 49–50, 51, 52
    spatial values, 53
    strings, 46–49
    time, 52–53
    unique identifiers, 53–54
    validation, 155–156
    video, 61–62
data usage, 333–334
data versioning, 313
data warehouses, 101, 115
databases
    Azure Data Studio, 27–28
    DBeaver, 28
    joins, 91
    MongoDB, 27
    nonrelational, 94
        column family databases, 95
        document databases, 94–95
        graph databases, 96–97
        key-value database, 94
    normalization, 98–99
    NoSQL, 27
    relational (*See* relational databases)
    relationships, 45–46
    SQL, 26–28, 90
        MySQL Workbench, 27
    SQL Server Management Studio, 28
    Toad, 28
date, 52–53
date functions, 124–125, 226–227
DBA (database administrator), 92
DBeaver, 28
DDL (Data Definition Language), 26–27, 120
deep learning, 11–12
de-identifying data, 333
deletion, 178
delimited files, 70
derived variables, 177–178
descriptive analytics, 10
descriptive statistics, 204–205
designing reports
    branding, 269, 271
    clarity, 267
    color schemes, 271
    concentration, 268
    consistency, 267
    control, 267
    correctness, 267

cover page, 268–269
executive summary, 269, 270
fonts, 272–274
graphics, 274–275
layouts, 271–272
DFD (Data Flow Diagram), 302–304
dimension tables, 101
dimensional data, 65–66
dimensionality reduction, 163, 164
dimensions, dashboards, 281
discrete data, 64
distribution, 215
 Bessel's correction, 218–219
 bimodal distribution, 216, 218
 normal distribution, 215–216
 skewed distribution, 216, 217
 special normal distributions
  standard normal distribution, 221
  t-distribution, 221–223
  Z-distribution, 221
 standard deviation, 219–221
 variance, 218–219
DML (Data Manipulation Language), 26–27, 120–121
document databases, 94–95
documentation
 appendixes, 278–279
 data dictionary, 306
 data explainability report, 304–306
 data lineage, 304
 DFD (Data Flow Diagram), 302–304
 FAQs, 278
 hierarchy structure, 306, 308–309, 310, 311
 references, 278
 version numbers, 277
DUA (data use agreement), 334

E

EDA (exploratory data analysis), 7, 236–237
EKS (Elastic Kubernetes Services), 34
encryption, 327–331
ERD (entity relationship diagram), 86–88
ETL (extract, transform, and load), 107–108
 data lineage, 304
 data redundancy, 148–149
 nonconformity, 188
 reporting validation, 288
exploding, 168

F

fact tables, 101
file formats
 HTML (Hypertext Markup Language), 75–76
 JSON (JavaScript Object Notation), 72–74
 text files, 70–72
 XML (Extensible Markup Language), 74–75
files
 data sources, 113
 extensions, 63
 storage, 34
filtering, 123
 logical operators, 123–124
fixed-width files, 72
fractional numbers, 50
frequency, 209–211

G

GCP (Google Cloud Platform), 33
 public cloud computing, 36–37
GenAI (generative AI), 12–13
geographic data, 53
geographic maps, 252
geometric data, 53
GKE (Google Kubernetes Engine), 34
governance, 13–14, 300
 analytics and, 3
 compliance
  audits, 323
  classification, 323–324

governance (*Cont.*)
    data ethics, 318–319
    incident reporting, 325
    jurisdictional requirements, 316–317
    NIST, 315–316
    PCI, 319
    PHI, 320–323
    PII, 320
    replication, 317–318
    retention requirements, 316
    storage, 318
  ethics, 318–319
  MDM (master data management), 14, 341–342
  privacy
    anonymization, 332–333
    data sharing, 334
    data usage, 333–334
    encryption, 327–331
    masking, 332
    permissions, 327
    RBAC, 326–327
  roles, 313–315
graph databases, 96–97
grouping, 130
  binning, 163
  clustering, 162
GUIDs (globally unique identifiers), 54

H

heat maps, 252–253, 257, 258
hierarchy structure, 306, 308–309, 310, 311
histograms, 165, 210, 251, 255, 256
HTML (Hypertext Markup Language), files, 75–76
HTTP (Hypertext Transfer Protocol), 110, 330
HTTPS (Hypertext Transfer Protocol Secure), 330
hybrid cloud computing, 36

I

IaaS (infrastructure as a service), 33–35
IDE (integrated development environment), 22
images, 60–61
imputation, 171–172
inconsistencies
  data completeness, 156
  data duplication, 146–147
  data outliers, 153–154
  data redundancy, 147–150
  data type validation, 155–156
  invalid data, 152–153
  missing values, 151–152
  nonparametric data, 153
  specification mismatch, 154–155
inferential analytics, 10
infographics, 258–259, 262
information sensitivity, 200
insights, 198
integers, 50
integration, 107–108
invalid data, 152–153
IQR (interquartile range), 223
ISO (International Organization for Standardization), 335
iteration, 9–10

J

joins, 91
  cross joins, 134–135
  inner joins, 131–132
  outer joins, 132–134
JSON (JavaScript Object Notation), files, 72–74
JVM (Java Virtual Machine), Scala, 24

K

key-value databases, 94
KPIs (key performance indicators), 200–201, 279
Kubernetes, 34

L

line charts, 247, 253, 254
link analysis, 236
live data, 280–281
LLMs (large language models), 12–13
local storage, 34–35
logical functions, 125–127, 223–226
logs, data sources, 113–114
Looker, 31

M

maps
    geographic, 252
    heat maps, 252–253, 257, 258
    tree maps, 253, 255, 259, 260
masking, 332
mathematical functions (statistics), 205
    date functions, 226–227
    logical functions, 223–226
    measures of central tendency, 211–214
    measures of dispersion, 214–223
    measures of frequency, 206–211
    measures of position, 223
    string functions, 227–228
MDM (master data management), 14, 341–342
mean, 211–212
measures of central tendency
    average, 211–212
    mean, 211–212
    median, 212–214
    mode, 214
    outliers, 211
measures of dispersion
    distribution, 215
        Bessel's correction, 218–219
        bimodal distribution, 216, 218
        CLT (central limit theorem), 215
        normal distribution, 215–216
        skewed distribution, 216, 217
        special normal distributions, 221–223
        standard deviation, 219–221
        variance, 218–219
    range, 215
measures of frequency
    count, 206–207
    frequency, 209–211
    percentage, 207–209
measures of position, 223
median, 212–214
merging, 174–175
metadata, 313
Microsoft Excel, 14
    data visualization, 20
    table example, 19
min-max normalization, 161–162
missing values, 151–152
ML (machine learning), 11–12
mock-ups, 201
mode, 214
MongoDB, 27
Moore, Gordon, 5
Moore's Law, 5
MySQL Workbench, 27

N

nested structures, 73
NLP (natural language processing), 13
nominal variables, 176
nonparametric data, 153
nonrelational databases, 94
    column family databases, 95
    document databases, 94–95
    graph databases, 96–97
    key-value database, 94
normal distribution, 215–216
    CLT (central limit theorem), 215
NoSQL, 27
notebooks, 26
null values, 151

O

numeric data types, 49–50, 55
numerosity reduction, 163, 165–166

O

object storage, 34, 318
OLAP (Online Analytical Processing), 100–101
OLTP (Online Transactional Processing), 97–100
ordinal variables, 176
outliers, 153–154, 211

P

PaaS (platform as a service), 35
packages, R programming language, 21–22
pandas, 23
parsing, 172–174
PCI (Payment Card Industry), 319
percentage functions, 207–209
performance analysis, 236
PHI (Protected Health Information), 320–323
pie charts, 247, 248
PII (Personally Identifiable Information), 320
pivot tables, 255, 257–258, 260, 261
Power BI, 29
predictive analytics, 10–11
prescriptive analytics, 11
privacy
    anonymization, 332–333
    data sharing, 334
    data usage, 333–334
    encryption, 327–331
    masking, 332
    permissions, 327
    RBAC (role-based access control), 326–327
private cloud computing, 35
programming languages
    Python, 23–24
    R, 21–22

SAS, 24–25
Scala, 24
public cloud computing, 35–37
Python, JSON in, 73

Q

qualitative data, 63
quality assurance
    automated data quality monitoring, 339–340
    data health checks, 339
    data profiling, 341–342
    ISO (International Organization for Standardization), 335
    requirement testing, 337
    source control, 335–336
    stress testing, 337–338
    UAT (User Acceptance Testing), 338–339
    unit testing, 336–337
quantitative data, 63
quartiles, 223
queries, 130–131

R

R programming language, 21–22
    JSON in, 74
RBAC (role-based access control), 326–327
RDMS (relational database management system), 45
recoding data, 176–177
rectangular data, 85
reduction
    dimensionality reduction, 163, 164
    numerosity reduction, 163, 165–166
reidentifying data, 333
relational databases, 88
    cardinality, 87
    DBA (database administrator), 92
    entities, 85

entity instances, 85
ERD (entity relationship diagram), 86–88
foreign keys, 90, 91–92
joins, 91
primary keys, 89–90, 92
providers, 94
queries, 90
referential integrity, 91–93
relationships, 87
    associative tables, 89
    binary, 87
    many-to-many, 89
    ternary, 87
    unary, 87
schema, 88–89
    dimensionality, 104–107
    snowflake schema, 103–104
    star schema, 101–103
SQL, 90
reporting, 9, 263–267
    ad hoc, 285
    blended approach, 266
    corporate standards, 275–277
    data explainability report, 304–306
    data versioning, 286–287
    delivery, 283–284
    design
        branding, 269, 271
        clarity, 267
        color schemes, 271
        concentration, 268
        consistency, 267
        control, 267
        correctness, 267
        cover page, 268–269
        executive summary, 269, 270
        fonts, 272–274
        graphics, 274–275
        layouts, 271–272
    documentation, 277–279
    frequency, 284–285
    pull approach, 266
    push approach, 266
    recurring reports, 285–286
    research reports, 287–288
    tactical reports, 287–288
    validation, 288
        data filtering, 289
        data structures, 290–291
        monitoring alerts, 291
        reviews, 289–290
        sources, 290
repositories
    data lakehouses, 117
    data lakes, 117
    data marts, 115–116
    data silos, 114–115
    data warehouses, 115
requirement testing, 337
RPA (robotic process automation), 13
RStudio, 15, 22

S

SaaS (software as a service), 33
sampling, 165
SAS, 24–25
Scala, 24
scaling, 160–161
scatter charts, 249–250, 251, 252, 253
schema
    dimensionality, 104–107
    snowflake schema, 103–104
    star schema, 101–103
Schmidt, Eric, 2–3
SCP (Secure Copy Protocol), 331
semi-structured data, 69–70
SFTP (Secure File Transfer Protocol), 331
shape libraries, 202
shared drives, 330
shared storage, 35
skewed distribution, 216, 217
sorting, 124
source control, 335–336

source of truth, 309–310, 312
spatial values, 53
special normal distributions
    standard normal distribution, 221
    t-distribution, 221–223
    Z-distribution, 221
specification mismatches, 154–155
spreadsheets, 18–21
SQL (Structured Query Language), 26–28, 90
    aggregate functions, 127–128
    Azure Data Studio, 28
    data manipulation, 121–123
    date functions, 124–125
    DDL (Data Definition Language), 26–27
    DML (Data Manipulation Language), 26–27
    grouping, 130
    logical functions, 125–127
    queries
        full table scans, 137–138
        indexing, 137–138
        nested, 130–131
        parameterization, 136–137
        subqueries, 130–131
    system functions, 135–136
    tables, multiple, 131–135
    troubleshooting, code, 230–231
SQL Server Management Studio, 28
stacked charts, 249, 250
standard deviation, 219–221
standard normal distribution, 221
standardization, 168–170
star schema, 101–103
static data, 280
statistics
    census, 203
    correlation, 253
    descriptive statistics, 204–205
    mathematical functions, 205
        date functions, 226–227
        logical functions, 223–226
        measures of central tendency, 211–214
        measures of dispersion, 214–223
        measures of frequency, 206–211
        measures of position, 223
        string functions, 227–228
    observations, 204
    parameters, 204
    populations, 203
    sample size, 204
    samples, 203
    symbols, 204, 205
    univariate analysis, 203
    variables, 203
storage, 3–5
    audio files, 62
    block storage, 34, 318
    cloud-based, 330
    costs, 3–5
    file storage, 34
    local storage, 34–35
    object storage, 34, 318
    shared storage, 35
    video files, 62
stress testing, 337–338
string functions, 227–228
string manipulation, 156–158
strings, 46–49
structured data, 66–68
subject area data stewards, 314
system functions, 135–136

T

Tableau, 29–30
tables
    bridge tables, 66
    joins, 91, 131–135
    temporary, 138
tabular data, 45–46, 85
TDE (Transparent Data Encryption), 329
t-distribution, 221–223
technological advances, 5
text editors, 25–26
text files, 70–72
tidyverse, 22

time, 52–53
TLS (Transport Layer Security), 330
transposition, 167–168
tree maps, 253, 255, 259, 260
trend analysis, 235–236
troubleshooting
    connectivity-related issues, 229
    corrupted data, 231–232
    log files and, 232–233
    online resources, 234
    source validation, 233
    SQL code, 230–231
    user-reported issues, 230
    vendor communities and, 233–234
TSV (tab-separated values), 70–71

U

UAT (User Acceptance Testing), 338–339
unit testing, 336–337
unstructured data, 68–69
UUIDs (universally unique identifiers), 54

V

validation, 188
    automated, 182–183
    cross-validation, 190
    data audits, 189
    data profiling, 189
    reasonable expectations, 189
    reports, 288–291
variables
    categorical, 176
    derived variables, 177–178
    nominal, 176
    ordinal, 176
variance, 218–219
video, 61–62
visualization, 8–9
    charts, 246–247
        bar charts, 247–249
        bubble charts, 250–251
        histograms, 251, 255, 256
        line charts, 247, 253, 254
        pie charts, 247, 248
        scatter charts, 249–250, 251, 252, 253
        stacked charts, 249, 250
        waterfall charts, 259, 262
    infographics, 258–259, 262
    Looker, 31
    maps
        geographic, 252
        heat maps, 252–253, 257, 258
        tree maps, 253, 255, 258, 260
    Microsoft Excel, 20
    pivot tables, 255, 257–258, 260, 261
    Tableau, 29–30
    word clouds, 263, 264
VMs (virtual machines), IaaS, 34

W–Z

waterfall charts, 259, 262
web scraping, 112
web services, 110–112
whole numbers, 50
word clouds, 263, 264
XML (Extensible Markup Language), files, 74–75
Z-distribution, 221

Printed and bound by CPI Group (UK) Ltd, Croydon, CR0 4YY

14/10/2025

14752885-0002